D0983503

The Battle of Fort Donelson

The Battle of Fort Donelson

James J. Hamilton

South Brunswick
New York • Thomas Yoseloff • London

Library of Congress Catalogue Card Number: 67–10488

Thomas Yoseloff, Publisher
Cranbury, New Jersey 08512

Thomas Yoseloff Ltd
18 Charing Cross Road
London W.C. 2, England

Maps prepared for publication by Elizabeth Csanigo.

6575

Printed in the United States of America

Contents

	Preface	7
	Dramatis Personnae	9
1	An Idea Germinates	15
2	A Plum Gets Picked	24
3	The Buildup	32
4	The Advance on Fort Donelson	66
5	Thursday—Envelopment and Attack	83
6	Friday—Maybe a Siege	122
7	Naval Catastrophe	132
8	Ecstacy, Gloom, and a Conference	150
9	Saturday—Smite With The Arm of Gideon	163
10	Issue in Doubt	179
11	Thc High Tide of Gray	190
12	Diversion and Reclamation	252
13	Nervous Relaxation	283
14	The Incredible Conference	289
15	Unconditional Surrender—The Beginning of a Legend	304
	Epilogue	340
	Notes	352
	Bibliography	365
	Indcx	369

Preface

HIS NAME WAS REALLY HIRAM ULYSSES GRANT, BUT WEST Point had him on its rolls as Ulysses Simpson Grant, so most of his life he was saddled with the initials U. S. While the appellation "United States" Grant lends some distinction, it does not express the man's character with such clarity as does "Unconditional Surrender" Grant. The theme of this book is how Grant inherited this title and, with it, consequent success and fame.

Strangely, Fort Donelson has not been treated in depth in Civil War literature. Certainly in its day it was hailed as a decisive battle, but subsequently has been eclipsed by bloodier carnage, showier leaders, and more romantic military units.

Perhaps the most important result of the battle at Dover was its raising of Grant to national prominence at a low point in Union fortunes. Not only was it the first major breakthrough in the offensive on land but it bagged a large, if exaggerated, haul of prisoners. The North had found a name with proven success and Grant possessed the ability not to disappoint them.

Yet his initial important triumph (outside of Fort Henry, which was no army feat) came to him through events which can only be described as highly fortunate. True, he had the initiative to push hard for the expedition to Fort Henry and then the clarity to see an opening for a blow at Fort Donelson.

After this, however, his efforts became mediocre and often contradictory.

Largely the Confederacy created the image and legend of Ulysses S. Grant. Entirely independent of Grant's plans, the Confederate generals, through indecision, quarreling, and misunderstandings, delivered the fruits of victory to the Union army, not to Grant.

The one day of severe fighting saw the issue decided by the tenacity of the Northern infantrymen and through the exhaustion of resources at the Confederate garrison. General Grant only arrived on the field after the Southern army was in retreat, and his one significant lodgement of the day came when a diversion attack caught the enemy with his defending forces still absent from the trenches.

Then that night came the incredible Confederate conference which not only relinquished the accomplishment of the day but surrendered the fort and army as well. At this late date questions as to reasons can never be fully answered, but I have attempted by relating the events to lend some insights into the motivations of the participants.

Thus was the inception of the legend of Ulysses Grant really formed. From Fort Donelson he would go on to hammer the Confederate armies to death and become President of the United States.

For assistance in this endeavor I would like to express appreciation to John and Mary Boyers for their encouragement and aid. Also I am very grateful to Benjamin F. Cooling III, first historian at Fort Donelson National Military Park, for taking time to read the manuscript and for offering many valuable comments. Further thanks go to Alec Gould, present historian at the park, for his conducted tours of the field and the providing of valuable information and leads. Also Superintendent R. G. Hopper and his staff have been most cooperative and hospitable.

Dramatis Personnae

UNION

Major General Henry W. Halleck.
Brigadier General Ulysses S. Grant—commanding general of expeditionary force.
Brigadier General John A. McClernand—commanding First Division.
Brigadier General Charles F. Smith—commanding Second Division.
Brigadier General Lew Wallace—brigade commander, later commanding Third Division.
Flag Officer Andrew H. Foote—commanding naval flotilla.
Colonel J. D. Webster—chief of staff to General Grant.
Colonel Jacob Lauman—commanding brigade, Second Division.
Colonel John Cook—commanding brigade, Second Division.
Colonel John McArthur—commanding brigade, Second Division, later attached to First Division.
Colonel W. H. L. Wallace—commanding brigade, First Division.
Colonel Richard J. Oglesby—commanding brigade, First Division.
Colonel Morgan L. Smith—commanding brigade, detached from Second to Third Division.
Colonel Charles Cruft—commanding brigade, Third Division.

Colonel John M. Thayer—commanding brigade, Third Division.
Commander Henry Walke—commanding gunboat *Carondelet.*
Commander Benjamin Dove—commanding gunboat *Louisville.*
Commander Egbert Thompson—commanding gunboat *Pittsburgh.*
Colonel John A. Logan—commanding 31st Illinois.
Colonel Michael K. Lawler—commanding 18th Illinois.
Colonel John E. Smith—commanding 45th Illinois.
Colonel William R. Morrison—commanding 49th Illinois.
Colonel C. C. Marsh—commanding 20th Illinois.
Colonel Isham N. Haynie—commanding 49th Illinois.
Colonel F. L. Rhoads—commanding 8th Illinois.
Colonel Leonard F. Ross—commanding 17th Illinois.
Colonel Isaac C. Pugh—commanding 41st Illinois.
Colonel Crafts J. Wright—commanding 13th Missouri.
Colonel James C. Veatch—commanding 25th Indiana.
Colonel James M. Tuttle—commanding 2nd Iowa.
Colonel James M. Shackelford—commanding 25th Kentucky.
Colonel Hugh B. Reed—commanding 44th Indiana.
Colonel John B. McHenry—commanding 17th Kentucky.
Lt. Colonel Augustus Chetlain—commanding 12th Illinois.
Lt. Colonel Thomas E. G. Ranson—commanding 11th Illinois.
Lt. Colonel James C. Parrott—commanding 7th Iowa.
Lt. Colonel Elias S. Dennis—30th Illinois.
Lt. Colonel Thomas H. Smith—48th Illinois.
Lt. Colonel James B. McPherson—staff engineer.
Major Frederick Arn—commanding 31st Indiana.
Major John A. Rawlins—aide to General Grant.
Major John J. Mudd—cavalry.
Major Francis M. Smith—17th Illinois.
Captain Jasper M. Dresser—battery commander.

Captain Edward McAllister—battery commander.
Captain Ezra Taylor—battery commander.
Captain Henry Richardson—battery commander.
Captain W. S. Hillyer—aide to Grant.
Captain Samuel B. Marks—18th Illinois.
Lieutenant James O. Churchill—11th Illinois.
Dr. John Brinton—Grant's staff physician.

CONFEDERATE

General Albert Sidney Johnston—commanding Confederate armies in Kentucky and Tennessee.
Brigadier General John B. Floyd—commanding all units at Fort Donelson.
Brigadier General Gideon J. Pillow—second-in-command at Fort Donelson.
Brigadier General Simon B. Buckner—commanding division.
Brigadier General Bushrod R. Johnson—commanding division.
Brigadier General Lloyd Tilghman—commanding Fort Henry.
Colonel John W. Head—commanding fort and 30th Tennessee.
Colonel John C. Brown—commanding brigade, Buckner's division.
Colonel Adolphus Heiman—commanding brigade, Johnson's division.
Colonel Joseph Drake—commanding brigade, Johnson's division.
Colonel Gabriel C. Wharton—commanding brigade, Johnson's division.
Colonel John McCausland—commanding brigade, Johnson's division.
Colonel Davidson—commanding brigade, Johnson's division.
Colonel John M. Simonton—commanding 1st Mississippi, later Davidson's brigade.
Colonel William E. Baldwin—commanding brigade, Buckner's and later Johnson's brigade.

Colonel J. E. Bailey—commanding 49th Tennessee and later garrison of fort.
Colonel John M. Lillard—commanding 26th Tennessee.
Colonel A. E. Reynolds—commanding 26th Mississippi.
Colonel Edward C. Cook—commanding 32nd Tennessee.
Colonel Roger W. Hanson—commanding 2nd Kentucky.
Colonel Joseph B. Palmer—commanding 18th Tennessee.
Colonel John Burch—aide to General Pillow.
Lt. Colonel Nathan Bedford Forrest—commanding cavalry at Fort Donelson.
Lt. Colonel Jeremy F. Gilmer—engineer.
Lt. Colonel Milton A. Haynes—river batteries.
Lt. Colonel Randal W. McGavock—10th Tennessee.
Major Alexander Casseday—aide to Buckner.
Major George B. Cosby—aide to Buckner.
Lt. Colonel Hylan B. Lyon—8th Kentucky.
Major William N. Brown—commanding 20th Mississippi.
Major Nat F. Cheairs—3rd Tennessee.
Major W. L. Doss—commanding 14th Mississippi.
Major J. E. Rice—aide to Pillow.
Major W. H. Haynes—supervising commissary stores.
Major Gus Henry—aide to Pillow.
Captain B. G. Bidwell—water batteries.
Captain Joseph Dixon—water batteries.
Captain Reuben R. Ross—water batteries.
Captain Jacob Culbertson—water batteries.
Captain Frank Maney—field battery.
Captain Rice E. Graves—field battery.
Captain J. H. Guy—field battery.
Captain D. A. French—field battery.
Captain Porter—field battery.
Lieutenant John W. Morton—Porter's battery.
Lieutenant Hunter Nicholson—aide to Pillow.

The Battle of Fort Donelson

1

An Idea Germinates

WINTER GLOOM SETTLED OVER THE ILLINOIS TOWN OF CAIRO. Outside standing at the Point one could not mistake the signs that the Ohio and Mississippi Rivers, swollen by precipitation to the north, were on the rise. Even though levees had been constructed, old-timers had not yet freed themselves from fears of rampaging flood waters seen in previous years.

There were reasons, in addition to meteorological, for the prevailing gloom. The Federal garrison had been considerably reduced. This was in spite of the fact that 15 miles down the Mississippi stood a well-manned Confederate fortress. Some residents voiced the opinion that Cairo, supply depot, terminus of the only southern Illinois railroad, and located at the junction of the two most important Union-held rivers, was being needlessly exposed.

In the Ohio Building brooded a short, stocky man with a rather long and neglected beard. Occasionally he puffed from a drooping, foot-long meerschaum pipe. Only his blue uniform with the insignia of a brigadier general belied the impression that he somehow was a fixture of a bank or of some shop in town. The general's name was Ulysses S. Grant.

Grant's worries were not the same as those of the citizens of the town. The Confederates downstream had no fleet of warships or transports of any consequence. Also they apparently had an insufficient number of troops at their Columbus, Kentucky fortress with which to protect their Missouri flank or, for that matter, to launch an offensive. In addition, a disastrous defeat in eastern Kentucky had been experienced by the Rebels at Mill Spring on January 19.

The general's depression stemmed from the fact that in spite of commanding one of the North's most vital military departments and having a large force of men under arms he was forced to remain idle. Originally when Grant arrived at Cairo his department included southern Illinois and Confederate-occupied southeast Missouri. The day after his arrival, however, the South violated Kentucky's "neutrality" by seizing and fortifying Columbus, along with several other locations. On his own initiative Grant, on the following day, September 6, 1861, seized Paducah, a railroad city at the mouth of the Tennessee River and less than ten miles from the mouth of the Cumberland River. This move added western Kentucky to Grant's command. Soon he acquired an army of roughly 12,000 men.[1]

This was a post for a man of alertness, vision, and action. Although his appointment had originally come through political influence, General Grant proved to have these qualities. He constructed forts and maneuvered troops to threaten Confederate operations. Exactly two months after the occupation of Paducah he loaded a large brigade aboard transports and, accompanied by a squadron of gunboats under Flag Officer Andrew Foote, set out to harass the Columbus "Gibraltar."

The fortress being too strong, Grant landed about 3,000 men

for a reconnaissance-in-force on the Missouri side of the river at the village of Belmont. In command of a nearly equal force of Confederate troops was Gideon Pillow, a man for whom Grant professed no respect. Pillow, beginning to show age at fifty-five, bore a look of distinction, leadership, and confidence. Medium-length gray whiskers fringed the lower half of his face. Beneath his determined, flashing eyes were a snub nose and a set of firmly pressed lips. Pillow's military bearing stemmed in part from his Mexican War reputation and a pair of wounds from the Mexico City campaign. Being President Polk's law partner he had risen swiftly from brigadier general to major general of volunteers in that war. Pillow had even won Presidential support in a dispute with General Scott. After the war he offered himself for Vice-President in 1852 and 1856. In November 1861, he was a Confederate States brigadier and the senior Tennessee major general of volunteers.

After the landing, the two opposing brigades advanced toward each other and engaged in a lively skirmish. After a time the Confederates broke and ran for the protecting shelter of the river bank and the heavy artillery of Columbus. While Grant gloated over the 175 prisoners he had taken, General Leonidas Polk, commander of the Columbus fortress, became alarmed for his detachment and under cover of his guns, he dispatched a strong reinforcement. On the Missouri side Pillow managed to rally some of his forces and, with the complement from Columbus, counterattacked.

Meanwhile, the discipline among Grant's green troops had completely broken down. Their pursuit had led them into the enemy's deserted camp and, as is so often true of raw recruits and sometimes of veterans, curiosity and greed got the best of them. Much of Grant's command engaged in looting the camp. Pillow's counterstroke swept them back as quickly as they had come, and Grant, on horseback, was barely able to follow his retreating men aboard the transports.

In succeeding weeks Grant was not able to find much satisfaction in the escapade at Belmont. True he had destroyed and captured some enemy artillery and for a time routed a Rebel brigade. He could also say that some of his men had received needed experience in warfare and had returned with souvenirs from an enemy camp. On the other hand, it was also true that he and his force had finally been ignominiously repulsed, and he had suffered heavy losses (inaccurately minimized in his report), including the capture of half his wounded and one of the two brigadiers with little to show for them. The Confederates could gain confidence in the security of their position.[2]

In spite of the continued importance of his military district, it was natural that some of those around Grant, and perhaps the general himself, began to wonder if his star was not quite as bright as it seemed to be. In the subsequent three months after Belmont, almost no action took place, other than some bickering with contractors. With the victory at Mill Spring the fulcrum of action was apparently shifting toward the east. In central Kentucky a Union invasion army under Don Carlos Buell was assembling. Unless Grant could do something spectacular, he might find his department diminished in size, denuded of troops, or completely removed from his jurisdiction.

Because of his background, necessity compelled Grant to rely almost entirely on successful contemporary activities to maintain his position. While his Mexican War record brought him great credit, his departure from the regular army had been under a cloud of condensed alcohol and his subsequent business career had not brought him any fame. Most dangerous of all, there was already some talk that Grant had been drinking at Belmont.[3]

To further his own cause and that of the Union, Grant turned to a strategic plan in early January. From Columbus on the Mississippi the Confederate line of defense ran eastward to the junction of the Tennessee line and the Tennessee and Cumberland Rivers. From there it advanced north to cover Hopkinsville and Bowling Green and then dipped again to meet the Tennessee line in the mountainous eastern section. Columbus was garrisoned with 14,000 men and General Polk commanded the western Department to the Cumberland River. General Hardee led the chief striking force, the Central Army of Kentucky (35,000 troops), based at Bowling Green. The eastern Department in the mountains commanded less than 8,000 men.[4] To even the most casual map observer it was obvious that the potential strategic if not tactical weak spots of this defense lay at the rivers Mississippi, Tennessee, and Cumberland. Since the Mississippi route seemed effectively blocked by the Columbus fortress, Grant had turned his attention on the Tennessee and the Cumberland. The former, if opened, would allow the superior Federal flotillas to isolate western Tennessee from the East and would give the Union armies a convenient base of supply as far as the shoals at Florence, Alabama. Not only would this probably doom Columbus but it would severely threaten Memphis, the rail center at Corinth, and even central Tennessee. The penetration of the Cumberland by Union armies would lose to the Confederacy the vital armory and munitions center of Nashville and would allow complete envelopment of the army at Bowling Green.

Since the Tennessee was nearer to Paducah and since it offered the greatest long-term strategic advantages, the crux of Grant's plan lay with the capture of Fort Henry on the eastern side of the river near the Tennessee–Kentucky border. It appeared to be the sole Confederate endeavor to block access to the Tennessee. Twelve miles east of Fort Henry by road lay Fort Donelson, the main enemy fortification on the Cumberland. Thus two successful quick strokes in co-operation with the navy could bring the remainder of Kentucky and nearly half of Tennessee back under Union control.

Grant's immediate superior was General Henry Halleck, an able strategist but a dilatory tactician. On January 6, Grant requested permission to visit him in his headquarters in St. Louis, to explain his plan. When permission was not forthcoming, Grant sent Brigadier General Charles Smith, commander at Paducah, with Flag Officer Foote on a military-naval reconnaissance up the Tennessee. With an expedition so strong that it terrified Confederate military headquarters, and with the expectation that the attack on Fort Henry had arrived, Smith marched two brigades up the bank of the river against quickly strengthening Rebel opposition, boarded the gunboat *Lexington* north of the fort, and with his staff surveyed the strength of the entrenchments on January 22. With this accomplished he counter-marched his command over weather-worsened roads to Paducah.[5]

Armed with Smith's report that the rising Tennessee had gravely undermined the effectiveness of low-lying Fort Henry, Grant again requested permission to leave Cairo for St. Louis. Reluctantly and with ill grace Halleck granted him leave. While Grant was using a map to explain his project, Halleck periodically shuffled papers at his desk. Finally Halleck interrupted and asked if the proposal had anything to do with Grant's command. He then proceeded to answer his rhetorical question by notifying the junior general that such matters fell to the jurisdiction of the department commander.[6]

Back in Cairo, after the lapse of a few days, Grant again wired Halleck in one sentence requesting permission for his expedition. This time he had prevailed upon Foote to briefly and separately recommend the identical course of action.[7] Now on the following day, January 29, 1862, he pondered his next move in his headquarters office. While still discouraged and apprehensive lest the river might fall, Grant determined on one more attempt, this time writing the plan in a more detailed paragraph.

In his slow way, Henry Halleck, just recovering from a bout with the measles after meeting with Grant, was coming to a decision. Instinctively he reacted against this general and his plan at Cairo. Grant had a reputation for being impulsive and so far had lived up to it. In independent command he might make himself inaccessible to orders. Also it was the dead of winter. Traditionally the weather brought so many obvious problems, especially in the days of unpaved roads, that these months became an off-season, militarily.

On the other hand there were definite reasons for adopting his plan or something like it. General George McClellan, Halleck's superior in Washington, had forwarded reports that Confederate General P. G. T. Beauregard, victor at Bull Run, was coming west with reinforcements. Winter might not wait. Rumors were circulating that a strong force had been dispatched late in January, to Paris, Tennessee, west of the Tennessee River near Fort Henry. Finally, the spinal column of communications between Bowling Green and Columbus ran part way along the Memphis–Humboldt–Paris–Bowling Green railroad. It crossed the Cumberland at Cumberland City and the Tennessee a few miles above Fort Henry. If the railroad could be broken and mastered at the Tennessee, Confederate east–west communications would be irreparably harmed and Fort Donelson would be blockaded from reinforcements from the west. It might then be expected that after a short wait it would be evacuated.

Naval sanction for Grant's project and the fact that General Buell had earlier recommended action along the same lines decided Halleck.[8] On January 29, he directly answered Foote that he was awaiting further information but to make preparations. On January 30, in his best professorial manner, Halleck approved the plan "to take and hold Fort Henry." The navy was then to cut the railroad. Curiously he wrote to Buell on the same day, speaking of an attack on Dover (Fort Donelson) in the same sentence as Fort Henry. On the 31st Halleck allotted Grant 15,000 men with immediate reinforcements promised.[9] On February 1, he telegraphed that he was unable to supply all the horses, mules, and wagons requisitioned by Grant to maintain his supply line, but recommended instead that he rely more heavily on communications by water. "The object is to move rapidly and promptly by steamers, and to reduce the place before any large reinforcements can arrive," Halleck concluded.[10]

On receipt of his superior's permission, Grant, who had been making preparations all along, sped to Paducah, the base of operations for the new campaign, to organize his expedition. There he consulted with his subordinate, General C. F. Smith. There were many reasons why Grant felt uneasy in the presence of this officer. First, Smith had been in the United States service as commandant of cadets when Grant attended West Point. In military service for 35 years, Smith wore the soldier's look of distinction. His figure was slim, tall, straight, and square-shouldered. Above his quite ruddy cheeks shone a pair of clear blue eyes. His mustache, long and white, lent the impression of discipline and fierce courage. Smith had wide command of the most activating words on the battlefield. Through the fortunes of politics Grant had become this veteran's commander.

The First Division came under the command of Brigadier General John A. McClernand. The Union owed a debt to this energetic former Illinois congressman for his organization and planning in rousing many soldiers to the cause. Although his military experience was limited to some Black Hawk Indian War campaigning and brigade command at Belmont, McClernand was assigned two Illinois brigades under the commands of Colonels Richard Oglesby and W. H. L. Wallace.

Reports that rains had made the roads along the Tennessee River next to impassable were instrumental in deciding for Grant to accept Halleck's advice about naval transportation. When informed of this, Flag Officer Andrew Foote could not hide his discomfort. He privately fumed at the lack of naval preparation for the expedition. There were neither enough transports to haul this sizable army up the Tennessee nor were there sufficient crews to man both the transports and the gunboats detailed for escort and bombardment. Foote solved the latter problem by "borrowing" replacements from other naval craft under his jurisdiction and by requesting Washington for reinforcements.[11] Grant helped here by forwarding seafaring recruits from the army. The transport difficulty could be worked out only by sending the army up the river in shifts. This was, after all, nearly the largest combined operation ever undertaken by the United States Navy.

In the darkness of the early morning of February 3, regiment upon regiment filed silently aboard the transports at the Paducah docks. Three of their number and a battery had already been bloodied at Belmont. After equipment, artillery, horses, and supplies had been placed on board, Grant, tense with the expectation of recall, gave the signal for the leading steamer to proceed. With several gunboats in the lead the column slowly steamed into the Ohio River. Around the bend waited the Tennessee. Even at six o'clock in the morning Ulysses Grant knew that his destiny was in his own hands.[12]

2

A Plum Gets Picked

BRIGADIER GENERAL LLOYD TILGHMAN HAD BEEN ASSIGNED BY General Johnston in November to defend the Tennessee and the Cumberland.[1] Neat and dashing in appearance, this former construction engineer, with experience in the Mexican War, found the choice of locations for defense already forced upon him. Shortly after the secession of Tennessee in April, 1861, Adna Anderson, a railroad engineer, had been given charge of surveying sites for the defense of the two rivers. On the Cumberland, Anderson selected a hill slightly downstream from the village of Dover for a fort. Work on the fort began in May and Anderson moved west to survey the Tennessee. Here, however, his recommendation was overruled by the Confederate officer on the spot, Major Bushrod Johnson. Unprepossessing in appearance with his domed forehead, broad mustache, wide nose, and large eyes, Johnson nevertheless had the engineering authority in the area, and the major fortification on the Tennessee was placed five miles downstream from the point recommended by Anderson. Construction had begun on June 14 and the first gun had been mounted on July 12.[2]

This work, named Fort Henry for Confederate Senator Gustavus A. Henry,[3] was anything but a source of pride to Tilghman. Planned and constructed in the dry season, Fort Henry during the wet season had become an unhealthy, treacherous, and nearly defenseless swamp-lake in which a half-dozen guns were submerged. Tilghman further feared that the placement of an enemy battery on the western side of the river would add to the danger of the fort and so began the construction of another fort on the western side, but this one on higher ground. Fort Heiman, the new fortress, was named after Tilghman's second in command, Colonel Adolphus Heiman, originally a native of Prussia, a veteran of the Mexican War, and Nashville's leading architect. In addition Tilghman saw the need to improve his communications so he constructed two roads to connect his forts and strung a telegraph line from both forts to Cumberland City, which would connect him to headquarters at Nashville.

On the 4th, a rocket signalled the approach of an escorted Federal convoy coming up the Tennessee. It needed little confirmation when gunboats began intermittent dueling with Fort Henry's water batteries. In spite of his weak position Tilghman decided to wait and see what his opponent's strategy would be.

Selecting a landing point out of gun range and more than three miles downstream, Grant began disembarking his troops. Keeping his force immobile while the transports shuttled back for the balance of his army, Grant took stock of his situation. Originally intending to lay siege to Forts Henry and Heiman by sealing off their lines of supply on the landward side, Grant's view of the terrain, influenced by the recent wet weather, brought doubts as to how speedily the maneuver could be effected.

On the 5th, the transports returned and Grant had assembled his entire force. While the apparent lack of activity and the unfinished condition of Fort Heiman might normally cause little worry, its location above the water line made it potentially more ominous. Grant therefore allotted to the smaller division under General Smith, with its two brigades under Colonels John Cook and Morgan Smith, the task of reducing Fort Heiman. Grant, with McClernand's 9,000 men, would march and attempt to encircle Fort Henry. He assumed this latter task could be completed early on the 6th, and his orders to Foote were to begin a naval bombardment on that date.

On the afternoon of the 5th, an interesting and humorous incident took place on the Tennessee. The gunboat *Conestoga* had spied and fished out of the water a Confederate device known as a torpedo. These had been planted in the river as hazards to the navigation of Union vessels. Now it rested on the fantail of the *Cincinnati,* awaiting inspection. With Foote at his side Grant suggested that the torpedo be taken apart. Several ratings were carefully selected for the project but before long their subject let out a hissing sound. Both Grant and Foote dashed up a nearby ladder. No explosion followed and Foote turned to Grant: "General, why the haste?"

"That the Navy may not get ahead of us," responded the general quickly. It indicated a matter which was uppermost on his mind.[4]

Meanwhile Tilghman had discovered his situation to be extremely precarious. Having marched all the men he could spare from Fort Donelson, he still could muster barely 3000 soldiers. Observing the unfolding strength of the Union army, Tilghman was convinced of the futility of attempting to withstand a siege. Even though the guns in his water battery were on practically the same level as the Union flotilla and there was no high spot in the fort for observation of effect, the strength of his ordnance decided Tilghman on the rather slight hope of defeating at least the Union navy. Thus he ordered Heiman to march his entire force, except for the heavy artillery company of 75 men, back to Fort Donelson. Tilghman, in remaining, thus condemned Fort Henry to certain doom in the vain hope of getting a crack at Foote's gunboats. As the heavy artillery could not be evacuated, they might at least serve some purpose before being captured or spiked. Also the ensuing artillery fire would cover Heiman's withdrawal to Fort Donelson and perhaps gain time for the further swelling of its garrison.

Tilghman was not to be disappointed in his desire for an engagement. Foote's flotilla of seven gunboats approached, feeling out the range. Four of these vessels were new ironclads, their slanted sides having 2½ inches of iron over 24 inches of oak. They mounted a total of 48 guns, while the other three unarmored boats fought with 27 guns.[5]

Against a potential total of 75 enemy cannon, Tilghman brought a river battery of 12 guns led by a 6-inch rifled gun. He had, however, the advantages of a steady firing platform, more room in which to work, and the fact that not all of the flotilla's guns could be brought to bear on him at once. This was due to the distribution of the guns on two to four sides of the boats and to the fact that the gunboats often obstructed each other's fire.

Almost from the beginning the struggle went against the Confederates. Barely five minutes of fighting had gone by when the important 24-pound rifled gun burst. Soon a cannon firing a 32-pound projectile became disabled. Then it was followed by a 42-pounder. After a while the priming wire jammed in the vent of the 10-inch Columbiad.[6]

After 2 hours and 10 minutes of firing Tilghman surveyed the situation. His "torpedoes" or electrically-fired mines in the river had had little effect. Only two guns were working, the other six having no one to work them. Dead and wounded were strewn over the battery. In spite of superior Confederate markmanship, the only appreciable effect had been the disabling of the *Essex*. There was no choice; Tilghman ordered the Stars and Bars hauled down.

Normally a party from the besieging land army would approach the surrendered fort to accept the surrender. In the case of Fort Henry, impassable conditions had prevented the Union army from taking even initial positions. The navy, not aware of this, was anxious to accept the rewards of a victory they had obviously won. With dispatch, a detail from the flagship *Cincinnati* lowered a rowboat which had not been splintered by fire from the fort. Quickly a crew rowed an officer bearing a white flag up to the wall where the sallyport was opened; the boat rowed inside to be beached on the parade ground. With ill-disguised joy at besting the army the naval officer escorted the Confederate general to the boat which would carry him to Foote. General Lloyd Tilghman could no longer be responsible for what happened at Fort Henry or at Fort Donelson.[7]

Meanwhile, Heiman's retreating garrison was experiencing terrain difficulties similar to Grant's. Avoiding interception by the slow moving Union infantry, the column was nevertheless harassed by outriding patrols of blue cavalry. Confederate cavalry became panic-stricken and earned the derision of the Southern infantry. Three miles beyond the fort the Federal horsemen made a rather determined dash and scooped up two straggling officers of the rearguard. Heiman, showed signs of distraction as a result of the cavalry forays. While the brigade retired in relatively good order, the artillerymen with their two light cannon complained of the condition of the road and the high swift-running creeks they were constantly required to ford. Finally on another threat by a body of Federal riders the already upset Confederate colonel consented to the abandonment of the two pieces. The cavalry, outnumbered, inexperienced, and unfamiliar with the territory, found contentment with their four trophies and retired in the direction of Fort Henry. Shortly before midnight on February 6th, Heiman's force, having marched more than 14 miles, found rest behind the earthworks of Fort Donelson.[8]

To all intents and purposes Grant found his orders fulfilled. Foote had been instructed to send an expedition up the Tennessee to destroy the railroad bridge and raid at will. Fort Henry was solidly in Federal hands and prisoners and cavalry reports left no doubt about the impossibility of a counterattack by the scrawny Fort Donelson garrison against Grant's impressive and fast-building army. The Tennessee was now safely a Federal turnpike.

Two other thoughts, however, lurked in the Union general's mind. One was that the element of surprise must not be lost. A delay would permit the enemy to bolster Fort Donelson to a point where it could withstand a direct assault by his army. The second thought was directed to the circumstances of the fall of Fort Henry. To some it might appear that a mere reinforced naval excursion could have brought about the capitulation of the fort on the Tennessee. Doubtless, reports would go out to Halleck and Northern newspapers to that effect. Already the engineer, Lieutenant Colonel McPherson, was suspected of being a spy for Halleck.[9] Succeeding these reports could come the dispersement of his formidable army or his replacement as its commander. Grant's future demanded the playing of greater roles than his part in the fall of Fort Henry.

At his request, John Rawlins, his assistant chief of staff, now entered the cabin. According to standard military procedure Rawlins could expect to be given a formal report of the operation along with a request for further orders from Halleck. The expectations were met in the first part with a short report, but it was followed by the blunt statement (not a request) that

Grant immediately march on Fort Donelson and take it on February 8th. Evidently considering Donelson little more than an outpost, Grant added that he would either destroy it or occupy it with a small force. Because of the "intolerable" roads he would take no transportation and little artillery.[10]

Halleck, a fretter, felt enormously relieved on the 7th when he read the report, even though the victory took on the aspect of a bear swatting a fly. Twenty-four hours previous a bulletin had reached him that the feared General Beauregard had arrived on the 5th to add prestige and experience to the defense of Fort Henry. Forthwith Halleck had seen to it that Colonel Charles Cruft's brigade, under Buell's overall command on the Green River, covering and threatening Bowling Green, was ordered to the area of conflict.[11] Now Fort Henry was conquered and the rail line severed. Fort Donelson was next. If failure resulted, the responsibility would rest on Grant's shoulders. If it succeeded, the operation was all part of the original nebulous operation approved by Halleck. From St. Louis he telegraphed McClellan that Fort Donelson would probably fall on February 8th. By withholding comment to Grant. Halleck purposely left his field commander in anxiety.

On the morning of the 7th, as Lloyd Tilghman wrote a full report to his superiors, and brushed off Federal reporters, Grant set out to fulfill his promise to Halleck by making a personal reconnaissance. With his staff and the bulk of a regiment of cavalry he rode east meeting no opposition. At the foot of a hill, near a cabin called the Crisp house, about a mile from the fort, scouts supplemented the particles of information already gathered on Fort Donelson from isolated gunboat reconnaissance. The fort itself stood on a hill commanding a straight stretch of the river. Its right flank was effectively protected, as Grant could see, by naturally flooded Hickman Creek. The Confederates were apparently improving upon the fort's defense by building outworks and cutting abatis (logs felled in the direction of enemy lines with selected strong branches trimmed to points).

The total result of the ride, however, did not encourage Grant. Intermittent rain and snow had brought the two roads to an impassible state.[12] The march of Heiman's brigade had not improved them. The countryside was hilly and lent itself easily to ambush and infantry defense, should the enemy choose to do so. The fort's situation was stronger than he had supposed. Inasmuch as he was bound by orders to defend Fort Henry at all cost, a land campaign was called for to prevent a sudden foray from Donelson on Henry.

With the roads in that condition the Union army could not reach Donelson as quickly as Grant had originally and over-optimistically hoped, particularly since he would need more artillery than planned. This meant a longer baggage and supply train and more horses for possible double-teaming, which Grant didn't have, and the building of a base of supplies at Fort Henry. Fort Donelson could not possibly be captured by the 8th.

3

The Buildup

ON THE MORNING OF FEBRUARY 7, 1862, FEW ADMITTED TO believing that Fort Donelson could be successfully defended. Least optimistic was General Albert Sidney Johnston, commander of Southern armies in Kentucky and Tennessee. Johnston, with a distinctive bearing as "regular army" as Union General Charles Smith, was a high ranker in the old U.S. Army and possessed a superior military rating in Richmond. Try as he would to cash in on this reputation, Johnston could not obtain what he considered sufficient troops to man his department. Now with the flanks of western and middle Tennessee exposed by the loss of the Tennessee River, he was profoundly discouraged.

Frightened by C. F. Smith's January exploratory raid, Johnston had, on January 20, ordered Brigadier John B. Floyd's brigade-size division and enough of Brigadier General Simon Bolivar Buckner's division, which would bring the detachment to 8,000 men, to entrain from Bowling Green to Russellville where it could be employed as a strategic reserve for either Bowling Green or the Cumberland–Tennessee region. Now on February 7, orders were in effect for General Floyd, commanding at Russellville, to tranship his troops to Clarksville on the Cumberland where a detachment was engaged in making the city secure.[1]

Johnston's next reaction to the threat to Fort Donelson was to order a senior officer to take command there. Late on the 6th, he telegraphed from Bowling Green to newly appointed Brigadier Bushrod Johnson (the engineer who had mislocated Fort Henry) at Nashville to make all speed for the danger spot. The second move was to order Generals Hardee and Beauregard to a conference in his quarters on the 7th.

That morning Hardee and Beauregard met according to Johnston's instructions. On Johnston's polite inquiry as to the state of his health, the victor of Fort Sumter and Bull Run felt forced to reply that the recurrence of a throat ailment made an assignment to a field command unwise at that time. Reviewing their reports on the garrison, the equipment at hand, and location of Fort Donelson, the generals agreed unanimously that the place was "not long tenable." With the results of Fort Henry, Johnston even expressed the opinion that the Federal Navy could independently pass and render impotent the water batteries and the fort.

In this despairing state of mind the generals made plans for even larger strategy. Attempts must be made to choose a site or sites and defend the Cumberland between Fort Donelson and Nashville. The threat to the positions in Kentucky were already too great and Bowling Green and vicinity must be evacuated by stages. Were Nashville to fall, Hardee and Beauregard would retreat to Stevenson, Alabama to prevent further advance up the Tennessee River. It was agreed that Polk was now situated in a semi-independent command and, leaving a token garrison at Columbus, should be charged with the defense of Memphis, even though the circumstances might necessitate his retreat into Mississippi. With little confidence for the future, Johnston ordered a brigade marched from Hopkinsville, Kentucky to Clarksville; he then set out to return to departmental headquarters at Nashville.[2]

Through an aide, Bushrod Johnson received the time of departure of the next steamer down the Cumberland. (The Confederacy had only ten on the entire river.) A former teacher and, until the war, head of Nashville's Western Military Institute, Johnson thought it prudent, while he waited, to briefly refamiliarize himself with the location of Donelson on an area map. From Nashville the Cumberland flowed northwest for roughly 40 miles to the city of Clarksville. Besides being the river crossing point for the Humboldt–Bowling Green trains, Clarksville terminated another rail line from Nashville. It also was the nearest point on the Cumberland to Hardee's troop concentrations at Hopkinsville, Russellville, and Bowling Green. Even with its past strategic supply position, the present fluid situation made it much more vital for military assembly defense and for supply to operations farther downstream. Almost directly west of Clarksville lay Fort Donelson. Between the two points, the Cumberland formed a "U." At the base of the "U" was Cumberland City, less important because of its poor road connections and its small size.

It was a natural reaction for a general not to become ecstatic about assignment to a defensive command known to be outnumbered at least two to one by enemy land forces. Furthermore no notice had been given Johnson about the eventual disposition of the forces gathering at Donelson. Nevertheless he steamed on to Clarksville and found his orders confirmed by the general in charge there: General Gideon J. Pillow.

After the battle of Belmont, Pillow had been commended in General Polk's account of that action. Nevertheless a bitter quarrel soon ensued between the two over the legality of an appointment. With his orderly legal mind Pillow found it necessary to dispute Polk's use of his authority, which, in this case, he said infringed upon that of the President of the Confederate States. Feeling deeply on the matter, Pillow resigned his position in Polk's department; he claimed that Polk asked his forgiveness and withdrawal of the resignation. In Columbus, because of Pillow's great popularity among the junior officers and rank and file, a movement caught fire to present Polk with a petition expressing confidence in the former Tennessee politician. Privately Polk denounced this mass action as being inspired by Pillow. He also attacked his former subordinate as being overly proud of his Mexican War record and consequently unwilling to serve under subordinates from that war. Polk, who a few months previous had been an Episcopalian bishop, held that much of the argument stemmed from Pillow's intense ambition for higher rank. Finally the bishop-general began to criticize the Tennesseean's "blunders" in posting his men and selecting his ground at Belmont. Meanwhile Pillow had retired "ill" to his home in Columbia, from whence in late January he was sent to command at Clarksville.[3]

From Clarksville, where it took aboard the 2nd Kentucky regiment, the steamer bearing Brigadier General Johnson proceeded to the hamlet of Dover, one mile east of Fort Donelson. At the Dover Upper Landing in the early darkness of evening, Johnson could distinguish little of the town except from the dimly lighted tavern just up the slope. As is their custom tavern owners construct their establishments athwart main avenues of travel. The tavern of Dover was no exception to this rule. Lying in a corner of the village, it nevertheless would probably be noticed by anyone who set foot in Dover, for few visitors came to Dover who did not either arrive or depart by boat. Roads had been built from the town to haul supplies to a few inland farmers and some iron furnaces. Now, however, even the light from the weather-beaten tavern revealed a more purposeful, if more brutal, reason for existence of the hamlet. On the landing and along the road from it, supplemented from the steamer on which Johnson had jorneyed, military necessities were accumulating.

Commandeering horse and guide the general struck out for the fort. A crooked road led them to the brink of a deep, swampy valley, and after the highly treacherous winter footing was negotiated, Johnson rode past nervous sentries into Fort Donelson.

The situation encountered was far from encouraging. He was ushered into one of the largest of the 400 cabins[4] in the fort. Assembling the chief officers, Johnson was startled to discover that a vacuum of command existed. When Tilghman had departed for Fort Henry on February 4, Colonel John Head of the 30th Tennessee had been assigned to lead the Donelson garrison. Adolphus Heiman was shaken by the sudden experience of his retreat less than 24 hours before. In this condition and believing Head to be a difficult personality, Heiman did not assume the command of the fort from him. The difficulty was that this important detail was not widely known among the personnel, many believing Heiman had taken the authority and a report was even sent to Polk to that effect.[5] In addition most of the officers were surprised and showed some disappointment to see Johnson appear, as they had been led to expect the arrival of Pillow.

The agenda moved on and Johnson was briefed on the situation and activities at Donelson. Major Jeremy Gilmer, Chief Engineer of Polk's Western Department, and born in the North, had just arrived that day but had busied himself in marking lines of "infantry cover" outside the fort. A scant 750 feet southwest of the fort lay the northern extremity of an X-shaped ridge, which, by its height, dominated the already constructed earthworks. Gilmer had labored to establish works on the southern portion of this "X." In this task he discovered that the left flank of this complex was threatened by a wide Indian Creek Valley through which ran the Pinery Road. Not only would an enemy deployment penetrating the valley outflank the works on the "X," but it would lead them to the rear and the weakest portion of Fort Donelson. Gilmer thus found it necessary to survey the ridge on the eastern face of the valley.[6] This rise of ground was triangular in shape and was brought to a point some slight distance to the rear of the left flank of the "X" works by another creek running almost directly south. To prevent the opposing forces from advancing along the length of the ridge Gilmer seized upon a hillock in the center, its left and right flanks well defended by intervening ravines. Daylight had run out and, anyhow, this line if occupied would tax the resources of a garrison of the present size.

Lieutenant Colonel Milton Haynes, bearing the impressive title of Chief of Tennessee Artillery (Volunteer), had been directed by Tilghman to take charge of the artillery of the fort on January 16. He outlined some of his problems to Johnson. On Haynes' arrival the fort possessed artillery but no cannoneers. With permission of Colonel Head a company of infantry from his regiment, under Captain Bidwell, and another company, under Captain Beaumont, were detached for temporary artillery duty. Neither had a knowledge of or experience with artillery, but in their drills they were assisted by Haynes' commissioned assistants. (These latter had been sent from Polk on request.) Since not all guns in the water batteries, especially the most effective, were mounted, the fort was quite ill-prepared to meet an attack from the river. An underground bombproof 100-round magazine had been constructed to serve the ten 32-pounders, the 8-inch howitzer, two questionable 9-pounders, the 10-inch columbiad, and the 6½-inch rifled gun. The latter had only arrived on February 1, and the columbiad had been damaged in trial, but had been repaired with new wheels and now worked "like a charm."

Parenthetically Haynes added that the garrison was also served by a battery of light artillery under Captain Frank Maney.[7]

On being questioned, the supply officer mentioned that the situation with regard to munitions and subsistence stores building up in the town was reaching an impossible state. The medical officer stated that the number of sick due to the inclement weather and Heiman's forced march were mounting and many should be evacuated.[8]

News arrived that about 300 men of the 51st Virginia under Colonel Gabriel Wharton had arrived at the wharf. After arranging for their encampment near the landing, Johnson initiated a tally of the number of troops at his disposal.[9] Even with the addition of the two regiments that had arrived in the evening, Johnson discovered there were only 5,300 men to man the entrenchments.

At the close of the meeting, Heiman mentioned the clashes with cavalry pickets during the day and predicted the possibility that the Federals would mass in force before the incomplete entrenchments on the 8th. His spirits taxed, Johnson retired for the night.

Robust Lieutenant Colonel Randal McGavock, son of Nashville's most distinguished family, prepared to check in at Dover's crowded Brandon's Hotel. When Heiman was given brigade responsibility, McGavock naturally assumed command of the largely Irish 10th Tennessee. Little notice had been taken of them after their retreat from Fort Henry, and the regiment was consequently lacking in tents, utensils, blankets, and overcoats. Enough tents had been borrowed from cabin-housed units at the fort to allow the regiment to encamp along the eastern bluff of Indian Creek near the Dover Cemetery.[10]

Meanwhile, General Ulysses Grant, unaware of the wretched state of the paper-thin Confederate defenses, found or thought he found more reasons on February 8 for not launching his announced offensive. For one thing precipitous action was ruled out by the fact that Halleck was not about to forbid the endeavor. (If he had, Grant could always, like Nelson at Copenhagen, turn his blind eye to the signal and proceed immediately with his own plans.) All that the St. Louis-based Halleck was doing was speeding reinforcements up the Tennessee. This in itself was a cause for delay. The weather, nature, and the Confederacy had not designed Fort Henry and environs to be either a hostel or a depot for an army of over 15,000 men, much less both. The inundated territory was becoming crowded and unhealthy for men and supplies. The troops, without tents, had to subsist on hardtack and coffee.[11]

Aside from political and logistical considerations, Grant encountered other problems. Foote had complained about the post-battle condition of his gunboats and had pursued the severely damaged *Essex* down the Tennessee to Cairo, along with the bulk of his flotilla, for repairs. In the Illinois town he promised he would seek to legally replenish his crews. Without the navy Grant would lose his ace in the hole. That day also brought increased reports of indiscriminate burning, pillaging, marauding, and destroying of the countryside by Union forces. Idle men become restless, so Grant had orders drafted to put his soldiers to work developing the fortifications at the former Fort Heiman.[12]

In spite of some latent discontent at the inaction among his subordinates—notably McClernand—Grant decided to allow the second day following the fall of Fort Henry to pass without marching or planning for a march. After all it was coming up Sunday—the day of rest.

In St. Louis, Henry Halleck shuffled papers like a beaver. From departments as far away as Kansas he had assembled an immediate reinforcement force of 8,000 men for Grant. Buell, according to telegrams received, was cooperating by sending a four-regiment brigade up the Tennessee and offering eight more regiments. Knowing that Buell was a favorite of McClellan's, Halleck had become suspicious of this evidence of sudden interest in his campaign and on the 7th had suggested to McClellan that he himself would go to Fort Henry on the 10th or 11th. If he and Buell were both going to be there, Halleck would have the ranking authority. While steeling himself against further encroachments upon his realm, Halleck found time to send Grant his sanction to impress slaves if necessary to construct appropriate entrenchments at Fort Henry.[13]

Unknown to Grant, Halleck was busily striving to bring a new commanding general to the Tennessee. A Department of the Mississippi would be created, making its general equal in rank with Buell and preventing poaching on Halleck's prerogatives. Suitable to Halleck's plans were Brigadier William Tecumseh Sherman at Paducah and a General Hitchcock (neither of whom were the slightest bit interested in the propriety of supplanting a successful field commander).[14]

Unlike his opposite number, Halleck, Albert Sidney Johnston lay in the throes of indecision. To Richmond, capital of the Confederacy, he telegraphed a report on the activities of the past few days. In part it said, "The capture of that fort [Henry] by the enemy gives them the control of the navigation of the Tennessee River, and their gunboats are now ascending the river to Florence. Operations against Fort Donelson, on the Cumberland, are about to be commenced, and that work will soon be attacked. . . . I think the gunboats of the enemy will probably take Fort Donelson with the necessity of employing their land force in cooperation, as seems to have been done at Fort Henry." The "7000" men at Donelson, Johnston stated, were "not well armed or drilled, except Heiman's regiment and the regiments of Floyd's command."[15]

Ever since the Crimean War, ten years before, military authorities had disputed the future of fortifications, especially earthworks, against the developing ironclad vessel. In that war the Russians had been singularly unsuccessful in repelling Allied ironclads. To Johnston the battle of Fort Henry served only to further drive home the lessons of the Crimean campaign. Back in his headquarters at Nashville his disillusionment drained from his will most of the initiative required of him as commander in chief of the western contingents.

Johnston had several alternatives. On one hand he could pick a site for a defensive stand downstream from Nashville. Also it would be a natural expectation of the commander in chief to oversee the front-line situation at the fort himself. The rail line at his disposal could speed Hardee and his army to Donelson where Grant could be crushed before he mounted an overwhelming army. Possibly, in spite of the swampy landward approaches, Fort Henry might even be retaken. The most apparent and unimaginative course was to abandon to the Union the line of the Cumberland and Nashville with its precious storehouses, field artillery factory, and arsenals. These were the obvious choices facing Johnston.

Yet as he meditated in his Nashville office, Johnston took no direct action on the 8th. Somehow it seems as if he felt the loss of the rivers was pre-ordained. He seems not to have been greatly surprised by the quick demise of Fort Henry. Certainly, consciously or subconsciously he felt a twinge of guilt that after five months in his current post the river forts were not in a more advanced state of preparation.

Here enters a puzzling factor. Rationally, with Johnston's belief in the invulnerability of the ironclad gunboats, how could he possibly tolerate the maintenance of a large garrison at Fort Donelson, of all places? If, as Johnston predicted, the ironclads could easily overcome the water batteries, where would this leave the garrison? With the beneficent assumption that the Federal army would not yet have invested the place, the advance of the gunboats would have cut off the only convenient line of retreat. The commander would be compelled to march his troops over roads more miserable than the ones Grant now faced. Not only would a retreat along these lines still run the risk of interception or overrunning by the Union army, but it led almost nowhere—away from avenues and centers of strategic importance—and it foolishly violated the famous military dictum against dividing one's force in the face of the enemy by hopelessly separating the garrison from Nashville.

Johnston's initiative remained paralyzed in spite of hints and suggestions from subordinates. General Buckner, at Russellville, relayed a report heard from a private source in Cairo, Illinois, that five Union gunboats had been sent up the Tennessee and that the remaining warships with 16 transports were ascending the Cumberland with 12,000 confident men in blue. The report obviously denoted an immediate threat to Fort Donelson. General Floyd, while he shared Johnston's opinions about the invulnerability of the ironclads, telegraphed Johnston that he was greatly impressed with the potential strength of Clarksville.[16]

General Pillow at Clarksville had determined to be as formidable an antagonist to the Northern horde as he had been to his superiors, Generals Scott and Polk. Out of a situation which could easily have led to chaos, Pillow used his great energy and organizational talent to make Clarksville the most efficient supply post on the river. His cheery spirit was infectious and touched most of those with whom he came in contact. With these advantages the military units and stores which came pouring into Clarksville from the north, east, and south were effectively directed or unloaded.

To Pillow there lurked no doubt that the area of decision centered upon Fort Donelson. While personally he had not inspected the post at Dover, his nature dictated that the enemy must be met and stopped on the front line. Thus, while it is true he had little heavy artillery, he did little to put Clarksville in a state of defense. It was chiefly he who was responsible for the plentitude of supplies at Dover, as he had continued their flow past Clarksville downstream. As regiments of the divisions of General Floyd and General Buckner arrived at the city, Pillow forthwith dispatched them to Donelson. For this the reasons were dual. His uncomplicated mind assumed that the threatened work would be defended and to accomplish this it needed soldiers. Rumors already had him destined to be given the responsibility of the garrison and he was only doing his duty and preparing for that eventuality. Also, while it would seem that the retention of these piecemeal reinforcements at Clarksville would elaborate on his own power, Pillow fully realized that Floyd and Buckner would soon be along to reassume the direction of these portions of their divisions.[17]

As a matter of fact, on the 8th General Floyd was already at Clarksville. One year older than Pillow, Floyd stood out among the men of that day but not in physical magnificence. He was short in stature and his long face, distinguished by its lack of beard or mustache, was bordered by a receding hairline and a weak, receding chin. Age had brought flabby jowls but had not altered the Roman nose with its wide nostrils. On first notice one might categorize him as a politician or an orator, and Floyd was just that. From a disastrous cotton-planting venture in Arkansas, he rose to occupy the Virginia Governor's Mansion in 1848. President James Buchanan had appointed him Secretary of War and Floyd bore heavy responsibility for the quantity of Federal arms and ammunition falling into secessionist hands, for the dispersion of government land and sea forces to the time of Lincoln's inauguration, and to some degree for the preliminary maneuvers at Fort Sumter. (In Union camps he was commonly referred to as "the thief.") His distinguished background supposedly compensated somewhat for his lack of active military service, and Floyd was made one of the early brigadiers of the Confederate army. In 1861 he saw some action in the mountains of western Virginia against McClellan's invasion, and in the latter part of December orders came to him to evacuate that theater by way of Kentucky. It was there that the combined facts of not proving himself incompetent and of having seniority and his own troops secured him the command of a division. To complete his complement Buckner was required to provide some regiments.[18]

Floyd's arrival in Clarksville produced difficulties between Pillow and Floyd. The difference of time between May 27 and July 9 (their appointment dates to brigadier general) made Floyd the senior officer present. Also Pillow had consigned two of the regiments (a brigade) from Floyd's much cherished original Virginia brigade to Fort Donelson. The result was, however, that while Pillow conducted his operations more cautiously, Floyd did not greatly exert his authority, other than in giving Johnston the recommendation already mentioned and requesting him to make a personal visit and give directions.[19]

In turn Floyd had received instructions through Johnston's assistant adjutant general:

> Although the employment of your forces after arriving at Clarksville has been left to your discretion, I deem it proper that you ascertain whether the enemy will hold his force to attack Fort Donelson in conjunction with gunboats or move them against Clarksville direct.[20]

Because of this doubt as to the intentions of Grant the Southern forces along the Cumberland were literally split into two camps.

With his rising early on the 8th, General Bushrod Johnson forlornly prepared to meet his responsibilities. Although he possessed an imposing military background—West Point, Seminole War, and Mexican War—Johnson was unaccustomed to, and insecure in, tasks where no general direction from a superior was given him. In addition the reporting of the rumor that Pillow had been scheduled to assume command tended to fluster him. Weakly then, he devoted his attention to the tasks in which he felt the most happiness and proficiency.

One of his first orders was to the medical officer to prepare the sick cases for removal to the Dover landings. At the landings they were to be carried aboard the empty transports and steamers which had disgorged their charges and were prepared to trudge back up the Cumberland. Inasmuch as possible the military stores were removed from exposure.

At the water batteries, Lieutenant Colonel Haynes continued serving each gun with 15 artillerists, if possible. The time was divided between drilling inexperienced crews and mounting the remaining guns in position. Captain Beaumont, with his infantry company of 80 men, served five 32-pounder guns. The 75 foot soldiers of Captain Bidwell worked the columbiad and four 32-pounders.[21]

Johnson did order the bulk of his cavalry under Lieutenant Colonel Gantt to make an advanced picket of the roads, especially the northern or Telegraph Road. While this was being done, Major Gilmer, often stroking his long beard in agitation at the lack of attention he was receiving, continued laboring on the outer works with the few men placed at his disposal.

With the sun beginning to dip behind the tallest of the trees, the 56th Virginia of Wharton's brigade arrived around 4 P.M. Also coming to the scene that day was the 18th Tennessee of 685 men belonging to Buckner's division and under the command of Colonel Joseph Palmer and the 3rd Tennessee, 750 troops in assorted excuses for uniforms, under the command of Colonel John Brown, who had been assigned to brigade command.[22] Altogether the force at Donelson amounted to about 7,000 men, the exact figure Albert Sidney Johnston had communicated to Richmond, only earlier in the day.

On the bleak, wintery morning of February 9th, the Northern army of General Ulysses S. Grant roused themselves reluctantly. Early inspection of the river clearly indicated that the water level was falling.

This piece of information had not escaped the notice of the commanding general. Aside from ordering the cavalry patrols to be a bit more active and to observe more closely the height of the water in the creeks, however, Grant made no preparations for an immediate forward movement. Instead he devoted his attention to logistics, procedure, and paper work. He ordered Major Rawlins to warn the colonels who commanded the brigades that were involved in the vandalism and stealing. A hurried communiqué was dispatched to St. Louis asking for the assignment of the 2nd Iowa regiment to his army. It seems that the 2nd Iowa had originally been destined for the western Missouri campaign (which would soon culminate in the battle of Pea Ridge).[23]

In the Queen City, General Halleck busied himself over the jurisdictional dispute with McClellan and Buell and efficiently assured the flow of military necessities and reinforcements to the army on the Tennessee. Foote had bluntly refused his suggestion to run the Donelson river batteries with three ironclads to destroy that haunting railroad bridge. That evening the 1st Nebraska departed for the front. Before he left his office that night Halleck approved the reassignment of the 2nd Iowa to Grant's theater. There was one provision, however. Due to the suspicious occurrence of the robbery of a St. Louis museum under the guard of the regiment and because it happened during the temporary absence of Colonel Tuttle, the unit was under instructions to board their transports with folded colors and silent drums. Halleck made a note that he would address a further communiqué to the regiment on the morrow.[24]

At Cairo, discovering the minister to be unavailable, Flag

Officer Andrew Foote took upon himself the obligation to preach the morning sermon at the Presbyterian Church.[25]

Bushrod Johnson was not the only Confederate general who at that time was adroitly avoiding difficult decisions. His near namesake, Albert Sidney Johnston, reckoned that with the possibility of attack and pursuit from Buell, many miles to the north, the Bowling Green front was more worthy of his attention. This reasoning occurred in spite of the existence of and confusion in the growing corps of over 10,000 Confederate soldiers between Clarksville and the Tennessee River. Thus the unique situation developed of a major general (Hardee) and one healthy and one sick full general dedicating their personal attention to a dwindling and slightly superior force unthreatened by the enemy, while much nearer to the commanding general dwelt the main striking army, facing the enemy but scattered and ruled in portions by four brigadier generals of differing seniority.

Johnston was well aware that his professional reputation rested to a high degree on his ability to handle military personnel. Knowing Pillow's contentious nature, he sensed a storm brewing at Clarksville. For one thing Floyd had ordered a large amount of foodstuffs returned to Nashville instead of having them forwarded to Donelson or even kept in readiness at the Clarksville depot. Also with an inkling of Bushrod Johnson's paucity of self-confidence when not in a subordinate position, the commanding general found it convenient to order General Pillow to take himself immediately from Clarksville to Fort Donelson and take direction of the crisis.[26]

Meanwhile, Pillow, suspecting and expecting something of that sort—after all, he was the senior Tennessee general—had briefed himself as much as possible on Fort Donelson. He was well aware, for instance, that the fort had been named for General Daniel Smith Donelson, an old acquaintance in politics of Pillow's and former Speaker of the statehouse.

Technically in charge of the choosing of the fort, Donelson, famous for being a nephew of Andrew Jackson, was not too surprised to discover the work named after him.[27] Pillow also reckoned that with the despairing mood at Clarksville, the reinforcements from that place could not have raised the morale at Fort Donelson to any degree.

Not long after the departure of General Pillow on the 9th, General Simon Bolivar Buckner lowered himself from his railroad car at Clarksville. In appearance very similar to Albert Sidney Johnston, Buckner boasted an impressive military build, crowned with a magnificent mustache on an oval, square-jawed face. A Kentuckian of thirty-nine, he had been graduated from West Point and had been twice promoted in the Mexican War. Shortly after his resignation from the regular army in 1855, and after living near Nashville for about a year, Buckner became commander of the Kentucky State Guard and in that capacity raised morale to a high point. As an inducement to leave the service of that "neutral" state the Federal government offered him a commission as brigadier general, but he accepted an offer instead to command a division in Johnston's army.

It was certainly no accident that General Buckner had postponed his entry into Clarksville until the arrival of his rear guard from Russellville. With Pillow's presence in that city Buckner had good reason to avoid a face-to-face encounter. The cause dated back to 1857 when Pillow had declared himself a candidate for the Tennessee seat in the United States Senate. In the campaign Pillow's war record was brought into question. In the Mexico City campaign incident, when Scott had testily relieved Pillow of command and tried to court martial him for insubordination, Pillow retaliated by levelling acusations against General Scott. Scott's friends rallied to his support and among them stood Buckner. As the controversy continued after the election, in which Pillow was defeated by

Andrew Johnson, Buckner wrote three sarcastic articles under a pseudonym in a Nashville newspaper. Pillow, of course, replied with spirit to the ridicule, and the talk of the town was that a duel was imminent. The smoke blew over, but no reconciliation was made.[28]

Buckner could have enumerated many reasons, other than the proximity of Pillow, for being unhappy with the current situation. In the required move to Russellville in January, he had been able to retain only the 2nd Kentucky of General John Breckinridge's Kentucky brigade. He had also sacrificed the 1st Kentucky cavalry. These favored home state units would stay with Hardee wherever he marched. This left Buckner with a residue of about 5,000 men, many debilitated with recent camp sickness and demoralized by the withdrawal from Kentucky.[29]

Meanwhile Gideon Pillow steamed with his rather large staff toward Fort Donelson. Somewhat addicted to writing proclamations, he was quite conscious of the army's need for firm leadership and for a boost in morale. He therefore outlined for his chief of staff, Gus Henry, an order of the day to be read or posted before all units after his landing.

Special Orders No. 1 — Headquarters, Dover, Tenn., February 9, 1862

Brigadier General Pillow assumes command of the forces at this place. He relies with confidence upon the courage and fidelity of the brave officers and men under his command to maintain the post. Drive back the ruthless invader from our soil and again raise the Confederate flag over Fort Henry. He expects every man to do his duty. With God's help we will accomplish our purpose. Our battle cry, "Liberty or death."

By order of Brigadier General Pillow:

Gus A. Henry, Jr.,
Assistant Adjutant General.[30]

These aggressive intentions took a jolt with Pillow's arrival at the wharf. He received the disturbing report that at a location halfway between Forts Donelson and Henry on the northern or Telegraph Road a cavalry engagement had decidedly gone against the Confederates. A Union troop of 200 men had attacked the approximately equal picket force of Gantt's 9th Tennessee battalion. In the restricted area a score of Rebel troopers were knocked or had fallen from their mounts to become prisoners when their companions precipitously galloped away in the direction of Fort Donelson. A handful of dead Rebels also remained as trophies.[31]

Dismissing this incident as a misfortune of war, Pillow left Major W. H. Haynes at Dover in temporary charge of the commissariat, obtained horses and rode off to the fort. There, with General Johnson, he devoted his attention to the point of primary importance, the water batteries.

The batteries were divided into two sections—the lower and the upper. In his research Pillow had discovered that the Cumberland River often would fall in depth from 5 to 6 feet in 24 hours, and with the current lowering of the water level this worked to the advantage of the defense. Pillow was impressed not only with their narrow embrasures but with the probability that no more than three gunboats could bring their weapons to bear on the batteries at one time because of the narrow confines of the river at that point. All guns but the columbiad and the rifled 32-pounder were in place.[32]

On the other hand the general manifested shock at the indefensibility of the field works on the landward side of the fort. Not only were they dominated by the higher features of the "X," but on their own they were tactically weak. On the eastern face of the fort lay a large, fairly steep valley through which ran a tiny stream—Hickman Creek. The works across the floor of this valley were easily dominated by the eastern topography which would be in enemy hands. Even worse, the crest of the ridge 50 feet above the valley was so narrow that a consequent withdrawal to it would place the defenders back-to-back with the lower water battery. Enemy artillery from the river and valley sides could then play havoc with these cramped troops on the ridge. Fortunately, Pillow soon discovered, the approach to this vulnerable valley in Fort Donelson had been largely sealed by the works laid out by Major Gilmer.

Pillow went on to concern himself with the labors of this worthy officer. Gilmer's complaints about the scarcity of labor received immediate attention. Pillow placed special emphasis on continuing the field works to the east so as to render safe the base of supplies, Dover.[33]

Returning to town, Pillow established his headquarters in the Dover Tavern.[34] He instructed his aides to see to the procurement of a larger quantity of ammunition for the heavy artillery from Nashville. Even though it was getting late in the evening, he still took time to draft reports to Floyd and to issue orders for the organization and disposition of his forces.

First of all Buckner loomed as a touchy thorn. Of his division, the 2nd Kentucky (Colonel Hanson), most of Brown's brigade, and a regiment of Baldwin's brigade had arrived at Donelson. To try to avoid further controversy with the man, Pillow wrote that Buckner, even though he was not present, would command his own division and control the right wing. General Johnson was issued instructions to direct the left wing, which comprised Heiman's brigade with Captain Maney's battery, the just-arrived brigade from Hopkinsville under the command of the senior colonel—Davidson—and the brigade under Colonel Drake, made up from Heiman's Fort Henry evacuees and the original fort garrison. The command of the fort proper went to Colonel Head in charge of three regiments. Pillow displayed sensitivity to Floyd's superior rank by not assigning his regiments to anyone. Altogether the garrison could now muster around 9,000 fighting men.

At 8.30, Pillow interrupted other tasks to complete his letter to John Floyd on the state of affairs:

Fort Donelson, February 8 [sic] 1862

General Floyd:

I reached this place in time to walk through the works before dark. The works are not completed nor do I consider them well conceived. But I find them fully as well prepared for defense as I expected. I will push everything with all the energy I can command. The trouble is the want of everything—tools, lumber, and the necessary equipments of the artillery. From the imperfect examination of the ground and its surroundings I feel very confident of holding it against an assault by the infantry and if I am allowed time to complete the works and mount all the guns I have confidence in being able to resist an attack of their gunboats if they are vulnerable to all metal. The enemy are reported in strong force both sides of the Tennessee River and on the road approaching this place. He still occupies Fort Henry and holds Tilghman there yet. Their body of infantry is still below Fort Henry. It is said by scouts and citizens that there are two gunboats eight or ten miles below here. It is absolutely necessary for the health of the troops that their tents shall be pushed forward as rapidly as possible and I shall stand in great need of General Buckner. Will you order him down as early as possible. I will communicate more fully to-morrow, and advise you by telegram via Cumberland City and couriers frequently that you may keep General Johnston well informed of our condition and wants.

Your obedient servant,

Gid. J. Pillow
Brigadier General, C. S. Army

Fearing it would be near morning before the steamer reached Clarksville, Pillow dashed off a telegram to Floyd at 9 P.M.

I have reached this place and find everything quiet. Enemy said to be [in] force on Tennessee River, and two gun-boats ten miles below. I have written you.[35]

Not all Confederates in the gathering army at Dover had welcomed the arrival of Pillow. Through his prominent position in Nashville, Randal McGavock had pre-war association with the lawyer-politician. He had no confidence in the man, but was determined to make the most of the situation, especially since his wife had sent a box of blankets for himself and his men. The weather was cold and disagreeable, he wrote in his journal.[36]

A number of events stirred Grant from his lethargic state of inaction on the 10th. Among them was the successful patrol of Captain Stewart who, on the 9th, had routed a considerable force of the enemy. Another was the obviously improving condition of the water routes. Certainly not least but definitely most surprising was pressure from General Henry Halleck. In Grant's hands lay a dispatch from his superior urging destruction of the railroad bridge at Clarksville.[37] With the navy still not up to par, the most obvious way in which to accomplish this was to capture Fort Donelson.

There could be no more delay. Grant picked up his pen and scribbled a plea to Foote, in Cairo. A minimum of two gunboats would be required for support on an advance to Donelson. Could Foote furnish them? If necessary the army could supply artillerists. He did not "feel justified in going without some of your [Foote's] gunboats to cooperate."[38] The wheels were set in motion, for not only could the flag officer make ready at least two vessels, but Grant had challenged his pride in his service with the offer of army artillerists.

With efficiency the stocky general dismissed another complication. So many reinforcing regiments had made their way to Fort Henry that they could no longer be assimilated into existing brigades. He therefore ordered that the 17th, 43rd, and 49th Illinois be grouped into the Third Brigade of McClernand's division. The 14th Iowa, the 25th and 52nd Indiana, Birge's Sharpshooters, and a battalion of cavalry were to become the Fourth Brigade of Smith's division. Each brigade would be led by its senior colonel.[39]

Orders went to Brigadiers Lew Wallace, McClernand, and Smith to meet him on the gunboat *Tigress* at 2 P.M. With Rawlins in attendance, the senior officers of the army gathered in the comfortable ladies' cabin. There in reserved tones Grant inquired, "The question for consideration, gentlemen, is whether we shall march against Fort Donelson or wait for reinforcements. I should like to have your views."

"There is every reason why we should move without loss of a day," Smith responded abruptly, almost impatiently.

General McClernand removed from his pocket a document which was obviously of some length. As McClernand read from it, Grant could not suppress some inward amusement at the time his associate had taken to impress upon everyone the necessity for aggressive action. There, of course, existed the latent threat that if the course recommended did not get approval, the contents of the paper would be sent to important Northern personages. After all, McClernand received his brigadier's appointment the same day as Grant and would therefore suffer no embarrassment at being appointed commander of the army. Smith, bored by a political and legalistic harangue, began to wish that Grant would permit in his presence a beverage stronger than water.

At the conclusion of McClernand's reading, Grant turned to Wallace, nodded with the assumption that there was no disagreement, and said, "Let us go, by all means; the sooner the better. We will set out immediately. Orders will be sent you. Get your commands ready." At least one general returned to the shore convinced that Grant had sometime before that council determined his course of action.[40]

Grant then set Rawlins and his staff to work by issuing verbal instructions to prepare general orders to the effect that the army was to be in readiness to move on the dawn of Wednesday, February 12th. To facilitate this, 40 rounds of ammunition and two days' rations were to be issued to each man.[41]

All over the encampment the eyes of officers lighted up as they surveyed their orders. It looked as if the Union army would finally march on Donelson.

In St. Louis, Halleck remembered to issue his final instructions to the embarrassed 2nd Iowa before their departure that night. The stigma under which they were marching to their boats (folded colors and silent drums), he stated, could be removed for all time by the regiment proving itself valorous in action. Grimly the men of the 2nd Iowa resolved to heed this admonition.

Grant's indecision and immobility had begun to cause Halleck pain. He was faintly amused that Grant, since his hasty announcement that he would capture Fort Donelson on the 8th, had communicated his reports through the Federal commander at Cairo. Now, however, Halleck demanded action. On the evening of February 10, he transmitted a dispatch by boat again urging the destruction of the bridge at Clarksville. He firmed this request up with the statement, "Run any risk to accomplish this." He also communicated his desires for an advance up the Cumberland to Flag Officer Foote.[42]

Gestures deemed threatening on the part of Federal forces before Bowling Green consumed the attention of General Albert Sidney Johnston that Monday. The evacuation of the 20,000 men left to Hardee was taking place by stages. No consideration appears to have been given to routing any portion of the Central Army to the strategic reserve center of

Clarksville. Johnston's concern was primarily that the commands on the Cumberland cover his left flank until the retirement to Nashville could be completed.

In Clarksville it had not occurred to General Floyd to request further reinforcements. For one thing he remained unsure of actual conditions at Donelson and of future plans of strategy for the defense of the region. Two days previous, it must be recalled, Floyd had requested Johnston to personally pay a visit and take charge of the situation and the reply was only to order further intelligence gathering on Grant's intentions. Having only tenuous confidence in his own military judgment, Floyd tentatively decided to allow the upper echelon determinations for the Cumberland to rest with the superior authority and experience of Albert Sidney Johnston.

Even then, however, pressures mounted for the altering of this resolve. General Buckner continued to face a dilemma in regard to his relationship with General Pillow. By now most of Buckner's division were laboring on the Fort Donelson entrenchments. It was almost obligatory, especially since he had been assigned a responsibility, for Buckner to journey to the front and lead his troops. Indeed, that very day Pillow repeated his request for Buckner's presence. Other ideas, however, developed in his fertile mind.

More than halfway between Clarksville and Dover lay the town of Cumberland City. Buckner reasoned that a forward movement of Floyd and the reserves to that location combined with a retrograde movement from Donelson would return his division to his command and give him equal if not superior status to Pillow. Adroitly he initiated the task of planting this plan in the mind of Floyd.

In Donelson, Pillow supervised the implementation of his orders of the 9th. To assist him he added to his staff Major Haynes, who was then relieved of his duty at the commissary. While Pillow enjoyed some grandeur from a coterie of neatly uniformed, high-ranking officers, the usefulness of aides in commanding a large group of men was not overlooked. All indications are that Pillow's staff was kept busy in his service.

Under pressure from Pillow, Major Gilmer, with ample assistance, had extended his field works to the left so as to embrace Dover. Advantage had been taken of a defensible ridge fronting the town. While Pillow approved of the sites of the entrenchments, he showed concern over the length of the works (two-and-a-half miles) with the garrison he possessed to defend them.

With alacrity the regiments were rushed to their respective positions with available tools for entrenching. Parties of slaves cleared space before the prospective defenses by cutting breast-high abatis. Some units found difficulties, however. Cavalry clashes between patrols made the green troops quite nervous. Worse yet some regiments possessed insufficient or inadequate tools, and sharing among detachments became necessary.[40]

Some units, however, had no part in the erecting of their own defenses. Lieutenant Colonel McGavock's 10th Tennessee moved out to occupy the south end of a ridge south of Erin Hollow.[44] They found constructed parapets of logs and brush covered with dirt.

Even with the press of his duties Pillow found time to transmit the following hurried communication to Floyd:

> I am apprehensive, from the large accumulation of the enemy's forces in the neighborhood of Fort Henry, that the enemy will attempt to cross the country south of my position and cut my communications by river, thus depriving me of supplies from above. The country south of me is exceedingly broken and rugged, so much so as to be nearly impracticable, but the enemy may possibly make it. His difficulty will be in procuring supplies for his forces which is one almost (if not altogether) insurmountable. I think that is my safety.
>
> The conflict of yesterday between our cavalry and that of the

enemy resulted in 3 of ours wounded and 20 of ours taken prisioners by being thrown from their horses and in 3 of the enemy killed and 6 mortally wounded. Three of the enemy's gun-boats have gone up the Tennessee River above the bridge. The *Eastport,* which we were converting into a gun-boat, was burned and sunk, as was one steamboat, to keep them from falling into the hands of the enemy. The enemy have destroyed the high trestle work on the left bank of the Tennessee River, but have not damaged the bridge.

I am pushing the work on my river batteries day and night; and on my field works and defensive lines on the river also day and night. In one week's time (if I am allowed that much time) I will try very hard to make my batteries bomb-proof. I am now raising the parapets and strengthening them. I got my heavy rifle 32-pounders and 10-inch columbiad in position today, and tried them and my whole battery. The trial was most satisfactory. I need two additional heavy guns very much, and if I am not engaged by him in three or six days, I shall apply for the 42-pounders at Clarksville. It is certain that if I cannot hold this position, the two 42-pounders at Clarksville will not arrest his movements by Clarksville. Upon one thing you may rest assured, viz., that I will never surrender the position, and with God's help I mean to maintain it.

I send up the Hillman for a boat load of flour and meat. Let her bring a full load. You will please give orders accordingly to the commissary of your post. I shall continue to draw supplies of subsistence to this place until I have a heavy store on hand.

I have established a line of vedettes [sic] on the right bank of the Cumberland to within 8 miles of Smithland [on the Ohio], so that I will be posted of the movements and advance of the enemy.

I hope you will order forward at once the tents and baggage of General Buckner's command, as they are suffering very much for want of them this cold weather.

I must request that you will forward this letter, after reading it, to General Johnston. My engagements and duties press me so much that I cannot address you both, and knowing his anxiety, I am anxious to place before him the intelligence contained in this letter.[45]

By this letter Pillow demonstrates that the realities of the situation at Donelson have deferred any thought of counter-stroke against Fort Henry. He held confidence in his river batteries to fend off the Union flotilla, but he projected the Federal land strategy to accomplish the same purpose by a southward envelopment of Dover. Implied in this letter is his determination to make any encirclement of his position even more hazardous by armed intervention. Pillow also indicates, as he had on the 9th, by the tone of the portion requesting supplies and the forwarding of the report that he has little respect for the superior seniority of General Floyd.

Pillow received great comfort that evening by the arrival of advance elements of 800 cavalrymen commanded by Lieutenant Colonel Nathan Bedford Forrest. A man of piercing eyes and coal-black short beard and mustache, Forrest was a prime example of a self-made man. The son of a blacksmith, he had built enterprises from plantations to slave trading to real estate. A former Memphis alderman, Forrest first enlisted in the Confederate service as a private, but he soon received permission to raise a battalion of cavalry. Although inexperienced in military combat, he proved adept in handling cavalry by repulsing enemy horsemen at Sacramento, Kentucky in December. (There he also showed a propensity for exaggeration in his reports.) Ordered from Hopkinsville on the 7th, his command rode to the north bank of the river, where they were now in the process of being ferried across.[46]

Further solace was brought to the garrison commander by the disembarkation of the last of Colonel Brown's brigade, the 32nd Tennessee under Colonel Edward Cook. Embarrassed by the reduced strength of his regiment (555 effectives), Brown found it necessary to explain that numerous sick had been left at Russellville and Bowling Green.[47] Even so, Pillow's force now contained nearly 11,000 men.

With the change of pace on February 10, Ulysses Grant had become a changed man. Not that his shopkeeper exterior bore any alteration. Now action loomed imminent and inwardly the general was stimulated.

He took enough time away that morning from the organization of preparational details to have Rawlins send a staff officer to all brigade commanders to assemble early that Tuesday afternoon on the *New Uncle Sam* steamboat. At the appointed hour Grant appeared before them, confirmed the orders for a Wednesday march, and announced that it would probably be initiated in the forenoon. He called for questions, and as most officers realized that incidentals could be reviewed with division commanders, there were few. The Union brass then departed to bring their brigades to readiness for a march in the face of the enemy. General Lew Wallace stopped at Grant's request and received orders, to his chagrin, to remain behind for the defense of Forts Henry and Heiman, principally the latter.[48]

Room in the Federal encampment had always been a thorny problem, but now with word of imminent reinforcements Grant found drastic action necessary. In response to orders then, McClernand moved his division somewhat eastward on the roads to Fort Donelson and made a new one-night camp. On the night of the 11th, transports docked with their contents of a brigade from Buell and two regiments from Halleck.[49]

Amid additional prodding from Halleck, at Cairo Flag Officer Foote consented to deliver the minimum naval support required by Grant. Foote had his own obstacles to face. His request to Washington for 500 additional sailors had snarled in red tape. With a larger flotilla to man he again had to resort to the tactic of removing crews from vessels not on the expedition. From 8.30 to 9 on Tuesday night the Federal gunboats slipped their moorings at Cairo to steam quietly into the darkness of the Ohio River.[50]

The screech of iron on iron rent the usual stillness of the morning air as steam engine after steam engine hauled its quota of flatcars and boxcars into the Kentucky town of Bowling Green. Another military force was in the process of moving. Gunners manhandled caissons and wheeled artillery up steep ramps onto the cars. Soldiers crammed themselves into and onto every conceivable space within or without the rail vehicles. Toward evening, on the rutted roads, the last of Hardee's rearguard hurriedly departed on the partially winter-damaged highway to Nashville. With the Central Army of Kentucky about to lose its name and its headquarters in the face of some threats of enemy armed action, Albert Sidney Johnston would take precious little time to fret about Fort Donelson this day, except to wire full authority to Floyd on the matters of Fort Donelson, Clarksville, and the Cumberland River.

A small steamer pushed off from a wharf at Clarksville. Aboard were Brigadier Generals Floyd and Buckner. Buckner had managed to interest Floyd, now armed with *carte blanche,* in his project of concentrating at Cumberland City, and the officers took themselves downriver to make a personal reconnaissance of the area. While en route Floyd made quite clear his paramount fear that the Federal ironclad gunboats were invulnerable. Adroitly Buckner pointed out the extremely hazardous situation of the army at Fort Donelson if the warships should conquer the water batteries.[51]

Floyd took it from there. His failure to acknowledge Johnston's first telegram had brought a second. While it smacked strongly of impatient irritation and official morale boosting, the piece of paper also gave Floyd further written proof of his authority:

Twice today I have telegraphed to you to command all the troops and use your judgment. Your report of the effect of our shot at Henry should encourage the troops and insure our success. If [at] the long range we could do so much damage, with the necessary short range on the Cumberland [we] should destroy their boats.[52]

On inspection of the town he noticed that the railroad was not within range of naval artillery there. Thus between Cumberland City and the Tennessee River he would have a small railroad to help ease his supply problems. Floyd also imagined he would block the land route to Nashville here, although with control of the Cumberland practically defaulted to them, why the Union generals would want to use a nearly impassable land route is unknown. While it is true the road communications would be better protected by the geographical location of and distance of Cumberland City from the Federal concentration, the Confederate army would relinquish its simplest supply line, the Cumberland River. The garrison Floyd would leave at Fort Donelson proper was impractical for any purposes. First, Floyd harbored no delusions about it arresting a serious advance by the Union navy. Second, he had neither been informed about nor had he investigated the defensibility of the fort, i.e. it was doubtless untenable against infantry and artillery assault.

With Buckner's smiling approval Floyd had adopted for himself a plan. Buckner already had established a portion of his division at Cumberland City, and word went back to Clarksville to rush the remainder of the generals' units to that point. To the 1st Louisiana Cavalry Buckner gave the responsibility of patrolling the eastern bank of the river and forbidding the enemy to establish batteries against Fort Donelson there.[53]

By telegram to Pillow at Donelson, Floyd released the substance of his intentions. Pillow responded negatively in shocked surprise and strongly advised delay in effecting the plan, at least until a joint conference could be arranged. Nevertheless, Floyd directed Buckner to himself journey to Donelson and supervise the withdrawal of both Floyd's and Buckner's divisions.[54]

Meanwhile Pillow had rejoiced at the completed ferrying of Forrest's cavalry command to the entrenchments that morning. Not only would this effective reinforcement make his reconnaissance more effective, but morale of both infantry and cavalry services would be enhanced by some successful action on the part of the horse corps.

From Pillow that afternoon Forrest read orders to take less than half of his battalion and scout in the direction of Fort Henry. After briefing himself from the map, the colonel advanced his troopers to the crossroads and up the Telegraph Road. One mile in this direction they encountered a larger body of Union cavalry. Not having aggressive intentions, the latter withdrew toward Grant's army, losing a prisoner and several wounded to Forrest's pursuing riders. After a chase of nearly six miles, Forrest reined in his command. Ahead glistened the bayonets of a substantial force of Federal infantry (belonging to McClernand's division). Interrogation methods not being then so highly developed, no information was gleaned from the captive trooper in blue about the impending Federal approach.[55]

At the fort, dark and broad-faced Captain Reuben R. Ross of the Maury Artillery had set his battery ashore. After being ordered to the left of the line in front of Dover, Ross received personal instructions to report to headquarters at the tavern along with the other light artillery commanders. There Pillow confided to them one of his major problems. The heavy artillery on the river required a company of experienced artillerists. "It was the post of danger, but the post of honor," spoke the general. Ross immediately volunteered.

After distributing his cannon among the other batteries, Ross hurried to the fort with his company to familiarize them with the heavy artillery drill. Captain Dixon, commanding the batteries and recognizing the value of experienced cannoneers, assigned the rifled gun, flanked in the upper battery by two 32-pounders, to Ross. Downstream on the same hill the lower battery of the other eight emplaced 32-pounders and the columbiad went under the overall supervision of Captain Culbertson.[56]

Other problems confronted Gideon Pillow. At the extreme right of his line of defense, the point most likely to be first engaged by the enemy, stood Colonel Hanson and the 2nd Kentucky. Hanson estimated that his responsibility extended over a half mile (actually it was closer to a quarter mile) and with only a regiment at his disposal he felt compelled to spread them out in a series of rifle pits. To his right stood the flooded slough of Hickman Creek. His rifle pits, located more than 100 yards apart, were placed along the southwest arm of the "X." To make matters worse, after laboring day and night on Monday, his men found orders being given to relinquish their tools to other units further to the left. Consequently the 2nd Kentucky sat in abatis-fronted shallow unconnected ditches with the dirt thrown to the front. Consoling them was the observation that the slope in their front was relatively steep.

Darkness had set in as Simon Bolivar Buckner strode down the steamer's plank onto Dover's wharf. Inquiring as to the headquarters of General Pillow, he was directed up the bank a few feet in front of him. Making his presence known in the tavern headquarters, Buckner made himself comfortable while staff officers scurried to establish the whereabouts of the commanding general.

It was some time before Pillow arrived. As the older man entered the room, Buckner stiffly pushed himself up from his chair and smiled politely. Pillow with more friendliness removed his gauntlet and offered his hand. He apologized for the delay, but it seemed that Colonel Cook of the 32nd Tennessee on the southeast arm of the "X" had nervously reported the active presence of enemy artillery and sharpshooters in the woods before him. On inspection Pillow had found nothing really threatening.

Buckner hastily denied any inconvenience and then brought up the reason for his visit. He informed Pillow that he had arrived to remove his own and Floyd's divisions. Pillow, astounded that this action had come so soon, reached quickly as was his nature. He regretted, he said, that he must refuse Buckner permission, but he was sure that misinformation had been responsible for Floyd's disposition. The troops must remain at Donelson, he continued, until Pillow could adjust the matter with Floyd in a personal conference.

The two stood facing each other, eye meeting eye. One was young, erect, and assured, but inclined to act in deliberation. The other, while graying and somewhat bent in stature, bore in his eye the attitude of instant self-confidence. Buckner, taken aback, somewhat curtly inquired when this confrontation would take place. Pillow replied that with the circumstances of transportation, etc., it must await the following morning. Buckner, seeing no recourse, offered no argument, and Pillow had an aide see him to his quarters for the night. The Kentuckian consoled himself with the belief that it would be a one night stand at Donelson.[57]

4

The Advance on Fort Donelson

THE SUN HAD BARELY RISEN ON WEDNESDAY MORNING, February 12, when General Buckner awakened to a message delivered by one of Pillow's aides. Placing himself in his uniform, Buckner met with his temporary superior downstairs in the dining room. Pillow informed him that he was about to steam to Cumberland City to confer with General Floyd. In his absence he was giving the command to Buckner. He also relayed the information that the previous night he had assigned Colonel Forrest command over the cavalry as acting brigadier. A few minutes previous Pillow had instructed Forrest to assemble his total force and feel out the enemy in the direction of Fort Henry but not to bring on a general engagement which would require infantry support.[1]

Unaware of the imminent Federal approach to Fort Donelson, Pillow boarded his steamer, which began the 15-mile voyage upstream. It had not particularly pleased him to leave Buckner, who was totally unfamiliar with the terrain and with the disposition of troops, in command. Pillow suspected, however, that he saw Buckner's hand in these sudden orders to withdraw to Cumberland City; he was not about to accompany himself with a contrary influence to play upon Floyd's indecision, and the only way to eliminate Buckner from supreme authority at Dover was to take him on the steamer. Appreciating Buckner's situation, Pillow had placed all of his cavalry in an interposing position and ordered them not to bring on an engagement which must bring the army from the entrenchments.

Very shortly after Pillow had set foot aboard his steamer, General Grant had placed in motion his entire Federal army, with the exceptions of General Lew Wallace, who was defending the west bank of the Tennessee River, and six regiments, just arrived Tuesday night, which were kept aboard their transports and sent to the Cumberland. At 8 A.M., McClernand, looking for all like a Russian monk in uniform, was in motion to the west on the Telegraph and Ridge Roads, with Smith bringing up the rear via the Ridge Road. With the cavalry patrolling the intervals between the brigades, McClernand, with the four-mile headstart provided on the 11th, aggressively set out to add a substantial victory to his laurels.[2]

Traversing terrain highlighted by the rust-colored iron-bearing soil and made effective for ambush or delaying action by nature, the army of high-spirited rugged Westerners made good time against an absence of opposition. In the center of McClernand's column rode General Grant and his staff, including Dr. Brinton, the army's medical officer. The doctor, riding a mighty stallion just purchased at Cairo, had a large satchel attached to his saddle. In this was borne all the luggage—collars, combs, brushes, and toilet articles—of the staff. Grant himself carried nothing in the satchel; his toothbrush lay in his pocket. Possibly part of the reason was that Brinton, under instructions, had placed the only liquor in the group, an eight-ounce flask, in the bag and Grant would have no excuse for looking at its contents. He had been admonished by the general that this was to be reserved strictly for professional use.[3]

As the Union army was in transit, Pillow had arrived in Cumberland City only to discover that Floyd was up at Clarksville preparing the shifting of his base to Cumberland City. As a mater of fact, unknown to Pillow, Floyd had just sent a dispatch to Johnston outlining his plans:

There is but little known satisfactorily of the enemy or their movements; up to 10 o'clock last night all was quiet as usual at the fort. General Buckner is now there. I have thought the best disposition to make of the troops on this line was to concentrate the main force at Cumberland City, leaving at Fort Donelson enough to make all possible resistance to any attack which may be made upon the fort, but no more. . . . I am making every possible effort to concentrate the forces here at Cumberland City. I have been in the greatest dread ever since I reached this place of their scattered condition. The force is inadequate to defend a line of 40 miles in length, which can be attacked from three different directions. We can only be formidable by concentration. A strong guard is all that can be left here [Clarksville], and this no longer than your movement can be made. I shall begin today, if the engineers report favorable, to blockade the river at the piers of the railroad bridge. I have taken up an idea that a raft, secured against this bridge, can render the river impassable for the gunboats. If this is possible, it will be an immense relief to the movements above. I am quite sure this blockade can be made at a lower stage of water; but the present stage of water renders this experiment somewhat doubtful; still I will make every exertion to effect the blockade, if possible. I received by telegraph your authority to make any disposition of the troops which in my judgment was best, and acknowledged it by a dispatch immediately. I am acting accordingly.[4]

Pillow, assuming Floyd would be returning soon to his new base of operations, decided to wait for him at Cumberland City.

The morning of February 12, 1862, beamed with unusual intensity of sunlight and warmth. The two roads leading from the site of Fort Henry became increasingly littered with blue overcoats and U. S. blankets. Billy Yank had discovered that a rising temperature, long marching, and heavy equipment do not make for great personal comfort. Many officers attempted to prevail upon their commands to consider the nights and future winter weather, but a number of officers themselves in a carefree manner were divesting themselves of non-fighting equipment. It was a day of impatience, of optimism, and of free spirits. The volunteers did as they pleased.

Doctor Brinton discovered it demanded all of his energies to keep his black stallion in check. Indeed, the frisky horse insisted on passing the general, seated on his favorite stallion, "Jack." Finally Grant turned to Brinton and said in good nature, "Doctor, I believe I command this army, and I think I'll go first."[5]

Nathan Bedford Forrest was unaccountably dilatory that Wednesday morning. True, he had an enlarged command to organize, but he also had specific orders for a reconnaissance to implement. Sometime after 11 o'clock he marched his body of men westward along the road which embraced the entrenchments.

At 11 A.M. after three hours of marching, McClernand's vanguard on the Ridge or Paris Road, under Colonel Richard Oglesby, screened by cavalry, were three miles beyond the fort. In spite of their proximity to the enemy, Grant issued no orders to execute battle lines. Having discovered that Pillow commanded at Donelson, the Northern commander had determined that he had little to fear from astute military moves from that direction.

At roughly 11:30, Major John Mudd, leading a detachment of the 2nd Illinois cavalry, first encountered and pushed back enemy cavalry pickets. Meanwhile Oglesby had reached the juncture of the Telegraph and Ridge roads. McClernand reached the scene and ordered Oglesby to march through some old farm fields to the south until he came upon a major parallel road.[6]

Forrest, receiving his withdrawing pickets, surveyed the situation. While the valley before him was one of the few locations between Donelson and Henry disposed to cavalry action, occasional ridges made infantry a necessity. Forrest then effected one of the major alterations in cavalry since the use of the stirrup in the late Roman Empire. The gentlemen of the horse were dismounted and deployed as infantry.[7]

Three companies of Confederates advanced on foot to repel the enemy skirmishers, which they did successfully. Oglesby, commanding the 8th, 18th, 29th, 30th, and 31st Illinois regiments of infantry, the latter two veterans of Belmont, formed his line of battle across the slope of a ridge. Forrest himself moved to the left of this thickly wooded ridge, where he mounted a concerted flanking assault with cavalry. After a spirited 10-minute engagement the men in blue took definite charge of the situation, and Forrest recalled the attackers, sending one dismounted squadron as skirmishers.

Oglesby's men pressed forward and fiercely engaged the skirmishers, who fought with carbines. The Confederate squadron leader begged Forrest for relief. Four squadrons from the left and center of the line responded with a concerted mounted assault. Commanded by Major Kelly, these men in gray drove the Union cavalry through intervals formed in their infantry. Kelly reformed his line and swept on toward the supporting infantry. The latter, comprised principally of the 8th Illinois (Colonel F. L. Rhoads) at this point, responded with rifle fire in volley fashion. Here they were supported by several artillery guns loaded with grape shot. Kelly's men never reached the line; they fled the field in considerable confusion. Forrest, however, had achieved his purpose in withdrawing his hard-pressed skirmisher squadron.[8]

A messenger from Forrest had informed Buckner of the sudden alarming situation which was developing. The sound of large scale firing added considerably to the tension of the newly arrived general. A decision became necessary. The enemy obviously would press forward to invest the entrenchments. No one could expect the cavalry alone to fend them off. Should he commit substantial quantities of infantry to Forrest's support?

As he paced restlessly up and down along a portion of the still expanding entrenchments, Buckner well recognized that nothing he had seen between Dover and Fort Donelson had cheered him. In his opinion the works were little more than one-third complete. Disgustedly the trim Kentuckian pondered on how the few logs—rolled together, covered with dirt, and called breastworks—could be expected to withstand the effects of Union field artillery. Furthermore, he at any moment expected confirmation of his orders to detach most of the defending troops for service at Cumberland City. Therefore, to his mind there existed no question of exposing men about to be evacuated in a fruitless stand against odds.

Minutes later couriers from Forrest breathlessly disclosed that the cavalry was in the process of withdrawing, some in a state of disorganization. To the colonel's request for instructions, Buckner issued orders for the horsemen to retreat all the way to the entrenchments.[9]

To the east, three miles away, prisoners captured in the skirmishes with Forrest had furnished Grant with some disarming news. Their spoken estimates of the army entrenched before Dover brought the numbers to between 20,000 and 25,000 men. With the arrival of Smith's division Grant could muster only 25 regiments of infantry, seven field batteries, and certain units of cavalry to make a grand total of less than 20,000 blue-uniformed recruits.[10]

To McClernand, Grant sent a messenger with directions to proceed forward only in line of battle. The mood of the rather reckless approach of the morning came to an end. Grant also dispatched a heavy detachment of engineers to prepare a landing on the Cumberland downstream from the fort for the reception of the naval flotilla and the waterborne reinforcements.

An interesting communication had just reached Grant's hands by courier from Fort Henry. It was Halleck's prodding letter of the 10th. In private amusement Grant chuckled at the bespectacled general's caution that he should be fortifying Fort Henry. The injunction to destroy the railroad bridge at Clarksville at "any risk" made no permanent impression on his memory.

Meanwhile the forerunner of the naval arm had made its presence known. The ironclad *Carondelet* under Commander Henry Walke had commenced firing from her bow guns on Fort Donelson at 12:50. To the south Oglesby's volunteers in the waning minutes of their struggle with Forrest took heart at these loud reports which they knew could only augur the arrival of naval support.

Walke had departed from Fort Henry on the 10th, and finding the going against the currents of the Cumberland uncertain, had obtained towing assistance from the transport *Alps*. At a slight bend in the river his charts informed him that he had sighted Fort Donelson. Its steeply rising height of over 100 feet made a distinctly threatening impression on the gunboat's commander. He nevertheless proceeded with his orders from Grant—to signal his arrival with his guns, to demonstrate against the fort, and to control the river. With no menacing displays or replies from the fort, he accomplished the first two portions of his task with 10 or 11 shots from his bow guns. The *Carondelet,* assisted by the strong current, removed itself three miles downstream.[11]

No one in the fort proper had been caught napping. Lookouts could observe nearly 2½ miles down the river. Colonel Haynes and Captains Dixon and Ross had decided, however, perhaps from experience gained at Fort Henry, not to give the enemy any information which could be achieved with a duel at long range. Still, the silent batteries brought no cheer to an uncertain garrison.

Upstream, Gideon Pillow was doubly alarmed. A steamer had only shortly before arrived with the news of a Federal advance and now the heavy booms of the naval cannon downstream echoed over the hills and rippling river. He wasted no time getting to the telegraph office and wired Floyd a message which was to be repeated to Johnston:

> Steamboat just arrived brings me dispatch from my picket below Eddyville; says gun-boat and transports passed up 10 o'clock last night. I have heard ten heavy discharges of artillery. I leave immediately for Donelson. Shall suspend order for Buckner to fall back at present.[12]

Commandeering the steamer, Pillow made all speed for Dover.

McClernand had decided to skirt the Rebel defenses by marching his three brigades in an easterly direction over a complex of roads to the south out of enemy view. While waiting for W. H. L. Wallace's Second Brigade to catch up, Oglesby on McClernand's instructions advanced to a ridge facing Buckner's earthworks. Captain Jasper Dresser of Battery A spotted Wharton's brigade of two regiments which had reinforced Brown lying exposed some distance before him. Lieutenant Gumbart's howitzers not having the range, Dresser unlimbered his rifled 6-pounders. Before the completion of the expending of 21 shells from these guns, the Confederates had packed their tents and disappeared.[13]

Wallace having crossed Hickman Creek and formed in his rear, Oglesby wheeled his command southeast to the Paris road. Meanwhile the Second Brigade, encountering thickly wooded and brambled country, moved behind him in an easterly direction with a cavalry detachment scouting the distance between his left flank and the trenches. To his rear struggled the three regiments of the Third Brigade under McClernand's personal inspection.[14]

Gideon Pillow had returned to Dover. Briefed by Buckner on the rapidly unfolding developments, he did not waste time on fault-finding, but tersely informed the Kentuckian that his orders for evacuation were cancelled and that he should return to the post of his division. Unaware of Grant's inflated estimate of the number of Confederates, Pillow nevertheless realized he possessed scarcely more than half of the army which was rapidly spreading its tentacles around him. From flooded Hickman Creek on the west to overflowing Lick Creek and tributaries on the east, his command was spread out on a line of over 2½ miles. The "X" was held by Buckner, and across the valley of Indian Creek the ridge fortified by Gilmer was blocked by Heiman's brigade supported by Maney's battery. Bushrod Johnson directed Heiman and the two brigades laboring on breastworks across the valley to the east of the ridge. Forrest had been placed along the vulnerable Pinery Road paralleling Indian Creek.[15]

A few yards northeast of the site of Forrest's and Ogleby's battlefield, General Grant and his staff drew to a halt at a log house which had caught their eye on the penetrating reconnaissance of the 7th. Grant assumed his privilege of choice and laid claim to the large size kitchen with its double feather bed. With somewhat less dignity than befitted their rank, the staff officers distributed themselves among the smaller rooms of the two-storey building. Outside a garden and an orchard were in winter hibernation.

Simon Bolivar Buckner faced an uncertain future as he cautiously guided his mount down and up the precarious roadway across dangerously flooded Indian Creek, stretching to the Confederate right. A general of a division, Buckner now commanded nothing more than Brown's brigade. To intensify his moodiness Brown reported that his entrenchments were not yet half finished. Buckner initiated preparations for reconnoitering his front.

To patrol the dense woods to the south Buckner selected the 18th Tennessee, which held the cross of the "X." Colonel Palmer detailed Company C under Captain W. R. Butter. Shortly before two o'clock Butter scattered his men over a long line and cautiously advanced toward the expected enemy approach. It was some time before his slowly walking men in gray sighted any cause for suspicion. Suddenly in battle array there loomed before them a massive line of full-grown men in blue uniform with menacing muskets. Butter kept his head and ordered a withdrawal, but he kept the enemy in view. Finally within hailing distance of the rifle pits, the company fired a ragged volley and scampered off. Butter reported what he had seen to Palmer, who in turn rode in person to the field headquarters of Buckner and Brown.

Buckner without delay placed his brigade-size division in battle order. It was not long before Dresser's artillery shells were placing Wharton's men in discomfort. That situation was changed, if not improved, by the reining of a horde of horses drawing guns and caissons. With them the artillerists brought orders for the withdrawal of Wharton's brigade to the left. In their place to the salient of his line Buckner sent the fresh battery under Captain Porter.[16]

General Pillow had taken alarm at the slowly developing signs that his opponent was gradually slipping across his front.

To prevent the eventual investment of Dover, his army would have to have a strong countering reserve on the left flank, and to this end he ordered Wharton's withdrawal. No action was taken, however, to counterthrust the enemy envelopment.

Morrison's Union brigade of McClernand's Division had become impatient with the necessity of traversing countless areas of prickly underbrush, fences, brooks, and ravines while lugging full equipment. Soon their progress became traceable by countless knapsacks, overcoats, and other baggage which the soldiers found were impeding their good relationships with their officers as they stumbled cross-country in something resembling a battle line. Once they were halted and the lines dressed. The consequent assault, however, netted the brigade only an empty cleared area of burning campfires.[17]

With General Smith's Second Division taking up the slack vacated by the First Division, McClernand exhorted his subordinates to fulfill his instructions to extend his line to cover the enemy's fortified left. Oglesby, followed closely by Wallace, continued to press forward in battle order to the east of Indian Creek. By dusk the First Brigade was positioning itself on or near the Wynn's Ferry Road leading to the center of Johnson's entrenched ridge.

In front of the village of Dover, Bushrod Johnson had spent the day, when not in consultation with Buckner or Pillow, in fretfully expediting the completion of his defenses. To Captain Frank Maney, serving his battery in the centre with Heiman and to Captain Green, in charge of the only artillery–a seven gun unit–on the left, Johnson sent orders to set up emplacements before their guns. With the near disappearance of the sun he instructed a party of pickets to precede, protect, and alarm a work detail which would follow them out the Wynn's Ferry Road to widen the strip of abatis in that vicinity.

Heavy-set Colonel Michael Lawler, commanding the 18th

Illinois and mindful of the wishes of General Grant to outflank the Confederate left, urged his First Brigade vanguard forward along the Wynn's Ferry Road. While complaints from his jaded troops found their expression in the diminishing light, the colonel and his officers bolstered the regiments with praise for the day's achievements and appeals to personal and state pride.

Suddenly from the roadway scarcely 40 yards before them rolled the disturbing crackle of rifles being fired in succession. Lawler immediately sped reinforcements to his obviously embattled skirmishers. Sweeping boldly and fearlessly to the front, the supporting companies discovered to their chagrin that the Confederate skirmishers were already in full and startled retreat, carrying their wounded through the trees or up the road. Lawler on his arrival was relieved that not a Union man had been shot.[18]

Several hundred yards nearer the river the story of the rout of the picket and work party spread quickly through the Secessionist trenches. More disturbing to Johnson and Pillow than this minor reverse was the progress which the enemy van had made toward Dover. Pillow had counted on several days respite while the Union army engaged nature's growth. Already, however, in less than 12 hours the enemy had marched from his base to a point opposite his center.

At the center, pickets of Heiman's brigade had detected voices some distance ahead of the jutting point which enfolded Captain Frank Maney's four guns. Maney himself, although perhaps disgruntled that Heiman could not or would not furnish the tools to accomplish Johnson's orders for protection of the battery from counter-fire, with the information pinpointing the location of the Federal forerunners became aware that these voices were unfriendly. Pointers sighted their pieces and exploratory fire was directed toward the Wynn's Ferry Road.

Realizing suddenly the discovery of his approach, Colonel Oglesby was doubly shocked to find that Lawler had placed himself within range of this battery, which had previously made itself known with nuisance fire. An aide dashed up the road to have the 18th Illinois retire from the exposed position. Unfortunately an exchange of friendly fire killed and wounded several. Darkness being well upon them, the brigade bedded down for a fireless night.[19]

W. H. L. Wallace had little difficulty in keeping pace with Oglesby. Following the crossing of Indian Creek Valley, the leading brigade encountered broken country with thick entanglements. Consequently with night setting in, McClernand instructed Wallace to retrace his steps, cross Indian Creek and establish the Second Brigade to the west of the valley. Directly north of them Morrison's brigade steeled themselves to ward off a problematical night assault.

To the left the leading brigade of the Second Division under Colonel John Cook had been placed by their discerning general on a long ridge at least equal in height to Hanson's crestline. Feeling secure in the possibilities of his location, Cook took time to reflect on the day's events. Supporting McClernand in his line of march, his brigade had arrived before Hickman's Creek at 3 P.M. Contact had been insured with Morrison's unit, and he had then advanced to his present encampment. In immediate support to his right stood the brigade of Colonel Jacob Lauman. Less than two miles to the southwest lay three regiments under the authority of Colonel John McArthur. All in all it was comforting.[20]

Along the ridges guarding the river no one felt very comforted. Any enthusiasm lurking within the rank and file was dampened by the sudden chill of the night river air. Buckner nursed his reinvigorated disgust. Johnson considered the lack of success of his first skirmish an ill omen. Thoroughly frightened at what he considered the remarkable progress of the rapidly enfolding Union advance, Pillow telegraphed Colonel William Baldwin at Cumberland City to immediately embark his three remaining regiments for Dover.[21]

Pillow then transmitted a report to his immediate superior. Not having high confidence in the judgment of Floyd, *Pillow instructed the operator to repeat the message on to Albert Sidney Johnston,* the excuse being the lack of time. Thus he assured himself that precisely the same information would be in the hands of both generals:

We shall have a battle in the morning, I think, certainly, and an attack by gunboats. The enemy are all around my position and within distance to close in with me in 10 minutes march. One gunboat came today and fired fifteen or twenty shells and retired. We gave no reply. I have sent to Cumberland City for Baldwin's two regiments. Feel sanguine of victory, though I am not fully ready. I have done all that was possible to do, and think I will drive back the enemy.

At this news Johnston started. No longer could he trust in the discretion of Floyd to maintain the garrison at Dover. Moving to the nearest flat surface, he scratched with a pencil on a pad and handed the results to an aide. The order from Bowling Green went to Floyd:

My information from Donelson is that a battle will be fought in the morning. Leave a small force at Clarksville and take the remainder, if possible, to Donelson tonight. Take all the ammunition that can be spared from Clarksville. The forces at Elksford and Whippoorwill bridges have been ordered to Clarksville.

Floyd had had a bad day. Earlier even Hardee had put himself into the act with an urgent request for information on troop dispositions and defenses.[22]

On joint consultation Colonels Heiman and Drake com-

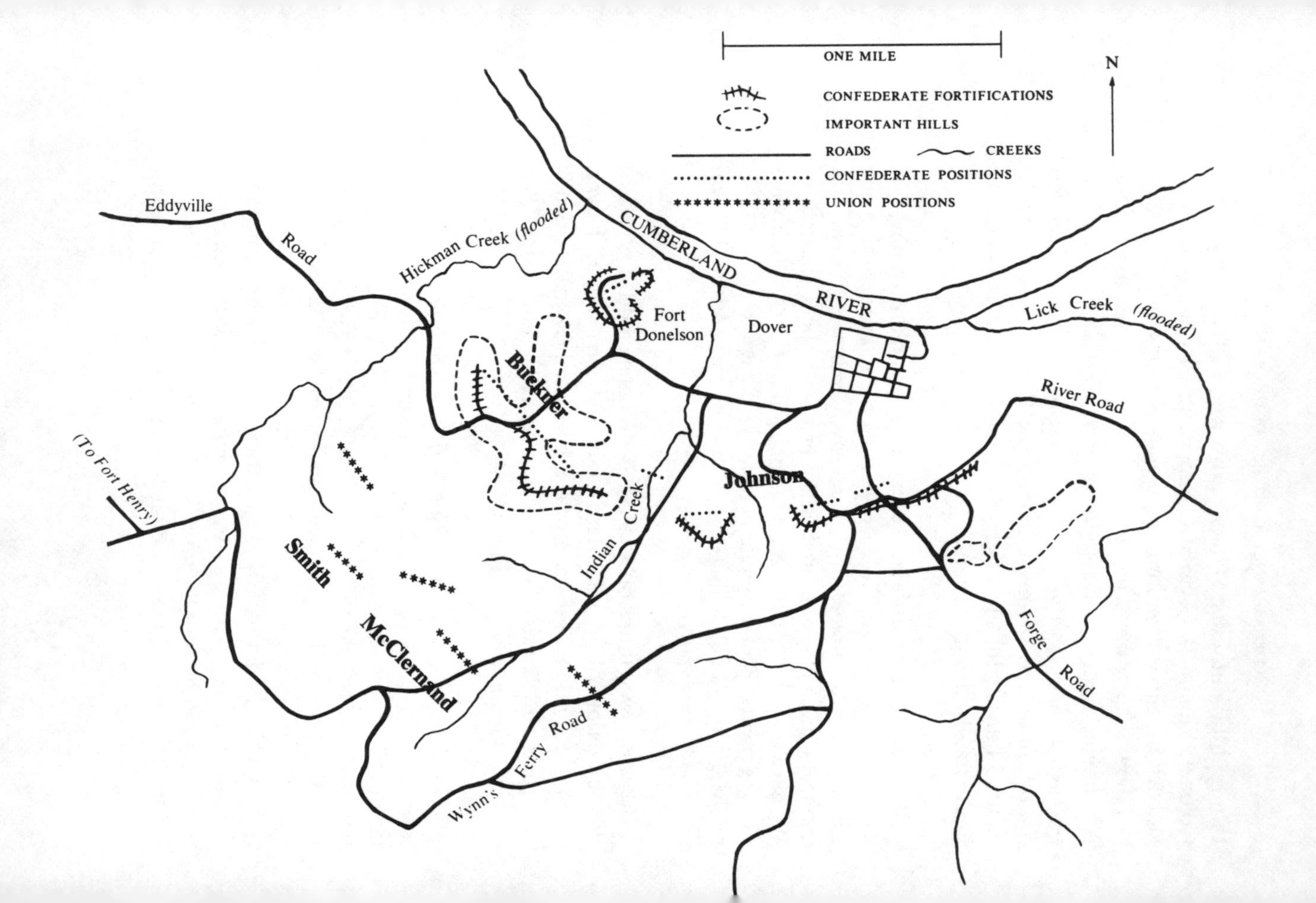

ONE MILE
CONFEDERATE FORTIFICATIONS
IMPORTANT HILLS
ROADS
CREEKS
CONFEDERATE POSITIONS
UNION POSITIONS
N
Eddyville Road
Hickman Creek (flooded)
CUMBERLAND RIVER
Fort Donelson
Dover
Lick Creek (flooded)
River Road
Buckner
Johnson
Indian Creek
(To Fort Henry)
Smith
McClernand
Wynn's Ferry Road
Forge Road

plained to Pillow of the gap caused by a small creek, Erin Hollow, between their positions. With Union regiments almost directly before this stream, Pillow issued a message to Colonel Head to march his 30th Tennessee to the unentrenched head of the valley. Heiman received the impression that the 30th was attached to his brigade.[23]

The valley of Indian Creek had become a source of concern to both Heiman and Brown. The 10th Tennessee of Heiman's brigade was directed to push a strong detachment across the road and to begin felling abatis and constructing rifle pits in this undefended area. A co-unit from their state, the 32nd Tennessee from Brown, joined them in this endeavor.

Nearly 75 feet above the swampy borderlands of the stream Palmer's 18th Tennessee had remained in a readiness which was typical of the whole Confederate line. Before the crossroads of the " X " a battalion of three companies was to receive the brunt of any assault. To the rear, prepared to dash to the support of the front line, lay seven more companies. Upon orders from Colonel Brown, Palmer advanced selected units into the darkness to complete the abatis and the breastworks. Those to the rear considered the work details the lucky ones, for the weather had returned to its norm and the air had become intensely cold. Buckner's blankets still had not arrived.

All along the Rebel line, soldiers, including Forrest's cavalrymen, swung axes chest-high against the saplings, trimmed branches to points with bayonets, and wielded spades and picks against the hardening soil to bring a few more cubic yards of earth before their slim trenches.[24]

In St. Louis and Louisville, Halleck and Buell stepped up the transmission of telegrams and dispatches to each other. Buell, with advice from McClellan, had informed Halleck of his resolve to move his army on the lines of the Tennessee or Cumberland Rivers instead of the overland route in central Kentucky. He was of the opinion, however, that it would take at least 10 days to transfer his troops to those lines of operations. Halleck, desiring Buell's troops but not his presence, telegraphed back that he understood that the enemy had amassed 40,000 recruits at Dover and Clarksville. And so on it had gone.[25]

Happily oblivious to these maneuverings, Ulysses Grant near the close of the day took himself in a well-satisfied state to his double feather bed in his log cabin. For the first time in six days he had ample reason to be pleased with himself. Under his direction his volunteers in their marching and fighting had rendered a good account of themselves.

A mile and a half to the east, over and down ridges and ravines, Battery A and Captain Dresser huddled on the frosty ground, wearing their equipment and keeping their teams in hitch. Away from the river, though, the air was still and the temperature mild for the season.

5

Thursday–Envelopment and Attack

THE FIRST INKLINGS OF SUNLIGHT HAD BARELY BEGUN TO SEEP over the cloudless horizon when an aide knocked at the door of the quarters of General Gideon Pillow. On being beckoned to enter the officer announced that he had two items of information to relate. One, as per expectations, Colonel Baldwin and two regiments of his brigade had made their appearance at the landing at one o'clock in the morning. Baldwin had followed the standing orders awaiting him and had positioned his command in support of Green's battery in Johnson's wing. Pillow had thus contradicted his original published pledge of keeping Buckner's division intact under the Kentuckian's leadership. In view of the developing threat on the left, the decision was necessary and wise, but it was not inclined to endear him to his unhappy right wing commander.[1]

The actual reason for disturbing Pillow, however, was that in the company of McCausland's brigade and three batteries of artillery, General John Floyd had set foot upon the Dover shores. Pillow no longer directed the half-encircled garrison.

Shortly after midnight at Cumberland City his chief of staff had roused General Floyd from peaceful slumber to discover the directions listed in the wire from Johnston. Hastily Floyd dispatched a courier to McCausland's Virginia brigade to prepare to decamp for Dover. After assuring himself that transport was available or would be, Floyd had telegraphed Johnston that he had already anticipated the order and had received it at Cumberland City. (The implication was that he had read the instructions while on his way to Dover. The fact was that Johnston's telegram had been sent to Cumberland City.) Fearing the future of his military cereer at stake, Floyd had busily gathered his personal effects and records so as to be enabled to arrive at Dover at first light.[2]

Greeting his brother in arms for the first time in four days, Pillow suggested that the two have a quick breakfast before any further action be taken. At the conclusion of the short meal Floyd accepted his second-in-command's offer of the escort of several staff officers on a tour of inspection of the works, while Pillow would undertake the necessary placing of the newly arrived units so as to counter the imminent enemy approach.

As Floyd and his reinforced escort rode west toward the fort, the Confederate army was in a state of incipient activity. In spite of the semi-darkness, men clad in innumerable varieties of gray and civilian dress filed silently but determinedly forward to relieve the companies which had manned the trenches during the cold night. If poor morale did exist, it made no impression upon the new commanding general.

At the fort proper Floyd made the acquaintance of Colonel J. E. Bailey, directing the garrison, Captain Dixon, commanding the water batteries, and on crutches the injured Lieutenant Colonel Haynes. On reviewing their respective detachments

Floyd was pleased to observe that the field of fire was impressive and that the entrenchments for the guns with their sandbag reinforcements had received considerable attention. In spite of certain misgivings he tried to impart notes of confidence to these troops placed at the most crucial point of his jurisdiction.

From the fort the body of horsemen proceeded southwest along a ridge for a quarter of a mile until they reached the command post of General S. B. Buckner. The two officers, of similar sympathy, greeted each other warmly. Buckner immediately offered to lead his compatriot in an inspection of his front lines. In the course of the journey Buckner explained how his men had been forced to labor the previous night to bring the works to even their present state.

In company with their staffs, the two generals guided their horses along Buckner's positions. The commander of the right wing lost no opportunities to emphasize threatening hills of imposing height under the control of the enemy. He explained how it was necessary to protect the base of supplies at Dover, and how consequently the lines of defense must stretch for nearly three miles from right to left. Every location where the abatis was thin or non-existent was spotted. Buckner hinted at difficulties encountered when soldiers were forced to silhouette themselves as they passed forward over the actual crest to the military crest where the works had been constructed. Also in Buckner's opinion they were generally built too far down from the brow of the ridge. With all of these observations and conclusions Floyd lent his enthusiastic concurrence.[3]

Meanwhile at Dover, Bushrod Johnson notified Pillow that his works were nearly finished. In general they were dug to a depth of 5 feet and a width of 2 feet. Before the trenches the laboring troops had interlaced small saplings in a line and thrown the dirt from the ditches over them. The average thickness of this natural shield was about 5 feet.[4]

Replaced by McCausland's three regiments, Colonel Baldwin directed the head of his column from Green's position to the extreme left of the Confederate line, where he placed his 26th Mississippi in the trenches and the 26th Tennessee in reserve. On Pillow's direction French's four-gun battery arrived to aid Drake to the east of Erin Hollow. Jackson's battery was dispatched to Buckner's disposal and Guy's Virginia-served guns reinforced Davidson to the right of Baldwin.[5]

A mile to the southwest the assemblage of human males which had created all this fuss had begun to stir. To some degree the activity of Oglesby's vanguard was hastened by projectiles borne aloft from the Rebel lines. Officers controlling Maney's four Confederate guns had spotted something interesting. When daylight was sufficient, guarded fires sprung up to cook a hot breakfast for the somewhat tired and nervous bluecoats.

Near the Wynn's Ferry Road the tall and thin McClernand engaged in anxious conversation with his subordinate, Oglesby. The general, his beard more bedraggled than usual, announced that most of the responsibility for carrying out Grant's directive of enveloping the enemy's left fell upon the colonel's brigade. McClernand himself would remain near at hand as much as possible. For the time being he ordered that no reply be made to the artillery fire.[6]

On the extreme left front of the Union lines, Colonel John Cook, satisfied with his vantage position, received orders in the midst of breakfast to march his brigade to the southeast to the vicinity occupied that night by Morrison's brigade. General Smith notified him that his advantageous hill would become the possession of Colonel Jacob Lauman's brigade, and Colonel John McArthur's three regiments would be the division reserve.

Between 8 and 8:30, Cook set his whole command in motion, marching down the road littered with souvenirs from McClernand. Behind him Lauman advanced his regiments to

Cook's former campsite and deployed his men across the ridge in battle order.

Across the Indian Creek hollow the steady incessant bombardment of Maney's guns for the past hour and a half had begun to wear upon McClernand's nerves. Captain Jasper Dresser received a direct order to place his three rifled pieces in readiness to silence the Confederate nuisance. Dresser responded with alacrity and within 15 minutes of the roar of his first gun Maney had second thoughts about his intrusion and ordered his gunners to cease fire.

With this success McClernand instructed his Illinois cavalry units to carefully scout and precede Oglesby's advance up the Wynn's Ferry Road.[7]

On the river Captain Walke of the *Carondelet* held in his hand a dispatch from General Grant. Of immediate concern to the naval officer was the statement, "If you will advance with your gunboat at ten o'clock in the morning, we will be ready to take advantage of any diversion in our favor." Walke had no reason not to comply and had ordered the chief engineer to raise steam. Soon struggling against the swift current the great revolving cylinder in the stern began to make progress. Reaching a heavily wooded point within range of the fort, the captain ordered the anchor cast overboard and the crew to battle stations. At 9:05, his guns began their belching of fire, smoke, and 64- and 70-pound shells. There was no urgency and time was taken to feel out the range.

The steady approach of the *Carondelet* had been carefully observed by Captain Dixon in the fort. Cannoneers, feeling their first trial to be at hand, assumed their posts. Dark and broad-nosed Captain Ross, with his experience in the field artillery, carefully inspected the cherished columbiad and rifled gun.

At a distance of approximately a mile the vessel fired its first test shot. No sooner was it arching overhead than Ross had powder and shell inserted into his prize long-range pieces. The first shot from the rifled 68-pounder splashed the water some distance from the gunboat. The duel was on.[8]

Inland and over the hills McClernand had concluded that Oglesby could use the services of extra artillery and had requisitioned part of Taylor's battery serving with Wallace. Wallace himself swung behind Oglesby to lend the necessary support.

Down the road galloped a courier with a report from the cavalry commander that the way was clear ahead. Along the line of Oglesby's brigade, sergeants bawled out orders bringing their charges into line. Artillery teams hitched up to caissons. Led by the 18th Illinois the regiments cautiously worked their way east. General Grant in his orders of the day had emphasized that he desired no general engagement to ensue.

About 600 yards away, overlooking most of the Wynn's Ferry Road, Captain Maney, scion of one of Nashville's foremost families, remained alert for significant opportunities to wield his guns effectively. His best opportunities would be as the Union forces crossed his line of sight through a cleared field bordering Erin Hollow to the southeast. Meanwhile the battery commander fretted at the lack of protection which had been afforded his weapons. Then, about 9:30, his chance came; heavy columns of blue-uniformed troops appeared through the break in the forest.

As four hurtling shells whistled through the trees and men of the North scrambled for cover, Lieutenant Conrad Gumbart, commanding Schwartz's battery, signaled his drivers to halt. Horses, with appropriate objections, reined in sharply and brakes squealed against the wheels. Animals, caissons, and guns were unhitched. By sheer brawn muzzles were swung toward the offending hill and wheels ground forward so the pieces would have a safe recoil. In a matter of minutes all four guns had spoken at least once. In this engagement Gumbart relied principally on solid shot, designed to smash guns and their servers.

In the vicinity clusters of Federal soldiers had found shelter in and around a farmhouse near the battery which was defending their lives. Down the road to the west several hundred feet, Captain Ezra Taylor switched his target on Heiman's hill to the impudent set of guns.

Maney, exposed and without shelter worthy of the name, endured the attention of the two Union captains for some time. Finally, however, their sightings had become too accurate, and with the difficulties of diverting his fire between two widely separated opponents, Maney ceased his fire.[9]

Judging that Gumbart and Taylor had rendered the Confederate battery impotent, McClernand and Oglesby jointly agreed to pursue their original intentions. Barely had the brigade resumed its previous status in its line of march, when from the ridge to the east of Erin Hollow issued a volley of projectiles from French's newly established battery. McClernand, highly irritated at these distractions which compelled his volunteers to scatter into the brush for protection, sent aides to bring a concentration of all available artillery units upon French. Dresser, forward with the advance of the column and fresh from a successful 10-minute engagement with a Southern section of guns, selected a spot with a promising view, and deployed his three rifled guns. While continuing to direct his fire upon Heiman's hill, Taylor spared a two-gun section to the new point of crisis. Gumbart unlimbered a section very near the enemy battery. Subject to the wrath of seven Union cannon, French soon deemed it discreet to discontinue his annoyance. For his part, Dresser cursed vehemently for the time and effort he had wasted in firing only 15 shots.[10]

On the Cumberland the *Carondelet,* with its deadline of ten o'clock fast approaching, moved from its sheltering shore toward the bluff of Fort Donelson. Mindful of the lurking presence of Rebel sharpshooters, Walke, at the appointed hour, anchored about a mile from the water batteries. Here he increased the rate of activity from his 10- and 15-inch guns.

With the feeling that up-to-date reports would impress his superior, Floyd dictated a note to be carried to the telegrapher a short distance away. In the telegram he informed Johnston that the gunboats were advancing. In spite of his conference with Buckner, he felt constrained to venture the opinion that the army could defend themselves against the land forces of the enemy.

On the guardian hill, concern mounted. Was one gunboat by itself going to attempt to pass the batteries or was this merely an effort to test the strength of the fort? Cautiously Dixon allowed only the columbiad and the rifled gun, principally the latter, to reply.[11]

Actually Grant had neither plan immediately in mind. Very early in the morning he had consulted with General Charles Smith of the Second Division. They jointly agreed that a reconnaissance-in-force by Smith would both test the Southern right and tend to facilitate McClernand's objective of establishing himself on the Cumberland.

Accordingly the brunt of infantry duty fell upon Lauman's and Cook's brigades. At the approximate site of Cook's evening camp location, Lauman dressed his three regiments into battle order near 10:30. The volunteers checked the percussion cap priming on their weapons, and the colonels in short addresses exhorted their followers to sweep forward into the enemy entrenchments. The 14th Iowa on the right and the 25th Indiana on the left were to be the shock force. The 7th Iowa, just brought up from battery support, became the reserve.

Down the slope in an orderly swarm surged the men of

Iowa and Indiana. Near the foot of the height Colonel James Veatch of the 25th Indiana, deploring the thick timber which prevented pinpointing of the obstructions ahead, halted temporarily and pushed his two flank companies before him as skirmishers. At the foot of the hill the brigade emerged into the clearing which had been deliberately chopped for a field of fire by the Confederates.

Atop the confronting ridge Hanson had been forewarned by his pickets of the impending assault. A section of two guns (Porter's) from Buckner had just been emplaced on his lengthy line. The general, who held the opinion that his defenses were not in the best state but were tolerable for the first time, had instructed Colonel Palmer on Hanson's left to keep two companies ready as a reserve for Hanson. Now E and K companies of the 18th Tennessee marched to the northwest to assist their menaced comrades.

Greeted in the depth of the valley by a fusilade of rifle shot, buckshot, and charges of grape from the summit above, Lauman's novitiates nevertheless strived to accomplish their assignment. Discovering in the sudden exposure of the enemy front that the 25th was outflanked by entrenchments to the left, the two skirmisher companies of Veatch trotted by the left flank to give coverage to the open end of the battle line.

Under Colonel William Shaw the 14th Iowa had paused to reform because of the uneven ground and abatis. To his right Porter's Confederate battery suddenly showed themselves to be in a perfect position to play their shot in enfilade down his line. As much as possible, while maintaining contact with the 25th, Shaw placed his men to shelter them from flanking fire.

Bayonets extended, the Hoosiers with a hearty cheer ascended the Minie-ball-swept slope, which rose more than 100 feet into the air. On the left the original skirmishers had managed to silence a saucy six-pounder. Ignoring the volleys bursting in their faces and their suddenly fallen comrades, detachments cleared the abatis and the regiment poured through the entanglements. Almost within spitting distance of the rifle pits, the blue line, distraught by the grape, shell, and cannister whistling and exploding down the whole length of their line, fell into confusion. Fearing the disastrous results of a retreat under fire. Veatch shouted for his men to lie down. The portion of the Union attack under Lauman was effectively pinned down.[12]

To the southeast Cook's entrance into the fray had been delayed by his long march to his point of departure and the heavily wooded country. The 52nd Indiana on the left and the 7th Illinois on the right comprised the flanking skirmish lines. Where necessary the remaining three regiments threw their flanking companies forward to complete the scouting line.

As the brigade in battle formation advanced down the side of a ravine, the left portions were subjected to the unpleasant attentions of some of Porter's guns. On the right the 7th Illinois, progressing nicely along the edge of the Indian Creek valley, silhouetted themselves on the crest of the Confederate side of the ravine. From an unexpected quarter reports of cannon followed by the smash of missiles suddenly occurred. A captain fell dead, terribly mangled. Before some of the wounded had touched the earth, a substantial number of the survivors were fleeing down the hill. Finding that, with the location of Graves' Rebel battery previously undisclosed to them, the 7th Illinois to some degree became demoralized, John Cook removed them to battery support duty in the Federal lines.

The remaining four regiments progressed under crossfire until sheltered two-thirds of the way up the opposite hill. Attended by several officers, Cook crept cautiously to the summit and with field glasses surveyed the ridge they intended to storm. In Cook's opinion the enemy's works were too strong; word was passed down the line for the bulk of each regiment to rest under arms and for the colonels to send skirmishers and sharpshooters forward.

On Buckner's left flank, unrecognized by the unengaged infantry, General John B. Floyd sat astride his war horse. He had happened on the spot during the repulse of the 7th Illinois and the consequent loss of momentum of Cook's assault. This fracas would later enter his reports as the fiercest engagement of the day.

At 10:30, the narrow streets of Dover became crowded with the men and baggage of the 41st Tennessee. This unit, a part of Baldwin's brigade, was marching on its arrival to join its old commander, General Buckner.[13]

In the fort after a half hour of more intensive bombardment, sprays of earth had annoyed the cannoneers but no further impression had been made on the batteries. To the rear, all within easy range of the Union naval Parrots, Colonel Bailey's garrison had suffered several casualties. Near the crest Captain Ross endeavored, with limitations of heat on metal, to keep the rifled gun in rapid fire. Suffering great pain, Lieutenant Colonel Haynes visited the lower batteries to visually test the range. Hobbling on his crutches from the guns to the officers, he recommended that fire from the 32-pounders be withheld until the man-of-war advanced much nearer. In his condition the very distant transport, *Alps,* appeared to him as a gunboat in reserve.[14]

In the Federal First Division Oglesby, followed by Morrison, had resumed his march unhindered by intersecting artillery fire. Not for long, however, for Maney had bided his time long enough and instructed his gunners to sight on a new Yankee military element passing through his clear field of vision.

For McClernand this was too much. While Union guns

were again deploying in counter-battery attitudes, the general transmitted to Colonel Morrison his desire that he move his two regiments into Erin Hollow and maintain them there until attacked or until he received further instructions.

McClernand mulled over in his mind a bold plan. The battery in this center redoubt would be attacked by Union artillery until and after it was silenced. He would then reinforce Morrison's skeleton brigade and throw them upon this center hill. The result after all this artillery pounding, he ruminated, would be the breaking of the Confederate line in a strategic and vulnerable place.

As he watched his guns bring the Southern cannon into inactivity, it suddenly dawned upon McClernand that, with Grant's instructions of the morning not to bring on a general engagement, permission of the commanding general would be required. Meanwhile, Oglesby, facing the danger of creating a gap between himself and the immobile Morrison, halted, spread out his line, and devoted his attention to countering sharpshooters, who had annoyed him all morning, and shelling the Confederate left[15]

On the Union left Colonel Lauman and his three regiments remained in desperate straits. While they were near to their goal, the enfilading fire of Porter's battery prevented the bringing up of the supporting 7th Iowa to the bogged-down assault regiments. The 25th Indiana especially was in an awkward position. Rifle shots from the pits above made it extremely uncomfortable for the infantrymen to bring their weapons to bear. To complete their discomfort two of Porter's cannon insisted upon raining death and injury upon the unit. The 14th Iowa, confronted by more imposing abatis, stayed put.[16]

All along the Union front, since the break of dawn, individuals in blue uniforms were seen taking station in tree tops or clumps of brush. No stragglers, they belonged to a unique Federal detachment–Birge's Missouri Sharpshooters–attached administratively to Lauman's brigade. Armed with repeating long and accurate Demmick rifles,[17] each member of this unit had been recruited especially for his marksmanship. Every morning in the meagre light they would glide from the campsites alone or in small groups to select a sniping slot for the day. Any officer or soldier who showed his head above the Rebel trenches did so at his own risk, because, even at this early state of the war, the reputation of the skill of this Missouri unit was well known.

At the river batteries the officer commanding the silent short-range 32-pounders, Captain Culbertson, looked at his watch. A few minutes would bring 11:30. The heavy portion of the engagement had lasted nearly an hour and a half. In Captain Beaumont's command a man had been injured by a cannister shot glancing off one of the barrels.

Culbertson turned suddenly, startled by the presence of another individual. He faced Captain Dixon, who suggested in tones of welcome drama that the 32-pounders might test the range. Together they walked to Captain B. G. Bidwell and explained their proposed course of action. (If Bidwell looked tired, it was because he had spent the night and morning assisting gunners with incapacitated legs to the warmth of shelter.) Bidwell moved to one of his flanking guns and ordered it raised to the highest degree of elevation. This done, someone jerked the lanyard. The shot splashed short.

On the *Carondelet* through an embrasure in a casemate, a gun captain noticed the smoke wisp up from the nearer entrenchments. He concluded that the lower guns were being brought into action and decided to discourage them. His Parrot loaded, he lowered the elevation screw on the weapon, stood back, and ordered ignition.

As the solid ball of iron arched its way from its launcher to its target, Dixon moved to the adjoining loaded cannon to supervise its elevating. Bending over the side of the breech, the captain's eyes started at the unexpected impact of a chunk of metal at the opening of the breastwork. In the next instant the cannonball bounded upward to the left and shattered the right cheek of the gun and carriage. From the consequent scattering of wood and metal, a solitary bolt flew back, striking the senior captain with full force in the left temple. Without a word Dixon crumpled on his side, dead. The hurtling missile and its side effects also injured Lieutenant Shuster and a couple of his gunners.

At the battery to the rear one of the volunteers servicing the rifled gun informed Captain Ross that the warship had apparently drawn its first blood among the water batteries. Not taking time to confirm the observations (another cannonball was unmistakably coming in their direction), Ross personally sighted his favorite weapon and commanded that the conical shot be ejected. Almost from the moment of its departure, Ross felt certain it would strike home. His predictions were verified by a clear ringing reverberation as the heavy ball pierced the armor plating.

Plunging through the corner of the broadside casemate, the 128-pound projectile smashed through the wooden beams beneath the metal exterior. Splintered wood spit in all directions. A dozen sailors fell beneath the onslaught of wood and metal.

The cannonball itself had only begun. Before it lay the compact and cramped interior of the gunboat. Almost as if it had a mission, it sped toward the vital and vulnerable boilers. Here a precautionary temporary barricade had been erected. The shot glanced off this semi-partition and jumped over the steamdrum. As seamen scattered precipitously to left and right, the solid iron missile knocked itself against the beams of the upper deck and tore away the railing around the engine room. Until its momentum was spent, it then rolled the deck as a wild beast, causing many to believe they would never escape its forays.

With the damage halted chaos reigned aboard the *Carondelet*. His orders fulfilled to the best of his knowledge, Walke directed that firing not be resumed and allowed the current with the aid of the engines to take him to the sheltering wooded point.

In the fort any rejoicing had been tempered by the losses suffered in the lower battery. As Colonel Bailey was being informed that a new commander of the river batteries would have to be appointed, Captain Ross, in surveying the damage done to the Southern side, saw his men gather 14 cannon balls in an area with a radius of 14 yards. Floyd dutifully told Johnston of the gunboat's retreat.[18]

McClernand was at the point of making two errors in judgment. Being acquainted with Colonel Isham Haynie of the 48th Illinois of Wallace's brigade, the general decided to make him, in accordance with his seniority, the attack leader. This was in spite of the fact that Morrison's Third Brigade, minus a detached regiment, had successfully endured the trials of the approach to the fort under their own senior colonel. Now they were being asked to follow a strange officer in their most crucial exercise. The second error came when McClernand oddly neglected to notify anyone else of his intentions of command for the Third Brigade.

It was near noon when Colonel W. H. L. Wallace heard a verbal order transmitted through an aide to detach Colonel Haynie ahead to join the Third. Haynie himself received word through Captain Stewart of divisional staff. Meanwhile, Morrison, subjected to accurate artillery fire from Graves across the Indian Creek Valley, felt obliged to withdraw the 17th Illinois from the crest of the ridge leading into Heiman's position to a location beneath the brim.[19]

The shaken crew of the *Carondelet* had barely been able

to place a few morsels of sustenance into their nervous stomachs, when a request from Grant to unleash another demonstration was signaled to them. In a few minutes the *Alps,* which had completed its requested approach, was lashed alongside and the wounded, seven of them being in critical condition, were transferred from the exposed warship.

Walke examined his magazines and discovered that 139 shot had been expended in the morning's bombardment. Having developed a healthy respect for the armament of Fort Donelson, the captain ordered the anchor kept in place and elevated the bearing guns to range on the bluff. At 12:15, sheltered by the wooded point, the *Carondelet* resumed a slow steady shelling.

The commandant of the fort sat listening to the recitation of an aide of General Floyd's to the effect that he, Colonel Bailey, should place the next in rank in command of the river batteries. This posed something of a dilemma, since a number of captains stood on the scene. A joint conference was called, and almost immediately, because of his responsibility and previous artillery experience, attention focused upon Captain Ross. However, because of his own new arrival on the scene, Captain Culbertson's senior appointment, long familiarity with the fort, and extended service under the United States flag, Ross yielded any claim to superior authority. With Culbertson in command the officers returned to their charges. As long as no direct threat was made at running the batteries, the long-range gun attendants were instructed to fire only on discretion.[20]

Meanwhile acting Brigadier Lauman recognized that the Fourth Brigade would either perish on that slope or would have to retreat very soon. After the hours of close fire they had endured, there was no question of storming the rifle pits. The spell broke with the request of Colonel Veatch for permission to withdraw. Lauman assented and word passed down the

Indiana line to prepare to retire. Word, however, did not reach the more sheltered 14th Iowa.

As had been feared, raw troops retreating from a protected position under fire could not be expected to retain their composure. Grape and Minie balls splintered their ranks and with difficulty, aided by the thick natural growth, the officers rallied the remnants part way up the reverse slope.

Colonel Shaw of the 14th suddenly found his left wing hanging in the air on the hillside. With the bulk of his regiment under cover at the foot of the incline, Shaw deemed it advisable to bring back these exposed companies.

While his other engaged brigade was still ducking animated Confederate rifle and artillery fire on the right, General Charles Smith and the Second Division had badly fumbled on their first play in the siege. Smith, himself, was responsible for not being able to better co-ordinate the approaches and for not being on the scene to exert personal leadership when it might have been decisive. Lauman, leading his brigade in battle for the first time since it was organized on Monday, had a high numerical advantage and the asset of being opposite one of the weakest constructed fortifications in the Confederate line. The artillery enfilade, however, had a drastic effect upon his men and in the remaining time he was unable to resume the initiative. No one could complain of the bravery of the 25th Indiana; in a crossfire for more than two hours, the Hoosiers left some of their 14 dead and 61 wounded on that bloody and bullet-scarred slope.[21]

The other newly organized brigade of the army steeled itself for its baptism of fire. While Lauman revitalized his brigade at the base of his ill-starred ridge, Colonels Morrison and Haynie, assisted by McClernand's Captain Stewart analyzed their pending assignment.

Confident in his rank, Haynie hoped to ascend to command of the brigade, except he was unsure of his division commander's intentions in this matter. A rather frigid discussion on the matter developed, with Haynie consciously referring to his seniority but unwilling to assume the responsibility of superseding Morrison. Both looked to Stewart but he was as mystified as the others. Morrison, seeking to resolve the impasse, offered a compromise. He would lead the brigade to the jumping-off spot for the attack, and then the responsibility would devolve upon Haynie. Cryptically, Haynie responded: "Colonel, let us take it together." To Haynie this meant a duumverate, with Haynie as senior member, had been created. To Morrison the remark gave him the responsibility over his own two regiments.

To the right had assembled the remainder of Wallace's brigade. While Morrison had moved forward of the Wynn's Ferry Road in response to McClernand's request, the Second Brigade had maneuvered to their rear and formed to the east. Even further to the east the rifled pieces continued their thundering display to one and all of their magnificent range.[22]

On the river with wood-burning engines puffing black smoke over the horizon, a transport with a cargo of the last regiment from Clarksville hove into sight of the Dover landing. On board no one was left in doubt that the region was under siege. Many saw debris from shell explosions in the town shooting into the air. Even at that moment, evidently attracted by the smoke from the stacks, shells splashed into the water near the wharf.

Alarmed at the inhospitable reception, the men of the 42nd Tennessee, in spite of the cramped quarters, formed in company line on the decks of the steamer. As a frightened crew made the vessel fast at the landing, unit after unit sped at double-time down the gangplank. In the shell-pocked streets of the town, a staff officer straight from Pillow (who was near to the scene) directed the commanding officer and his volunteers toward the defenses of Heiman's menaced brigade.[23]

Before returning to the head of his regiment, Colonel William Morrison rode into the area of the 17th Illinois. In the absence of its colonel the regiment would be led into action by its senior major, Francis Smith. Finding everything in order, Morrison proceeded to his own unit, the 49th Illinois. To his right in a location to come to their assistance if necessary lay the 45th Illinois lead miners under Colonel John E. Smith, Swiss watchmaker and resident of Grant's home town, Galena. For the Union it was to be a battle of the "Smiths."

Meanwhile Haynie, giving command of his own regiment to Lieutenant Colonel Thomas Smith, instructed each regiment to contribute to the skirmish line which preceded the assault force by about 100 yards. The 49th would debark from the floor of the western branch of Erin Hollow. Between the left of the 49th and the crest of the ridge which led straight to Maney's guns, marched the 17th. The 48th would have as its field of operations the top of the ridge, lacking any notable ascent but exposed, as the 17th had already discovered, to the guns of Graves across the wide valley to the left.

Heiman, while he had not seen fit to construct appropriate earthworks for Maney, found himself with adequate infantry defenses along his line. Directly supporting Maney at the apex of his line was the 53rd Tennessee under Colonel Voorhies. To their left stood the 27th Alabama and the 48th Tennessee respectively. The 10th Tennessee held the duty of barring the Indian Creek Valley and occupying the works fronting on a deep, almost impassable ravine. Maney, in spite of the unwelcome attention he had received from Federal cannon in the early hours, mustered his full strength, with the exception of a gunner who had lost both hands in an accidental explosion. It was 12:45.[24]

Colonel Morrison scanned the ominous incline over which his troops were about to tread. The downhill portion, above the small creek known as Erin Hollow, grew thick with woods and underbrush. By this time, however, his skirmishers had emerged from this tangle at the foot of the hill into the extensive clearing which had given Maney such an open field of fire. Instructing some privates to cut a way for him through the more wicked parts of the leafless jungle, Morrison decided he could remain astride his steed to give himself more mobility in the attack.

The 17th and 48th Illinois, while not needing to overcome such steep slopes, found their paths barred by a blackjack undergrowth. Already the skirmisher line had disappeared. Officers assured their men that there was open land ahead, but they neglected to include the information that it was directly before and beyond the abatis.

Meanwhile, a desperate fire fight had initiated at the base of Morrison's clearing. As the skirmishers of the 49th stepped beyond the small trees marking the perimeter of the cleared hill, the four Confederate guns discharged their lethal shells. The widely spaced Federals were not slow to reply. One of the first musket balls struck the exposed section commander, Lieutenant Burns, with a horrible wound. As most of the Union advance party knelt or crouched to reload or dodge return fire, Lieutenant Massie gasped and plunged forward beside his guns. Many of his gray-clad gunners recognized that he would not live long.

On the Federal left the glitter from emblems and bayonets had attracted the attention of the alert Captain Graves, and he launched a worrisome hail of missiles upon the 48th. The left flank faltered noticeably.

The 17th Illinois in the center, behind which strode acting Brigadier (in his own mind) Haynie, encountered their own troubles. A man could travel in a straight path for a few feet without having to pause to batter away a pricker limb or a slim, low-lying branch of a tree. The alternative to this dodging was bleeding hands and faces or tripping and stumbling solders.

In addition a healthy distance was maintained between the ranks of the storming troops, for the whiplash of branches and thorns from the first line would catch the second line full in the face. With officers understandably concerned over the alignment of their companies, the progress of the 17th became very slow.[25]

At that moment the sweeping rows of the 49th Illinois were gathering momentum. They had left the worst of their terrain behind them, and with the exception of the foreboding abatis the entrenchments lay visibly before them.

At this point the assault plans, poorly laid to begin with, rapidly disintegrated. The assumption on which the movement had been predicted—the silencing of Maney's battery—had been proved distinctly false. No particularly intensive artillery bombardment had preceded the attack. Now, with the lack of obstructions before Morrison and the lack of coordination due to the difficulties of the country or the feelings between Morrison and Haynie, the gap between the 17th and the 49th began to widen noticeably. Gaps also began to materialize between the 17th and 48th, the latter encountering practically the same natural hindrances as the 17th as well as being under fire.

His skirmishers near the entangled abatis, Morrison rushed supports forward. The usual military procedure at this juncture was to maintain the lines and shoot at the enemy until one side broke. In this case, however, Morrison intended to break through the pointed logs and carry the works by storm. For this reason the shock troops received explicit orders to reserve fire until point-blank range on top of the breastworks was reached.

Seeing the Union advance at the obstructions Heiman instructed the infantry to commence firing. In the angle surrounding the battery, gun attendants were dropping regularly. Maney himself had just been wounded. The Confederate infantry, well sheltered, had up to this time sustained next to no casualties. Observing no immediate threat in their fronts, the troops of the 53rd Tennessee on the right of the angle began to slide by their left flanks to the area of potential impact.

Heiman's well-aimed and executed volley had a predictable effect upon the green Union troops. Halted either by the abatis or the stalled rank in front of them, each volunteer endured several moments of shock at the sight of their dead and wounded comrades lying about them. Frustrated at their immobility and desiring to retaliate, they suddenly cast to the winds all remembrance of discipline and their rifles and muskets spoke for them.

A barrage of oaths from the mounted Morrison brought the regiment back to its senses. Swiftly they reloaded their weapons. Before this project could be effected, another blast of shot and lead issued forth from the earthworks. While many Rebel riflemen had trained their pieces on the angry horseman, Morrison managed to remain unscathed.[26]

Observing the sudden bottleneck through his field glasses, McClernand rushed an aide to Colonel Smith of the 45th Illinois on the left flank of the Second Brigade. The verbal orders were for Smith to make the utmost speed to give Morrison what he needed to seize the battery. At 1 P.M., the 45th, directed toward the right of the 49th, tramped down the hill into the hollow.

Meanwhile the front line of the 49th with hands and axes endeavored to hack a passage through the interlaced lumber. While some in blue were falling, others dashed forward to assume their places. Suddenly a tremendous cheer rumbled along the whole Union battlefront. From the forest on the left the blue-uniformed 17th Illinois had emerged into the open area.

Here Major Smith, finding his left flank unattended, halted

and marched some companies by flank movement until they reached the deep ravine on the western face. The prospects of his attack secure, Smith prepared to resume his approach to the abatis.

The sudden presence of another regiment had caused some consternation in the Southern trenches. Tennesseeans clambered over one another to reach posts to repulse this sudden threat. Under the circumstances the next volley upon the 49th nearly 40 feet away was not among the most effective. Nevertheless, scattered cheers rose above the echoes of the musketry. The enemy officer on horseback was down.

Staff and nearby infantrymen gathered around the fallen Morrison. Trying desperately not to expose his intense pain, the colonel attempted to encourage the survivors to press the attack. A quick look at the savage hole in the right hip convinced the huddled group that the officer should be evacuated to the hospital. As tenderly as possible they carried Morrison down the incline.

The occurrence or its significance was not lost on the Illinoisans of the 49th. Without their trusted leader they hesitated, undecided. Then as Captain John W. Brockaw collapsed dead, a company to the right of Morrison's fall broke and retreated swiftly down the hill. The other survivors needed little encouragement to follow suit.

Without warning the 17th found its right flank exposed. Major Smith did his best to temporarily remedy the situation with some help from Haynie. Now, however, the remaining wrath of Captain Maney and Voorhies' regiment and others who could train their muskets on the standing bluecoats descended with full force. The 17th could not stand alone and unsupported against such attention and withdrew into the undergrowth.[27]

The 48th Illinois finally reached its sector only to find it preempted by the 17th. Consequently it assumed a rear area support role. Major Smith, although finding himself at a disadvantage without artillery backing, promptly sent his high-spirited young men back into the fray.

A few hundred yards ahead of him the 42nd Tennessee had arrived to bolster Heiman's defense. Not feeling himself to be in any desperate straits, Heiman nevertheless guided forward three companies of the fresh troops to relieve sections of the pressed 53rd on the left side of the angle.

Soon rejoined on the right by rallied remnants of the 49th, the 17th endeavored to maintain a heavy volume of musketry from behind the abatis. The left wing was plagued, however, by a steady rain of shot from all six of Graves' cannon, whose gunners were generally unable to observe the effect. While the proximity of the Union line to the Confederate forces prevented the Southern gunners fom executing their trade as well as they had previously, it served to divert Yankee attention from the immediate task at hand.

It was not long before two gun captains dashed up to Maney with the news that their crews lay on all sides of their weapons and not enough remained to service them. Maney ordered the survivors to reinforce the other two pieces. A few feet away some of the Tennesseeans from the 42nd moaned about the accuracy of the 49th Illinois which had knocked down a number of their companions while approaching and fighting from the trenches.[28]

On the fight went, neither side even considering withdrawal. The muzzles of the Rebel six-pounders smoked and fairly glowed from the heat of the rapid fire. Sunburnt Midwest faces turned even darker from the effects of the gunpowder they manipulated. On both sides certain individuals seized upon the opportunities of wounded neighbors to take themselves out of rifle range by escorting the wounded to the hospitals.

Finally Major Smith and Colonel Haynie, seeing no hint of

a Confederate retreat, decided that no purpose would be served by continuing the engagement. Bugles sounded retreat. With dignity and spirit the 17th and 49th backed down the hill, replying to their opponents in kind as best they could. The time was not quite 1:30.

At this point on the extreme right the flags of the 45th Illinois stuck their heads from the forest on the border of the clearing. During their struggles with nature's gowth in Erin Hollow, the regiment had been free from enemy interference, due to their attention being occupied by Federal artillery. A few pickets from the 30th Tennessee had been scattered, and the 45th found itself with its center on an unassailable ravine leading to the base of the angle. Thus Colonel Smith found himself compelled to infringe upon the front of the 49th to the left.

At that time no one in the 49th was in a mood to argue the matter. While Haynie, unaware of the presence of the 45th, continued to withdraw the 17th and the 48th, the 49th agreed to stand and support Smith's effort to improve the situation.

At quick time the 45th took themselves right to the abatis. Just at that moment the ignition of gunpowder in one or a number of spots caused leaves on the clearing ground, dropped in the autumn, to spring into flame. The smoke and the heat brought panic to the Federal wounded still sprawling on the earth, and their desperate cries unnerved both the 49th and the 45th. Smith retired his flanks in succession, and the smoke from the wetter leaves helped to disguise the evacuation.[29]

Near the Wynn's Ferry Road Dr. John Brinton and his surgical staff had set up a field hospital in a ravine nearly within sight of the Confederate works. For more than 30 minutes wounded cases had been flowing in. The doctor full well realized that in many circumstances it was incumbent upon able-bodied soldiers to bring non-ambulatory injured to the station. What thoroughly disgusted Brinton was the skulkers who hung around the medical center thinking they appeared to the world as surgeon's aides. At this time in his first major engagement Brinton displayed concern lest the large gathering attract unusual notice from the enemy. As a precaution the doctor had brought the reserve medical supplies to that spot, and he well knew the army could not afford their loss. He now sent his second complaint to General Grant, warning of the potential danger of a Confederate assault.[30]

As the jaded and crestfallen survivors of the Third Brigade filed or stumbled up the ravine to the road plateau amid the resumed booming of Taylor's guns, Colonel Webster, Chief of Staff of Grant's army, and Major McPherson, the engineer, discussed their impressions of the assault. Both had been present when the writhing form of Colonel Morrison had been carried to the hospital shelter. Naturally, assuming he had been in command, the two officers now agreed that the bullet which felled the colonel had brought the climax of the attack. In their view the brigade would have swept on to victory had it not been for this misfortune.

After a short respite in the hollow, Colonel Smith of the 45th received orders to proceed with his unit east on the road until he reached the right of McAllister's battery. Haynie, who had received McClernand's sanction to withdraw the brigade, now listened to instructions to rejoin Wallace with his regiment. It was two o'clock.

Moved by the plight of the Federal wounded in the flaming leaves, Heiman had instructed a party to advance to their assistance. Several of them returned with two suffering Illinoisans. The others soon stacked in piles more than 60 abandoned muskets and quantities of assorted Federal government equipment. Further down the slope bodies of dead and wounded Federals were being consumed by the accidental conflagration.

As the collection mounted, runners related the casualties of the various detachments. Preoccupied with other matters, the Confederate colonel did not keep an accurate count, but to the best of his mental powers the casualties did not exceed 10 killed and 30 wounded. The 42nd Tennessee, exposed on the dispatch of the three companies to the breastworks, accounted for 20 per cent of this figure. Almost all of the remainder was divided between Maney and the 53rd Tennessee. The latter regiment had performed yeoman service that day; in the morning cannon balls and shells meant for Maney injured some of their men and now they had just taken the brunt of the battery defense. Maney's artillery crews, highlighted against the sky and unprotected by defensive works, had lost just about 50 per cent, about 16 being dead.

To the North the chief losses in the first phase of the attack had been borne by the 49th. The burden of the second phase fell upon their companion, the 17th. In total the rolls of the brigade were reduced by more than 10 dozen fighting men, nearly 10 per cent, high for the Western theater at that time. Ashamed at his own regiment's performance, Haynie reported one killed and eight wounded in the 48th. Taking part in the final phase of the storming, the 45th suffered only a few more casualties than the 48th.[31]

The burden of responsibility for the abortive advance rested heavily upon John McClernand. His intentions were not only to remove the thorn in his side of the battery but to hold the hill against any further annoyance. He did not lay down adequate artillery preparation. The question of who commanded was never clear. Obviously reconnaissance had been sparse. Worst of all, no strong supports were in position to hold the hill if the angle had been carried. Heiman, with a brigade equal in number to the assault force, had three regiments practically unused. Later the 42nd marched to his succor, and the 30th Tennessee was within supporting distance for a counter attack. McClernand could not very easily have used more of Wallace's brigade as support, because this would have jeopardized Oglesby by isolating him before the large opposing Rebel left wing. Only McArthur of Smith's Divisions was available for support on the left, and he was needed to block the Indian Creek Road. McClernand had earlier requested to Grant that the navy and General Smith be brought into action.[32] The former was certainly fulfilled and the latter partially, for Lauman was just retreating at 12:30. In addition a long time had elapsed between conception of the plan and its implementation. The most McClernand could have hoped for under the circumstances was to capture or spike the battery. As it was, he reduced its effectiveness by one-half—but at a high cost.

Again Dr. Brinton attempted to alarm Grant about the danger to the medical supplies. Finally the general took time to send a written message. It stated that he knew the enemy's leader (Pillow), and he was completely confident the Confederates would not leave their trenches.

Grant's actions, however, show no great reliance upon his own assuring words. McClernand acknowledged instructions to proceed no further with his attempt at envelopment. Instead he was to consolidate his present position and harass the enemy at a distance. Thinning his own line could only make him vulnerable if the Southerners sortied from their own works.

With the news of the complete failure of the lunge at the center, Grant became highly depressed. Suspecting superior numbers to be facing him, he could, with his present force, no longer stretch his right flank. With the Confederates "in such great strength," even the prospective reinforcements made this plan unsure. The fortifications were strong and seemingly would withstand direct assault. It appeared that for the third time in four months Grant would have to watch the Navy pull his fat from the furnace. Possibly the fortunes of his career hung in the balance.

Thoroughly alarmed, Grant penned a note to Brigadier Lew Wallace in command of two brigades of 2,500 men at Forts Henry and Heiman. According to the order Wallace was to bring one brigade of two regiments to Donelson immediately. Already the Henry garrison, smaller even than Tilghman's, held a precarious post, threatened as they were from Paris and the Columbus garrison. Now with the defending force even more dangerously reduced, Grant attempted to allay Halleck's fears for Fort Henry by sending a second message. From his commanding general he requested a shift in the destination of reinforcements to Fort Henry.[33]

On the diminishing waters of the Cumberland successive steams of smoke denoted the progress of the vanguard of Flag Officer Foote's flotilla and convoy. In the breezy air above the casemates of the *St. Louis,* a small, somewhat frail, stooped figure in gold buttons and epaulettes glared at the shore. Too bad it was inhabited by so many of those near-heathen secessionist sympathizers. Typically New England in features and with a typically New England religious outlook, Andrew H. Foote chugged upstream on his way to "save" General Grant. A final message from Henry Halleck emphasized the urgency of reducing Fort Donelson immediately.

From the port holes sailors stuck their heads out to view the oncoming shore, and beyond that the land with the ominous name—no man's land. Already the excitement of the voyage had submerged the displeasure of some at being shifted from their assigned vessels. The homes of the natives were viewed with cynicism and even elicited comments that individuals so poor and stupid could never hope to sustain themselves against the mighty technological giant of the North. The primitive log cabins in some cases were built so close to the water that they were now under water. Here and there Negroes had gathered in small clusters to dance and sing and frolic at the supposed advent of their freedom. Some of the bluejackets, irrespective of the feelings of their abolitionist messmates, took the opportunity to imitate the Negro dialect to their companions. Whether well or poorly done, the mockery invariably brought peals of laughter from those around them.

A two-gun Union section planted their train on the skirt of the ridge directly opposite Buckner's left. From his vantage point the menacing crashes from across the valley did not go unnoticed by Confederate Captain Rice Graves. He thereupon strode over to his most accurate rifled gun and aimed the piece while the assistants performed their necessary evolutions. Ten minutes later the Southern artillerists let loose a deafening cheer. A solid ball had smashed the wheel off one of the howitzers. The whole battery opened fire as perplexed Federal gunners endeavored to rescue their responsibilities. By this time, however, Porter had taken his bearings on this martial activity and found it within range. In a matter of seconds General Smith had to chalk off another gun to enemy action. In addition Cook's infantry support disappeared in the face of the Rebel grape and cannister.[34]

Observing the effective use of artillery, in the very manner that he himself had suffered, McClernand determined to repay the Confederates by blasting then into quiescence. Accordingly, before and during the time of Morrison's attack, Taylor, Dresser, Welker (with Parrotts), and McAllister all massed within close proximity of each other to hurl death at the earthworks near where the road made its entry. During this exercise the Southern batteries of Green and French condensed their own replies.

Shortly after it was definitely decided that Heiman would make no counterattack, several batteries were moved along the Wynn's Ferry Road to the point of Oglesby's advance. There, one section of Taylor's guns and two of Dresser's rifled James pieces joined Gumbart's artillery. Here the newcomers found Gumbart heavily engaged, not only with enemy artillery but with swarms of sharpshooters too. Lieutenant Joseph Hauger had already fallen victim to a sniper.

The reinforcement of Parrotts under Captain Welker had signaled the move. The sudden diminishing in battery fire, however, notified the gunners of the light artillery under the supervision of Captains Green and French that something was up. Welker was unwise enough to openly display one gun by setting it up on the road. Long-range missiles began to rain down on the unfortunate blue-clad gunners as they struggled to bring the weapon to bear. Even so, they managed to get off five shots before one nearly direct hit mangled one soldier horribly and sent his compatriots into the brush.

Nearby McAllister sought to retaliate. The projectiles from his 24-pounder arched high above the ridge positions of the garrison. In a few minutes, however, one lucky solid ball of iron skipped crazily along the crust of the earth and straight into the wheel of his Number Three.

McAllister, himself, galloped up to the still useful howitzers and shouted peremptory orders to get them to the cover of the reverse slope of the ridge a few feet away. This his men succeeded in doing. Here they found a gunner's paradise. With a little digging the surviving pair of howitzers would be in ideal fortress position. The servers would stand exposed only as long as it took to run the piece up the slope and ignite its powder. The recoil would send the wheels spinning backwards and out of enemy view. Still, French and Green were able to throw four shots for every one the howitzers could unleash.

As Union batteries on the far right resumed their interdiction, the din of musketry in the vicinity rose in crescendo. For one thing the Confederate pickets had not only increased in numbers but also in vigor. Another reason was that Oglesby was pushing his regiments nearer the Southern lines. The 18th Illinois, which had taken the point of the drive and had been compelled to beat off enemy scouts and sharpshooters all day, was particularly unlucky and suffered one killed and four wounded in a single one-sided skirmish.[35]

The Confederate cavalry also found opportunities to get in their licks. All day long individual riders had been employed in giving warnings and carrying messages. Some, like Forrest, though, took time to accomplish more than merely digging their spurs into the flanks of their steeds. Something about the gray uniform or the squirrel-tail crested cap attracted the acting brigadier's attention to a lurking Birge rifleman. He drew rein and unobtrusively requested the loan of an aide's Maynard rifle. In less than a minute a ranking Union sharpshooter had plunged headlong from his perch to the leaf-packed ground.

The Birge men had some measure of revenge another time that day. *Tribune* correspondent Browne on a dare took a sharpshooter's rifle and silenced an insistent Rebel marksman.[36]

In the meantime the fragments of the three Union batteries on the right had achieved marked success. Enemy batteries at their fronts were beaten into silence. Oglesby's advance had kept the small-arms damage to a minimum. While Dresser took advantage of his long range to again direct shells near the river, the 12-pounders and 6-pounders of the other two sections concentrated on their front and on the extreme left flank of the enemy breastworks. On the latter the batteries were in position to enfilade.

Within the confines of the entrenchments the infantry of Johnson had begun to suffer heavily from the bombardment. The Texans of the 7th, poorly armed and inexperienced, became so unnerved at the shell fragments which skipped through their trenches that the 20th Mississippi, held in reserve since their morning arrival, was sent by Johnson as a replacement. Dissatisfied with the state of their cover, the Mississippians began to burrow downward like moles.[37]

In the fort there were many beaming faces as Generals Floyd

and Pillow together paid a visit and congratulated the rank and file and officers alike for their stout defense.

The overcast sky was bringing an early darkness. As a few gunners commented on the noticeable moistening of the air, Captain Dresser glumly listened to tales that the caissons were now empty of shell. Not wishing to expose a defenseless command, he withdrew his pieces from danger. Anyhow he felt strongly that his men deserved a prolonged respite, especially after their animated and extremely successful activity of the day.

Before Wallace's brigade Gumbart found that the section he directed had exhausted their cannister. He so informed McClernand who ordered Taylor with two sections to assume Gumbart's place.

Enlightened by cavalry scouts or pickets, the sections on the right flank experimented with reducing the powder charges propelling their shells. Darkness had set in before true observation of the effects could be recorded. Colonel Baldwin, defending the Rebel left with his brigade, could have told them. All day long the enemy's explosives had whistled overhead and had only terrified the volunteers. Suddenly the troops ducked for cover as each shell seemed directed at the exact spot where they were standing. The 26th Mississippi in the trenches saw one of their men chewed up so badly he could not live. The 26th Tennessee in support heard the cries of two men wounded by one burst.

The moisture in the atmosphere condensed and finally settled into a light cold rain. John McClernand, inspecting Oglesby's location, fretted that the enemy might utilize a road to the right which could not be occupied. He therefore instructed the brigade commander to withdraw his line 100 to 150 yards to better protect his rear against surprise.

With McArthur's brigade of Smith's division advancing to occupy the eastern slope of Indian Creek Valley, W. H. L.

Wallace, on orders from his general, marched his brigade east into closer contact with Oglesby near the sallyport of the Wynn's Ferry Road.[38]

Darkness brought its enveloping mantle over the contingents of blue and gray. Johnson's left wing enumerated its losses. McCausland's contingent, aiding Green's battery, was minus five men, all wounded. The shaken 7th Texas had lost two, one dead and one wounded. The 8th Kentucky with a group of opposing guns directly before them had suffered two killed and ten wounded during six hours of steady bombardment.

In the center Adolphus Heiman had heard from Pillow that a section of guns under Captain Parker would be moved up to supplement Maney during the night. The comparatively fresh and unworked 42nd Tennessee was put to work digging a parapet of some strength to shelter all the guns. Some of the infantry men were overheard voicing concern that with the great chill and dampness in the air the brigade would spend a miserable evening without any blankets.

On the right Buckner estimated the day's loss at 39 killed and wounded in his portion of the army. At the river fortifications Captain Culbertson issued instructions that in view of the *Carondelet* maintaining pressure in her boilers troops manning the guns would sleep by them that night. Receiving a reprieve from duty, Captain Ross journeyed to Dover and in discussion with exuberant residents heard one and all "verify" that both Federal vessels in sight that day had been crippled, if not sunk.[39]

With the rays of the sun no longer available to reveal their movements, Lauman's three regiments discreetly withdrew from the woods at the perimeter of the clearing leading to Hanson's rifle pits. At the position of the morning's debarkation a halt was called and the rattled men initiated their preparation for dinner and a night of rest.

Briefly the cold rain turned to sleet. Then to the temporary relief of the exposed volunteers of both sides, the driving pelt changed to the soft steady patter of snowflakes. The volume from the skies increased more, then more. At that rate it was not long before a layer of snow had secured a lodgment atop the deceased leaves.[40]

Amid their labors to build and bolster the height and thickness of their breastworks, the 20th Mississippi found it to their comfort and advantage to keep their feet dry by bailing the accumulated water and melted snow out of the trench. Elsewhere the effects of the days and nights spent at construction and the alerts of the day were taking their effect. The 2nd Kentucky, however, tired or not, was employed in building earthen protection for Jackson's reinforced battery of four pieces. In the fort the infantry garrison cooked rations and accumulated spirits from hoarded private stocks to send to the heroes of the river-side batteries.[41]

The 18th Illinois found human companionship only on their left. The assumption could be made that men heard or seen in their front, right, or rear would denote the presence of the enemy, for the regiment was on the flank of Grant's army. A few soldiers tried to recline and rest their weary limbs, but shortly they found the wetness of the packing snow much more to their distaste. All along the brigade troops stood to arms amid frequent picket skirmishes.

While Wallace's unit maintained a like readiness and Morrison's survivors licked their wounds, McArthur's brigade found some consolation in the precipitation. It was easier to dig to complete their assignment of throwing up two small earthworks for one pair of 20-pound artillery pieces and another pair of 10-pounders. Strong detachments here too were alert for any sortie under cover of the snowfall.

Couriers from brigade and division commanders began to stream regularly into Grant's dilapidated one-and-a-half story headquarters. The most consistent complaint was the shortage or non-variety of rations. The activity of Confederate artillery during the day had kept those available in the rear, and now darkness and the worsening condition of the roads prevented their moving to anyone's relief. One almost insultingly terse note from McClernand notified the stubby general that the First Division was limited to hard bread and coffee for its evening meal. (In many cases the coffee was cold, for few fires were permitted.)[42]

A telegrapher in a large hut at Fort Donelson beat a tattoo on the line to Nashville. His text was a report from General Floyd to General Albert Sidney Johnston:

> The day is closed, and we have maintained ourselves fully by land and water. The cannonade at one time was quite sharp. The attack on our trenches was not very severe. The gunboats, after two assaults, retired at an early hour in the evening. I presume battle will be fought tomorrow. We will endeavor to hold our position if we are capable of doing so. Our casualties are not great; the enemy's, I have no doubt, are much greater.

While the message was not highly sanguine, it at least contained no request for permission to retire. Significantly, neither did it ask for reinforcements. Floyd thought it necessary to give no recommendations to Johnston. Johnston would not ask for any.

In the Dover tavern Floyd and Pillow busily weighed the evidence submitted from intelligence sources on the Tennessee and Smithland, the Union temporary base at the mouth of the Cumberland. The news they sifted was fairly accurate but distorted just enough to create a psychological imbalance. Floyd felt obliged to pen another, less confident, telegram to Johnston:

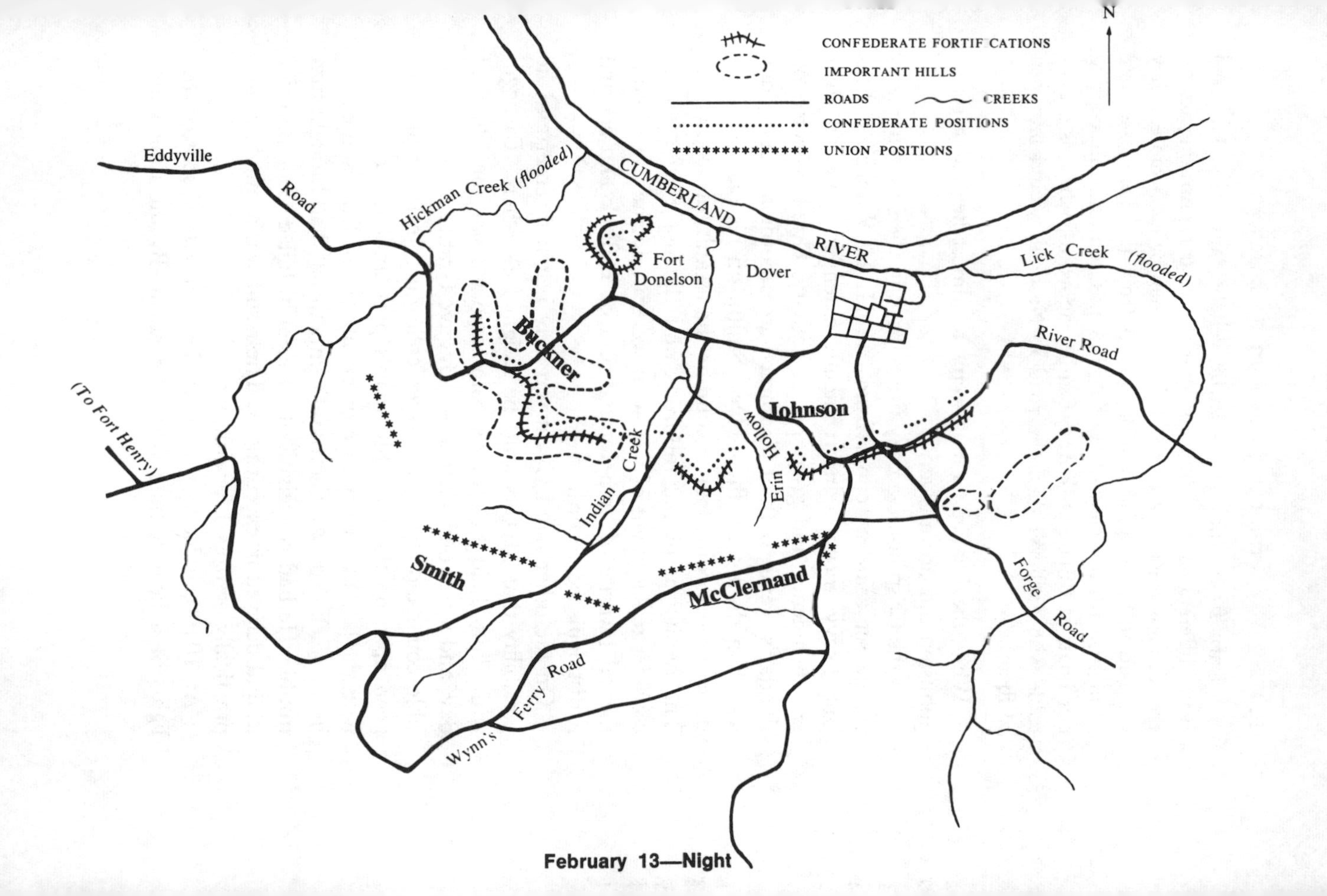

February 13—Night

I learn from what seems to be reliable authority, gathered from different sources, that the enemy are concentrating up on the Tennessee River a force of 50,000 men or even more. They are said to be bringing reinforcements from the Tennessee here to-night, with the view of turning our position and intercepting our boats at Randolph Forge, 6 miles above us, which is practicable with artillery; then the road to Nashville would lay open to them.

While the final statement seems to almost beg for a reply, Johnston did not answer.[43]

In the Crisp house a cozy fire burned in the stone fireplace. As he set aside a report from W. H. L. Wallace indicating heavy enemy reinforcements, extended work on their entrenchments, and great picket activity, Grant reflected on the day's events. Both of his immediate subordinates had done less than distinguish themselves. Smith, on his part, was not present to coordinate or encourage the assaults of his division. The result was dismal failure. Grant did not even begin to consider replacement of the aging veteran, for he was a sentimental favorite of both himself and of Halleck and sported a distinguished record.

On the other hand Grant seriously began to entertain the possibility that McClernand be assigned elsewhere. To begin with, both held brigadier's commissions from the identical day, and it was only chance which gave Grant a more responsible command than his lawyer colleague. Jealousy had not been open on the tall, thin man's part until his impatience with the lack of celerity of movement toward Donelson earlier in the week. Now McClernand's impetuosity had brought him trouble. He had conceived of an assault, failed to prepare for it, and delayed in executing it. The result was a small brigade practically destroyed for combat.

At 10:00, a lookout aboard the *Carondelet* spotted the lights of a boat coming from the north. By the time Commander Walke reached the deck, the faint lines exposed her as the *Pittsburgh,* forerunner of the flotilla. Walke inwardly rejoiced, for he had expended all of the ammunition of his main guns that day.[44]

A few minutes later Colonel McArthur heard the recitation of an order from McClernand to move a quarter of a mile closer to Wallace.

In Dover the generals learned of the arrival of the first installment of the gunboats and transports from cavalry videttes posted across the Cumberland. Pillow advised Floyd to await more exact news in the morning before reporting to Johnston. To the Tennessean three lengthy telegrams in one six-hour period were much more than the situation called for.

At Mrs. Crisp's meanwhile, Grant in his restless mood had abandoned the double feather bed to seek peace in another room. The temperature had plummeted down to such low depths, however, that he soon straggled back to the kitchen with its warmth and comfort.

There was no warmth and comfort on the hill of the 14th Iowa. Regretting the discard of blankets and overcoats on Wednesday, the men grouped in rings and trooped around in circles Indian fashion. Between trembling and nearly blue lips one of the Iowans muttered to his predecessor that he had overheard one of the officers say it was nearly 10 degrees Fahrenheit.[45]

6

Friday—Maybe a Siege

NEITHER THE HUDDLED ROWS OF SLEEPNESS BLUE OR GRAY soldiers cared that it was the morning of Friday, February 14, 1862. As long as there was no light in the sky, there was no prospect of relief from the wintery north wind or its accompanying packets of snow, which had by now accumulated to three inches. Those enlistees lying in fetal position under blankets with the C. S. A. emblem muttered imprecations at the ugly President of the United States whose election had brought them to these inhospitable hills and dales. On the other hand volunteers sworn to pacify these same Rebels found it some comfort to curse and belittle the ancestry of the individual upon whom the blame for the separation of the Union could so illogically be centred—Jefferson Davis.

The most fortunate Federal infantrymen that morning were the new arrivals sheltered aboard the transports anchored in the Cumberland. The messmates of six regiments in particular, however, took the opportunity to grumble about their lot. Cruft's brigade, the 1st Nebraska and the 2nd Iowa had spent the bulk of the hours since Sunday cramped aboard these steamboats. On Wednesday morning there had been anticipation at the scheduled opportunity to regain terra firma at Fort Henry. Then instructions had come from General Grant to proceed back down the Tennessee and up the Cumberland. In their uncomfortable journey north and then east, they reinforced at Smithland the second brigade from Buell —the first was Cruft's—and picked up an escort of gunboats.

Now at six o'clock, with the shore becoming sprayed with filtered sunlight, the first of the troop carriers began to unload. A particularly nasty flurry of combined snow and hail was just beginning to subside.

In the dim interior of the Crisp house Major Rawlins pored over the returns for the effectives of the new nine regiments. Taking into consideration losses in action, to the best of his calculations the addition brought the Union army to just over 25,000 able-bodied men.

More were on their way. Handsome General Lew Wallace had been routed from his cot barely five hours earlier to take from the hands of an exhausted courier the expected command to report with reinforcements before Donelson. Complying with the admonition to leave a strong guard at Fort Henry, Wallace told a disappointed colonel of the 23rd Indiana and the cavalry commanders that they were entrusted with defending the base. After boats had spent the dark morning hours ferrying marching units to the east bank of the Tennessee, Wallace found himself ready to leave his headquarters boat. At that time the friendly naval captain presented him with a picnic basket of food for the trip.[1]

Shivering from the effects of the 12-degree weather outside, General John Floyd stared glumly at the cavalry messenger who had just related the latest intelligence from the pickets on the northern side of the Cumberland. The news was bad; the enemy had received substantial waterborne reinforcements.

Up to this point Confederate estimates of the Union army had been remarkably accurate. Knowing his own corps to now number 14,000 and no worthwhile reinforcements to be forthcoming, Floyd allowed an exaggeration to influence his despairing mind. Before, the enemy gunboats had been the prime threat. Now temporarily they became secondary. Floyd then and there resolved to prepare a sortie to extricate himself and the garrison.

To Albert Sidney Johnston he communicated his reasons but only a hint of his purpose:

> The enemy have reached the ground near the fort with eight or ten gunboats. I am uncertain which, and fifteen transports, reported to have on board near 20,000 men. They are now landing. This makes their force nearly 40,000 strong. I will fight them this evening.[2]

On the Union left acting Brigadier Cook was fit to be tied. The 13th Missouri had vacated its frontline position against his wishes. Out of earshot of the rank and file Colonel Cook and Colonel Wright of the 13th argued the matter out. Cook had arrived on an ordinary tour of inspection to discover Wright seated on a log before a fire wrapped in a blanket—and a considerable distance behind his post. Wright replied that his men had been drenched and frozen and he had deemed it advisable to get some fires built. He therefore had requested (and thought he had received) permission at three o'clock to retire a half mile and build fires. Disgusted, Cook uttered a final reproof and ordered the regiment back to its original line.[3]

As his large body hunched over his freshly brewed steaming coffee in a tin cup, Colonel Richard Oglesby learned the extremely discouraging news that the supply wagons would be unable to reach the eastern extremity of the army before Saturday. The only rations available to his bedraggled group were pots of boiling coffee.

The commander of the First Division, John McClernand, was fortunate enough to supplement this meager diet with a piece of hard roll. He had just given his best wishes to his favorite Captain Stewart and a Lieutenant Freeman, who were leading a reconnaissance party to investigate the enemy's potential avenues of escape to the east.[4]

In Buckner's division Colonel Hanson voiced apprehension lest the Union army, now being reinforced from the west, take the opportunity to take the shortest route to the goal. Colonels Brown and Buckner readily agreed to the merit of the fears and released the five reserve companies of the 18th Tennessee to the disposal of the 2nd Kentucky. Enemy sharpshooter activity was already on the increase.[5]

General Ulysses S. Grant was up and about. In spite of Thursday's dismal omens, he was now confident of his eventual triumph. As he trotted along the lines, quipping jokes to right and left, Grant foresaw the navy isolating the Confederate army, being unable by itself to force surrender, and looking on while the army carried the day. To his aides he commented that this affair had hung fire long enough, and that he would like to end it that evening, if possible, with a night attack.

To the amalgamation of the new arrivals Grant turned his attention. The 2nd Iowa was absorbed by the predominantly Iowa brigade of Jacob Lauman. The 1st Nebraska was led by Colonel John Thayer, and since he outranked by far the commandants of the 58th, 68th, and 76th Ohio organizations, he became a brigade commander. Together with Colonel Cruft's unit of Kentucky and Indiana regiments he would be placed in Wallace's new Third Division. After all, Wallace too wore a star on his shoulders and could not be expected to command less in this army with its excess of brigades. On consultation with McClernand it was decided to place this new division on the left of the First Division to allow it to extend more to the right.

Later that morning Grant undertook to keep Halleck informed about his operations. His information, he wrote Chief-of-Staff Cullum at Cairo, indicated that General John Floyd had arrived at Donelson with a reinforcement of 4,000 troops. He enumerated his losses of the 13th (they were only Morrison's, however) and placed a request for ammunition for his 10- and 20-pound Parrotts and 24-pounder howitzers. Transportation for his field supplies, he emphasized, had reached an acute state.

Then, for some enigmatic reason, Grant stated that he expected a protracted siege of Dover and environs. Meekly he excused his stand by saying that he feared storming entrenchments with raw troops. Possibly this was a ploy to keep Halleck in St. Louis.[6]

On board the *St. Louis* Flag Officer Foote had just terminated a conversation with Commander Walke on the situation before the river batteries. The upshot of the conference was that Foote decided to take precautions against quick disabling injuries such as occurred at Fort Henry. Shortly, orders greeted the captains of the flagship, the *Carondelet,* the *Louisville,* the *Pittsburgh,* and the wooden gunboats, *Tyler* and *Conestoga,* to armor their upper works with all materials available on board. To General Grant went the notice that the flotilla would be unable to run the fort's guns until that afternoon.

Hurried consultations took place among the naval officers aboard the vessels of war. Inventories of unnecessary ballast and supplies were taken and decisions evolved as to methods to strengthen the vulnerable portions above the waterlines. Soon all hands were hard at work stacking and attaching chains, lumber, bags of coal, and other impediments on the decks and sides of the boats.[7]

It was not long before the entire body of foot soldiers on both sides of the line became aware of the arrival of the Union gunboats. It was a natural instinct, then, on the part of officers and infantrymen alike to avoid exposing human life until a crucial event of the battle had been settled. At most points only sporadic skirmishing took place.

General Lew Wallace with his two regiments and battery of artillery had switched from the Telegraph Road to the southern Ridge Road. On the latter route the passing soldiers took in the sights of the Peytonia Iron Furnaces.

Captain Ezra Taylor on the Union right found his horses to be suffering badly from the effects of the weather, and he retired his guns some 500 yards to the rear to a ravine for food and water. To the right of his prior position the shaken 48th Illinois huddled behind any natural protection they were lucky enough to get, as Confederate sharpshooters kept their nerves on edge and heads down. To Haynie's right the 20th Illinois replied vigorously and W. H. L. Wallace's point regiment, the 11th, proudly watched the marksmen of the 4th Illinois Cavalry accompany their men into no man's land.[8]

On the Union left there came a sudden eruption of a vigorous duel between Captain Henry Richardson's Missouri artillerists and a battery of Buckner's cannon. To the immediate supports of both North and South this was not a spectator's sport, and they scrambled over one another to reach the bulwarks of trenches, rifle pits, and earth indentations. For 50 rounds no one at Richardson's battery was heard to complain about the low temperatures. As a matter of fact, the air was alive with clods of half-frozen dirt as Rebel-aimed shells and shot fell in near proximity. Finally Richardson could take no more, and gunners manhandled their pieces out of sight and waited silently while the Secessionist fire abated.

On the center hill Colonel Heiman had detected a skirmish line in process of formation on his right. Determined to get the jump on this possible attack, he sent Maney's guns flying down the hill to disrupt the ominous gathering. The Federals moved no closer, and in spite of artillery crossfire and persistent sniping, Maney continued to cover Indian Creek.

Inside the entrenchments moving figures stayed in constant dread of Birge's camouflaged riflemen with their dyed-black squirrel tails perched on their caps and their rifles aimed from high limbs. At the dock one man would be free from these worries. Lieutenant Colonel Haynes of the fort lay on a stretcher being carried up a gangplank. Because of his aggravated leg condition, the chief surgeon had ordered his evacuation from the battleground.[9]

At the Union landing the unloading of the transports had reached its completion at ten o'clock. Colonels Cruft and Thayer assembled their regiments and marched them off to their points of duty.

The 2nd Iowa proceeded alone to its assignment at the Second Division. Arriving at General Smith's headquarters at 11:00, Colonel Tuttle was sent to the left of Lauman's brigade. There they established themselves on a hill and sent two companies forward to make contact with the enemy.[10]

Meanwhile in Dover, Floyd and Pillow had just unlocked themselves from an earnest discussion. Floyd had felt an obligation to review with his second-in-command his determination to fight his way out of the net which was gathering about them. With the issue at the forts batteries more than in doubt, Pillow did not argue too enthusiastically against the plan. After all, if the gunboats passed the fort and the garrison became trapped, the responsibility for thwarting Floyd's intention would rest heavily on his shoulders. He did raise enough doubts, though, for Floyd to summon Buckner to join them.

At the second stage of the conference Buckner joined cause with Floyd from the beginning. Pillow in defense of his views pointed to conflicting reports which placed the number of

Federal transports lower than the estimate of 15 communicated earlier by Floyd. From this Pillow deduced that Grant's army might total only around 30,000. Even he had to admit, however, that more than two-to-one odds were not the most encouraging. Floyd and Buckner, having been stationed with the disease-ridden encampment at Bowling Green, held the opinion that Johnston had spared all that could be from the Central Army.

Weakly then Pillow accepted from Floyd the responsibility of opening the road to Charlotte. (This was the narrow way known as the Forge Road, which issued from the left flank of the Confederate line and passed just to the right of Oglesby.) In the mood of the moment no one thought to discuss any details. Pillow would open the road, and Buckner would cover the retreat.

At his divisional headquarters Buckner notified his brigade chief, Colonel Brown, who in turn began to instruct the regimental commanders. Pillow meanwhile rode to the left to survey the situation. There he decided the sortie would be spearheaded by Baldwin's brigade, reinforced.[11]

At noon Lew Wallace learned from Grant that he was to turn over his two regiments to C. F. Smith and assume command of the two brigades just off the boats. Just as he took leave of his escorts, excepting the artillery, the brigades of Thayer and Cruft appeared on the route from the river. The new division then crossed upper Hickman Creek and directed itself toward a small valley settlement near the site of a field hospital, where they would rest until a position was established for them between Smith and McClernand. Grant also had in mind holding the division in reserve in the event a naval attack was a success. Wallace's reinforcing brigade was positioned by Smith on the lightly guarded Indian Creek Road.[12]

By 1 P.M. General Pillow had begun to muster his striking force, supplemented now by Forrest's cavalry. The 20th Mississippi, serving with Davidson's brigade, received orders to march at double time to the extreme left of the line to be thrown in with Baldwin's infantry.

For an event of such potential consequences to the army, the maneuver was conducted in surprising secrecy. Outside of Buckner's division few high ranking officers–not excepting Forrest or Baldwin–were aware of the operation or its intention. By this time Pillow had determined to sabotage its initiation, and the gross errors of omission might well be attributed largely to him. Floyd, however, the father of the scheme, could not escape a role of responsibility.

On the Forge Road Baldwin assembled his brigade with the 26th Mississippi in the lead, followed by the 26th Tennessee and with the 20th Mississippi trailing. Forrest covered the flanks and provided a scouting detail. No sooner had the march begun when alert Federal sharpshooters caught sight of the unusual activity and voiced their displeasure. One hundred yards from their starting point the vanguard suffered its first casualty.

Meanwhile Pillow had guided his mount to a hillock from which the commanding general surveyed the scene. To Floyd Pillow gave voice to a thought which had just occurred to him. Only about four hours of daylight remained for the army to guarantee its retreat, to evacuate, and to establish a distance between itself and its pursuers. Floyd pondered for a moment and, not being able to refute the logic of the observation, ordered the advance cancelled.

As orderlies scurried from place to place, Baldwin halted after progress of 300 yards. Completely puzzled at these meaningless exercises, the infantry returned to their former stations. The cavalry, however, with the presence of ornery riflemen in the area, found employment in flushing out and dislodging them.[13]

Disgruntled, the dumpy Confederate commanding general

reluctantly urged his horse toward the point of imminent armed conflict, the fort. At the site he found alarm with just cause. Wisps of smoke against the horizon indicated the Federal gunboats were raising steam.

7

Naval Catastrophe

ULYSSES GRANT, IN SPITE OF HIS WRITTEN COMMUNIQUÉ to General Halleck, intended to do his utmost at once to render the Dover works impotent. To this end he conferred with Flag Officer Foote on the importance and the methods of forcing a naval passage of the garrison. General Grant, understanding little of marine technique, left the matter of tactics to Foote, but he did strongly recommend that the water batteries be bypassed instead of silenced. Agreeing to this plan, Foote took leave to attend to final preparations. Meanwhile Grant would ready a culminating infantry assault, which would completely surround Floyd.[1]

The flotilla Foote directed was not the one which had scored the signal success at Fort Henry. The *Essex* had been punished severely for its audacity at the Tennessee post and needed major boiler repair; the *Cincinnati* was raiding on the Tennessee. Moreover, the rearranged crews aboard the gunboats had not worked together as a smoothly functioning machine.

The vessels themselves, while imposing, were not invulnerable. The bursting of the boiler of the *Essex* and the scalding of half her crew under fire remained uppermost in everyone's mind. As a matter of fact, only a fraction more than the front half of the gunboats were covered with iron plating. Possibly this could pose problems not only at point-blank range but also after passing the batteries. Otherwise, the four ironclads measured 175 feet from stem to stern, possessed a 50-foot beam and drew 5 feet of water in action.[2]

As the delicate-looking Foote braced himself against the rail of the *St. Louis,* he detected natural problems confronting him. The volume of the Cumberland had been declining for days and the current breadth of the stream allowed reduced room for safe maneuver. As he had already discovered, the channel at that time of year possessed a mighty current which would extend greatly the time spent under the muzzles of the landward cannon.

At two o'clock sharp Commander Walke weighed anchor, followed 10 minutes later by the *Pittsburgh* and then the rest of the flotilla. Battle orders directed each succeeding gunboat to take station on the left of its predecessor. The wooden gunboats, *Tyler* and *Conestoga,* were to form in the rear.[3]

On the highest bluff in view gray-uniformed individuals felt a certain tautness. Some of the rank and file serving the guns began to loudly joke about how close the Yankees would approach before they would skedaddle, or perhaps how many hull punctures their gun would force. Almost invariably a nervous officer, charged with more responsibility, growled an order to desist. Usually this was a command gratefully accepted by the men.

In the besieged village of Dover news that their impending fate was about to be decided quickly spread like a torrent about the civilian population. It was an occasion at which to be an observer: the danger to non-combatants was not large, and whichever way the issue went it would be something the grandchildren would like to hear.

Many of the residents had to compete for choice vantage points with personnel of the Confederate army. Few military representatives along the slopes of the Cumberland were authorized, but this made little difference to the more adventurous. Word had swept down the line that the gunboats were moving, and with a dull afternoon in store in the trenches they individually and in small groups made their way to the banks.[4]

The better disciplined Union army had also found its front-rank strength suddenly depleted. A number of soldiers, Jesse Young among them, vanished from their camps only to appear near the water. Among the watchers in blue were General Ulysses Grant and staff. It was hardly an engagement he wanted to miss.

In the fort Captain Reuben Ross glowed with the assumption that the gunboats were entering a foray to cause an abeyance to some random shelling the batteries had been making on the transports. Hardly had the cannonade been under way when smoke issued from the funnels of the ironclads.

On the scene was General Pillow, fresh from his abortive sortie, and Ross passed his impressions on to him. Pillow gave consent to long-range fire on the approaching flotilla, but remarked that the other artillery should be reserved for later at point-blank range.[5] General Floyd had stationed himself by the telegraph, ready to report instantly to General Johnston.

Just then the leading *Carondelet* began to emerge into distinct view. Captain Ross snapped an order to the gunners of the rifled gun to commence firing. Through the gloomy atmosphere arched the first projectile of this momentous battle, to burst with little effect some distance above and away from Walke's ironclad.

The *Carondelet,* the old nemesis of the fort, continued to

expose her broadside as she angled for the north bank of the Cumberland. To her starboard rear steamed the *Pittsburgh,* Commander Egbert Thompson in charge. As an officer made a notation in the log, the *Pittsburgh* at 2:40 belched flame from her three bow guns. With fifteen-second fuses eating away, the shells sped toward the bluff and exploded without damage to the works. Each antagonist had now bared its teeth.

As the *St. Louis* and the *Louisville* approached their stations, a bend in the river obstructed sight of the opponents. As Captain Culbertson chafed at Pillow's order allowing the exposing of his prize rifle and columbiad, Captain Ross instructed Lieutenants Sparkman and Bedford of the columbiad to withhold their fire until the range was certain.

On the water the animated flag officer directed his shock force into a semblance of a battle line and instructed the captain of the flagship to commence shooting. Following the *St. Louis,* the three companion ironclads boomed forth, followed by the 8-inch weapons of the *Tyler* and *Conestoga* about 1,000 yards to the rear.[7]

The effect of this rain of iron on the fort was fearsome.

In partial shock a green gunner neglected to adequately sponge out the bore of the rifled gun and a sphere of solid shot stuck midway down the barrel. As the rammer would not budge it, Sergeant Cook and Corporal Dockery led ten men forward in a search for a log of the bore's diameter. Shortly, amid the explosions and showers of deadly iron, they found one and cut it to size. Then as a group, within clear visibility of the approaching vessels, they stood on the parapet, heaved together and drove the shot home. With a bucket of warm water they calmly scrubbed out the bore, and completed the reconditioning with a cleansing of caked powder from the six rifled grooves with a rifler.[8]

Sparkman and Bedford had determined that their weapon could effectively operate in a very few minutes. Nevertheless, inactive gunners and infantrymen alike cringed behind their piles of dirt and sandbags, fully expecting never to be granted the opportunity to strike back.

Upstream with the spectators, Captain Jack Davis of the 7th Texas overheard voiced alarm that apparently only the " small " guns of the fort were replying to the bombardment. Others scoffed at this statement, saying that the newly initiated methodic deep boom (of the columbiad) indicated that at least one high calibre piece was in use.

Peering from the pilot house Foote had detected that the ships to port and starboard, the *Pittsburgh* and *Louisville,* were not keeping pace. Immediately he had seized up his megaphone to voice his displeasure and the " steam-up " order had soon been carried out by the laggards.[9] For the purposes of gunnery and the battle line a moderate speed remained the rule. This allowed at least the bow guns of each gunboat to be trained on the fort without inordinate risk of masking by a colleague.

The rear echelon of the wooden gunboats threw only shells. The embattled gunners in the front rank, however, alternately loaded shot, shell, and grape into the mouths of their death-dealers. In spite of the metal fragments of the shells bursting just over the decks of several of the ironclads, no serious damage had been suffered.[10]

Matters were going no better in the fort, even though the naval cannoneers were beginning to overshoot their targets. The soldiers serving the rifled gun again manifested overexcitement with their unfamiliar weapon. After cleaning the vent with a wire, a gunner carelessly forgot to retrieve his tool and a powder cartridge was rammed home. In the process the wire was so bent it could not be removed and the rifled could no longer be fired safely.

Further to the left, Captain Bidwell, at the 32-pounders, silently prayed for Foote to pour on the coal. His worst fear remained that enduring the assault without reply would demoralize his detachment and cause defections before the maximum 1,200-yard range was reached.[11]

On board the *Carondelet* Walke considered a signaled order from the *St. Louis* that he desist from firing so rapidly. Either the flotilla commander concerned himself over the *Carondelet's* stock of ammunition, thought Walke, or he held the opinion that no cannoneers could aim accurately and fire so fast. In any event the gunboat reduced its volume of output.

Already its ratings were aware they were not on a daisy-pickng expedition. Barely seconds before a 128-pound cone-shaped shot had smashed the anchor under the horrified gaze of several seamen. Not yet satisfied, the projectile rebounded high into the air, tore away a portion of the smokestack, and sheared off a set of boat davits.[12]

On shore Colonel Nathan Bedford Forrest galloped in company with the Reverend D. C. Kelley toward the entrance to a ravine which would carry them to the riverfront and provide a vista for the developing struggle.

Captain Culbertson felt a grim satisfaction. One of his major worries had been that the flotilla would utilize their more numerous long-range artillery to silence the batteries. Now very shortly he would be able to demonstrate the full might of his gunpower.

At just about 3:30, as the gunboats approached a difficult point in the river, Culbertson instructed the short-range batteries to commence firing. The increased crescendo was instantly obvious to anyone with normal hearing and especially to the Union navy, which soon saw more than half-a-dozen cannonballs skipping wildly toward them after ricochets with the water. With the trajectories thus being kept low and the angle of the water batteries to the warships, it was apparent the ironclads were entering the critical phase.[13]

Nearly a mile to the south of the fort naval ordnance began exploding behind and among the positions of the 30th Tennessee. Colonel Head and his subordinates rushed to the desecrated areas and made efforts to keep the rank and file cool. Not far to the east Colonel Wharton observed that shells from the wrong direction were landing near his lines.

General John Floyd was in a cold sweat. Nervously he inspected his watch; it pointed to five minutes after three. To a staff officer standing near the telegrapher he rattled off a message at breakneck speed to General Johnston:

The enemy are assaulting us with a most tremendous cannonade from gunboats abreast the batteries, becoming general around the whole line. I will make the best defense in my power.[14]

On the *Carondelet* there was sudden pandemonium. Without warning the inactive stern quarter had been penetrated seriously by ominous shell fragments. Immediate investigation by several officers at this unarmored portion of the ship resulted soon in the conclusion that a missile had gone awry from one of the two wooden gunboats. For a moment there had been a lurking fear that the Confederates had concealed a battery which was now in flanking position.

Damage began to tell. The *Pittsburgh* had the iron casing of the pilot house soundly dented by a direct hit. Other shots from the 32-pounders were smashing into hulls dangerously near the waterlines. Already some iron plating on the *Carondelet* had been badly ripped.

Still the ironclads ominously proceeded. In a nearly complete panic the telegraph operator at the fort appended a footnote to Floyd's message. The company superintendent farther down the line deciphered and repeated it with authority:

General Johnston:

Operator at Donelson says gunboats passed and are right on him.

Trabue[15]

Five hundred yards from the fort matters took an even worse turn for the flotilla. On the left flank gunboat one of Walke's gunners loaded the forward port rifled gun too quickly and as the lanyard jerked back, the piece exploded. Miraculously no one was killed, but rescuing seamen discovered a dozen sailors seriously wounded. Everywhere in the vicinity sailors were blinded and coughing from the drifting gunpowder. The gun burst into three parts.

Trouble had only begun for the ill-fated *Carondelet*. Somewhere the gunpowder had ignited and the bone-chilling cry of " Fire " echoed throughout the ship. The carpenter and his assistants supervised the manning of the pumps. At this moment a 32-pound shot smashed itself partially into the pilot house, and a pilot crumpled to the floor, screaming and bleeding, riddled with slivers.

Meanwhile in the bow near the squirting pumps, two solid shot almost simultaneously entered the gunports. One, two, three of the gunners and seamen were transformed into headless corpses and another fell crushed beneath the force of the projectile.

Two of the decapitations had been eager young gunners at the middle bow gun who had needlessly exposed themselves at the open ports in spite of repeated warnings. The other took place next to a starboard gun which was subsequently disabled. Green sailors, nauseous from the three sharp " spats " and the bloody debris which was strewn in their wake, suffered further discomfort in slipping in the gore until sand was spread to roughen the decks. Despite the chaos of these fatalities and other casualties the fire soon came under control.[16]

On shore Federal enlistee Jesse Bowman Young observed the explosion with his companions, and all around assumed the explosion had been initiated by a Rebel shell. The pitiful cries of the wounded, the shouts of the officers, and the noise of the damage control party were discouraging even to those not engaged in combat.

To the *St. Louis,* word had been passed from shore that shells from the navy were coming close to even the Union lines and could therefore be of little effect against the fort. From the flagship signals informed the commanders of their error, and powder charges were consequently reduced. On the *Pittsburgh* Commander Thompson also cut his fuses from fifteen seconds to five seconds.

The flagship itself was enduring a teriffic pounding. Plating had been battered, split, and curled. At least one shot had entered between "wind and water." The *Pittsburgh* and the *Louisville* too had their tribulations. The former suffered a second strike, this time from the columbiad, on the identical spot on the pilot house. On this occasion the ball passed through the armor and the wall and through the oak of the opposite wall and then bounced to the deck. The four uninjured pilots took a few moments to recover from their shock, but once again brought the *Pittsburgh* back to course.

As the line of awesome floating machines neared the 300-yard mark those on shore knew that the next few minutes would tell the tale. Jesse Young stood fascinated by the terriffic splashes caused by cannonballs bouncing off the armored hulls. Those around the Southern Captain Jack Davis were beginning to lose the confident expressions they had exhibited when the 32-pounders had first roared. Tension mounted.[17]

At the 32's Captain Bidwell swiftly recorded among his observations that his riddled earthworks had been receiving less enemy attention as time passed. Nearby one of his busy gunners showed no evidence of apprehension. John Frequa, standing straight as the flagpole he defended, called to his colleagues, "Now, boys, see me take a chimney."

The heavy artillery piece roared, the shot flew out and downward, finally carrying off a funnel and the flag of the

United States. In the midst of the plaudits of his comrades John threw his cap in the air and bellowed, " Come on, you cowardly scoundrels, you are not at Fort Henry."

The gunboats had reached a point 250 yards from the fort. Upstream at the mouth of a ravine emptying into the Cumberland, Nathan Bedford Forrest turned to Reverend Kelley, " Parson! for God's sake, pray, nothing but God Almighty can save that fort."[18]

At that moment General John Floyd was even more emotional, but in agreement. Scarcely pausing for breath he dictated the message to be wired eastward to Albert Sidney Johnston:

The fort can not hold out twenty minutes. Our river batteries working admirably. Four gunboats advancing abreast.

At Nashville the same General Johnston suffered through the worst of the process of decision making–awaiting the returns. All of his departmental reserve and more had been committed to the affair at Donelson. He had not been in favor of the place from the first. He could think of better generals to put in charge. Now he held in his dampening hand a foreboding note from an eyewitness telegraph operator written at the bottom of a less-than-optimistic report from General Floyd.

No, he would not wait any longer; he would send his first order in more than a day to the region.

Edgefield, February 14.

General Floyd, Fort Donelson:

If you lose the fort, bring your troops to Nashville if possible.

A. S. Johnston[19]
General

With that Johnston ordered his couriers and aides to keep him informed of developments and then devoted his attention to his favorite task, the well-being of Hardee's Central Army.

The gunboats reached the 200-yard point. John Frequa sighted along the barrel of his beloved 32-pounder, aimed at the second ship from his right. Someone pulled the lanyard, smoke issued forth, and a solid cannonball sped to its destination. It penetrated the *Pittsburgh* through the middle bow port, sliced through swinging hammocks, tumbled pipes, bags and equipment, entered and left the wheelhouse, and finally departed through the stern.[20]

From his observation post high on the hill the alert Captain Culbertson noted several gunners for the first time looking over their shoulder to determine how far it was until the batteries would be passed. With Captain Ross, Culbertson quickly discussed the moving of at least half of their eight useful pieces to play on the gunboats after they had passed the current field of fire. There, Culbertson observed to Ross, the vulnerable rear section of the ironclads would be exposed and at their mercy. As he spoke he watched units of Colonel Bailey's infantry garrison moving into position to repel any landing. Culbertson suggested to Ross that he cooperate by supporting them with any unemployed artillery.[21]

Aboard the gunboats reports circulated that the battle was won–the enemy was fleeing from their guns. Others began to agree; to them the rate of fire from shore seemed to be slackening.

Perhaps, but the accuracy was never better. A 32-pound sphere of iron forced its way into the pilot house of the *St. Louis,* crushing one of the pilots. Splinters from the entry imbedded themselves in the left ankle and left arm of Flag Officer Foote, distracting his attention from the engagement. To make matters worse the missile rebounded from wall to wall, making a shambles of the pilot house. In the course of its swath of action the ball severed the wheel ropes, and the ship became unmanageable.

To starboard, almost simultaneously, the *Louisville's* pilot house had become a virtual wreck. The pilot lay writhing on the deck, desperately wounded, and the wheel ropes no longer directed the rudder. A volunteer repair party instantly prepared to venture to approach the tiller ropes on the stern deck but were dissuaded by shrapnel bursts from misguided short-fused shells from the *Tyler* and *Conestoga* much farther downstream.

In the bow a brain-stained Commander Dove of the *Louisville* struggled to return his craft to full fighting efficiency. A heavy shot had just entered a bow port, wrenching a gun captain in two before Dove's horrified eyes and dismounting the second starboard gun.[22]

All this while the *Carondelet* had added tribulations. Again the walls of her pilot house had been breached and a pilot winced in pain from the effect of his injury. Worse yet, a wheel had jammed.

The *Pittsburgh* to starboard had by this time taken two waterline hits in the bow and shipped water badly. The aggregate effect of her sister gunboats staggering in their alignment, the unresponsive and sluggish helm, and the shattering experience which the pilots had just suffered caused the *Pittsburgh* suddenly to shift to port.

Understandably preoccupied with restoring the efficiency of the wheelhouse and the nuisance of fretting over the Federal shells exploding near his stern, Commander Walke stood transfixed at the rapid-fire report from a seaman that the *Pittsburgh* was swinging on them like a giant door. His transfixation was broken by the collision, not great in magnitude but possibly vulnerable in location. Making his way to the starboard stern section, Walke listened to a crestfallen subordinate explain that the accident had sheared off the starboard rudder iron.

Taking observations through the stern casement, Walke

noted the unmanageable condition of the *St. Louis* and the *Louisville,* with the *Pittsburgh* taking on the appearance of retiring and his own precipitously moving toward the northern shore, he determined his immediate course of action must be defensive. Correcting his course with the port rudder, the harassed naval officer took no more chances with the erratic *Pittsburgh* and proceeded straight ahead upstream so as to clear a point of rocks jutting from the shore and to give himself ample room for maneuver. To make matters even worse he learned that bad leaks had developed underwater both fore and aft.

The fighting front line of the flotilla was meanwhile engaged in weird orbital movements in last minute efforts to resume management of their directional control. Within minutes of the sudden blow, Foote, standing with great difficulty, gave the signal to withdraw. Aided immeasurably by the swift current the *St. Louis,* followed by the *Louisville* and then by the *Pittsburgh* floated north, away from the guns of doom.[23]

The reaction on the summit and its eastern vicinity can easily be imagined. Soldiers jumped up and down, cheering at the top of their lungs. Artillery officers had difficulty maintaining crews at the smoking and heated guns. Citizens on the hills excitedly lofted their hats in the air, caring not where they came to rest. Colonel Forrest, himself, had rarely seen such jubilation. Old men broke down into tears amid the tumult raised by their companions.[24]

The volunteers on the front lines had not missed the significance of the occasion. Runners from the fort competed to be the first to Buckner's regiments with the news. As unit after unit received or guessed the news a wave-like mammoth cheer rose from the trenches and rifle pits and swept to the east until it reached the last outpost on the left flank.

In the Union lines soldiers too had guessed what had occasioned the joy of the enemy. A cloud of profound silence hung over the Blue positions.

At the telegraph station General John Floyd scribbled out a message to be tapped out to his commanding general. Timidly he still worried about the outcome:

The fort holds out. Three gunboats have retired. Only one firing now.

That one was the *Carondelet*. Battered but still defiant, she had stopped her advance and spat fire from her two remaining guns from the closest point yet reached by a Federal gunboat. Then, bowing to the fickleness of chance, her engines swung into reverse and, keeping her scarred face to her respected enemy, she backed off downstream.

Being well aware that the water batteries would level all their combined attentions on him, Commander Walke worked out a defensive strategy which would conserve as much life as possible. Acting Gunner John Hall, new to his job, had come forward to take command of the starboard bow rifled gun. From Walke he had heard specific instructions to personally give warning of the approach of enemy shot. As Hall soon found out, this was no simple task. Not only did he have to supervise the operation of his gun and spot iron missiles in mid-flight, but he was forced to keep track of projectiles skipping along the surface of the river and guess their destination. Hearing the call, " Down," the gunners would scamper away from the ports as Hall made the breech of the rifle his shield. There was little trouble with obedience to these orders since the three instances of decapitation which had occurred just a few minutes before to the left.

Confederate General Floyd had just consulted his battery commanders and felt secure enough to send a culminating report to department headquarters. It stated:

The gunboats have been driven back. Two, it is said, seriously injured. I think the fight is over to-day.

Backing his unwieldy ironclad down the Cumberland, Henry Walke reached into his trousers and pulled out his watch. His tired eyes read 4:10. Still the fore part of the *Carondelet* rang with an occasional strike from Southern iron. Despairing of victory, Walke had just finished the issuance of an order to increase the rate of fire to spread concealing smoke.[25]

In the marshy lowlands upstream of the Union landing small knots of blue-outfitted individuals gazed out at the piles of wreckage, once called warships, now drifting toward them. To a man they were overpowered by a possessive enervation in the pits of their stomachs. Their navy, which had made such singular achievement at Fort Henry, now fled the scene, relinquishing the upper river to the Confederacy. Some turned to look toward the elevation from which the commanding general and his staff had been spectators. It was empty, as if it had never been occupied.

A couple of miles south General Gideon Pillow, his face beaming, strode up to Lieutenant George Martin, part of the fort's original artillery staff. During the struggle Martin had been called to the attention of the Tennessee general, and among other things Pillow had watched him strip off his coat and ram it down the muzzle of a cannon when the gun's wadding had given out. Now he offered Martin his congratulations for energy and judgment.

Already Confederate officers gathered to voice their post-mortems and relate their experiences. At about 4:30, as the echoes of the shots from the *Carondelet* became lost in the trees, Captain Bidwell expressed his opinion that the turning point of the battle had taken place on the first volley from the 32-pounders. Captain Ross was just about to concur when

Pillow broke in with the emphatic statement that with all due respect to the lower guns they had provided a good deal of encouragement and noise along with some good scores, but the telling shots had been struck by the long-range columbiad and rifled gun. As young and indiscreet Captain Bidwell hastened to contest the point, Captain Culbertson, the artillery commander, mused to himself how apparent it was that Pillow did not know that the rifle had been disabled early in the duel by inexperienced cannoneers. The same thought ran through Ross's head and another one joined it; someone should tell the general that the heavy columbiad had fired only 27 times. In deference to rank everyone remained silent until Bidwell had sputtered out of gas. Pillow departed sure of his opinion.

Profoundly irritated that a major officer had missed the contribution of his battery, Bidwell sulked back to his station to wind up the battle reports. In conferring with individual gun commanders he found that 45 to 50 rounds had been expended per piece. This brought to about 350 the total artillery output on that afternoon of crisis. (The gunboats, he felt, had fired about 2,000 shots.) No noteworthy human casualties had been suffered.[26]

As the flotilla retired out of range, commanders initiated rough mental copies of their final reports of their historic engagement. In considerable pain Flag Officer Andrew Foote opined that his task force had done well with 12 guns against 20 (in reality, though, the Confederates had used nine at the most). Also he began to wonder if a gift from God of 15 more uneventful minutes would not have brought victory. From the commander of the battered flagship Foote discovered that the *St. Louis* had survived 59 hits and four holes at the waterline. Signals from the other warships notified him that the casualties had reached 54. All this in an hour and a half.

Thompson of the *Pittsburgh* considered himself lucky even though his ship was nearing a sinking condition. Only two men had been hurt and these by concussions through the hull. More than 30 projectiles had struck his vessel, two of them between wind and water. In return he had fired off 111 rounds.

The last to fire, the last to be fired at, Commander Walke fumed at the role the *Carondelet* had been forced to assume in the struggle. Within her wood and iron bulkheads four seamen lay dead and the crew cared for the wounds of 32 more. Bad leaks had sprung both fore and aft. So in addition to having to feel the range and the strength of the fort on Thursday and consequently suffering grievous casualties, the next day he had to lead the flotilla into battle, suffer two-thirds of its personnel losses, and then set up a smokescreen for it as it fled. True, he had received only 35 hits, but these had been telling. In Walke's estimate the battle line had fired no more than 500 shots and the two reserve vessels could barely have equaled that, making a total of 1,000 rounds launched against the fort.[27] (This was half of what Captain Bidwell had just guessed.)

On shore among both civilian and military observers, many stories about the extent of the damage to the fleet were in vogue. In the Confederate army itself the image of a great " Sword of Damocles " had suddenly vaporized. For the first time the rank and file were sure that destiny could do them no wrong at Fort Donelson.

Heady with success attributed in no small degree to himself, General Pillow floated directly to the telegraph station. From one of his several aides he secured a leaf of paper, sat down at a table and began writing. No thought of military protocol entered his satisfied mind. He had won the victory; he should send the report directly to General Johnston. To the telegrapher he handed the sentences, and then Pillow strode out into the gathering dusk mulling over new ideas as to how he would save the Confederate cause. The message to Nashville read:

> We have just had the fiercest fight on record between our guns and six gunboats, which lasted two hours. They came within 200 yards of our batteries. We drove them back, damaged two of them badly, and crippled a third very badly. No damage done to our battery and not a man killed.

A few hundred yards downstream one by one the injured gunboats made fast to shore, tying to good-sized trees there. Emergency parties scurried over every inch of the ships, attempting to render them floatable at a minimum. Obviously some, if not all, would need the major repairs of a shipyard. It was after 5 P.M.

Scores of miles to the east General Albert Sidney Johnston and his staff showed great pleasure at the conclusive evidence offered by the telegram of Brigadier General Pillow. Johnston immediately forwarded the exact same message to Secretary of War Judah P. Benjamin. General Floyd's messages were dutifully filed away.[28]

8

Ecstacy, Gloom, and a Conference

WITH THE ECHOES OF THE LARGE-CALIBRE CANNON ON THE river lapsing into silence, Colonel John Brown, commanding Buckner's front line, gazed out into the thickets from behind his parapets, confident the enemy would give them no more trouble than routine, half-hearted skirmishing. Nearby Colonel Hanson of the 2nd Kentucky finally felt able to overlook his expectations of a renewed assault. Enigmatic reports, however, of some fierce shooting from the center of his line kept drifting back to him. Didn't these Yankees know they had lost the day.

Colonel James Tuttle's 2nd Iowa was no more happy about the disappointing river contest than General Grant, but for all they knew the army and the regiment would be retreating in the morning. So the two companies sent across the ravine as skirmishers were instructed by their comrades to do their all for the redemption of the regiment's honor. Until their recall at dark, these green farm boys would show more determination than the entire remainder of the Union army.

At 5 P.M., with the pall of darkness about to fall on the day of February 14, General Lew Wallace inspected the positions of his newly formed Third Division. Lying on the Indian Creek Road and to the east of it, none of the position, except for the artillery, was familiar to him. The first sound of the deep bass booms on the river had brought a headquarters courier speeding up to his cabin delivering written instructions for him to advance up the Creek Road to the point of the Federal lines and hold himself in readiness for orders. On arrival Cruft's leading brigade had found staff officers present ready to acquaint them with the territory and the neighboring positions of Generals Smith and McClernand. Having been standing in battle order since that time, the regiments were now dispirited from fatigue and from the morale-shaking rumor from the river. Wallace took it on his own to order the men to be at ease. It was quite obvious that no imminent serious attempt could be made to penetrate the Confederate outer works and then march on either the fort or Dover.[2]

On the Wynn's Ferry Road a group of dismounted horsemen congregated out of sight of the Rebel lines. Two officers stood apart from the others. One, short and stubby, had the look of a shopkeeper who had just learned of his impending foreclosure. The other, more demonstrative than the first, bore the look of a fervent and dedicated missionary. General Ulysses Grant and General John McClernand had met to solve the problems of the right wing.

McClernand spoke not of his immediate trials but of what he feared for the future. True, at three o'clock on the left of the First Division, Southern shells began exploding among the infantry but these were soon silenced by protecting Federal guns. The most important crisis was, in short, that McClernand had too few troops to defend his area against a likely Confederate counter-assault.

The two generals pored over their rough maps and devised a temporary solution until the expected arrival of reinforcements. McArthur's brigade from Smith's division would be marched to the extreme right to fill the "400 yard" gap found between Oglesby and the flooded Lick Creek by Stewart and the cavalry in the morning. Grant had given up the idea of encircling Dover by land, since any force to the east of Lick Creek would lose touch with the rest of the army. Meanwhile McClernand could compress the remainder of his line while Lew Wallace spread out and filled the center of the Union position. McClernand was satisfied. Half of the army would now maneuver at his direction.[3]

As the generals and their staffs placed their boots in the stirrups to return to other responsibilities the quiet was shattered with the explosions of a vindictive artillery celebration from Bushrod Johnson's lines. Farther up the road W. H. L. Wallace's infantry scrambled for cover as a lieutenant of the 1st Missouri Light Artillery and Captain McAllister supervised the pin-pointing of the enemy and the training of the guns on the target. The three guns of McAllister combined with a 10-pounder cut short the Confederate festivities with about eight shells from each gun. To McAllister the satisfaction of the successful response of his battery was tempered with the news that the trail of the number one gun had broken irreparably on the frozen turf. To the commander of the 10-pounder, who had had a man killed and his piece silenced after only five rounds on Thursday, proof of his competence had finally arrived.

In the vicinity soldiers resumed their construction of gun emplacements. They would be completed by nightfall and these three guns would doubtless leave their exposure for these entrenchments at this time.[4]

Oglesby's brigade, guarding the right flank of the Union force, grew tense with its immobility in the face of impending enemy action. Earlier in the afternoon the commanding colonel had led his unit 100 yards to the east so that they lay athwart a three-road intersection. The defense of the southernmost segment of the Forge road had immobilized Lieutenant Gumbart and his four guns. The opposite section was sheltered by the protecting muskets of the 18th Illinois on the east. The 8th, 29th, and 31st Illinois straddled the connecting lane to the Wynn's Ferry Road. Oglesby held the 30th Illinois in reserve for these three assignments. He was relieved to hear of the forthcoming assistance of McArthur, but from conversations with McClernand's aides he felt they were to act as reserves rather than an extension of the right flank.[5]

While there was still daylight the playful Virginians of McCausland's brigade engaged in souvenir hunting. Large Federal ordnance and fragments of it had descended into their midst during the naval engagement and the opportunity for future glory and profits was not to be missed. While they scoured thickets and brush for any hiding shells, another group of guns was drawn to the left wing and their front. As some grumblingly anticipated the probable assignment of constructing field works for their cannoneers, other more astute foot soldiers thought that the build-up signified that something very important was in the offing.

Darkness brought relative peace and tranquility to this embattled section of Tennessee. But it also brought significantly colder weather. At six o'clock a heavy rain beat down on the armies.

Tired of line duty and uncomfortable in the chilly rain, Colonel Woods of the 12th Iowa of Smith's division gathered up eight of his companies and sneaked off into the blackness in search of a site for campfires. Two companies remained to hold the ground.

Not far away a recall order had sent a regiment into near spasms of disgust. The 2nd Iowa had been having such a fine time and keeping so warm skirmishing that its components resented vacating the battle line. Even more uninviting was the stark fact that the regiment was desperately short of blankets. In some cases there was only one per squad. Colonel Tuttle was deeply depressed to see the enthusiasm of his fighting men, burning so brightly only minutes before, flicker and become extinguished.[6]

The largest fresh unit in the Union army, Wallace's divisions, spread themselves from the crest leading to Heiman's hill on the right to the east side of the Indian Creek Road on the left. Neighboring were Wallace's two regiments from Fort Henry. The division posted their pickets and slept on their arms, ready for any eventuality.

To the right of Lew Wallace's flank lay the remnants of Morrison's old brigade resting in line of battle. Continuing east on the other side of Smith's 45th Illinois, Colonel Haynie of the 48th felt it permissable for the first time that Friday to relax his frayed nerves. It seemed to him that the opposition had given him no peace all day, and that every showing of the blue brought a musket or cannon shot response. Haynie told one and all that he did not know what service his "exhausted" regiment could perform on Saturday or whether they were in condition to even follow his leadership. Now it appeared night would bring no peace. The staccato cracks of skirmishers harassing his line rolled back from the front.[7]

To the north in Kentucky an aide to Union General Don Carlos Buell blinked his eyes, which were watering from the smoke of his lantern. He was working after hours transcribing the report of his commander to General McClellan. Pending a successful development of the advance on Bowling Green, he wrote, Buell would be ready to leave for Donelson with two divisions on Monday. According to Buell's estimate Grant had a force of 30,000 men poised to strike at Dover. At the same time he voiced concern for the gunboats, as there was only a reported 10 feet of water in the Cumberland.[8]

The night of Friday, February 14 wore on. Among the briars

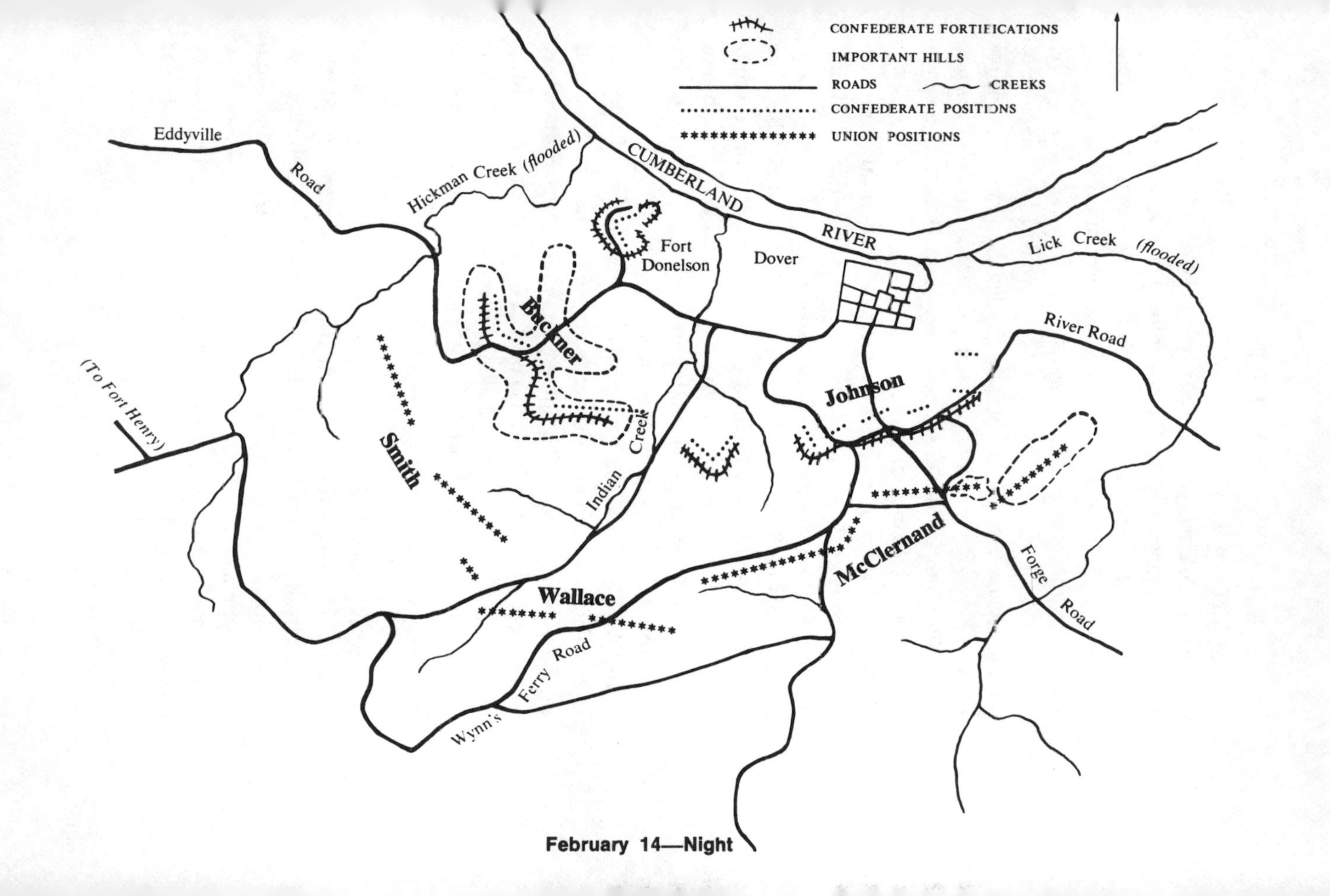

February 14—Night

and blackjack of the southeast outskirts of the village of Dover, an uneasy Colonel John McArthur nervously fretted at the foot of an apparently significant hill over his position. Now assigned to McClernand, he had received no instructions from that general. Neither did he have knowledge of his surrounding terrain. In the course of his march from 5 P.M. to 7 P.M., the last vestiges of glimmering light had revealed his presence to the enemy and they had heavily shelled him on his trek up Wynn's Ferry Road. Now unwilling to reveal his full presence or blunder into Confederate positions. McArthur settled down to await the blessings of dawn.

Sleet and then snow began falling in substantial amounts.[9] Neither army really had an advantage in this whim of nature. True, the Confederates held the advantage of already constructed pits and trenches and some huts, but they also bore the first thrust of the northern gusts and most of the recruits were unused to freezing weather. Both sides had insufficient blankets, and fires could be maintained with feelings of security only in buildings or rearward areas.

In Smith's division the roughly handled battery of Captain Henry Richardson had a double welcome for the completion of the breastwork designed to house a section of guns. Somewhere to the left of Richardson, Colonel Tuttle of the 2nd Iowa observed an officer or two shaking their men to prevent their falling into a deep freezing sleep. At this rate, he observed to himself, it promised to be a long night for some of his officers.

Nearby the divisional commander, General C. F. Smith, sat defying the storm on a log and wrapped in a small rubber blanket. His sweeping mustache bristling arrogantly at the storm, Smith nevertheless at his advanced age felt the discomforts of the exposure. He wondered how his health would be at daybreak.[10]

The momentum of the storm did not prevent the primary officers of the Southern army at Dover from gathering at the tavern at about ten o'clock. Present were the generals and selected advisors, such as the bushy-bearded Major Gilmer, the engineer.

Following a light-hearted exchange of congratulations and comments on the success of the water batteries, Floyd revealed the purpose of the council. First he mentioned that he could see no significant reason for altering the decision of the same morning to evacuate the post, in spite of the startling victory of the afternoon. He expressed the opinion that Grant would now be forced into siege operations to secure his objective. In such an eventuality, Floyd stated, the army of the Confederate States could expect nothing but defeat and probable capture. The enemy was known to have received substantial reinforcements that Friday and further supplements from Buell and Halleck for operations on the Tennessee and the Cumberland could logically be expected. Thus, it could be only a matter of time until the Union army could force its way around the Southern left flank and seal off reinforcements down the Cumberland. Already, he noted, the events of the past two days had proved Federal artillery could reach any point within their lines.

The solution Floyd proposed was to assault the enemy right wing Saturday morning, force them back, "and thus pass our people into the open country lying southward toward Nashville." He did not expand further.[11]

Buckner, in agreement with Floyd and hearing Pillow's voice rise in response, wondered how the second senior general would react to the proposition this time. He was mildly surprised to hear his associate voice enthusiastic agreement with Floyd. The scattered prisoners brought in that day, reported Pillow, told that the Union army had reached 52 regiments or about 30,000 men. In regard to the siege operations he himself knew of 24-pounder cannon in the enemy encampments. Pillow did feel, though, that this sortie would be no easy proposition.

Indications were that heavy concentrations had been and were being made on the eastern sector of the Union lines. Also, if his recollection was correct, the heavy undergrowth near the Forge Road would impede troop movements.[12]

At the conclusion of this little address, Buckner and then Johnson expressed their opinions that the conditions of the decision of that morning had not altered. Although not wishing to prolong the deliberations, Buckner again mentioned his displeasure over the strength of his defensive positions; he also felt that with their numerical inferiority it was probable the army would eventually be trapped in Dover.

The decision had been made then to open the avenues for withdrawal to Charlotte, Tennessee. Interestingly enough, no attention was given to General Albert Sidney Johnston or to his preferences for reinforcement, attack, or withdrawal. As to the latter item, the telegram of that afternoon from Nashville was thought to be indicative of what the commander of the department had in mind for the garrison. Apparently, because of cognizance of the situation of Hardee's army, none of the discussion dwelt on the basic responsibility of requesting reinforcements before evacuating to superior numbers. It was assumed Johnston had none to give.

The conference turning to the tactics necessary to implement the strategy, Pillow brought up an extension of the scope. He envisioned a surprise attack from Dover being such a success that the Union army would be turned into a confused rabble resulting in a rout. Not pausing to throw this possibility up for discussion, Pillow proceeded to outline an alternate plan. The left wing, reinforced, would assault the Federal right in flank and front. As they began to roll up the Union line, Buckner with his division massed on the Confederate end of the Wynn's Ferry Road would strike McClernand on his salient flank and rear.

Details of this plan immediately brought queries. Buckner

questioned what forces were going to hold his breastworks and what reinforcements the left wing would expect.

Pillow reflected for a moment, looking over the roster of combat units. He felt Heiman's brigade could be stretched out to hold the right and center with the increment of the fort's garrison of two regiments. As to the reinforcement, Pillow stated that Hanson's Kentucky regiment would suffice.

Buckner, from whose division Hanson would be taken, fairly blew up at this. He had come to Clarksville, he said, with a division of reputable size. No sooner had his division begun to be forwarded to Donelson, than regiments and even brigades were detached to the command of other officers. Even after his arrival at Dover his division had remained emasculated. Up to this point he had made no issue of it, but now this further transfer was going too far. He appealed to Floyd's sense of justice.

Pillow, seeing Floyd in just the kind of predicament his senior dreaded, decided to make a strategic withdrawal, as his whole plan was obviously in jeopardy. Grumbling politely that he bore the lion's portion of the plan and that his troops were somewhat ill armed, Pillow relented and agreed to leave Hanson with Buckner.[13]

With essential conflicts resolved, General Floyd gave to Pillow, the originator of the sortie design, the command of the first stage of the assault—Johnson's division. With this point settled Buckner immediately proposed a modification of the timing of the offensive. During the meeting he had heard of a concentration of enemy guns on the Wynn's Ferry Road and suggested that these might be neutralized early in the contest. To achieve this Buckner thought he might attack simultaneously with Pillow.

All eyes focused on Gideon Pillow. With apparent lack of enthusiasm the second-in-command assented but with the compromise that Buckner wait until the sound of battle insured that the Union right was heavily engaged. Then the Kentuckian would move on the batteries and pin down the blue regiments in this sector.[14]

Floyd, obviously relieved that a potentially explosive situation had retreated from the critical temperature, said that he felt the plan had excellent prospects for success and that it met with his approval. Using Pillow's advice as the guide, it was agreed that all units would be in readiness at 4:30 A.M., and the march could be initiated at five o'clock. At 11:00 P.M., several important subordinate commanders were sent for.[15]

As he dismounted from his horse after a harrowing ride over the rutted, icy, snow-covered streets of Dover and its outskirts, Colonel Adolphus Heiman saw a tall, handsome figure close the door of the tavern behind him and step to the frozen earth. "What is going on, Colonel Forrest?" Heiman inquired thickly.

"Big things, Colonel," came the drawled reply. "We attack at dawn."

"And you, Colonel. You are to . . ."

"Just leading the advance and guarding our left flank," Forrest said.

"I see. Well, I must see what work they have for me. Good night." The Germanic gutteral was half drowned in a gust of wind.

At the conference table Heiman heard his assignment given without benefit of soothing words. He was instructed to assume command of both center and right wing. Buckner's position would be held by Head's 30th Tennessee. All other regiments, including the fort garrison, would defend their current positions.

Having just begun to feel comfortable in the presence of the roaring fireplace blaze, Heiman suddenly felt cold again. His English words came out with difficulty. Without a reserve, he said, he could not even be sure of holding his own hill with his measles-racked brigade. Likewise, he felt the other two works would fall prey to any assault. Floyd was not prepared to offer him any comfort. In such a case, he said, Heiman would fall back on the fort, *or* use his own judgment. Heiman knew there was nothing more for him to say; the original occupants of Fort Donelson would be the last to leave its premises—*if* they were very lucky. It was 11:30.[16]

To the orderly mind of Simon Bolivar Buckner, returning to his troops, all his preconceived objectives for the council had been fulfilled. Pulling his broad-brimmed hat farther down over his eyes to shield his face against the wind, he mentally listed them. The Confederate army would evacuate Fort Donelson immediately. He and his division would bear an active part in the glory of the breakout.

Leaving Pillow to issue instructions to his brigade commanders, he continued to pick his way toward the right of the line. The first thing he must do on his return, he planned, was to tell Colonel Brown the attack was on again. Orders must go out to assemble all equipment and to cook rations for the retreat. He made a note to take as little baggage with them as possible, for the division would be serving as rear guard.

At the very moment Buckner was taking so much for granted, General Pillow faced the realization that he would be getting precious little sleep that night. Following the instructing of the brigade commanders, there were innumerable other details to arrange. Already it was nearing midnight.[17]

Colonel Davidson staggered into the hut which served as his field headquarters. His own conference with Pillow had impressed him with the necessity of preparing his brigade for the hardships of a long retreat. Feeling highly indisposed and ill, Davidson ordered his aide to inform all his colonels to prepare three days' rations and to be ready to march early in the morning. He then crawled into his cot.[18]

Pillow in his explanations of his plan to the brigadiers seems to have been vague in his own mind as to what results it would bring. Later conferees would leave the inn prepared to drive the enemy from the field and with little thought of an evacuation.[19]

Floyd, in his extreme joy to be in the process of ridding himself of that gadfly, Fort Donelson, seems to have taken no thought as to the details of the operation. Nothing had been said in the conference about blankets or knapsacks being included in the field kits of the army; nothing had been said at all about rations. Neither had the order of march on the commencement of the retreat been organized; no provisions for a vanguard or a rear guard were set. The direction of the march —towards Charlotte—had been enough to satisfy General Floyd.[20]

On paper Pillow's plan had accomplished the magnificent feat of mustering 11,000 effective fighting men of the 14,000-man army against an enemy division mounting over 12,000 soldiers fit to rely on in battle. If the Confederates could maintain the advantage of surprise, it appeared that they might have at least an even chance of defeating McClernand. The rest would depend on who made the most mistakes.

On the right wing of W. H. L. Wallace's brigade, Lieutenant Colonel T. G. Ransom of the 11th Illinois fondled his watch; it told him it was midnight. Picket fire in his front had just become especially heavy and worrisome. Perhaps it signified something. Many of the men were predicting heavy fighting. Pondering a moment, he decided not to take chances and ordered the regiment into battle line. Ransom resolved to keep them there until he was sure the threat had subsided.[21]

9

Saturday—Smite With The Arm of Gideon

AT ONE O'CLOCK SATURDAY MORNING GENERALS PILLOW AND Johnson rose from their conference chairs in the Dover Inn. The last of the brigade commanders had just departed after being briefed with orders to prepare and assemble their brigades with the greatest dispatch. Well satisfied with the tenor of the council deliberations, Bushrod Johnson smiled confidently at the prospects for success for the sortie. Even if Grant's army was not driven from the field, a rallying point within the present Union lines had been provided. If, heaven forbid, a retreat to Nashville was then deemed necessary, the Confederate army could assemble its provisions and baggage with the escape routes firmly secured. The planning for this would require a second council, which Johnson cheerfully believed would never be needed. He anticipated victory.[1]

Several hundred yards away over snow-coated roofs and slopes the commander of the 20th Mississippi awakened to read a message from Johnson assigning him once more to the brigade of Colonel Baldwin. Quietly the men were roused and filed off in column to the east.

Sixty minutes later Union Lieutenant Colonel Ransom could see no more reason for maintaining instant readiness in his position to the east of the Wynn's Ferry Road. After all, the picket fire had died down to almost nothing. The Illini soldiers went back to sleeping on their muskets.

Another officer (but in a gray uniform) had just terminated a journey. At 2 A.M., he had received a somewhat confusing order to report to General Buckner. Finally locating the general's headquarters in the dark, Colonel Head of the 30th Tennessee was tersely informed that he would be expected to defend three-fourths of a mile of works with only 450 recruits. His reaction approximated that of Heiman earlier. Buckner shrugged and told him that his second line of defense would of necessity be the fort. Head saluted and wearily walked with slightly unsteady steps into the night, aware that he had the honor of being selected as a sacrifice.[2]

Hiding his weariness, Gideon Pillow looked sharply into the eyes of a mounted aide as he awaited his report. The young man announced that he had delivered orders to all brigade commanders in Johnson's division to march their units to a level area on the River Road east of Dover. He also added that an assistant to Colonel Davidson had informed him that the colonel was not feeling well. Pillow nodded shortly and continued the management and supervision of necessary details.

One by one the brigades made their appearance. Soon there were five including Forrest's cavalry. General Floyd had shown up. Nervous and fidgety at this major undertaking, Floyd found himself examining the faces of the male human beings that he was ordering into battle. The weather had taken its toll. Some soldiers, frostbitten in their trenches and enervated by camp sickness, could barely keep their eyelids open. Others exhausted by work details stood in a similar state. Still, not a complaint arose. In the aftermath of the victory over the Yankee navy, a glow of cocky confidence radiated from the entire division.

Minutes passed and the impatient Pillow began to worry over the non-arrival of the brigade of Colonel Davidson. He turned to Johnson and inquired whether he knew anything of the whereabouts of these men. Johnson replied that he did not but that he would find out; he then rode off into the blackness. Pillow continued to fret. He looked at his watch; it was after 3:30. He motioned a group of his staff officers over to him and charged them with finding the cause of the delay.

At Davidson's headquarters General Johnson was met by Lieutenant R. B. Ryan, chief aide-de-camp to the brigadier. Curtly, Johnson asked of him why the brigade was not on its feet and on the march. Ryan took on a look of puzzlement and then responded that he had just finished delivering orders that regimental commanders put themselves on a moment's notice to move out, but that he had been instructed to say nothing further. He then stated that his colonel seemed to be severely ill. Irritated but kindly, Johnson told Ryan to ride to Colonel Simonton of the 1st Mississippi and notify him that he had been placed in command of the brigade and should without delay march to the designated point of assembly.[3]

On the River Road one more item began to trouble Pillow. Reports had reached him that Buckner had not arrived to defend the Wynn's Ferry Road entrenchments and that there was now not a soldier in the area to defend it. To Pillow this was nothing but inefficiency, as he deemed Buckner had been provided ample time to assemble his regiments and march them to the left flank by four o'clock. He sighed, decided to make the best of a poor situation, and sent a chief aide, Major Rice, to Heiman with instructions to send a regiment to the Wynn's

Ferry Road to defend the gap until the arrival of General Buckner.[4]

The reason for this delay hinged in part on another clash of personalities in the army. While Head officially did and would come under the jurisdiction of Heiman, it was thought best to avoid confrontations; for that reason Buckner instead of Heiman gave Head his orders; also for that reason (and perhaps some petulance over his assignment) Head was delayed in replacing the division in the trenches. As Head inched his way along dangerous, rutted, and slippery inclines, Colonel Brown decided the situation could no longer bear waiting and he instructed the 3rd Tennessee to lead the division to Wynn's Ferry Road. Colonel Palmer, having followed his orders to send his wagons (non-ordnance) across the river, fell into line, along with two regiments. The 2nd Kentucky and the 14th Mississippi, *which had received orders at 3 A.M. to be ready to move in two hours,* remained behind in the entrenchments.

The winds, the snow, and sleet, and the temperature faced the division with an unexpected obstacle in its eastward march. An incline led sharply down from the complex of ridges of the fort and outer works to the valley of Indian Creek. The infantry could descend the slope with care, but transition by the ammunition wagons and the invaluable artillery of Captain Graves was another matter. Soldiers were detached to steady and guide the teams of horses by grasping their halters and leading them downhill. Other groups situated themselves around the spoked wheels of the vehicles to ease them on their way. After continued exertion all had reached the valley without major mishap.

As some of the rear elements of the division passed by Head's companies gingerly trudging toward their old rifle pits, the vanguard threw themselves into the task of ascending a more steep and tricky opposite ridge. Teamsters cursed and switched their whips while officers prayed the wind and the distance would disguise the sound from enemy pickets. Gradually with shoulders wedging the wheels forward and teams occasionally doubled all the transportation reached what could be called the crest.

Colonel Hanson kicked up a cloud of snow in impatient anger. An hour had passed since the vanguard of the division had passed and the relief column of the 30th Tennessee had not appeared. Just as he pivoted his body again to face the enemy encampment, a posted lookout sped up to him. Confederate troops were approaching just over the hill. As a Tennessean captain in a few minutes reported, Hanson was surprised that only two companies had shown up. But it was no longer his responsibility to defend the entrenchments and he hastened to place his regiment on the road leading to Wynn's Ferry.[5]

At the widow Crisp's house the clatter of a horse's hoofs was slightly muffled by the newly fallen snow and the whistling wind. Unfamiliar, at least recently, to his perch, a navy sailor slid from the saddle to the more predictable ground. A sentry admitted him to the cabin and a sleepy aide ascertained his business. From the anteroom the aide then ventured into the kitchen and gently awakened General Ulysses Grant from his fitful feather-bed sleep.

A tallow dip in the shadowy room revealed the message to be from Flag Officer Foote. Grant broke the seal and read on. His naval partner apologized for having to request the general to detach himself from his army, but a desperate situation had arisen in the flotilla and Foote's injury incapacitated any journey on his part over the several miles separating them. He hoped Grant would understand and would come at his earliest convenience.

Grant permitted himself the luxury of a grunt at the inconvenience. He knew the sleep he was getting was not lending him much benefit, so in spite of the cold, dark, and wintry conditions he resolved to travel at once. Before opening the door to face the icy winds, he instructed his aides to visit the division generals before dawn to instruct them under no conditions to bring on a general engagement during his absence. This would at least protect him against the machinations of McClernand. With a single aide as escort Grant struck out on the six-mile journey.[6]

At that moment there was more than one disgusted officer within the Confederate lines. In spite of the lateness of the hour, Pillow, with an effort, managed to hold his temper. He had hoped to initiate his surprise assault shortly after 5 A.M.; it was now 5.10, and he had just finished organizing and assembling all the brigades of his striking force. Daylight was 30 minutes away. It was unlikely that a line of battle could be formed without being perceived by Union pickets, but the plan must proceed. Five minutes later the column, many of them wearing white identification armbands, went into motion and marched south.

Concerned over the ability of his untried regiments to advance from their entrenchments in line of battle through the rugged, thicketed surroundings, Pillow had decided to assume the risk of marching out in column on a farm roadway connecting the Forge Road to the River Road by traversing the north slope of Barn Hollow at right angles to that trail. It linked with the Forge Road as an extension of a 90-degree left, the latter made just outside of the entrenchments. The success of this particular venture was heavily dependent upon lack of discovery and the method of assembling his units had been dependent upon that premise. Now with the delay from Davidson's brigade, timing had been thrown out of gear and strategic success was in jeopardy. In spite of the consequent delay of at least a half hour, however, nothing could be done but to press forward the implementation of the original idea.

Leading the way was Baldwin's brigade, followed by Wharton, McCausland, and Drake. Tagging along in the position of disfavor slogged Colonel Simonton with Davidson's former brigade.[7]

Given the impression from his own observations and from headquarters that the Federal encampments were more than one and one-half miles from the field works, Baldwin, on reaching the Forge Road where it made a right turn down into Barn Hollow, sent the 26th Mississippi to the front with instructions that a company should be sent forward as skirmishers. A simply dressed officer, whom he knew as Colonel Forrest, had consulted him as to their joint movements. Forrest had assured the square-faced Mississippian that he would do his best to screen the advance, but warned that the thick underbrush was far from an asset in the functioning of cavalry. In any event the dual commanders of the vanguard were well chosen—the terrain had been immediately adjacent to their defensive stations.[8]

A small cluster of Illinois infantrymen huddled in the weeds on picket duty. To keep their minds off the miserable weather pending their reliefs, they followed the time-honored military tradition of chatting in gossip fashion about their collective woes. Certain ones felt underprivileged in having been selected to stand guard in the coldest portion of the day. Others belabored the long march and shellfire of Friday's dusk. Someone piped up that the generals must all be drunk to send a brigade out into unexplored territory in the dark. No, the men of the 9th Illinois were not happy.

A muffled outcry from one of their more alert buddies brought the griping to a halt. In the dim grayness the voice cautioned that he thought he had seen a horseman. Others soon verified the impression. A challenge barked out. The mounted shadow jerked the reins, the animal's head swept back in the direction of its tail, and its motion spun on the fulcrum of its hind legs. Too late. A musket crackled, followed by others; the horse fell and the rider jumped clear. In the next instant the Union pickets had sprung their assigned positions.

The shots had not gone unnoticed in the vicinity of Colonel Baldwin. His spurs dug into the flanks of his steed as he made what speed he could down the miserable pathway. At the head of the column Baldwin found his point company rapidly ascending Dudley Ridge on the south side of Barn Hollow to investigate the cause of the disturbance. Here and there cavalrymen, their mounts bleeding from scratches, made their way toward the rear. While the former Mississippi book dealer was confident that the column had gone such a little distance that the firing could not have originated with the enemy, he worried that the sounds might carry to the Yankees and alert their right wing. It must cease immediately.

Suddenly a quick succession of shots initiated from the brush bordering the road. The Rebel company deployed and responded in kind. The truth known at last, Baldwin thought it wise to delay aggressive action until another company had been brought up. Meanwhile the exchange of gunshots continued in an animated fashion.

Behind the crest of Dudley Ridge, Colonel August Mersy and his battalion and company officers (only eight of the latter since Company H was still at Paducah and Company A was supporting one of the Second Division's batteries) scampered about raging at slow-rising volunteers. Most of the 9th Illinois of McArthur's Brigade had been jostled out of a fitful slumber by the fusilade in their immediate area. Instinctively they completed their attire and took places in the rifle line with their muskets. Knapsacks were generally forgotten but cartridge boxes hung conspicuously from their belts. By 5:40, ranks stood in order and Mersy ordered them over the crest to the support of the pickets. Across their front ran the Forge Road on its last dogleg—heading west.[9]

Colonel John McArthur sat up straight to the rapidly increasing roar of firearms. For a minute he hoped and wished he were asleep—an attack was the worst of nightmares he could have. Then watching the scurrying of staff and orderlies around him, he knew it was real and began to take stock of the reality. The 9th apparently was engaged. To its right lay the 41st Illinois. In reserve stood the 12th Illinois. Sending word to the orderlies to bring his saddled horse, McArthur ran to the battle front, buttoning his coat as he flew along.

Simultaneously Baldwin's second company and Mersey's first rank reached the skirmish line. With one company supporting the other the Confederates arose to the attack. Even before they could take many steps a withering blast issued from the top of the slope and the two companies withdrew in discouragement.

General Pillow now arrived with the bulk of the 26th Mississippi. A hurried consultation with Baldwin brought agreement that they must form their battle lines on the spot. A word of confidence, a pat on the back, and Pillow rode off to bring other brigades into battle order.[10]

As Baldwin struggled to bring his leading regiment into action, Buckner, as yet unaware that the battle was becoming general, surveyed his assigned territory in the vicinity of the entry of the Wynn's Ferry Road through the breastworks. Not a Southern soldier was in sight. The defenses were unmanned. Even worse a battery of guns stood untended in the frosty morning air. Immediately Buckner threw the leading 3rd Tennessee forward into the works while he deployed the remainder of the division to the rear. It had just become light enough to distinguish objects about them.

The 42nd Tennessee from Heiman's brigade belatedly reached Drake's former entrenchments, found them being occupied and settled down on the right wing of Buckner's division.

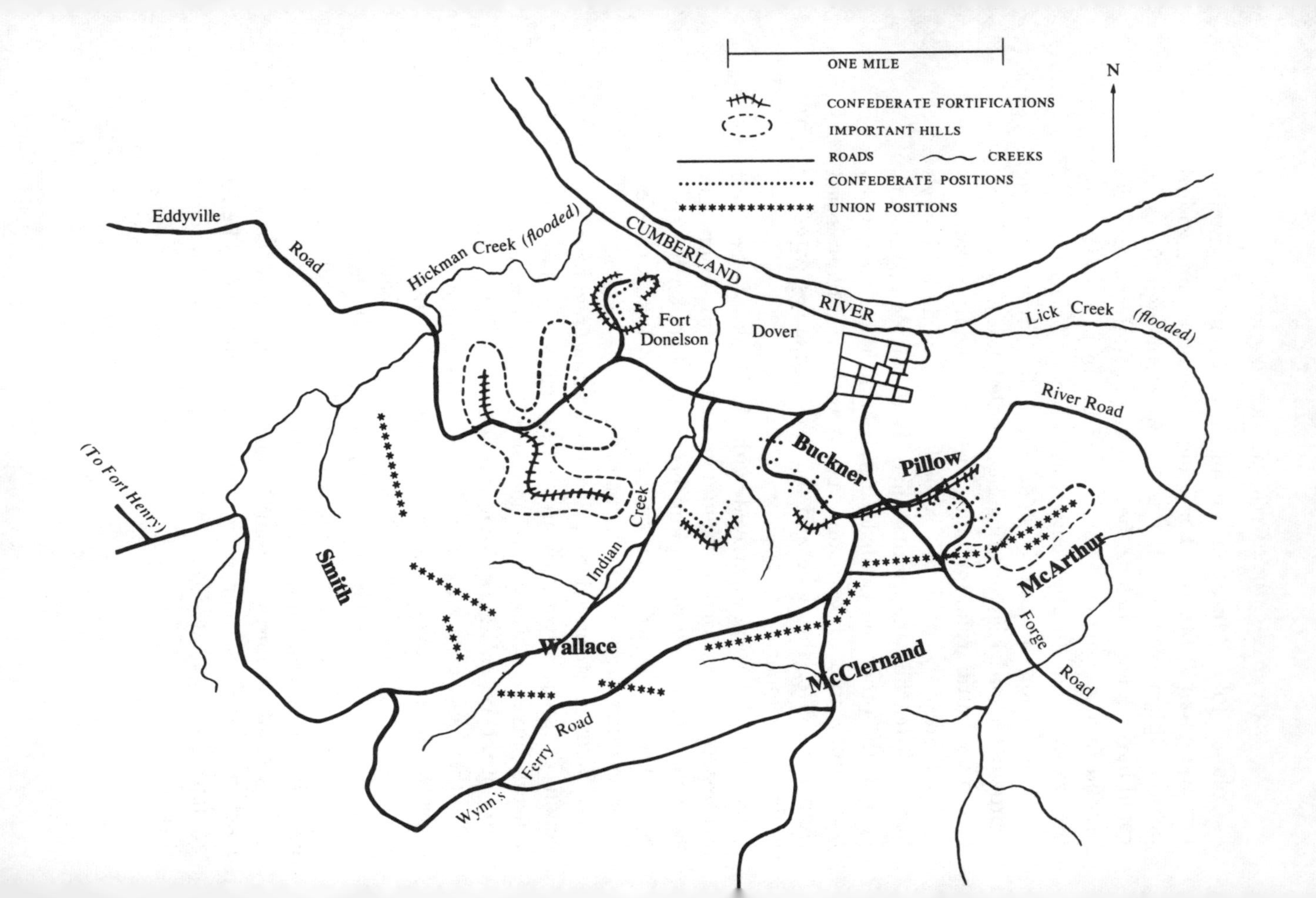
ONE MILE
N
CONFEDERATE FORTIFICATIONS
IMPORTANT HILLS
ROADS
CREEKS
CONFEDERATE POSITIONS
UNION POSITIONS
Eddyville Road
Hickman Creek (flooded)
CUMBERLAND RIVER
Fort Donelson
Dover
Lick Creek (flooded)
River Road
(To Fort Henry)
Buckner
Pillow
Indian Creek
Smith
McArthur
Wallace
McClernand
Forge Road
Wynn's Ferry Road

On the Confederate right Major Doss, commanding the large 14th Mississippi, found himself relieved of watch by companies of the 30th Tennessee. Colonel Head had decided to scatter four companies in the trenches to the east of the connecting road from the fort to the frontal positions. Behind the two companies in Hanson's rifle pits lay a reserve company, and three companies resided in overall reserve. Four hundred and fifty soldiers were to do the work of 3,800.[11]

By company the volunteers of Baldwin's 26th Mississippi fell into line under fire to the west of the road. Green as they were and forced to form in a thickly wooded area tangled with underbrush, the bronzed youngsters from the Deep South fell into confusion. Their officers and Colonel Baldwin hastened to set things aright. As a certain orderliness was just about becoming apparent, the regiment tumbled back in great disorder. Baldwin, spying a gap in his line developing to the left on the road, temporarily departed.

After instructing Baldwin, General Pillow had ridden down the road with his escort of aides to the brigade of Gabriel Wharton. Directing the Virginian to place himself east of the road and cut his way through the enemy right flank, Pillow caught sight of Bushrod Johnson, who had been supervising the rear detachments. Requesting Johnson to direct the deployment on the left wing of the striking forces, he wheeled his charger and galloped back up the road to the front.

In the valley of Barn Hollow to the east of the roadway lay a large open field. Between the field and the road—about 10 yards from the latter—stood a rail fence roughly parallel to the Forge Road. While the field offered no protection for mounting an attack within range of the enemy musketry, Pillow also knew he could not afford to expose his flank by leaving the enemy there unopposed. The newly assigned and idle rear regiment of Baldwin's brigade—the 20th Mississippi—was handed the task. The leg of the fence coming at right angles to the road and at the north end of the field gave the new regiment a fine bulwark behind which to string out.[12]

Colonel Isaac Pugh of McArthur's brigade had long since discovered that the biting cold of winter always brought on his most aggressive nature. His pickets had also been involved in raising the alarm for the brigade. Almost on reflex on the hearing of the news Pugh had shoved two companies of skirmishers of the 41st Illinois forward on the road, the right side of which was his responsibility.[13]

Before Confederate eyes patches of blue began to appear around the road dividing the two Mississippi regiments. Penetration of this gap could disastrously delay the assault. Instead of activating the third regiment of the brigade, Pillow decided to utilize the 20th—already at hand and already in formation. Speaking to its senior officer, Major Brown, he outlined a rather complex flank assault on the Union skirmishers. The Confederate line would swivel until it was parallel to the road, catch the Yankees in their right flank, and then remain in a position to cover the exposed gap. Pillow in turn would be responsible for filling the hole behind the fence.

Sensing further difficulties in the offing, Pillow sent a messenger back to pull the third brigade, that of McCausland, off from the left wing and forward as a reserve for Baldwin. Implicit in this action was the assumption that if the Federal right wing were in such strength so close to the Southern lines, their right flank must lie exposed nearby. The immediate requirement was to pin down McClernand's main forces in their front while Johnson swung the remaining brigades around into enfilade.

Meanwhile the gray-clad components of the 20th Mississippi had enthusiastically leaped over the fence which had so conveniently allowed them to dress their line. With the right flank company marking time the 500 Mississippians began one gigantic wheeling movement toward the west. Major Brown considered this less risky than moving his inexperienced recruits into position by echelon.[14]

Looking down from his elevation advantage of over 40 feet, Pugh could not believe his eyes. A large body of enemy troops was deliberately exposing its flank to him. A messenger rushed down the hill to ensure the alertness of the skirmisher companies. Small parties of the latter began to float to the east to locate themselves in the undergrowth and woods to fire down the wheeling line.

As the 90-degree turn had been fulfilled, the left wing of the Rebel regiment found itself in the predicament of being caught in a wicked crossfire. Obviously unless defensive measures were taken the situation of facing enemy in front and flank would go to pieces. Instinctively captains deployed their companies to shelter themselves and frustrate the enemy intentions. As one wing of his regiment fragmented itself, Major Brown dispatched messengers to locate General Pillow and acquaint him with the turn of events.

Pillow, on his saddle near the road, raised his field glasses and took in the crisis. After a few seconds meditation he instructed the messengers to cancel the previous orders and to return the 20th to its former position. To verify the correctness of the interpretation of his wishes, he then sent one of his own aides with identical instructions to Major Brown.

Minutes later soldiers under Brown's command were scampering over the fence and stretching themselves in security at its base. Not all the regiment had retired, however. Several companies of the left wing found it impossible to extricate themselves immediately; now they were the subjects of the attentions of the entire 41st Illinois.

In Company F at the base of the hill Confederate Lieutenant O. R. Eastland had fallen badly wounded. Several of his men offered to risk the gauntlet of enemy fire to carry him across the open field. The officer opened his pain-clenched lips long enough to say, "Never mind me, boys; fight on! fight on!"

By now Colonel Pugh had all eight remaining companies drawn up forward of the crest of the ridge. Fate had given him an opportunity, he speculated. It was his duty to make the most of it. A single order rumbled down the length of the regiment. "Forward."

Brown's left wing wasted no time packing up and hustling north through the level field. Behind the fence the breathless returnees added nothing to the morale of an already confused majority of the 20th Mississippi. They now had a clear view of the smart and trim Union rows marching upon them through the stubby vegetation of the field. Soon a volley coming their way reminded them they were scared. First a few, then more, then everyone drifted back from the fence. Officers spread to attempt to rally a line of defense on the southern rim of the hollow.[15]

At the same time the usually clear blue eyes of William Baldwin had clouded noticeably. The problem of filling the huge opening in the center of his brigade had consumed his attention. Riding toward the road he located his 26th Tennesseans and instructed Colonel John Lillard to form half of it into battle order and fill in the gap between the fumbling 26th Mississippi and the fence to the east of the road. The remaining five companies would maintain their post as the only brigade reserve.

As the Tennesseans were ominously threatening his left flank, Pugh had wrested the fence from the 20th Mississippi and he had thrown Wharton's flanking brigade off balance by seizing a clump of trees in their front. Suddenly the tide was turning again. Some yards behind the fence Major Brown was bringing his regiment under control. The right wing of the 41st in penetrating beyond the woods encountered fresh legions of

Southerners. These were not content with blunting the attack but were pushing to the east and forming on the flank. On Pugh's left a detachment of Confederates directed themselves south on the roadway, menacing his other flank. Seeing no reinforcements on the way, Pugh deftly removed the 41st from the hotly contested field. It was the first Federal retreat of Saturday, February 15.

For the third time the 26th Mississippi found itself unready to attack. Impatient officers trotted up and down the line moving companies into their battalions and locating companies for platoon. Finally amid much cursing and some rough handling of individuals the 26th reported itself in battle line. Unfortunately, noted Baldwin to himself, they were considerably to the west and rear of their intended area.

In the interim Pillow, being concerned that the aggressive activities of the opposition would soon manifest themselves in a counterattacking flank assault on Baldwin, began shunting McCausland to the right of the lead brigade. Necessity was bringing more weight to the hinge of the sortie than the general had originally intended.

On the other flank Bushrod Johnson was still leading Drake and Wharton to their assigned positions. He was especially anxious to keep a personal eye on the former's unit, made up as it was of ill-armed garrison troops. Forrest and the cavalry lent some little aid but Nature's dense vegetation worked too much of a hardship on the horses to expect substantial assistance from them.[16]

Colonel Richard Oglesby put his hand to the halter of his horse. The top arc of the sun had peeked over the horizon, even through the cloud cover. An aide exclaimed that it was a good omen. At that moment Oglesby was unconcerned with omens. Having, from the sound of firing, put on notice his brigade astride the Forge Road, he was off to see what assistance or coordination he could effect with the newly-arrived Colonel McArthur.

The latter was feeling in desperate need of something. From the rim of the hill he had taken note of the enveloping threat on his right. Unwilling to commit his reserve regiment yet, he notified Pugh that Mersy would in addition assume control of the front to the east of the road. As the engaged 9th marched by the right flank to broaden its responsibility, Pugh on its right concentrated on keeping hold of his little woods and preventing the Secessionists from passing his right flank.[17]

Miles to the west two horsemen in blue overcoats plodded along on the terrible road to the gunboat landing. It was 6 : 15.

Concurrently, less than a mile south of the village of Dover, the second in command of the Confederate army wryly observed aloud that the "surprise" attack was no longer such and was already an hour late in its launching.

10

Issue in Doubt

SHOUTING ENCOURAGEMENT TO ONE ANOTHER, THE TWO regiments of Baldwin's original command took the initiative for the Confederate army. Preceded a short distance by a thin line of skirmishers, the main body of the brigade swept through the stabbing thickets and tread over the stubby ground until they had reached an acceptable firing distance from the Union assemblage. Here they delivered their first volley as a unit that day.

On the road General Gideon Pillow felt the spark of new courage. One regiment of the brigade, the 20th Mississippi, had already been demoralized and withdrawn from the field of action. Another had formed only with the greatest difficulty. Yet still the brigade could throw itself boldly into the fray. With such material, he exclaimed, how could his cause lose?

As the extreme right of Oglesby's brigade dodged its first infantry fire, the remainder of the unit felt consternation over the artillery missiles whizzing in over the intervening brush.

There was no Union artillery support, for Gumbart's guns lay on the left with Oglesby.

The delay was bringing problems to Pillow. Only the artillery occupied the attention of most of the brigade of Oglesby—the force Pillow coyly was going to crush by inundating its right flank. Some of this artillery was unsupported by infantry reserves. Except for some companies of McCausland's undermanned brigade the Forge Road lay open for some sudden sally from McClernand's division. There was no choice here. He therefore directed his last brigade, Simonton's, to extend the line beyond McCausland's formation. From their position on the Forge Road the brigade moved between their own fortifications and the Union battle line by a right flank march.[1]

It was just in time. Skirmishers of the 18th and 8th Illinois were becoming audacious and nosy. Nearing their designated point, the head of the Confederate column ran into ambush. Simonton decided it was time to link up with the Confederate battle line. The 3rd Mississippi was detailed to take care of this. The pesky pickets brought confusion to the Mississippians and Lieutenant Colonel Hylan Lyon, his sharply pointed nose scenting out the enemy, swung his 8th Kentucky south to prevent a flank attack. Here at the point of the earlier ambush the fire grew hot as the enemy on the ridge to the south was able to enfilade his line. Major R. W. Henry, swinging his saber to guide his troops into position, had the sudden and weird sensation of finding everything giving way beneath him; his horse had expired instantaneously. In spite of severe losses the 8th kept its place and the 1st Mississippi and 7th Texas were able to move behind it from left to right and form on the right flank. It was past 7 A.M.

Colonel Lillard of the 26th Tennessee had already fallen victim to an accurate Federal shot on Baldwin's front. To avoid discouraging his men, however, he straightened up, shouted some encouragement and resumed setting his line to order. At the fence near the lane a cluster of figures gathered around the recumbent Captain D. H. Spence, whose head now bled profusely. Only a few feet from Baldwin himself, Spence had been hollering inspiration to the Tennesseans when a chance shot had tumbled him from the fence.

Across the fence Colonel Wharton had succeeded in deploying his small brigade and now urged them to drive the 41st Illinois from the field. As they stepped through the field in good order, Pugh's skirmishers gave out a cry and soldiers shifted their sights to attend to the new threat. One by one Virginians dropped to the ground as their brigade strode beyond them. In the field battalions wavered and fired a ragged volley. Finding it to have negligible effect, they stumbled back through the open space, picking up their wounded as they retired.[2]

Colonels Oglesby and McArthur had met at the brow of the hill. As McArthur explained his dispositions Oglesby nodded his approval. It had been good to extend the line to frustrate envelopment. Now, however, possession of the clump of trees left the flank highly up in the air. Judiciously Richard Oglesby began dropping hints that it might be prudent to bring up reserves to bolster this wing by bringing the line in a curve back toward the hill.

Reinforced by Colonel Forrest, who could operate more freely in the plain around the hollow, Drake, under Johnson's supervision, continued the drive of his three regiments. Both units proceeded cautiously in extending the left flank, however, because it was becoming increasingly obvious that the enemy was strong on their front.

General John A. McClernand had arrived at the positions of Oglesby's brigade. Ever since the arrival of information indicating Confederate aggressive action, he had found himself facing a dilemma. Grant had sent specific instructions stating no general engagement was to be entered into without his specific approval. Now McClernand was on the defensive. If the enemy intended only to make a reconnaissance-in-force, there was nothing to worry about. As it stood, in spite of the racket of battle rising to a tornado-like crescendo, his division seemed to be holding its own quite well. At the time of the final Confederate withdrawal McClernand would secure permission to employ his divisional reserve, the cavalry, in pursuit. The enemy was playing into his hands; there was glory to be won at Donelson yet. Until time for the counter-stroke, he would hold his counsel and act independently.[3]

General Ulysses S. Grant and escort had made their arrival at flotilla headquarters. On the way they had passed the spanking clean 20th Ohio, marching to add their numbers to the army. As naval ratings led their tired horses away to food and shelter, Grant fastened his eyes on a rowboat pulling the short distance from the *Louisville* to shore. A stiff coxswain in the stern barked sharp instructions to the impeccably dressed sailors pulling on the oars.[4]

General John Floyd had so far spent the morning surveying the conflict from the vantage points of his own constructed defenses. In the course of his travels the brigadier general had happened upon two unmanned light batteries. It occurred to him that the unemployed brigade of Colonel Heiman might put them to good use. Off on that errand he sent the chief of army artillery, Major Cunningham.

Simonton's brigade, poised at the 18th Illinois and 8th Illinois of Oglesby's command, struck its first blow. Flags pointing the way, drums pounding the pace, 1,500 trainees of Hardee's army steadily stepped onward. Enemy skirmishers pelted them with insistent harassment, but to a man they knew worse was to come. It came beneath the crest. A sheet of flame erupted from the top of the hill and the ridge. In front of the 8th Illinois, Confederate Lieutenant Colonel Clough felt a stab of pain and expired instantly. A regimental comrade, Lieutenant J. W. Nowlin, crumpled dead nearly on top of his superior. The captain of Nowlin's company of the 7th Texas, William Hill, fell victim to an ugly, gaping puncture in the torso only a few feet away. Simonton's line reeled backward.[5]

To the Confederate left Colonel William Baldwin expanded his horizons. Word had reached him through the active rumor mill (and from the lack of progress against the hills) that the prospects of the left wing were in peril. For two days he and his brigade had been stationed in a vantage point to oversee and observe the ground which was now so vital. Looking to the east to where the hollow spilled out into a little plain, Baldwin spotted a body of Southern troops apparently lying in reserve. Without a second thought he left his engaged brigade and rode to their presence. Locating the senior officer, Baldwin requested that he lead his detachment, which he supposed to be a regiment, through the marshy lowland to the east until he came to the Lick Creek bed. This hollow, Baldwin assured him, would lead the Confederates around the flank and to the rear of the unexpectedly occupied ridge. Somewhat confused, the officer consented, but on his way consulted his brigade commander, Colonel Drake. The latter, seeing his reserve already in motion and proposing to probe that sector anyhow, agreed and promised to support the enterprise with whatever he could muster.[6]

Meanwhile Wharton's Virginians had renewed their efforts to bring their right wing into play. Hurtling the fence, companies of threadbare veterans from the Dominion State dressed their line. A regimental standard waved near their newly-made army flag—a blue flag with a white globe. The field was not half crossed when the Midwesterners from their vantage point gave notice that they were awake by loosing a well-aimed barrage. The Rebel line never hesitated—just kept coming. A few yards from the edge of the field small lead balls whistled through the frigid air again. This time the Southern front ranks jerked. A few individuals resumed their pace then halted, looking back to their companions who either littered the frozen soil with their gray uniforms or who stood motionless. These audacious ones retired as did the first rank upon the second rank and both upon the third. Those in the effort to take station astride the trail drifted northward in defeat across the field.

Colonel Wharton dug his spurs into his stallion and guided him behind the fence. Within minutes he was returning the smart salute of Major William Brown of the 20th Mississippi. To Brown Wharton explained the awkward position of his brigade. The information he desired from the major was if the 20th was recovered enough to make a lodgement in the face of the Union firepower. The sparse resources of his brigade, he admitted, were not equal to the task. Brown responded that he could do no more than try. The two departed hoping for the best.

The Mississippians decided to take no chances in their re-entry into the fray. Whooping and hollering in unison they hurtled the fence and dashed pellmell through the clearing to a spot of advantage occupied by their dead and wounded. Here they unleased a volley upon the already hard-pressed 9th Illinois.

In spite of himself Colonel Richard Oglesby could not suppress a twinge of admiration for the formations of Confederates who had assembled their battle order and advanced through the apparently impenetrable blackjack on the right of his brigade. Not far from him, however, another colonel of the same organization had other problems. The left shoulder of Colonel Michael Lawler had been shredded by a speedy Minie ball. As Lawler clutched the bloody hole to stem the flow of blood and awaited the regimental surgeon, he sent for his next two senior officers, Captains Brush and Marks. In his incapacity the colonel allotted Sam Marks command of the left of the 18th Illinois and acting Major Brush was told to direct the more critical right five companies.

Colonel John McArthur surveyed the eastward limits of his defended territory. Here and there parties of hostile soldiery streamed ominously toward the right flank—exposed as it was—of the 41st Illinois. Now was the time, he determined, to call upon the 12th Illinois in reserve.

The 9th Illinois continued to reap the blows of a human whirlwind. Now almost the entire effort of Baldwin's three regiments fell upon their heads. The Confederates, under continual reminder, aimed their weapons low. Large caliber smoothbore pieces firing buckshot and bullets cut the Illini down in bundles. As so often with novices, particularly on the top of slopes looking down, the fire of the Yankees largely passed over the heads of the Mississippians and Tennesseans. In spite of heavy losses and non-effective return, the 9th Illinois clung tenaciously to their hillside.[7]

Uneasiness began to settle on General John McClernand. Nearly the whole morning Rebel artillery from the heights of the breastworks had been pelting his lines with grape and cannister.

Illogically McClernand removed Captain Jasper Dresser from near the Wynn's Ferry Road near the sallyport to the source of Erin Hollow under Heiman's hill. Throughout the campaign this height had remained uppermost in the division commander's mind. Now it seemed prudent to preempt any pincer attack from that direction.

In the discussion over Friday's naval battle as they sat for breakfast in the stateroom of the *St. Louis,* Grant could not keep his eyes from occasionally straying down to the Flag Officer's bandaged ankle. There was something about "Foote's foot" that brought wry amusement even to the general's businesslike mind.

The three batteries of Buckner engaged in a determined duel with two Federal groups of guns which had revealed their presence forward of the Wynn's Ferry Road to the southwest of the quadrilateral intersection which joined to the Forge Road and sent a spur south, parallel to the latter. The 14th Mississippi and the 2nd Kentucky had not long completed their journey from the west wing trenches amid the accompaniment of Union shells. Buckner deemed it wise to allow them to relax for a time. Likewise he considered it prudent to reduce the effectiveness of the Union cannon before proceeding to an assault. Anyhow, in spite of the assistance of a well-directed barrage from the efficient Captain Graves, Pillow had made no noticeable gains on the left.[8]

The shock troops of Simonton's brigade had long since recovered from the effects of their first hail of musketry. Demoralization was rare, especially in the 7th Texas around funny-looking Major Hiram Bronson Granbury. His protruding ears almost flapping in the excitement and his long, unruly hair flowing behind him, the major by his example brought new enthusiasm to the decimated ranks. In the center of the line former artillery captain Lieutenant Colonel Hylan Lyon took off his hat, revealing a shining domed forehead, and waved the 8th Kentucky forward.

A new menace to the South, however, projected itself on the right of the division. The unoccupied 29th and 31st Illinois of Oglesby's brigade ventured to unleash swarms of skirmishers on the flank of the 7th Texas. Colonel Gregg found annoyance at this operation and thought it wise to bend some reserve companies behind the line at right angles to it.

Distraught by events even before he witnessed this new development, Colonel Simonton felt increased concern for the ability of his brigade not to break under the pressure from two sides. In the last extremity he turned to Pillow for help. For this errand the brigadier turned to Davidson's aide, Lieutenant Ryan.

Lieutenant Ryan finally located a disconsolate General Pillow. For two hours the striking force had been in the process of denting the Union lines and no promising success seemed in the offing. Quick surprise had not been achieved; fresh Yankee regiments could be expected to arrive momentarily.

No wonder the harried extrovert turned impatient yet dull eyes upon the intruder. In a pattern of studied aloofness Pillow pondered the solution to the crisis as he slowly surveyed the battlefield. The closest thing to a reserve he now possessed was the lightly engaged weak brigade of McCausland to the left of Simonton. Ryan received permission to conduct one of the Virginian's two regiments no further than the left of Simonton's brigade. Beyond that the new brigadier was on his own.

Gideon Pillow was not the only general who began to worry. John McClernand, seeing the issue hanging in the balance and alarming signs of an impending ammunition shortage, began to think for the first time of assembling assistance. Lieutenant Carter was at hand. Verbal instructions were issued him to visit General Lew Wallace's headquarters, notify him of the desperate situation, and then ride to Grant for reinforcements. It was eight o'clock.[9]

Colonel Baldwin had rejoined his brigade, which remained stalled on the hillside. Wharton, at thirty-seven one of the oldest brigade commanders, recalled the time 15 years before when he was graduated second in his class at V. M. I. Knowing he had something to live up to, he rode down several stragglers attempting to shirk their duty in the line. Running, he snorted, would just bring people into the highly aimed Union fire.

Lieutenant Colonel Augustus Chetlain of Galena, Grant's home town, sat astride his restless horse as it walked over the crest of the hill. Behind him marched the columns of the 12th Illinois. The sight before him, however, jolted the officer out of his placidity. Ranks of Southern soldiers were gathering in the brush. He pulled at the reins and cantered his mount back to the regiment. The first two captains encountered received orders to run their companies to the brow and deploy them as skirmishers.

In front of Chetlain, Joseph Drake, in spite of the extremely steep slopes, was not about to give the bluecoats a respite to thwart his flanking drive. A running line of gray slammed into the skirmish line, which to seize the most commanding ground had doubled behind the 41st. Captain Hale, in the midst of aligning his Union company, slumped down into a bush, dead. The other Federal company barely won a race for a strategic group of buildings downhill near the angle formed by the two regiments. Braving substantial casualties, a couple of blue platoons reached a fence and leveled their muskets across it.

To the left the tamed Colonel Pugh bore the brunt of Johnson's storm. While Chetlain had arrived to shield his right and rear, the 41st was still being subjected to heavy pressure at the apex of the defenses and to slanting fire where its line had bent into a "U."

Chetlain began to flow supports to his front line, which by then had fallen into various reclining postures. Within minutes half of his regiment was committed and losses rose rapidly.

Signs of strain began to pop up in the 41st. Slightly wounded infantrymen required the "assistance" of three or four of their companions. Occasional cries of "More ammunition" shrilled above the chatter of detonations. As Pugh began to reproach himself for not stocking up on these materials on Friday night, stragglers, mostly on the right where their backs practically pressed on the 12th, darted by screaming, "We're flanked. We're flanked." The fighting front of the 41st Illinois sagged inward. Discipline might have restored order but in a volunteer regiment this would not materialize. The first break for which Pillow had been waiting had materialized. It was going on 8:30.[10]

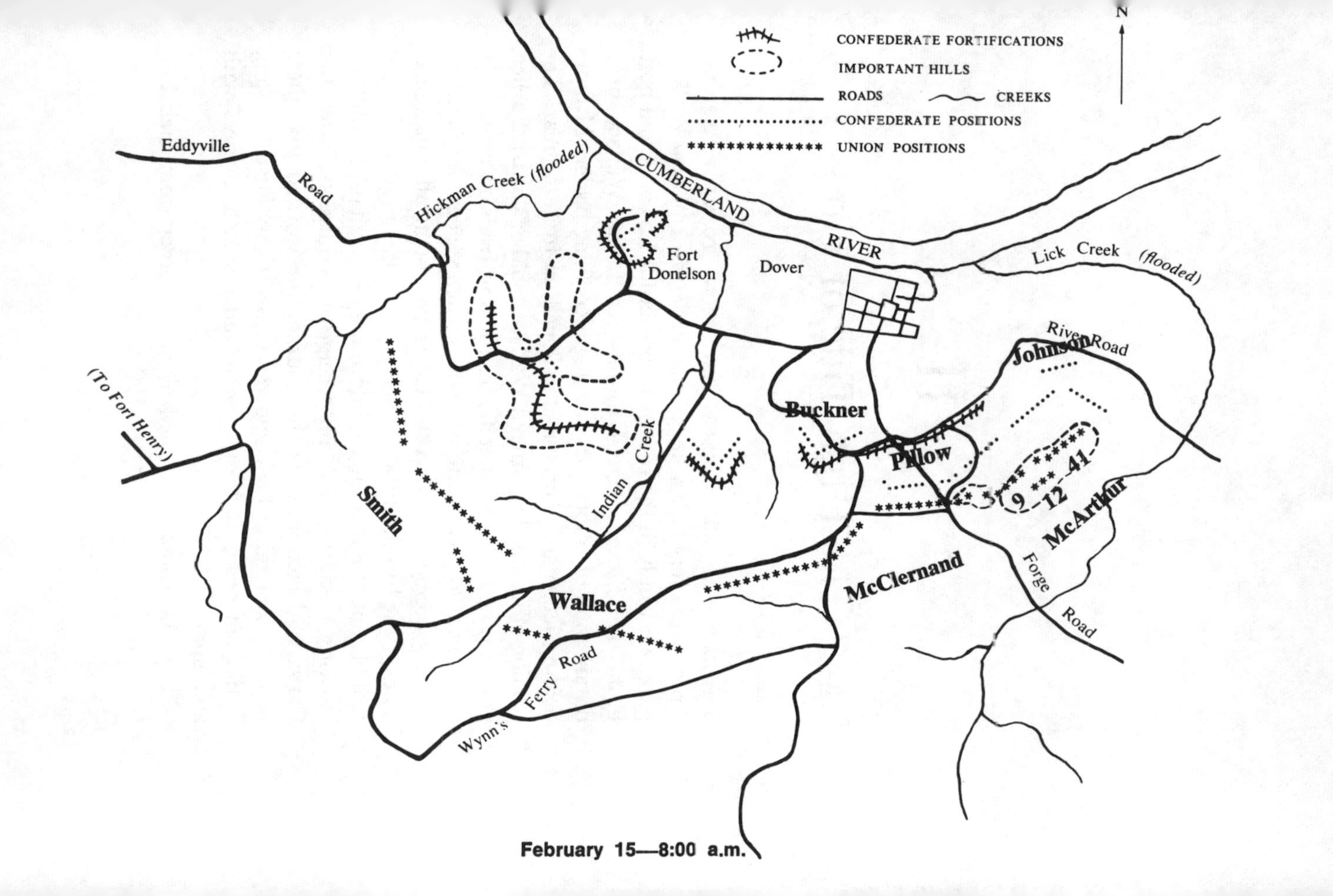

February 15—8:00 a.m.

11

The High Tide of Gray

THE LIGHT COVER OF SNOW HAD BEGUN TO MELT RAPIDLY. Trim, with every hair at its proper angle, General Lew Wallace paced nervously in the thawing turf outside his command post. From the distance issued sounds reminding Wallace of a distant train of empty cars crossing a creaking bridge. Minutes before Lieutenant Carter had galloped up from the rear. The relation of his tale had stirred Wallace's soldier's heart. Earlier, however, he had read specific instructions from his commanding general to precipitate no general engagement and to maintain his position at all costs. He could not in all conscience, he explained to the junior officer, violate these orders. He did scribble out a note, though, informing Grant that he would be instantly ready to move on receipt of permission. Now that Carter had continued on his journey, he worried that there was not something he could do to assist the First Division. It did not occur to him to load and dispatch carriers with ammunition.[1]

The 41st Illinois streamed in ragged order from their hill.

By now their officers realized the uselessness of trying to rally the dispirited men and struggled only to prevent the retreat from degenerating into chaos. In their haste and confusion the right wing of the regiment ran smack into the left wing of the 12th Illinois to their rear. Sizable segments of both units melded together and were borne off in the tide of defeat.

Reluctantly the survivors of the 9th Illinois saw that circumstances would bring their friends of the 18th to the left into greater jeopardy. Nevertheless, with their own right flank now up in the air, ammunition gone, and one-third of their number dead or wounded, the 9th grudgingly, on orders from the brigadiers, yielded their blood-marked battle line to Baldwin's surging battalions. After inching back for several hundred feet the 9th came to a halt on the instructions of Colonel McArthur, who had suddenly made an appearance. Out of the shell of the 9th Illinois McArthur attempted to manufacture a new line.

Under the supervision of Bushrod Johnson the beaming volunteers of Wharton and Drake paused on McArthur's lost easternmost hill to reorganize. Before them stretched forbidding thickets and intertwining saplings—an officer's nightmare. Imperfect as they were, the Secessionist ranks then resumed their victorious procession.

On the right of McArthur's brigade, Lieutenant Colonel Ansel Tupper strove to sort and reassemble companies of his 41st Illinois. Reasonable success had been achieved when the battle flags of the Confederate army waved against the sky once more, and the right wing practically melted into the underbrush.

Unsteady from lack of food, tears of remorse in their eyes, the gallant remnants of the 9th Illinois again were ordered to turn their backs on their comrades from Oglesby's brigade and retire to the south. All hope of maintaining a link with the 18th had vanished. McArthur determined to bring out his brigade intact and the 9th must be a nucleus of that effort. Confederate officers had detected the gap and Rebel infantrymen were moving rapidly through the void. The 18th Illinois was now left to its own devices.[2]

With the despair of defeat about them Illinoisans flowed down and across the Forge Road. In their defense it must be said that many of them had not eaten in more than a day. Finally after a considerable distance senior officers mustered a line and the extended bayonets brought to a close the retrograde movement. In the meantime, however, McArthur's brigade had taken itself literally right out of the battle area.

As Johnson paused once again to gather his scattered battalions and Baldwin swerved his front to bring it to right angles to Oglesby, the latter was taking rapid stock of his predicament. To an aide he shouted, " Find General McClernand. Tell him McArthur is retreating and my flank is exposed." Another rider dashed to the nearby 30th Illinois with orders for it to fill in the space being made by the 18th Illinois as it tried to block the onrush on its side. The dike was leaking and no one had enough fingers to stem the tide.

Lawler had exhausted his large blood-drained body in swiftly bringing the two wings of the 18th into position to meet the Rebels head on. Even as he saw that throngs of his enemies still hovered to the right, Lawler knew that there was no more he could do. He could not think clearly. The pain was too great; he sat down to rest.

McClernand turned ashen at the calamity. Only a few minutes before, he had envisioned pursuing a routed enemy; now, with a turn of the tables, it was he who faced the rout. Lieutenant Jones looked equally alarmed and on orders he grabbed a waiting horse from an orderly and sped off to tell Lew Wallace and Grant of the catastrophe.[3]

Baldwin, using his militia training, quickly re-organized his brigade and marched in columns of six toward the positions of the 18th Illinois. Under cover of the dense vegetation he formulated his line of battle and ordered it forward.

Oglesby began looking ahead. The two Parrotts supposed to be supporting McArthur were located and rushed to the crumbling right flank. Gumbart was given advance warning that his artillery duel might soon have to cease and his duties would switch to repelling infantry assaults. In preparation for their use as reserves or on another line of defense the 29th and 31st were told to recall their skirmishers and be ready to march.

Lew Wallace stroked his beard as he listened to the depressing tale of the excited Lieutenant Jones. Dismissing Jones to carry the news to Grant, Wallace pondered what his course of action should be. No word of any sort had yet arrived from army headquarters but the time had been too short for a messenger to go and return. Assuming permission was on the way, Wallace placed his foot in the stirrup and trotted his animal forward to the brigade of Colonel Charles Cruft. He briefed that officer on the turn of events and ordered him to lead his four large regiments up the road and place them at the disposal of the First Division. It was past 8:30.[4]

Colonel John Simonton breathed deeply in relief. Not only had the enemy mysteriously vanished after menacing his right flank, but Lieutenant Ryan had arrived at the head of a column of relatively fresh-looking graycoats. With the colonel's permission Ryan guided the 36th Virginia to a jumping-off spot for attack. Here at the left of the brigade a breach had developed between the 30th Illinois and the sharply jutting 18th. Ryan dropped a suggestion that the moment was remarkably good for exploiting the Union gap and taking the enemy in flank.

Oglesby had begun to feel as if the end of the world was near. McClernand was nowhere to be found. Hints of an approaching ammunition shortage were popping up. At this stage ammunition runners departing for the rear might stimulate a panic; no one was willing to assume the risk. All that could be hoped for was that reinforcements or replacements would arrive in time.

On his right flank the northern front, with the aid of the 30th, was being rapidly consolidated. The brigades of Wharton and Drake were building opposite the now doubled-over southeast flank. At the apex of this looping line Baldwin's ranks were taking on the appearance of a steady sheet of flame as rank after rank in turn advanced, fired, retired, reloaded, and advanced again.[5]

The visage of Gideon Pillow once more reflected the light of exuberance. Part of the Federal line had cracked. Now was the time to exploit the favors of the gods of war. He dispatched an aide to Johnson's wing to bring Forrest and his cavalry to the center of the line. Here were fresh troops, Pillow calculated, and the territory seemed more adaptable to cavalry maneuver. Also he must inform General Buckner.

Lieutenant Jones of the Union Army could feel his ears redden. Here he was galloping to General Grant's headquarters with news which might make or break the Union, and green troops marching along the road had the audacity to hurl jibes at him. If his business were not so pressing, he might consider stopping and teaching these newcomers the manner of respect an aide of General McClernand deserved. Down deep though, Jones felt gratified that reinforcements were pouring into the army and were directing themselves toward the battleground.

General Simon Bolivar Buckner unbent the folds of a hand-inscribed leaf of paper. The signature informed him immediately that it came from General Pillow. The senior brigadier wanted him to know that his embattled brigades were in the midst of success, everywhere. The time had come, he suggested, for Buckner to join him on the field of conflict. Together, Pillow continued, the two divisions would sweep the enemy from the territory and win a lasting victory for the Confederacy.

Buckner let his hand drop. His back erect and chest thrust out as usual, he turned his eyes to his smoke-framed batteries. Success had not come to them. The Federal batteries remained active in their front. But he would obey. To Pillow's young staff officer he said he would do his best to comply.

In central Kentucky, Buckner's name had been a byword in the enemy camps. There his antagonists knew and respected him and his division. Now sickness and political or accidental strife had emasculated his imposing array of fighting men. How many of these Illinois backwoodsmen knew the name Buckner? Now his attention turned to the matter at hand. For some reason he sent word to the regiment most recently under fire to be his shock unit. It was 9 A.M.[6]

Cruft's brigade stamped jauntily northeast on the Wynn's Ferry Road. They made no secret of their pride and amusement that regiments of Buell's army had been called upon to snatch victory from the hands of defeat in the western army. Some foot-soldiers grumbled, however, that so little notice had been supplied for their sudden advance that blankets, overcoats, and knapsacks were left lying in camp. Many blankets still hung from branches where they had been left to air out. The vanguard of ambulances hauling off McClernand's wounded hove into sight.

Colonel Cruft looked not quite so cocky as he rode along near the middle of the column. Soon he would be asked to cooperate with strange officers of a strange army. Would he be the senior brigadier at the scene? Would McClernand be present to direct operations? How would his troops behave in their first major engagement?[7]

Confidently the 36th Virginia tramped up the hill. In general their approach was oblique to the line of the 30th Illinois.

From that angle they were bound to take the 30th in flank. The Union commander, Lieutenant Colonel Elias Dennis, whipped a few choice companies northward in a valiant effort to forestall the Virginians. Instinctively the Confederates let loose with a storm of lead at the first trace of the enemy. The Federals paused, fired in return, and slowly retreated. The time these companies had given Dennis had been just enough to prevent a breakthrough.

In Buckner's opinion Major W. L. Doss was not taking his assignment with appropriate grace. Shifting his feet restlessly, Doss found it necessary to mention that his Captain Crigler seemed to have sacrificed his arm to an exploding shell a little over an hour before. In addition the commander of the 14th Mississippi noted that his recent arrival had given him little time to assemble knowledge of the territory he was supposed to transit.

Buckner then brought forward bright, young Major Alexander Casseday of his staff. In Buckner's mind Casseday's responsibility was now to direct the activities of the 14th Mississippi. To the major himself the assignment encompassed the supervision of the entire sortie. As near as Doss could make out, Casseday was sent to assist him in some ill-defined manner. In any event he felt insecure about the arrangement.

With only two of Buckner's remaining five regiments as supports the 14th Mississippi aligned themselves at the breastworks. With the battle line projecting itself forward the Confederate artillery suddenly assumed a silent posture. Down the slope strode the Mississippians. Suddenly they emerged into a small clearing obstructed with abatis, which most assumed to be of enemy manufacture. Skirmishers from Wallace's brigade peppered the regiment from the safety of the trees behind the abatis.

The Southern line paused. Doss shouted a command to be passed down the line not to return the fire. To the right the pointed impediments came to an end. The acting colonel detailed four companies to bypass them in that direction. These marched by the right flank obliquely up the hill. Once on the other side of the abatis they faced front again.

The bulk of the 14th wormed their way through a break, which had been discovered in the stakes. Reuniting with the right wing on the south side, it sent off a volley while the joining four companies reloaded after covering their approach. General Floyd reined up behind the line and stood in his stirrups and shouted, "Be steady, boys, and aim low. Fear not, the day will be ours."[8]

By this time the guns of McAllister and Taylor had readjusted to the menace and rained cannister and grape down on the aggressors. William Wallace's whole brigade, excluding the recently attached two former regiments of Morrison, joined in.

At the head of Cruft's relief column Colonel James Shackelford ordered a halt as a group of high-ranking officers beckoned to him near a cluster of farm buildings. One of them turned out to be Brigadier General McClernand. The general brought forth a guide for Shackelford and issued orders to move forward at the double quick–no time was to be lost.

Some distance farther on the guide negotiated a departure from the road. After the 25th Kentucky had hacked and chopped their way through the brush for a good number of yards, the guide called the colonel aside. Verbal instructions passed from his mouth as to how to march around the hill which he had pointed out. Then the man spurred his horse away from the direction indicated. Confused, Shackelford did his best to follow the directions, keeping his ear cocked for the sound of battle.[9]

General Grant thanked the handsome naval officer. The well-briefed young man had just taken him on a tour of the wrecked *St. Louis*. With the sailor pointing out pertinent details the two had interrupted their trip frequently in order to survey, through their field glasses, the damage to the other gunboats. Strongly suspecting that he already knew what he was about to hear, the general turned to listen to Foote's account of the reason for bringing Grant these five miles.[10]

The line of battle in front of Buckner had become too long for the 14th Mississippi to handle all by itself. The 3rd Tennessee scampered forward to place its ranks to the right of their suffering companions. Here they were in excellent position to march on the blazing guns of McAllister.

The combined attack drove the Yankee skirmishers back to the sheltering wing of their regiments. While their casualties were adding up, the Confederates maximised their advantage of high Union fire. In turn they could see that their consciously low-aimed muskets were wreaking havoc in the enemy ranks. Still their flags led them up the slope.

Under pressure from the 3rd Tennessee the 48th Illinois wavered. Lieutenant Colonel Thomas Smith had just slipped to the ground with a grievous wound. The Illinoisans fell back toward the crest of the ridge.

Puffing Tennesseans paused to take aim. Struggling Federal gunners above them were trying to raise the trails of their pieces to depress the muzzles. The crash of a volley. Gunners abandoned their project and fled into the woods. The overjoyed Rebels resumed their climb—a prize of three cannon lay within their grasp.

Colonel Hugh Reed stared into the eyes of a very excited officer, who was unknown to him. Apparently this personage was trying to convey the impression that the guns on W. H. L. Wallace's front were endangered and urgently needed infantry support. Somehow Reed received the impression that this was the desire of General McClernand. He therefore detached his 44th Indiana from its position at the rear of Cruft's column and pointed it north of the Wynn's Ferry Road.[11]

Meanwhile Simonton's brigade, with the addition of the 36th Virginia and the surplus of troops on the division's left, slid their regiments and their facing to the right. Now the 7th Texas was face to face with the 29th Illinois and Gumbart's cannon.

Oglesby, having just rejected the idea of a bayonet counter-attack because of the thick brush, had split the battery into two sections. The blast from one pair caused the rearward ranks of the 7th to look aghast. In spots the leading rank lay strewn across the ground, victims of grapeshot. Captain Robert Slaughter parted company with half of his Kentucky detachment at that moment. Oglesby still refused to allow Simonton to pick up momentum.[12]

Colonel F. L. Rhoads of the 8th Illinois sprinted through some prickers toward a group of horsemen he had recognized. Not even pausing for the usual formalities, Rhoads blurted out to Colonel Oglesby that his regiment had but few rounds of ammunition left, and it remained under heavy attack. Oglesby's knitted brows displayed his sympathy, and he promised Rhoads that the first relief unit would be sent to replace the 8th so it could renew its stocks. It was 9:30.

Meanwhile with Shackelford in the lead the brigade of Charles Cruft wandered through the irregular wilderness. With the sounds of battle rising larger as they marched, the nerves of the colonel and his men began to fray. Stragglers poured past them, running in all directions; they warned of the approach of corps after corps of Southern infantry. Friend or foe were continually taking pot shots at the 25th Kentucky.[13]

Yankee Lieutenant Jones quickly looked from face to face. Colonel J. D. Webster did not meet his appealing glance. Major John Rawlins did not return the look of reproach of this subaltern. Nor did Lieutenant Colonel James McPherson. All of the rest of General Grant's staff, including Captain W.

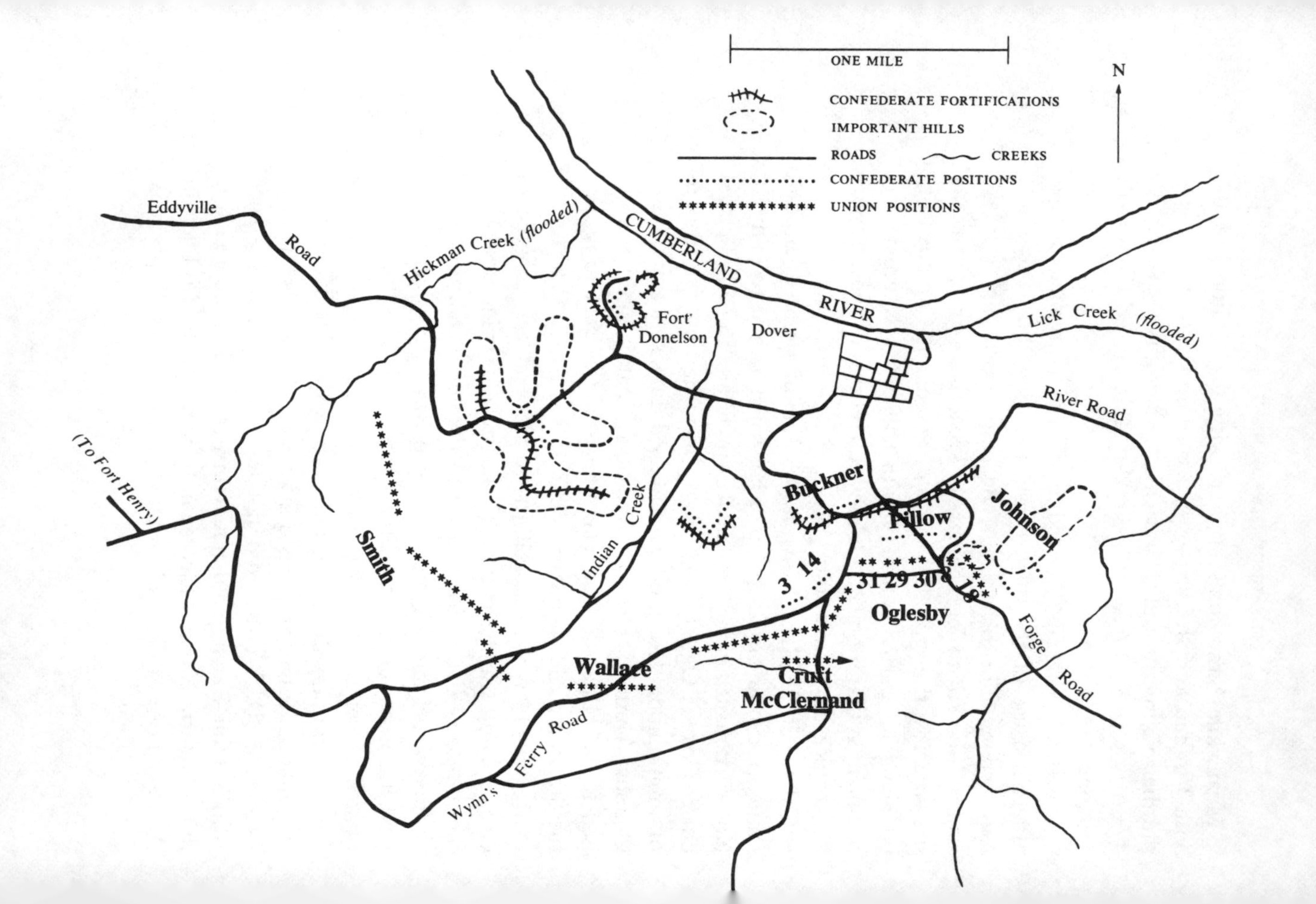
ONE MILE
N
CONFEDERATE FORTIFICATIONS
IMPORTANT HILLS
ROADS
CREEKS
CONFEDERATE POSITIONS
UNION POSITIONS
Eddyville
Road
Hickman Creek (flooded)
CUMBERLAND
RIVER
Fort Donelson
Dover
Lick Creek (flooded)
River Road
(To Fort Henry)
Smith
Indian Creek
Buckner
Pillow
Johnson
3 14
31 29 30
18
Oglesby
Wallace
Cruft
McClernand
Forge Road
Wynn's Ferry Road

S. Hillyer, sat confoundingly quiet. Yet no one spoke to dismiss Jones or give any order.

Finally the senior officer, Webster, slowly cleared his throat and spoke. "All we can do is send someone for the general."

Everyone, including Lieutenant Jones, could feel the atmosphere in the Crisp house warm up. No one had wanted to take responsibility either way. Yet everyone except Jones had known what reasoning had lurked in Grant's mind when he left with the order not to bring on a general engagement. McClernand was the next senior general. Grant had wanted no glory-hunting expedition during his absence. But now something Grant did not anticipate from Pillow had arisen. Webster had just expressed the unexpressable: The status quo must be maintained until the return of Grant. The colonel selected Captain Hillyer to take the fastest horse with the message to Grant. Everyone else readied themselves to ride east to investigate the crisis.[14]

An alert aide notified Oglesby that a fresh regiment was coming up from the rear. Delighted, the colonel excitedly galloped his horse in the direction of his succor.

A cannonball from the artillery positions in the Confederate works arched its way skyward. Its trajectory brought it straight to its target—Gumbart's battery. As its fathers would have hoped it smashed right into the trail of one of the guns. Nonplussed, Gumbart sent a crew of gunners to bring up the one in the rear as a replacement.

It was only with luck that the vanguard of the 25th Kentucky had not shot Richard Oglesby out of the saddle. Sharp commands from officers managed to restrain the overly alert recruits only at the last minute. Oglesby drew rein at the side of Colonel Shackelford. Words blurted out rapidly, amid desperate pauses for breath. The message, however, was that the 8th Illinois would any moment exhaust its ammunition. Would the 25th advance to its relief?

Shackelford pondered. He was under the command of Colonel Cruft, but if such a crisis loomed there was no time to send for authorization. He agreed and asked Oglesby to verify this disposition with Colonel Cruft to the rear. The brigadier pointed out the sector of the 8th and rode down the line to confer with Cruft.[15]

Minutes later on Oglesby's right the 18th Illinois again bent and stretched its right flank to keep it from being overrun. The gradual withdrawal had already forfeited to them and the 30th their strategic hill, and certain companies already sprawled to the west of the Forge Road on the south flank.

Captain Brush, commanding the right wing of the 18th, shifted his thin line of survivors more to the south. To compensate for the ensuing gap he sent a messenger to Captain Marks, of the left wing, to march by the right flank. Shortly after this order Brush gasped in great pain, a victim of an enemy missile. Another bullet cut down the runner he had dispatched to Marks.

A sharp-eyed young Confederate officer spied a widening break in the Union firing rows. The word spread to General Johnson who sat in the saddle nearby. The general himself called upon the 20th Mississippi and thrust them toward the spot, on the double. Meanwhile the two blue masses of five companies each continued in good order to gradually yield to the weight of the Southern lines.

Then a Federal officer questioned the wisdom of the gap. Before the word could reach Marks the Mississippians had penetrated the Yankee formation. Jaded Federal officers tried to string a new rank of men across the hole, to get the men on each wing to temporarily refuse their flanks, but the 18th Illinois had had enough. Some dropped Springfields, Harpers Ferries, and Enfields and ran for their lives. Others just trotted off in small clusters.

Events elsewhere prevented any redemption of the crisis.

Colonel Rhoads had been informed by an aide of Oglesby of the imminent arrival of the 25th Kentucky. Keeping his eyes peeled to the rear, Rhoads reflected on the extent his regiment had suffered during the campaign. They had been heavily engaged with Forrest on Wednesday and today had been thinned out by the ravages of enemy artillery. Now pressed by determined Southern battalions they were out of ammunition. No more than two out of three of his original complement could walk off the field.[16]

The flags waved with decidedly more boldness than the men felt, but still the Kentuckians drew up their line. From the clouds of smoke to the left of the regiment a few bullets began to whistle here and there in their direction. Jittery Union volunteers felt the need to return the " fire." Soon all the companies on that side of the line were industriously loading and unloading their pieces into the smoke—also into the 8th and 29th Illinois and Gumbart's sections. Officers from these units courageously ran to the rear waving their arms for a cease-fire.

Immediately the one-sided engagement died down. Colonel Shackelford demanded to know what the commotion was about. He was told that unknown officers had told them they were shooting Union soldiers. When the colonel asked where they were, he was told that they evidently had rejoined their commands. With their own officers in such indecision the Kentuckians grew more restive.[17]

Meanwhile the 8th had been moving out of line to march off to replenish their cartridges. Caught in a crossfire at an unexpected moment, the regiment halted in indecision. A spent ball ricocheted off the head of Major John Post and he stumbled in circles, talking nonsense. This helped matters not at all. The 8th Illinois suddenly folded and fled.

Unusually sensitive to his flanks, Lieutenant Colonel Dennis was rapidly retreating with the 30th Illinois. (It had lost less at Belmont than had any other regiment.) On the way they ran across a body of infantry men carrying the wounded Lieutenant Colonel Lawler of the 18th Illinois.

Retreat can be infectious. The 29th Illinois had been boldly supporting Gumbart's guns up to this point. With well-ordered volleys pouring into their rear the rumor floated down the ranks that the division had been taken in the rear. In minutes Illinoisans of the 29th added to the rout.

Gumbart's artillerymen stood by their guns. They had come a long way with these proud possessions and they were not about to lose them so easily. For a handful of minutes the heated barrels kept the reorganizing Rebel infantry at a distance. Then the enemy swelled into a conglomeration and advanced. Pistols, sabers, muskets, and pikes appeared for hand-to-hand defense.

Portions of the 25th Kentucky had withstood the overrunning of the demoralized troops of their army. West Pointer Hylan Lyon, however, had no intention of allowing any Federal fragment to save the day. The 8th Kentucky, C.S.A., pushed the 25th Kentucky, U.S.A., right out of the way.

Buckner's 3rd Tennessee had in the meantime been repulsed. The 45th Illinois to the rear of McAllister's battery had risen to the occasion and had reached the abandoned cannon before the Tennesseans. Here a ferocious fight raged while gunners as a precautionary measure removed the guns to the rear. Finally the 45th backed off somewhat, but their purpose had been accomplished.[18]

To the northeast the 14th Mississippi was even more desperately engaged with the 11th and 20th Illinois. While the Confederates were outnumbered by more than two to one, the Federals were enduring heavier losses. In the 11th Illinois a Lieutenant Boyce was killed at his post. Fifteen dead infantrymen littered the white landscape.

Suddenly on the right of the 14th Mississippi the shimmer

of bayonets caught the eyes of the embattled Secessionists. Apparently a regiment had been ordered to fix bayonets. Row after row of bluecoats surged forward. Alexander Casseday impatiently surveyed the line of his improvised Confederate brigade. On the far right the 3rd Tennessee had lost its major advantage. The 14th had suffered, he felt, dreadfully in the past 45 minutes. "Fall back," he called out. Some officers complied immediately. Others looked to Major Doss for clarification. Doss, with an attitude of resignation, shrugged his shoulders and waved on the withdrawal.

As the Mississippians retired in growing confusion, Colonel C. C. Marsh of the 20th Illinois confidently watched as his troops quickened their pace. Who knew where this counterattack would end?

Without notice Confederate cannon from the entrenchments released their lethal loads. Iron balls, both large and small, sprayed the ranks of the cocky 20th. Everywhere key men went down. Among them was Lieutenant Colonel William Erwin.

Since the organization of the unit Erwin had stood out as an inspiration to the rank and file. Many of his townsmen had memorized the tales of his distinguished service at the battle of Buena Vista in the Mexican conflict. It had stirred many of the young clerks and farmhands to hear recounted the instances where Zack Taylor's gallant little army had almost been overwhelmed on the first day. Now the colonel lay motionless, barely alive, bleeding at the side of his chest where a portion of cannister charge had crushed his ribs. Gently a detail set about lifting the body to bear it off to the hospital.

By this time Colonel Joseph Palmer, twisting his individualistic mustache, had thrown the 18th Tennessee forward to assist the 14th. Not without difficulty Doss rallied most of his men on these supports and urged them back up the slope onto the dispirited 20th Illinois.

Marsh himself was shaky. Just a few feet away from him only the corporal stood of the original color guard. First making sure of his reserves, he withdrew the foremost rank and ordered the second rank to commence firing.

The 14th and 18th had barely discharged their muskets for the first time in the renewed engagement when Major Casseday came riding up in great haste. Obviously excited, the Kentucky aide to Buckner swept his hand to the rear in a gesture at the firing Confederate cannon. Doss argued that they would soon cease fire on the clash of the battle lines, but Casseday stubbornly remained adamant. He then rode off to instruct Palmer to retire to the entrenchments. Back down the ridge tumbled the 14th Mississippi, this time in more disorder than before. Buckner rallied them at the trenches with a comparison to the victorious Virginians on the left.[19]

Tough Colonel John Logan had been disappointed. At Belmont he had fought and was commended for his tactics by fellow politician McClernand, but up to this point his 31st Illinois had seen little action. Then some time after 9:30, he began to see his services in demand. Regiment after regiment on the right of his brigade was being swept up in the tide of defeat. At the extreme left of Oglesby's position the 31st stood relatively aloof from the psychology of disaster. They were also determined to let the Confederates know of their presence.

Knowing that a continued facing to the north would mean quick eventual flanking of the 31st, Logan pointed out new positions to his battle commanders. A straight line would be drawn facing east. It was not easy. Many of their retreating Illinois comrades were determined that nothing should stand in their way, and in their panic plowed into stalwarts of the 31st. Finally, with the line in place, Logan saw to it that company commanders opened their ranks somewhat to permit the jetsam of defeat to pass through.

In general the Southern onslaught had stalled. An enemy

camp had fallen into their clutches. Easy and legal loot drew the attention of the poor dirt farmers who made up the bulk of the Confederate service. New rifles were everywhere within their grasp. Simonton's brigade and others searched through the ammunition boxes of dead and wounded enemy soldiers for suitable restoration of these essential elements. Several dozen prisoners were available for inspection. There was even an exhibit of a raving high-ranking Federal officer. Insensible Major John Post had bumped into Private George Blair of the 7th Texas.

Some Rebels, however, remembered the score they had to settle. Friends and relatives had been mercilessly cut down by certain Union artillery. They must be taken and turned against their oppressors.

Gumbart prayed for just a few minutes. The ground about him was too rough to drag his pieces away by hand. Some gunners had just departed to fetch the horses, but precious seconds were necessary to attach the limbers and move back the pieces. Now with the hostile mob rushing at him it appeared that these minutes were not forthcoming.

At that moment from the flanks to the right and left poured accurate, well-directed infantry fire upon the disorganized Confederate attack. While the graycoats did not retreat, they did not come any closer. Yankee gunners laid down their hand weapons and furiously worked to make the attachments of limbers to guntrails. In a couple of minutes they were on their way to the protective arms of the 31st Illinois yards to the west.

Between the Forge and Wynn's Ferry Roads Cruft's brigade floundered in confusion. The 25th Kentucky had become separated from the 31st Indiana. The latter, Cruft's own regiment, tried to maintain its battle formation but Union soldiers in flight were making it a shambles. Also in the chaos Lieutenant Colonel Osborn had mysteriously disappeared. Finally Major Frederick Arn decided it was either retreat or suffer the demoralization of the 31st Indiana. The 17th Kentucky came up for support but they were ambushed by Drake's troops to the right and never were able to get in line.

At the time of the cracking of his brigade Richard Oglesby had been in deep consultation with Cruft. The speediest of the flying infantrymen brought him the news he knew had been unavoidable. Encouraging Cruft to hold fast where he stood, Oglesby endeavored to rally the remnants of his brigade once more into fighting shape. Only slightly successful here, he instructed the small corps of undemoralized Union officers to continue gathering willing survivors and form them into a reserve. Meanwhile he directed himself north to determine if any portion of his line still held the field.[20]

Unaware that Buckner had relented in his aggressiveness at the most crucial moment, Gideon Pillow in the glow of victory cast his eye about for fresh units to hurl against the one regiment which stood between him and the rout of McClernand's division. Forrest was there, his dark eyes flashing in anticipation. The bellicose-looking McCausland still possessed a relatively fresh 50th Virginia. These two he dispatched to crush the last vestige of Federal resistance.

Oglesby arrived to find the reliable 31st Illinois in the midst of a fight for its life. Flags of countless Rebel regiments floated in the distance. A battery of guns valiantly contended with these hordes but Oglesby found out that their ammunition also was running low. As Logan voiced concern for his right flank, Oglesby promised immediately to oversee the placement of Cruft's regiments there. The time was after ten o'clock.[21]

By this time few officers in either McClernand's or Pillow's divisions could tell anyone exactly what was transpiring with their units. Lucky indeed was the officer who had half of his command under his eye. The rapid progress of the battle since 8:30 had mixed and confused so many regiments that everyone was dangerously under manned. The more individualistic soldier would pause with an organized fighting unit and add to its fire power no matter what his regimental badge said. The more insecure would wander around through the fields, up and down the firing lines, telling everyone he was searching for his regiment.

South of the Confederate entrenchments at the station of the 20th Illinois, a fork appeared in the Wynn's Ferry Road. The main highway angled east while a side road continued directly south. Finally it dipped into a ravine. Here stood a house provisioned as a hospital. Surgeon Thomas Fry was its director.

Beginning with the retreat of McArthur and increasing greatly with the flight of Oglesby, unwounded Union soldiers had lingered beneath the walls of the cabin. The surgeons had been too busy attending the wounded to worry about these stragglers. Now some in grave excitement began to herald the imminent approach of thousands of Rebel infantry. For the first time Fry realized that his malingering countrymen were using the hospital flag as a protection and an excuse for not returning to the fray. Hospital guards and surgeons alike started to attempt to chase the freeloaders away.[22]

Clouds of cavalry were making frequent incursions on the front of the 31st Illinois but with the aid of Gumbart's cannon they were repeatedly driven back. A massed infantry assault in the center, however, had resulted in the wounding of Lieutenant Gumbart and he was carried from the field.

Logan began to harbor worries over the security of his two flanks. First of all, columns of infantry were observed between his left and the Confederate works. A messenger had dashed off to the left to warn the 11th Illinois of Wallace's brigade. From the right rear a mysterious orderly bombardment was being made on his regiments. Staff officers were sent off to investigate.[23]

With the assistance of Oglesby, Cruft was stringing out a

semblance of a line of resistance. In the confusion of the retreat the nearly leaderless 31st Indiana turned itself north, toward the smoke and sound of battle. It was not from this direction, however, that danger threatened Major Arn's men. Johnson's wing was advancing on them from the east. Nevertheless, the Hoosiers with machine-like precision blazed out against the figures moving in the distance.

As the 17th Kentucky reformed in reserve and the 44th Indiana, relieved of its responsibility to W. H. L. Wallace, moved up in support, Colonel Cruft heard from breathless messengers that a body of men in his vicinity was firing into the 31st Illinois. Cruft looked to the east and immediately determined that the offenders were one of his regiments. The 31st Indiana was directly ordered to cease their firing into the 31st Illinois.[24]

Lieutenant Colonel Thomas Ransom of the 11th Illinois heard firing increasing in volume to his right. Riding to that flank he observed large numbers of enemy troops seeking to slip into the gap between Wallace's and Oglesby's brigades. At that moment a messenger from Colonel Logan informed him that enemy detachments were headed west in his direction. Implicit was the suggestion that the two regiments join forces. Ransom sent orders to the 11th Illinois to leave the Wynn's Ferry defenses and march to the right rear and link up with the 31st Illinois.

As he supervised the marshalling of his legions for the final onslaught, Gideon Pillow assumed the glow of victory. Two Yankee brigades had been wrecked. Only scattered units blocked their path. On his right he had seen Buckner move to the attack and assumed that W. H. L. Wallace was pinned down by these exertions.

In reality, however, during this crucial stage Buckner had relapsed into a passive pose. Attacking with only half his division, he had caused considerable consternation to W. H. L.

Wallace and Cruft. In the end, due in no small degree to inept leadership by a major of his staff, the three regiments had relinquished the field. Now with reinforcements marching to assist Logan against the encroachments of Pillow, Buckner was content to nurse the wounds of his dispirited troops while his batteries duelled in reply to the Federal guns.

Young, dark and bearded, Colonel Charles Cruft began to see some semblance of order appearing in his line of battle. The jumpy 31st Indiana had quit firing into Logan's regiment. The 44th Indiana had just been admonished to be cautious in using their muskets due to the presence of the 31st Illinois in their front. Their officers felt there was nothing they could do but await an attack. The 17th Kentucky lay in reserve.[25]

John Alexander Logan was too important a man to be pushed around, even by the army of the Confederate States of America. Although a Democratic Congressman, he had enthusiastically supported the waging of war. With his Mexican War experience, his square jaw, and his forbidding heavy black mustache, John Logan was a leader of men—whether from the rostrum or the saddle.

Matters were not going well, however. Party differences forgotten, Oglesby had recognized the superior ability of Logan and left him to manage his own affairs while he took his portly body off to salvage what he could of his brigade. Alone, Logan fended off the alternate cavalry and infantry waves sweeping toward his battery.

Just below the crest of the east slope of the ridge the thickets had become matted with dead horses and human beings. Lieutenant Jeffrey Forrest had suffered the killing of his mount beneath him at an untimely moment, severely injuring the young officer. Unaware of this personal loss, Colonel Forrest was at the same moment striding through the brush searching for a loose horse. His own had been shot just minutes before.

In spite of his apparent success Logan knew his volunteers

could not hold the field much longer under existing conditions. Ammunition for the riflemen was being consumed at a prodigious rate. (There had been little enough provided to begin with.) The battery was releasing its last rounds. Its leader had been carried wounded from the scene. Lieutenant Colonel John White of the 31st had collapsed with a lead ball in the neck.[26]

Pillow was troubled to no small degree that the rear guard stubbornly contesting every inch of ground had just been reinforced. It did not occur to him that these additions had been released for duty on a new front by the abortion of Buckner's half-hearted sortie. He began to wonder if artillery could not be brought up through the thickets.

Privates on the right wing of the 31st Indiana listened alertly as large groups of men tramped through the brush in their front toward their flank. As these troops seemed to be organized, it seemed unlikely that they belonged to the Union army. The soldiers decided to notify their officers.

Young Colonel Thomas Ransom realized he had moved his regiment to join up with the 31st Illinois just in time. Confederate musket balls were whistling through his ranks in large numbers. As he was riding back and forth steadying his Illinoisans, the bushy sideburns on his otherwise unbearded face twitched in a sudden start. The colonel had been hit.

Nathan Bedford Forrest had reformed his squadrons. Word had just reached him that the life or death of his brother was in God's hands. On a motion of his gauntleted hand the rows of horsemen galloped forward up the rise of ground. The muzzles of the Union cannon blazed and smoked. Scores of balls from these and Federal rifles whizzed through the morning air. The leader never faltered, nor did his cavalrymen yet in the saddle. In a flash everyone observing the scene knew nothing short of death would stop that colonel.

Artillerymen sprinted for their horses. Squads of infantry manipulated their weapons as some of the first hand-to-hand combat scenes in the long battle took place. Here and there individual Rebel horsemen broke through the crowd of infantry. Pistols reported, sabers arced. Artillery horses fell in singles and pairs. While striving to defend their transportation, the gunners now began to realize that not enough horses remained to evacuate even one gun.

Gumbart's guns were abandoned. The infantry, seeing the nucleus of their defense crumble, found disinterest could come quickly to them too. Twenty-three artillery horses sprawled in a tiny area behind the lonely cannon. More than 150 rounds of ammunition had been expended in the guns' defense that day. Now they were trophies of the enemy.[27]

Several yards to the rear the retiring front ranks rallied upon their supports. Even at that moment, however, a cluster of blue uniforms around a recumbent figure denoted a further calamity. John Logan had suffered a grievous wound.

His normally hard features disguising his intense pain, Logan asked his attendants to help him to his feet so as not to demoralize the regiment. Constantly runners and officers approached with the minimum of deference due the circumstances and reported that companies had reached the end of their ammunition. Through clenched teeth the colonel instructed an aide to inform Colonel Ransom of the 11th Illinois that the 31st could no longer maintain their position and request a relief[28]

Brigadier General Ulysses Grant toyed with his crooked pipe as he heard Flag Officer Foote drawing to the end of his report. No doubt lurked in his mind that the navy had suffered dangerously on Friday. Foote had just suggested that the most damaged half of the ironclad flotilla retreat to Cairo for further repairs. In its condition, the naval commander argued, the navy could do the enemy no further substantial damage. Remaining at anchor might even cause some of the gunboats to sink in the shallow water, further damaging the engines. As a bit of an inducement Foote offered to return with some mortar boats, the ironclad *Benton* and perhaps some other craft, then at anchor on the Ohio and to leave the wooden warships. He had warned, however, that his absence might be as long as ten days.

Grant summoned all his energy for a smile to reassure the doubly uncomfortable flag officer. He then agreed with Foote that the vessels had been damaged severely and that he would of course accept the seaman's opinion that major repairs were desirable. In reality Grant was well aware that the meeting was a formality of courtesy, as the older officer could always withdraw his forces at his own discretion. The gesture was appreciated, though. In the meanwhile, he concluded, the army would dig in and lay siege to the enemy. Foote then added that the ironclads would pull out as they were ready before nightfall.[29]

The 44th Indiana of Cruft's brigade stirred restlessly. Previous experience during the preceding hour had notified them that gray uniforms blended well with black branches and fallen brown oak leaves. Many volunteers and their officers harbored the fear that the enemy was at that very moment drawing near by stealthy means. Colonel Reed had come to the conclusion that silence was demoralizing his regiment and ordered the colors placed ten paces before his drawn-up line. Except for the intense roar of close action to the north, the field remained silent. For Captain Bingham these moments were agony and on a sudden impulse he sprang forward, seized the staff and waved the regimental banner aloft. Without delay Confederates responded to the challenge and the cloth was rent by musketballs. Now knowing the location of the enemy the 44th replied.

The cavalry foray had temporarily been thwarted. Infantry of the Rebel army had advanced and taken possession of the captured cannon—disabled or otherwise. Logan, his eyes still

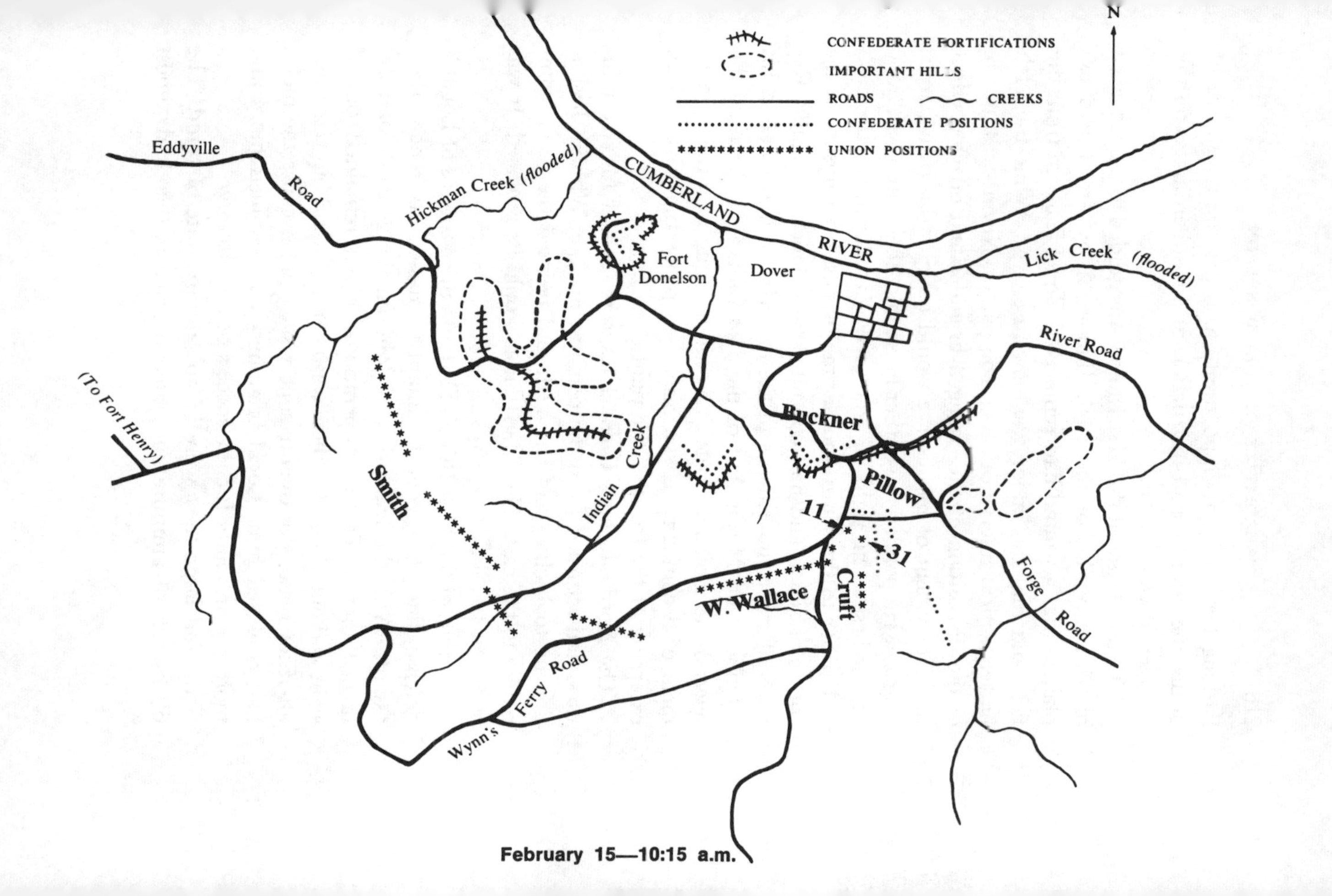

February 15—10:15 a.m.

flashing fire, took the opportunity to order the readjustment of his lines and to send instructions to his subordinates on the manner of withdrawal.

The messenger of the 31st Illinois was guided to the presence of Major Nevins of the 11th Illinois. A bystander had explained that a wound had removed Colonel Ransom from the field and that the major was now in charge. While the 11th had a tactical reserve of seven companies, Nevins was unsure of the disposition of the engaged brigades and of what effect the deployment of his reserve would have on his own parent brigade. He pondered whether he should act on his own, hope for the best on his right, or send to Wallace for instructions.

Farther to the south another major had been unsure of his course of action and had consulted his colonel of brigade. Reports of troop movements in the underbrush had come to his attention and Major Arn of the 31st Indiana had passed the news on to Colonel Cruft. The latter authorized the detachment of a company as skirmishers to probe the area and an extension of the front to the right.

The Nordic-looking Colonel Ransom, absent for five minutes, had returned from the rear just in time. Without hesitation he took charge of the 11th and pointed the seven companies to the east. The 31st Illinois would be replaced. It was going on 10:30.[30]

As units of the 11th Illinois filed into the positions of Logan's defense line, Confederate infantry massed to renew their assault. With the exception of Johnson the generals had detached themselves from operations. Floyd remained out of sight and out of mind. Pillow was nearer at hand but remained aloof for reasons of overall supervision and because the melee had confused him. Local brigadiers had assumed more and more responsibility for the success of the offensive.

By and large they were in no salutary state of mind. The 60 rounds of ammunition issued to each soldier had almost been exhausted. Some had been picked up from the Federal troops but there were problems of caliber here. Sometimes they were solved by exchanging firing pieces, but with the lessening numbers of opponents there were fewer bodies to pick from. Furthermore, the division had been engaged for nearly five hours and fresh troops were in great demand, but there was no supply.

The energetic Colonel Baldwin continued to be the guiding light of the Confederate thrust. His regiments had taken possession of most of the Federal guns and were now forming their survivors into ranks bent on driving the Yankees from the field. Colonel John McCausland, glowering fiercely at the temerity of the Union defense, dressed his lines once more. The regiments of John Simonton brought themselves into contact with the enemy as they saw fit.

Comparatively fresh troops had gathered to withstand the renewed onslaught. Logan, despite his grievous wound, had managed to pull out the 31st Illinois in remarkable condition, considering the fact that one-fourth of his complement was shot or captured.[31]

The smoke of battle approached the little Federal hospital in Bufford Hollow. Surgeon Fry had just presided over the last moments of Lieutenant Colonel William Ervin of the 20th Illinois and Lieutenant Colonel John White of the 31st Illinois. Both had died without struggle or murmur.

The withdrawal of the blooded veterans of the 31st Illinois had thrown portions of the 44th Indiana into confusion. To add to the problem, pursuing Confederates were spotted threading their way through the thicket. Colonel Reed sent to Cruft for assistance and rushed three companies to counter the threat to his left.

The lead company deployed as skirmishers and in a matter of moments brought the encroaching Rebels to a halt. Their withdrawal was only temporary, however, for soon new bodies of fighting men, including cavalrymen, assembled for a new drive. Eager to exploit their success the fresh horsemen assumed the initiative and spearheaded the charge. Once again their old problem frustrated them. Bushes and trees had grown so independently in this region for so long that no creature as large as a horse could pass except at his own jeopardy. The steady Union volleys hurled troopers back upon foot soldiers and the Southern units retreated to try some other stratagem.

The narrow eyes of Charles Cruft closed still further. Evidence from volume of fire was gathering of an enemy build-up on his right flank. His left flank was now endangered by the momentum of a Rebel victory. Should he commit the shaky 17th Kentucky piecemeal? Should he send it to the right? Should he send it to the left? At last he decided to keep the Kentuckians where they were, supporting the 44th on the left.[32]

The sailors of the boat's crew were not too unhappy to be assigned the duty of rowing from the *St. Louis* to the shoreline on that snappy morning. Besides they were serving a real army commander by returning him to his favorite element.

Around them they noticed that the improvised landing of the Federal army had never been busier. Other boats from transports at anchor shuttled cargoes of blueclad soldiers to the water's edge. Beyond that point in the mixture of mud and snow regiments were drawn up in marching order awaiting the completion of their complements.

With assistance from a couple of smartly uniformed navy enlistees, General Grant stepped on shore. In the distance guards approached to guide him to the horses. It was not to be an exciting trip—returning to a siege.

While waiting for the mounts to be saddled, Grant found time to pay attention to his personal appearance. Bits of tobacco and some soot from the shipboard activity had settled in his long beard. He ran his fingers through the hair with care.

In the background a rider had paused to question a sentry, and then had spun the head of his animal and galloped toward the general and his aide. Even at the range Grant could see that the horse had been ridden hard. His beard combing stopped as he recognized the erect outline of his aide, Captain Hillyer.

The dark-bearded messenger dismounted and remembered the formality of saluting. Then he broke the news. McClernand had been attacked. As of 8:30, the right wing had been driven off and the Confederates were advancing upon Oglesby from that sector. Grant said nothing but reached for the reins of his horse and, after hoisting himself into the saddle, led his party eastward.[33]

In dismay Cruft listened as a private related the story of the travels of the right wing of the 31st Indiana. The battalion had at first forced back the skirmishers of the Confederate detachment which had been seen moving through the brush. At this point, however, they had encountered a more numerous supporting force and, more ominously, had caught sight of large numbers of graycoats beating their way through the brush in the Bufford Hollow Valley far beyond Cruft's flank. The brigadier without delay unleashed his aides to bring off the retreat of his three regiments.

With his regiment now entangled in a furious fire fight, Thomas Ransom found an irresistable urge to turn his eyes rearward. In that direction lay his companion regiment, the 20th Illinois. Colonel Marsh had done next to nothing to replace the void caused by the relocation of the 11th as it hurried to the assistance of Logan. Certainly Marsh was doing nothing to assist the left wing of the 11th as it struggled to fend off Rebel forays from the northeast. A gap existed between the two Illinois units and nothing was being done to close it.

Marsh was well aware of the ordeal of Colonel Ransom.

His experience of the morning, however, had left him a shattered and timid commander. Bill Erwin, his experienced second-in-command, was dead. The hour-long stand and counterattack of the 20th had resulted in fearful casualties—one-fifth dead and wounded. With no one to advise him and with some of his best soldiers gone, Marsh had decided to await orders before undertaking any new projects. If anyone accused him of lack of initiative, he could always respond that he was awaiting fresh supplies of ammunition which he had sent for.

Looking for all the world like a thin warrior priest from a mystic temple, Colonel William Wallace had sat astride his sturdy mare peering through the trees to his rear. From his vantage point back of the line of battle he had seen the initial activities of Cruft's pull-back. Immediately he had ridden to the presence of General John McClernand. To the haggard general he voiced his worries that the Confederate encroachments to the east and south would soon surround his brigade. McClernand sighed, shook his head, and gave permission to Wallace to withdraw his brigade when he thought it necessary. There being no activity on his battle line facing Buckner, Wallace returned to keep posted on Southern progress behind the Wynn's Ferry Road.[34]

The tempo of the cavalcade with General Grant had diminished. True, reinforcing units of infantry clogged the roads. It was also true that the formerly snow-covered red soil was now turning into an amorphous mass of mud. But farther up the river the soil was taking on a different hue of red, and their leader, Ulysses Grant, was one of the most accomplished horsemen of his day.

What the associates did not know was that Grant in the turmoil of his thinking on this unexpected turn of events had made a quiet resolution. John McClernand had made no secret of wanting command of the army given to Grant. Well, he was now in charge of nearly half of it. Let the world see what he could do with it.

Also it seemed unlikely that the senior Confederate generals would undertake so bold a move as a design to destroy the Union hosts. From all accounts Floyd appeared to be in the lowest category of the political generals. Pillow, from what Grant knew of him from the Mexican War and Belmont, had few qualities to bring respect or apprehension. Bushrod Johnson had been an upper-classman during Grant's plebe year at West Point and was to Grant's mind an undistinguished individual. Buckner, a personal friend, was unlikely to carry the day against three such nonentities. It seemed likely that McClernand had exaggerated the threat. To the senior general there seemed no need to risk his neck in a classic ride when the destination was probably not one to stimulate the imagination of even a fourth-rate poet.[35]

To his horror Colonel Hugh Reed saw that there no longer existed a friendly line of defense to his right. His brigade had retreated. Sending a messenger to repeat the orders to the left wing, Reed rode up to the captain commanding the company on the right flank and instructed him to march by the right flank. When this order had been started down along the line of the 44th Indiana, Reed sped off to locate the encampment of the brigade.

The left wing was the most actively engaged portion of the 44th and the transmission of the message was garbled. The practical route of withdrawal to the battalion seemed to be to the west, so his detachment did an about-face and beat a hasty retreat.

Simultaneously Colonel Bedford Forrest and several infantry leaders detected the withdrawal of the flag Captain Bingham had so audaciously set to mark the position of the 44th. To them it signified one thing—a retreat and an opportunity to outflank the obstinate regiment blocking their victory. Sending word to put everything into an infantry frontal attack, Forrest led his eager squadrons across country toward a point where he could catch the Union regiment in flank.

At this point the Union line resembled a long, small-tipped hook with an acute angle bend. From the bend to the edge of the tip stood the 11th Illinois. Beyond this endpoint a piece had broken off the hook and stood poised in midair, quite close to the spine of the implement on the Wynn's Ferry Road. All this had not escaped the attention of William Wallace. He decided to withdraw his shaky brigade to a less threatened line of defense. Orders were rushed to regimental commanders. The time was about eleven o'clock.[36]

William Baldwin had just returned to his brigade after paying an official visit to his old associate, Captain Graves of Buckner's artillery. He had asked the battery commander to pass on his request for ammunition and reinforcements. While there he had also relayed information on the positions of Confederate and Union troops in Graves's front. As he rode along the line encouraging his men, Baldwin was gratified to hear the reports of the Southern battery and as a bonus to see two fresh companies from Hanson on their way as a reinforcement.

Unknown to Colonel Ransom the messenger from W. H. L. Wallace instructing him to withdraw had been killed. Ransom had been mulling over the problems of restoring his ammunition supplies, when to his right emerged a swarm of Rebel cavalry. At this sight many of his troops bolted. Already, enemy infiltrators on the unsupported left were shooting at their backs. A few clubbed their rifles or sprang forward probing with their bayonets. A melee ensued. Cavalrymen unloaded their revolvers, and swung their sabres and carbines. Union infantrymen lunged and leaped in efforts to unhorse their antagonists.

In seconds, however, Southern foot soldiers had arrived to

support their colleagues on the flank. Others of their uniform had broken through the Federal ranks in the center to tangle with those Yankees still determined to do battle. Everywhere Union officers called upon their men to withdraw and face to the rear. The wounded Ransom collected a body of picked men around him and slashed and shot and clubbed their way through the throngs of gray horsemen and foot troops.

Lieutenant J. O. Churchill had been hit in the thigh by a large-caliber musket ball early in Ransom's retrograde charge. He had fallen into a hole, but he got up and continued. A Confederate trooper wheeled in front of him and lowered his carbine. Churchill cocked his revolver but the Rebel fired first. Falling into a pile of dead and wounded, the lieutenant immediately felt the rush of the Southern infantry pass over him.[37]

Here and there segments of companies of the unsupported 11th found themselves completely cut off; so they threw their weapons to the ground and raised their hands. The left wing of the 11th fled through a field of felled timber, pursued by howling demons from Simonton's brigade, and intercepted periodically by groups from other brigades. Some fought their way through to the Wynn's Ferry Road. Others collapsed from wounds or heaved up their arms in sign of surrender.

Among the Federal soldiers who kept their heads was Corporal Armstrong of Company H. Serving with the color guard, Armstrong found himself surrounded by hordes of Rebel cavalry. Although wounded, he looked around himself and determined that he was the best able to carry the flag of the regiment from the field. The sight of the banner rallied Yankees around him sooner than it drew enemy marauders and Armstrong with luck was able to bear the colors out of reach of the Confederates.

Once outside of the encirclement most of the weary remnants of the 11th Illinois flung away all impedimenta including their arms and ran as if their shirts were on fire. Occasional rear guards were swept away by the surging Confederate legions who were not too exhausted to enjoy their supreme moment of victory.[38]

As Gideon Pillow rode slowly through the rows and bundles of the wounded and the dead, he sensed that something was wrong. He drew rein to his horse. Then he knew what it was. For the first time in over five hours it was quiet in his vicinity. No sound of sustained combat came to his ears. This was not as it should be. Directly ahead, seeing that they had not yet linked up, Simon Buckner should have had his division desperately engaged. Meaning to find out why Buckner was not participating in the struggle, Pillow sent for Forrest to bring his entire regiment. He might have need of them in the coming hours. It was approaching 11:30.

Lieutenant Churchill, whose part in the battle had been replenishing ammunition and removing dead from the firing line, felt that bones were broken in the vicinity of his hip. Confederate stragglers were everywhere, looting the fallen enemy. He protested vocally.[39]

Farther south Drake's brigade progressed westward through a large ravine bisected by a creek, Bufford Hollow. Since the rout of McArthur's brigade at 8:30, this unit had devoted its time to wandering through the wilderness, putting to flight scattered segments of the Federal right wing, and reorganizing the brigade and its battalions. Now their skirmishers spotted a sizable congregation of blue uniforms grouped around a house in the valley. They opened fire.

The sound of bullets pelting into the clapboards caused grown men everywhere in the hospital to become hysterical. Many of those who could move staggered, hopped, and crawled through the doors and began ascending the slopes to the west. Surgeons Fry and Thompson began organizing the non serious cases to assist the bed cases to the rear, wherever that was. In the midst of the evacuation the firing ceased. Someone in the Confederate brigade had seen the hospital flag. Nevertheless Thompson and Fry departed for the Wynn's Ferry Road, abandoning only those who could not accompany them.

North of the Wynn's Ferry Road a small knot of officers was engaged in a discussion of the military situation. Chief in importance among them were Major John Rawlins and Brigadier General Lew Wallace. Young Rawlins, sporting a thin semi-circle of beard hanging from his lips by a string of a mustache, appeared highly embarrassed at having to arrive from headquarters without orders and without the commanding general. Both officers were confessing their helplessness when a commotion arose behind them from the vicinity of the road. Wallace sent an orderly to investigate.

The panicking survivors of the 11th Illinois, in their haste to depart from the battlefield, had fled through the ranks of the retreating 20th and 48th Illinois. Certain of these shaky files began to waver and soon new flotsam was added to the gathering stream of Union soldiers heading away from it all.

Brigadier William Wallace had not the distinctive personality needed to quell a rout and he knew it. Instead he paused in his journey at the head of Erin Hollow and ordered Captain Edward McAllister to cover that approach along with one gun from Taylor's battery until forced to retreat. The 45th Illinois was ordered to continue in support of the artillery.[40]

Touched by the lifeless bodies of Union volunteers, Lieutenant Churchill called out to passing Southern doctors. The latter were selecting treatable cases of wounded to be removed by the ambulance corps. Three surgeons came to his assistance, conferred, and then told him that his case was hopeless and they would have to leave him.

As the numbers of stragglers pouring over the road and through the woods began to mount, a rider suddenly hurtled toward Lew Wallace and Rawlins from the foliage. His eyes transmitted a lack of self-control, his hair was in disarray, and his hat had been lost somewhere, but this man bore the rank of colonel commanding an Illinois regiment. Over and over he shrilled, "We're cut to pieces! We're cut to pieces!" In an outburst of disgust Rawlins reached his hand for his revolver. With a gentle motion Wallace restrained the staff officer, cautioning that it might be a bad example to the enlisted men. Not far away the colonel sped by "Black Jack" Logan, who was writhing in pain on his horse as he waited for a surgeon.

Minutes later Wallace's orderly returned and reported. A virtual stampede was rolling over the landscape, he said. Wallace turned his head to Rawlins, not needing to state the question on his mind. Rawlins cocked his ear toward the building tumult, nodded his head and indicated that Lew Wallace should march his remaining brigade toward the engagement. Relieved, the general dispatched a messenger to Thayer to place his brigade on the road and head it northeast.

At the vital trilateral intersection along Wynn's Ferry just captured by Pillow the scene remained relatively quiet. A soldier or two cavorted with the musical instruments abandoned by the band of the 11th as they assisted with the wounded. Details herded Yankee prisoners together while certain fighting men went about the necessary stop-gap task of searching the dead and wounded for appropriate ammunition. Certain units being withdrawn from combat lounged about or marched toward a prospective encampment.[41]

Accompanied by the engineer Lieutenant Colonel Jeremy Gilmer, a furious General Pillow spurred his horse up the ridge of entrenchments occupied by Buckner's division. Along almost the entire length of the position Confederate soldiers cowered behind the works showing no indication of a willingness to attack. Finding a regiment inactive behind the ridge to the rear of Green's battery, Pillow impetuously ordered it to march to the right and take the Union group of guns. This caused great discomfort to the recumbent division.

The enraged Tennessee general, knowing nothing of the circumstances, blamed the lack of spirit on a combination of low morale and harassing Federal artillery fire There was no one to confide in him the complete confusion lurking in the officer corps dating from the strange activities of Major Casseday of Buckner's staff. The despair of lost initiative had consequently passed through the ranks of the foot soldiers.

Buckner and Brigadier Brown came upon the transferring 32nd Tennessee with alarm in their faces. Colonel Edward Cook's story of Pillow's orders swept the reprimand right out of their mouths. The two officers and their staffs bolted off to conjure up supporting reinforcements.

Minutes later Pillow came upon Buckner surrounded by a rooting section of officers, throwing all of his commanding presence and experience of leadership into an exhortation to the troops to return to the trenches and assemble for a second assault.

As he drew rein, Pillow, in the best courtroom manner, placed a bridle on his temper. A partial state of shock had aided these efforts for he could not imagine a unit leader being reduced to such an ignominious station. Here was a general of the army pleading with his men to carry out their duty. Even in volunteer armies discipline had rarely reached such a bottom.

With an icy stare Pillow inquired stonily whether there was some misunderstanding of his own orders of 8:30 or of the decision of the conference of the generals on Friday night.

Buckner, realizing his current posture must put him on the defensive, responded that such was not the case. His men had just made a bold assault upon the most threatening of the enemy batteries, but the heavy volume of Union fire had thrown them into confusion. He concluded with a protest that just a little more time was necessary for the division to recover its composure.

Pillow offered no solace, but instead requested to see the offending battery. The combined groups of horsemen rode over the crest of the ridge to a point dominating Erin's Hollow. Pillow pensively took in all the surroundings. Then in terse terms he instructed Buckner to dispense with a frontal attack and instead to outflank it by maneuvering through the ravine.

As Buckner turned to the long-bearded Colonel Brown to have him implement Pillow's decision, the field commander rode off back to the left. Finding his staff at the rehabilitation area in the rear of his division, Pillow dispatched several of its members to track down Colonel Forrest and have him return immediately. He did not trust Buckner in view of conditions to remove this roadblocking battery with only his division.[42]

Once again Buckner did not deem it advisable to assail the Union front with his whole 3,000 men. Instead three regiments were given to Brown and two of them had been the associates of the hapless 14th Mississippi in the abortive sortie earlier in the morning. Colonel Cook's 32nd Tennessee would fill the spot of Doss's Mississippians. Two large regiments—the 2nd Kentucky and the 41st Tennessee—had so far remained unbloodied. Buckner was saving them as the nucleus of his rear guard.

As Palmer's 18th Tennessee approached, Cook gave the order for the advance. Two companies scampered down the gully through the brush. Filling in to the left of the 32nd, the narrow-faced Colonel Benjamin Palmer squinted his soft eyes to discern the outlines of the nemesis battery. All that served to locate it, however, were the occasional wisps of smoke and the bass boom of the reports.

Bedford Forrest, mounted on a war-horse nearly as spirited as the colonel's own exterior, came to a halt and saluted his superior officer. Pillow motioned the cavalryman around and directed his attention several hundred yards down the Wynn's Ferry Road. The faintest image of a depression to the north of the roadway could just be seen. This, said Pillow, housed a malicious enemy battery supported by a detachment of infantry. It would soon be engaged in a flank-frontal attack, but Pillow wanted to insure its capture by attacking it from the east. Such was Forrest's assignment. Pillow then took Gilmer off at high speed toward the vantage point of Heiman's hill.

Pillow's own jaded division was by then in a state of immobility. Many units were mere shadows of their originally diminished selves. Many brigade and regimental commanders were reluctant to proceed further until guaranteed fresh supports. Others halted to take their bearings.

In the latter condition was Colonel Baldwin. He was nearly a mile from the territory he had been observing for several days. Nothing was known of the probable line of retreat of the Union army or of the eventual direction of the various roads which stretched across their fronts. The brigadier was unwilling to march his completely exhausted unit aimlessly, so he halted and restored the soldiers' stock of ammunition from stores supplied by the 2nd Kentucky.[43]

Simultaneously the piercing eyes of Colonel Roger Hanson were centered on the warrior McCausland. The Virginia colonel had departed from his handful of men to personally scour the area for fresh supports. Like Baldwin he had come upon Hanson and the 2nd Kentucky. To the volunteer Kentucky lawyer McCausland hurriedly expressed his fears that Federal reinforcements were building up and would soon retake all the lost ground unless additional troops bolstered the line.

Meanwhile the columns of Colonels Brown, Palmer, and Cook were having considerable trouble in approaching the opposing battery. The brush was as overgrown as anywhere on the morning's battlefield, and thick melting snow disgruntled the shaken volunteers to no small degree as it began to soak through their varied uniforms.

Pillow and his staff, along with Lieutenant Colonel Gilmer, had ridden posthaste behind Buckner's remaining three regiments until they encountered the detached 42nd Tennessee under Colonel Quarles. In a quick conversation the general gleaned the information that the 42nd, mainly in the person of its colonel, had been forced earlier to rally stragglers from Buckner's right-most regiment, which had been discomfited in the trenches by heavy Yankee artillery fire.[44]

A ragtag rear guard of the Union army had been formed in a sheltered depression of Erin Hollow to the north of Wynn's Ferry Road. Remnants of the 11th Illinois and of Oglesby's brigade and the separated wing of the 44th Indiana checked their percussion caps and powder charges as they faced to the east and south to dissuade Pillow's division from any further penetration. Behind them the three guns of McAllister's battery roared as they discharged their deadly loads at Brown's two columns. Smith's 45th Illinois also faced north, prepared as per orders to repulse any infantry intruders. A number of yards to the west Wallace had approved the withdrawal of the guns of Taylor and these had finally ceased their harassment of the Confederate batteries and trench-bound infantry.[45]

Forrest, knowing that the numbing effect of the Confederate tide of victory would soon diminish on the Union ranks, personally led a hastily organized dash upon the small wooded ravine. The provisional Yankee rearguard, however, did not quake, but instead leveled their pieces calmly and delivered their volley when the cavalry had approached to a near distance. The horsemen reeled and scattered in several directions.

Northeast of this spot Roger Hanson stroked his jutting chin whiskers as an interested observer to the cavalry engagement. Appeals had been made for his assistance and he had even loaned two companies to another brigade without specific authorization. Now the last fresh detachment of Pillow's division seemed in danger of being thwarted in removing a serious obstacle to the army's progress. It would be too audacious to move the 2nd Kentucky out of its assigned position without authorization of Buckner so a staff officer sped off to contact the general.

By this time Pillow had arrived at the hill of Heiman's brigade. The latter brigadier had just read a request from General Buckner that the firing of his additional light battery be guarded as an infantry assault was being attempted in that area. In the conversation with Pillow the colonel inquired whether it would be helpful to lend any reinforcements to the attack. Pillow felt it would certainly be an asset to capture the battery at the earliest possible time. Accordingly the 48th Tennessee and the 27th Alabama were readied to march down the slope.[46]

John Calvin Brown's slowly progressing brigade had met only retiring opposition from the retiring Federal skirmishers. The provisional rear guard of Wallace's brigade had fallen back in some disorder as evidenced by the numbers of muskets littering the moistened turf and capture of five prisoners. Now, however, McAllister's prized pieces had opened up at telling range. Brown himself came up to Cook and Palmer with the 3rd Tennessee and peremptorily ordered the two regiments to move to the right into the hollow and deliver their assault from there.

Meanwhile Forrest again poised to drive the infantry supports away from the battery. Pillow had charged him with a mission of silencing these guns and the colonel was determined to do it. A motion of his hand signaled the cavalry forward.

By now, however, the Federal infantry was not only better organized but was also encouraged by the sudden disappearance of pressure from Buckner's front. A sharp volley spat forth from the ravine. Horses stumbled and convulsed, launching riders into space in various directions. Other mounted figures jerked on the reins, taking themselves away from the wall of fire. Some who approached closer found themselves handicapped because the trees and underbrush posed as natural abatis against their inroads; they too soon followed in retreat. Forrest, repulsed for the second time, determined to call for infantry assistance.

Colonel Roger Hanson was taking all of this in. As soon as it was apparent that the cavalry charge was to be abortive, he dispatched a swift messenger to solicit permission from Buckner to permit the 2nd Kentucky to turn the tide in this area. When the messenger did not return speedily (Buckner was at the right overseeing Brown) Hanson decided that no more time could be lost and marched the regiment onto the battlefield on his own responsibility.

The moment was high in its drama. The first fresh infantry to reach the fighting left wing was arriving. Resting companies in their path rose and called out encouragement. The figure of the magnificently mounted Colonel Hanson finally elicited a barrage of cheers from the recuperating legions.

Farther toward the front the sound of human voices to the rear swiveled the attention of the stalemated Rebel regiments in the vicinity of the three-sided crossroads. The square face of William Baldwin turned with them and took in the thrilling sight of nearly 500 marvelous specimens of Kentucky manhood striding in quick time toward the Yankee positions. In an instant his field glasses were to his eyes. Noting the identity of the regiment, Baldwin immediately rode off to release the two companies of the 2nd detached to his service.[47]

Men of the Union were also aware of the approaching

supports. Skinny Colonel William Wallace had lagged behind to supervise the evacuation of the last of his brigade. At his side stood Edward McAllister, his guns having expended the last of their potential on the skirmishers of Colonel John Brown. The colonel turned to the captain and said that he would allow the rear guard to smash this last sally. Meanwhile the guns must maintain their posts to frighten off attacks on the center.

The 2nd Kentucky paused as their leader consulted with Colonel Forrest. The two agreed upon a tactical plan whereby Forrest would dismount a portion of his force and maintain the remainder as a pursuit threat on the flanks.

Posted observers high in the trees had called the information to Pillow and his associates of the dramatic approach of the 2nd Kentucky. Lieutenant Colonel Gilmer's eyes glimmered with expectation at the news. In his mind the day's climactic moment was approaching.

Hanson strode through the weeds to address his regiment. The moment and the personal magnetism of the colonel brought the command to hang on every word. He uttered a few words in reference to the significance of the assault. Then Hanson concluded, " Hold your fire until you come to close quarters."

Not a word came forth from the ranks. Just a grim determination that their objective would be carried. The order to march brought a restless surge forward.

The area over which they trod had been cleared in peacetime and as such had been used as a camp ground by the Federal army. Now with their flanks covered by ample Southern cavalry the Kentuckians quickstepped across the unsheltered ground toward the tangled barrier of trees and bushes bordering the depression.

The Union infantry labored under no such orders to withhold the discharge of their weapons, and the crackle of musketry issued forth from the forest. On the flanks, however, signs of restiveness occurred as squadrons of mounted Confederates audaciously dashed forward, fired, and gave way in succession to the supporting line.

As the 2nd Kentucky sped across the clearing, officers in the supporting rank found it constantly prudent to fill in the gaps in the front line from their own material. The accurate fire of the Union detachment was taking its toll and the infantry had not yet proceeded halfway toward the timber. In spite of the losses discipline held firm and Hanson's order to refrain from firing was obeyed.

Onward moved the gray line. Two-thirds of the unsheltered ground had been transited. More Kentuckians dropped before the relentless aim of the Federal defenders. Still not a shot was fired in return. Forward pressed the attack. Only one-quarter of the distance lay before them. Seconds passed. Then as 80 per cent of the deadly field lay behind them, the order to fire rang true and clear down the Rebel ranks.

The effect was immediate. The once-solid Union firing position melted into the brush. The aggressors, noticing this, broke into a run, their throats letting out one vast cheer. Several Northern stalwarts paused to contest their advance, but in moments bayonets and clubbed muskets had beaten them into submission. The second line of the regiment pushed on forward and delivered a final volley to the backs of the bluecoats, whereupon they were halted by their officers to reorganize.

On the flanks and through the center of the cleared field littered with the bodies of some 50 sons of the Blue Grass State, the mounted and dismounted troops of the cavalry poured in pursuit. Once again, however, the horsemen found the terrain not to their advantage. Meanwhile the retreating Yankees had vanished into the tangled wilds.

At this time Forrest himself was in a predicament. His

horse had suddenly expired beneath him, leaving the brigadier of cavalry again without a mount. Turning this circumstance into an advantage, Forrest led his carbine-armed temporary infantry toward the last-known position of the worrisome Federal battery.

Meanwhile McAllister from his advanced position deep in the woods had dispatched his Parrott safely off on the heels of the supporting infantry. The left gun, however, was giving them considerable difficulty. The softening soil had allowed the wheels to depress themselves. Underbrush had entwined itself through the spokes of the wheels and butted against the axles of the caisson. The team of horses was doubled. Still the slope out of the ravine could not be negotiated. Precious time had been lost.

In desperation the captain decided to abandon efforts to evacuate this gun for the time being and to remove the more exposed piece to the east. Here he took no chances and hitched both available sets of animals up immediately.

Suddenly from the enveloping undergrowth came a series of shots. The gunners looked to their personal armament to ward off any stray Rebel skirmishers. Immediately it was apparent, though, that a large body of the enemy was falling on them, as defiant cries burst forth from the woods and the volume of fire increased. It was not long before their cannon had come to a jolting stop and with no Federal infantry available to defend them, McAllister's artillerymen relinquished the gun to the tender mercies of the enemy and took to their feet.

On Heiman's hill Gilmer was ecstatic with the rapidly moving developments as related by the observers in the trees. No obstacle stood in the way of the link-up of the divisions of Buckner and Pillow. With the fresh troops of Buckner in play the day appeared to have been won for the Confederacy.[48]

A few yards away General Gideon Pillow was anything but

sanguine. Messengers had been bringing reports to him from the cavalry posted across the Cumberland from the Union army's river landing. These told of the morning-long disembarkation of regiment after regiment of Union reinforcements. Lookouts along the Confederate right had spotted signs of heavy columns of troops marching to the east across their front. His own observations of the morale of Buckner's units had been depressing. His own men were spent after constantly fighting and marching for more than six hours. The situation for the Confederate army was not really too promising.

General Wallace and Major Rawlins had concluded their lengthy conversations near the Wynn's Ferry Road when a particular body of military on the roadway caught their eyes. The national colors and banners of a couple of regiments raised above the blue caps and the mounted officers.

In the midst of the throng the general recognized his namesake, W. H. L. Wallace. The colonel was in no hurry, nor was he particularly agitated. He guided his horse toward the division commander at a walk and was sitting peculiarly, with one leg over the horn of the saddle. To the simile-conscious Lew Wallace it was characteristic of an Illinois farmer returning from a hard day at the plow.

"Good morning," said the general.

"Good morning," tacitly returned the colonel.

"Are they pursuing you?" questioned the general.

"Yes."

"How far are they behind?" pressed Lew Wallace.

A disturbance behind the general diverted their attention. The brigade of Colonel John Thayer had showed its vanguard on the avenue amid scattered cheers, advice-giving, and catcalls from the retreating brigade.

Both Wallaces recalled their attention to the last question. The colonel turned his head to the northeast and calculated. His eyes once again fixed on the general. "You will have about time to form line of battle right here," he responded.

"Thank you. Good day," politely responded the general.

"Good day." Looking much like Ichabod Crane, the tall, thin brigadier rejoined the procession flowing away from the battle scene.[49]

A flicker of disgust crossed the pleasant features of Colonel William Baldwin as he saw a recognized figure ride toward him. Brigadier General Bushrod Johnson, technically commander of his division, was making his first appearance before Baldwin's brigade that morning. Following the introductory salutations, the colonel questioned the general on the location of their position and as to the direction of the proposed further line of march. Johnson excused his ignorance with the off-hand statement that he had been busy attending to matters elsewhere on the battlefield. Finally, betraying his lack of respect on his square features, Baldwin replied that he hoped that Johnson would not object if he maintained the status quo until these tactical matters were cleared up.

The 3rd, 18th, and 32nd Tennessee regiments worked their way up the slopes of Erin Hollow against almost non-existent opposition. At the crest the puffing Tennesseans found little more than a few dead artillerymen and infantrymen from the opposing army and through the trees the backs of the trailing portions of Wallace's brigade. Fruits of their journey, however, were realized by the seizure of two immobilized pieces of artillery. (Forrest at that moment was leading his command back to the road.)

To the relief of General Wallace the Third Brigade of his division had emerged relatively unscathed through the gauntlet of human wreckage from McClernand's force. Wallace chose the rise where Wynn's Ferry going northeast began to dip down into Erin Hollow as the point where he would make his stand. To his advantage were a dense thicket in his front and forbidding woods on both flanks.

As an aide from Wallace sped out to insure the arrival of Battery A, which had travelled with the general all the way from Fort Henry on Friday, Thayer guided his infantry through an opening in the woods into the line of battle. His responsibility was great for his spanking new brigade had become a catch-all for all of the reinforcements pouring into the Third Division. (In view of the crisis Wallace had deemed this preferable to culling out a senior colonel for command of a new brigade.) His fresh unit now outnumbered Buckner by more than a thousand men.[50]

With sudden enthusiasm Buckner and his staff reached the confused assembly of his three assault regiments. One of the general's handsome young associates spurred his horse off to bring a certain section of howitzers from Graves' battery down the Wynn's Ferry Road in company with Doss's 14th Mississippi. An equally ardent young man hastened on his trail to order Graves, Porter, and Jackson to hitch their horses to their available guns and rush them to Brown's assistance with the 41st Tennessee.

With Forrest scouting on foot up ahead, Buckner consulted with Brown on the best method of taking advantage of the enemy's confusion. Upon approach of the first section of artillery the 3rd Tennessee should attack to the south of the road while the remaining two regiments would advance through the north sector.

Wallace's Battery A, a Chicago unit, came up at a gallop. The general suggested to Thayer that it might be placed to best advantage on the roadway itself. To the southeast of the enlarged trail the leading 1st Nebraska had discovered units of Cruft's brigade occupying the ground. Thus it placed itself immediately to the right of the road. Thayer positioned his 76th Ohio in close support of the 1st. (The 68th Ohio had been left as a flank guard on the hill overlooking Indian Creek.) The new arrivals, the 46th and 57th Illinois, backed the battery on the roadway. To the left of Wynn's Ferry two more new regiments, the 58th Illinois and the 58th Ohio spread out in the impenetrable forest.

Battery A had barely unlimbered when they found use for their ammunition. Footmen and horsemen in gray cloth manifested themselves on their front. The guns roared. The intruders disappeared as quickly as they had come.

Colonel Bedford Forrest had managed to lay his hands upon a riderless horse and had vaulted into its saddle. Destiny did not have it in store for him to use this mount for long, however, for the first discharge from the battery on the crest had plunged a shell fragment into the rear flanks of the steed immediately behind the colonel's calf. Dismounted once again, Forrest retired with his cohorts to report the suddenly hardening opposition.[51]

Discovering everything to be going as well as could be expected in his immediate location and with reinforcements from Heiman preparing to stride down the hill to Buckner's aid, Gideon Pillow stepped into the saddle in preparation to riding behind the trenches back to the direction of the coordinated divisions.

Gray-uniformed skirmishers, discouraged by the interlocking arms of the deciduous trees, came filtering back to Brown's brigade with the report that the enemy could no longer be found or seen. North of the road Colonels Palmer and Cook set out to see for themselves. With a small escort they ventured into the forest and soon in peering up the slope they spotted a portion of Thayer's baggage. The return of the colonels after noon coincided with the retreat of Forrest's shaken vanguard.

Along Baldwin's stilled battlefront General Bushrod Johnson had again vanished, this time taking the 20th Mississippi under his wing. Baldwin, left with only his two hardest fought regiments, was furious.[52]

As Colonels Brown, Palmer, Cook, and Gordon hacked their

regiments through the timber, General Pillow rode upon a scene of energetic military activity. Battery mounts galloped to their limbers and guns were being attached to the same. Gunners stood around in preparation to assuming their seats on the horses or on the carriages. A thick column of company upon company of infantry was mustered on the rutted trail.

Pillow, having had during his ride a few detached moments to reflect on matters, now urged his horse slowly toward the senior officer of the infantry. Colonel Robert Farquharson of the 41st Tennessee spurred his stallion out smartly to meet him.

Following the exchange of salutes, the general inquired what was in the offing. Farquharson, a veteran of the Mexican War, replied that he and the battery commanders had just heard oral orders to proceed to the assistance of the engaged portion of the division.

This answer was not unexpected. A variety of factors began to effect their impression upon the general's mind. Fresh reinforcements were obviously reaching the enemy lines. While Buckner's command held the initiative, they were poorly armed, in poor spirits, and, Pillow suspected, poorly led. If the balance of power were about to change, the army must think defensively and not exhaust its last reserves by ill-judged marches.

On the strength of this Pillow made a momentous decision. He ordered Farquharson and the battery captains to remain at their stations until they heard further word from him. The guiding force of the morning's offensive had taken a backward step, which, if followed through, would insure that Grant's army would remain in partial possession of the field. The decision would also be destined to have its effect upon Pillow's military career, for at that very moment regimental commanders at Columbus, Kentucky, were answering a pointed questionnaire from General Leonidas Polk about Pillow's conduct at the battle of Belmont.

In his state of mind it did not occur to Pillow to consult General Floyd in this contradiction of the direct orders of General Buckner. While this courtesy was certainly owed the commanding general, Floyd had, since early morning, become the unseen and forgotten general of the battle. Both Union and Confederate armies had fought that Saturday morning virtually without direction from their highest ranking leaders. With Floyd's characteristic of vacillation, Pillow did not miss him in the least at the front and had found it easy to forget him.[50]

As Pillow rode on to probe the situation on his left, Union rifle and shell had fallen upon the massed marching columns of Colonel Brown's assault force. Colonel Palmer of the 18th Tennessee within minutes succeeded in deploying a reasonable facsimile of a battle line and ordered his volunteers to kneel and return the fire. This idea had been supplied by the example of the 32nd Tennessee under the personal guidance of Brown and Colonel Cook.

To the left of the road Brown's own regiment, the 3rd Tennessee, was in trouble. The first volley from the Union ranks had drawn a command from Lieutenant Colonel Thomas Gordon to lie down. The next enemy fire seconds later struck Gordon. Shortly thereafter an authoritarian voice was heard to order a retreat to cover farther to the rear. The 3rd Tennessee promptly withdrew from the struggle.

Riding over the melancholy battlefield and consulting Colonel Wharton, Pillow found further reasons for not pursuing the offensive. In his journey he had spotted shadowy groups of stragglers pointed toward Dover. Ammunition was at a premium and had to be transported by foot due to the lack of ammunition wagons on the field. Units were hopelessly confused in their makeup. Exhaustion was prevalent everywhere.

To top it all off, Pillow encountered Forrest on his way back to reform his scattered and jaded brigade. The cavalryman told of the fresh detachments of the enemy he had met in a strong position. In addition Pillow, through observation, inferred that the cavalry would not be a potent military force for some hours to come. He proceeded toward the crackle of Buckner's fire fight.[54]

In the opening moments of the afternoon Bushrod Johnson, with the recent addition of the 20th Mississippi, renewed his frustrated attempts to outflank Cruft's brigade with Drake's detachment. The radical refusal of Cruft's right flank, however, led to a confused wandering of this semi-amorphous unit in which they made little or no contact with the enemy Union battalions.

With McClernand rallying his shattered division around the solid nuclei of Taylor's and Dresser's batteries on the last parcel of high ground east of Indian Creek, Lew Wallace steeled himself to stave off disaster. Cruft, having his position approved by McClernand, now resumed his reports to Wallace by voicing his fears that a body of Confederate sharpshooters establishing contact in the vicinity of the abandoned Union hospital was a prelude to an assault on his center. Before leaving to investigate, the general quickly wrote a pithy emergency appeal to Charles Smith for assistance in this great moment of crisis.

As elements of Thayer's brigade continued to exchange volleys with the right and center of his striking arm, Brigadier John Brown wasted no time rushing to his left where the companies had retired a considerable distance in some confusion. Not without difficulty the colonel succeeded in stemming the tide of retreat in his former regiment. Finding its commander bothered by his wound, Brown placed the 3rd under the trusted Major Nat Cheairs.[55]

By this time the situation was clarifying itself rapidly. The volume of fire was doing a marvelous job of clearing no man's land of visual obstructions. Encouraged by the fact that the enemy on the heights was once again unloosing their barrage at a high angle which consequently passed over their heads, the 32nd and 18th Tennessee rose to their feet and initiated a steady advance.

At the end of 20 paces, however, a number of complicating factors set in. As they neared the enemy line their left flank became more exposed. Standing figures made better targets and the losses mounted, including Lieutenant Colonel W. P. Moore, who fell with his right knee horribly smashed. This left Colonel Edward Cook with no field officer to assist him. Worst of all the old-fashioned flintlocks carried by most in the two regiments were malfunctioning due to wetted priming from the snow on branches in their line of march. The line knelt once again.

Farther to the rear Buckner had observed the predicament on the left and, not being able to detect the approach of the first echelon of his reinforcements, he sent an aide to bring forward the elite 2nd Kentucky from its spot of rest.

Unknown to the Kentuckian, Pillow from another point of vantage had also witnessed the demise of the 3rd Tennessee. Spying the 14th Mississippi hurrying forward with two pieces of artillery, Pillow decided to defer his final decision on the direction of the battle until these reserves had thrown their weight on the scales.

None too happy, Colonels Cook and Palmer found themselves unable to prevent their soldiers from falling back. Just at the moment when the Federal ranks at the crest were slowly giving in, Tennesseans began complaining that they needed to wipe and dry their pieces out of range of the enemy. Even more ominously, for the third time that Saturday in Buckner's division, volunteers "reported" they had heard "an authoritarian" voice command a retreat. With the incident of the morning with Major Casseday fresh in everyone's mind, no one, not even Palmer and Cook, was in a position to deny that such an order actually had been issued.

Before Brown could return to the right of the road, the 18th and 32nd had retired as far back as the 3rd. Weapons were being refitted and details were actually on their way to collect their wounded comrades. Palmer had sent to the ammunition wagons behind the works for re-supply.

Highly irritated, Brown peremptorily ordered Cook on the right wing to send out two companies of skirmishers to ascertain whether the Union forces had really retired from their line of defense. The approaching 14th Mississippi was ordered to take the place of the 3rd Tennessee on the left.[56]

On the top of the crest Thayer held his ground. As a matter of fact, like Oglesby earlier in the day, he entertained notions of launching a bayonet attack on the heels of the Confederate withdrawal but decided against it on account of the thick brush. Battery A, however, continued to cause the Confederates no little annoyance by its sweeping of a section of the road with shell and cannister.

Under the personal direction of General Buckner, Graves unlimbered his two cannon at the top of a promontory south of the road. The Union gunners, however, lost no time in spotting this threat to their dominion. From the first the Northern missiles straddled the chosen position of the Confederate section. For the first time during the siege Graves found himself losing an artillery contest. With the disconcerting explosions all around them his men could barely concentrate on their primary task of locating and hitting the enemy battery.

Amidst all the tumult one of Graves' gunners stood motionless at his assigned task. Through the dust of powder and earth which enveloped the section he had caught sight of a party of horsemen just outside the circle of shrapnel. In the center he could distinguish a gray-haired officer with gold braid on his sleeves, lapels and hat motioning with great vehemence by his hand and then his forefinger back down the road. Immediately the gunner shouted out to Captain Graves, who with petulance at the interruption jerked his head in the direction indicated. The artillery captain was close enough and familiar enough to recognize General Pillow; without mistake he was motioning the battery section to retreat without delay from its perilous position.

Reluctantly the two companies of the 32nd Tennessee had marched forth to effect the reconnaissance demanded of them. Half-heartedly they disappeared into the woods, milled, and peered around for a while, then by orders of their captains they marched back to Colonels Brown and Cook. They could find no sign of the enemy, the captains reported dutifully.

At this time General Buckner rode up and Brown and he rode off to discuss some intelligence the general had just learned from one of his aides: General Pillow had prevented the batteries and the 41st Tennessee from leaving the entrenchments.

Having retired from the fray, Graves was now astounded to hear from the lips of Pillow himself the order to dispatch his section of guns back to the breastworks and to himself transmit this same order to the commander of the 14th Mississippi. He then heard Pillow issue a verbal order to one of his best known staff officers to instruct General Buckner to withdraw his division to the trenches. Pillow then rode off to arrange affairs on the left wing.

Palmer and Cook were locked in earnest conversation. On the strength of the "information gleaned" by Cook's skirmishers, Palmer, using to advantage the oratorical skill gained as mayor of Murfreesboro, urged Cook to place himself in readiness for their role as rear guard for the retreating Confederate army. Cook in turn gave a sudden start; in the interests of celerity his regiment's knapsacks, packed with provisions for the retreat, had been piled near the works. With no senior officer in the vicinity, the two decided it would be best for Cook to march back and get them.[57]

With matters going as they were, Buckner was not greatly chagrinned, nor did he protest or send dispatch riders in pursuit of the field general, as he received the instructions to retreat from Pillow's aide. Instead he began immediately to implement them.

Just missing Pillow by seconds, chubby General John Floyd sallied out onto the battlefield via Wynn's Ferry Road. Obviously his army was on the point of great success and he wanted to be at hand. The question of whether to initiate the retreat or to drive the enemy back to the Tennessee must now be resolved. It was time for the commander in chief to make his appearance.

Much surprised to see Floyd at this low point of the engagement, Buckner recovered quickly. His sharp eyes alertly caught the expression of dismay in the senior general's fleshy facial folds at the signs of iminent withdrawal. Craftily Buckner determined to see if he could not turn the situation to his advantage.

" I see you're retreating," observed Floyd, betraying his surprise in spite of himself.

" Yes sir, on orders of General Pillow," returned Buckner.

" I see. Do you think the situation requires a retreat? "

" No, General, I do not. We have maintained the initiative on this part of the field. We are in no danger here. My division is fully prepared to carry out its part as rear guard of the

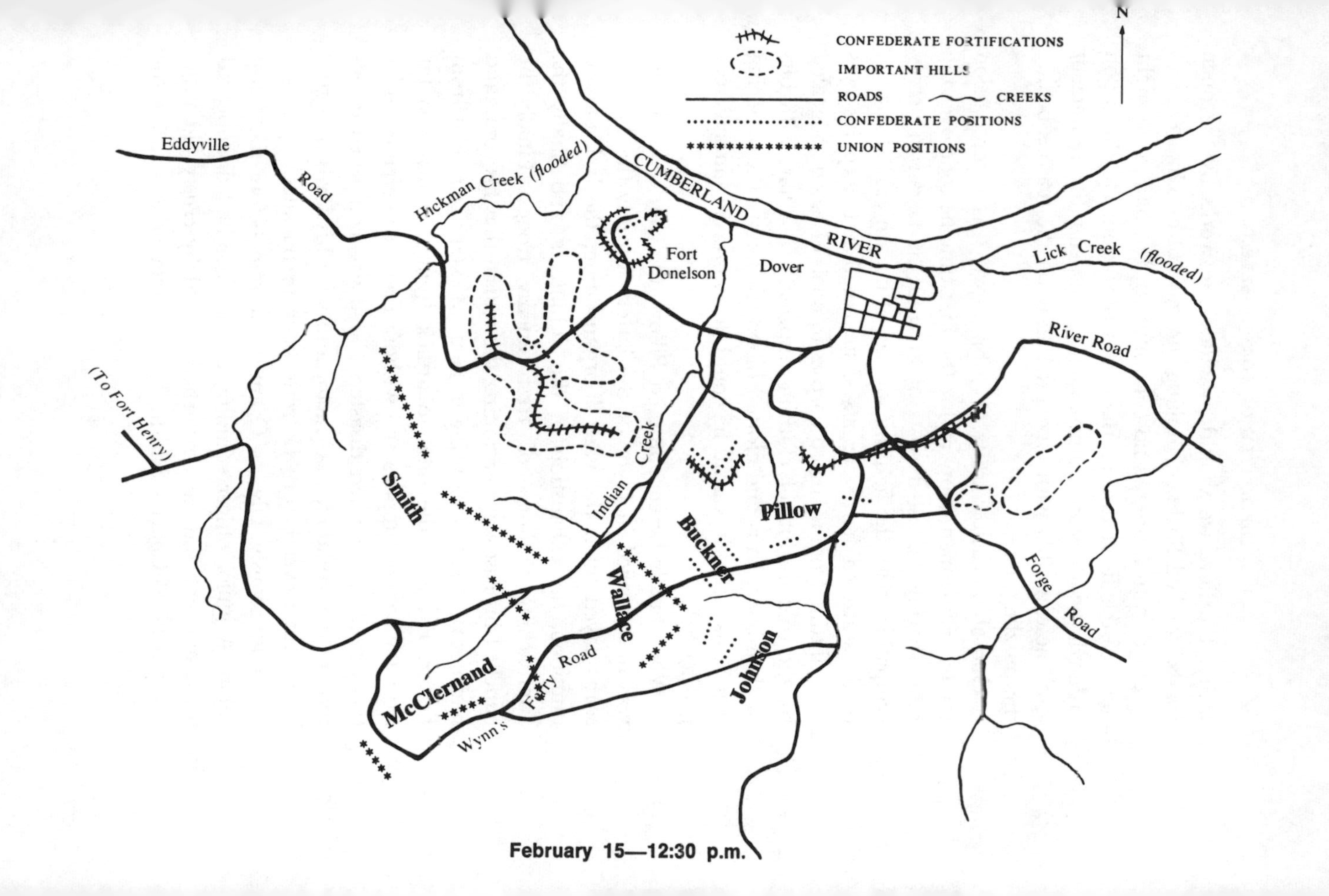

February 15—12:30 p.m.

army. I believe we should evacuate the works by the open roads," replied Buckner, making the most of his chance.

Floyd in turn uttered no commitment, but had given slight nods of the head during Buckner's recitation. He thereupon ordered the division commander to suspend the retirement until he consulted with General Pillow on the reasons behind the puzzling order.

One of the better traits of John Floyd was a compassion for his fellow man. Now as for the first time he rode over the most sharply contested plots of ground; he began to deeply sympathize with the fighting soldiers of his army. Dodging the oddly scattered horse carcasses, he could not keep his eyes from flitting from mangled corpses to pools of blood congealed by the cold, to bits of clothing, especially the hats with bits of skull bone, hair, and clotted blood sticking to them. Seeing war at its worst, it was all he could do to prevent himself from getting sick.

When finally he encountered Pillow, the courtroom setting was thus stacked in favor of the latter. Adroitly the Tennessean played upon the vast disorganization, the lack of ammunition, the exhaustion of the volunteers, and finally the approaching numbers of fresh enemy troops. Finally he clinched his case by mentioning the truism that his command had not the food or clothing to beat an extensive retreat from Dover. Exposing the men to attack from the enemy so far from the base of supplies and without prepared defenses under those conditions invited disaster. Floyd was compelled to accede to the situation, ipso facto, and with his jowls dragging longer than ever before he rode back to Buckner.[58]

Simultaneously Ulysses Grant drew rein before the Crisp cabin. A junior officer standing at the door had disappeared for a moment and then returned, joined by crusty old Brigadier General Charles Smith. The old regular was raring for action, and as Grant dismounted, he let the commanding general know about it.

Inside the house Chief of Staff J. D. Webster stared curiously at the tardy, mud-encrusted Grant. The general ignored it and asked the assemblage for the latest news. Smith handed over a message from Lew Wallace asking for reinforcements, and the erect brigadier informed Grant that his reserve brigade was being held in readiness for permission to march to Wallace's succor. Tersely Grant assented.

Webster reported that from what he had seen McClernand had been pushed back, but that no grand rout had taken place.

Grant turned back to Smith and instructed the keeper of the left wing to move up his regiments for an assault upon the Confederate entrenchments. No initiative was to be taken, however, until Grant himself had given the signal. Snatching up some newly arrived telegrams from Fort Henry, Grant strode through the door, remarked that he was taking any nearby fresh horse, and in a minute galloped off on the road toward Hickman Creek with Colonel Webster and a handful of aides.[59]

Floyd spent a few minutes explaining Pillow's viewpoint to the suddenly taciturn Buckner. Then he instructed the division commander to take his men on the long haul to the works occupied on Friday night and before. In an incredulous daze Buckner could not think of anything to say. Minutes before he had been ready to cover the army on its strategic withdrawal to the south. Now he was resuming the status quo before the battle.

General Bushrod Johnson loosened his grip on the reins of his steed. Before him enveloped the slightly cheery scene of a body of Southern troops probing the enemy lines not too far south of the just disengaged action on the Wynn's Ferry

Road. A reception committee of Cruft's brigade awaited this reconnaissance in force, among them some 50 separated bluecoats from the 17th Kentucky who found themselves defending the site of Friday's night campsite. With some chagrin several of these detached Federal Kentuckians observed that the coats and blankets thrown over tree limbs only a few hours before to dry were now being riddled by lead pellets.

The Confederate brigadier was not long in noting that the weary, half-hearted efforts on this sector were to be of no avail, and he sent an aide to Floyd for reinforcements. As the skirmish progressed, a mounted messenger pulled up beside him. Orders from the commanding general were for Johnson to accompany the officer to the presence of General Floyd.

By this time John Floyd had become a bundle of activity. At that moment he sat near the telegraph station at the fort dashing off a message to his superior in Nashville. He informed Johnston that the battle was still in progress, although the positions of the Union army had been "forced." Two hundred prisoners and four pieces of artillery had been captured. Losses had been heavy on both sides, he reported, and although the opposing army was bringing up reinforcements for counterassault, it must be considered, according to Floyd, that Confederate arms had been successful.

On the arrival of Johnson shortly before one oclock, Floyd asked politely how the battle was coming on the left flank. Aggressively Johnson stated that reinforcements should be assembled to continue the attack. Firmly Floyd informed his subordinate of the factors influencing him to the contrary. Johnson in turn became upset at the prospect of abandoning the hard-won territory. In the course of the consequent discussion the commander of the left wing offered the suggestion that at least a brigade be left in possession of the blood-soaked field. Sympathetically Floyd relented and issued instructions for Colonel Drake's brigade to take up defensive positions outside of the entrenchments and for the remainder of the units to withdraw within the works.[60]

The Confederate offensive of February 15, 1862, had run its course.

12

Diversion and Reclamation

ULYSSES GRANT AND HIS SMALL ESCORT HURRIED ALONG THE road leading circuitously to the scene of battle. He didn't have to ride far to discover evidence of a shaken army. Individual stragglers skulked here and there on the skirts of the rutted trail. Soon clusters of the more bold of the fastest runners began to manifest themselves on the roadway. Aides were detached to round these up. Later the rear areas of the overwhelmed brigades were reached. Here organization was at its loosest. Men of the ranks stood around talking with the officers, who were making no attempt to refit them or to re-establish military discipline.

Grant paused in his journey to talk with some of his men. In the free atmosphere of a volunteer army the soldiers did not hesitate to inform Grant of what was wrong: Other units had left them in the lurch. The regiment had run out of ammunition. The Rebels had more than enough ammunition. There were too many Secessionists. One youngster observed offhandedly that the Rebels also had plenty to eat.

Grant's trained military mind warned him that there was something of significance here. He singled out the volunteer and asked him to repeat his statement. This done, the general asked him how he knew. Others interrupted by shouting that at one point they had repulsed a Confederate assault and driven the enemy back. They had found Southern haversacks well stocked with rations. For the first time Grant had concrete evidence on the objective of the enemy offensive.

The general turned to his chief of staff, "Shout to them to get into line. They are trying to escape and we must not let them."

Setting their spurs to their horses the party rode on, Webster calling out, "Fill your cartridge boxes quick and get into line. The enemy is trying to escape and he must not be permitted to do so." While there was no cheering on that bleak day, soldiers of McClernand's brigades responded readily and positively.[1]

Colonel John Thayer had become slightly unsettled at the rapidly accumulating addition to his brigade in the midst of battle. Only the day before he had been serving as a regimental commander, and now he had charge of a half-dozen regiments. He resolved this difficulty by leaving each regimental leader to fight the battle on his own front while he directed Lieutenant Colonel McCord of his own 1st Nebraska and Battery A on the road. Thus, among other things, Thayer was not aware of the efforts of two guns of Taylor's battery with cannister furnished by Battery A, which aided in stemming the Rebel tide at the last minute, and that other regiments than his 1st Nebraska suffered casualties.[2]

Colonel Palmer of Buckner's division had been startled by the peremptory order to immediately retire to the entrenchments he had held on Friday; not all of the wounded had yet been collected. Nevertheless he hastened in the footsteps of the 32nd Tennessee. On the way Palmer encountered the main body of the 48th Tennessee and 27th Alabama, which had been sent by Heiman as support for Buckner. On learning of Palmer's instructions the regiments turned the heads of their columns back up the hill.[3]

Pillow's portion of the army was not making a textbook retreat. Across the length and breadth of the battlefield 400 wounded Southerners were left to suffer unaided. The Confederate columns streamed by the rows of frigid corpses of both armies without pausing to detach burial parties. On reaching the trenches most of them sank to the ground in exhaustion.

Perhaps little blame can be placed upon anyone, except Floyd and Pillow, for this too-hasty departure. Reasons for the retreat were not in most cases forthcoming to subordinates, and it might be logical to assume that this was a mere interlude to reorganize the army for evacuation. Under these circumstances neglect could be excused.[4]

As General Grant rode through the thickening crowds of his beaten army, he quickly collected his thoughts. While his men were not cheering him, they were responding to orders and discipline. He had noted that many who justifiably might be expected to be lingering around the hospitals were reporting for active duty in spite of buckshot wounds. This was indicative of a nucleus of good morale.

Reaching Indian Creek, Grant heard that the Confederates had long since broken off action. The general motioned Webster to his side and cried, "Some of our men are pretty badly demoralized, but the enemy must be more so, for he has attempted to force his way out but has fallen back. The one who attacks first now will be victorious and the enemy will have to be in a hurry if he gets ahead of me."

In spite of this cocky statement, Grant was still unsure of himself, as shown by the letter which he proceeded to dictate:

Camp near Fort Donelson, February 15, 1862

Andrew H. Foote

Commanding Officer Gunboat Flotilla:

If all the gunboats that can will make their appearance to the enemy it may secure us a victory. Otherwise all may be defeated. A terrible conflict ensued in my absence, which has demoralized a portion of my command, and I think the enemy is much more so. If the gunboats do not show themselves, it will reassure the enemy and still further demoralize our troops. I must order a charge to save appearances. I do not expect the gunboats to go into action, but to make appearance and throw a few shells at long range.

U. S. Grant
Brigadier General, Commanding

Apparently thinking only in terms of holding the field and preventing the withdrawal of the Confederate army from Dover, Grant sped toward the front, which he reached at 1:30.[5]

McClernand had ridden forward to consult with Lew Wallace on the situation. They saw the approach of Grant and without delay rode toward him. To their eyes Grant was a welcome, yet quizzical sight. In spite of being the commanding general, his detailing of associates to round-ups had left him almost unattended. He and his steed were covered with the mud of the trail. Wallace, however, noted something which stuck in his mind. Grant was clutching a sheaf of papers in his hand; these were the same he had taken from the Crisp house.

McClernand, in spite of his lack of success that morning, could not resist furthering his ambitions and growled, "The army wants a head."

"It would seem so," murmured Grant, returning a sharp glance to denote that the insolence had not been unnoticed.

Because of the objective which he had detected in Confederate tactics, Grant first directed a retirement beyond range of the last enemy artillery positions and the throwing up of breastworks. The purpose, he explained, was to maintain the siege, revitalize the right and center, and await the arrival of all the current reinforcements.

His face flushed slightly, however, and he crushed the wrinkled messages in his hand when McClernand replied that the road to Nashville was completely open to Southern forces.

Grant responded in his normal tones. "Gentlemen, the position on the right must be retaken." At that he turned and galloped off toward Charles Smith's positions, leaving the two divisional commanders astounded but assuming they were to effect these orders with their own resources.[6]

This time Grant did not bother about roads. With the assistance of those staff officers who could keep up with him, he raced cross country to give General Smith the order he knew could bear no further delay. His hopes for the success of the Second Division in capturing any enemy territory were slim. If they and the river gunboats could only divert Floyd's attention long enough to give Wallace and McClernand the edge in reclaiming the portal to the road to Nashville, success would be achieved. From the dismal results of the early days of the siege and from the detachment to Wallace of Smith's brigade, which Grant was now passing, little more could realistically be expected.

At 1:45 Grant found C. F. Smith awaiting him expectantly, sitting under a tree. Grant informed him that the situation on the right had deteriorated and his division must take Fort Donelson. Smith responded, "I will do it," and departed, after dispatching his aides on their already assigned errands. Grant could not resist staying to enjoy the show.

John McClernand was listening to his Captain Stewart relate the findings of the scout the aide had just made with a picked body of cavalry. In the sectors he had observed, Stewart said, the Rebel infantry was falling back in noticeable disarray with the officers apparently trying to stem the tide.

McClernand recalled Major Mudd of the 2nd Illinois Cavalry to reconnoiter to the right of the line. Colonel Leonard Ross, beardless, blond, and efficient, of the 17th Illinois, reported for duty and was given supervision of his own unit and the 49th Illinois. McClernand then rode forward to consult with Lew Wallace on the implementation of Grant's orders.[7]

The men of the Second Division had champed at the bit for hours while their comrades on the right fought and died. Now at last with orders to engage the enemy their commander, General Charles F. Smith, was ready with a plan of battle. His divisional reserve, the brigade of Morgan Smith, was now en route to bolster the right wing of the army. Cook's and Lauman's brigades would have to do the job.

Aides arrived at the command post of Colonel John Cook of Smith's Third Brigade. Cook actually hoped they brought word of action. Earlier in the morning with the battle raging to the east, he had been ordered to send the 52nd Indiana farther to the left to cover the roadway exiting from the far right of the enemy entrenchments to forestall any sortie from that sallyport. Beyond that the morning had been quiet on his front.

Now he had word from his chief to send out large numbers of skirmishers to distract the Southerners and guard the flank while Smith himself took the remainder of the division on a grand assault on the breastworks to the left. Thereupon Cook sent his own messengers to alert the regimental colonels.

Smith himself huddled with Colonel Jacob Lauman on the storming of the ridge. For shock troops Lauman personally recommended the 2nd Iowa which had been itching for enemy blood since setting foot on Tennessee soil. Abruptly Smith told him to proceed with the details while he supervised the the positioning of the batteries.[8]

In Dover Brigadier General Gideon Pillow paused as he dismounted in the rutted road fronting the Rice House, his new headquarters. On and below the bluff facing the landing sat and loitered multitudes of Confederates absent without leave from their regiments and gathered around improvised campfires. Pillow called his remaining aides to his side and instructed them to go among these skulkers and disperse them. Weary from exertion and lack of sleep, Pillow took himself into the building and upstairs to bed.[9]

At the appearance of Colonel Morgan Smith with his two regiments, Lew Wallace appealed to McClernand for them to be assigned to his division, which would in turn retake the territory ordered by Grant. After all, he argued, these regiments had formerly been under his jurisdiction and he knew their strengths and weaknesses well. McClernand, who knew better than anyone else that his own division was in no position to assume the initiative, offered no argument.

At that moment a courier from Major Mudd made an appearance. The enemy, he reported, had been discovered holding a position in some strength on the right. Sending some of his officers to bring Morgan Smith, Wallace rode ahead with the courier as a guide. While moving through the undergrowth they were startled by a sudden succession of explosions to the left. Wallace was the first to recover. Charles Smith certainly wasted no time, he observed to an associate.

The old war horse had indeed brought about a spectacular achievement. An efficient staff system and anticipation of orders had brought the batteries to readiness by two o'clock. Meanwhile, Lauman guided the assault forces through the forest to the point of departure. Here and there Northerners in the columns pointed up to moving figures behind the barriers of earth above. Others, not of the 2nd Iowa, gaped at the formidable abatis which stood between them and their objective. Someone said, "It's too thick for a rabbit to get through."[10]

Charles Smith and his staff galloped up to the head of the column. He singled out the blond Colonel Tuttle with his line-like mustache. "Can you go into the entrenchments?" his look fixed the Iowan.

Tuttle's eyes returned as much as they received. He responded determinedly that with support there would be no doubt of it.

Meanwhile after a feat of marching unrivaled on that day of military movements, Roger Hanson's 2nd Kentucky was drawing up at the intersection of the "X" forming the right of Buckner's divisional defenses. Only a little more than an hour before the 2nd had been stationed on the Wynn's Ferry Road within the former enemy lines. The circuitous return trip was more than equivalent to marching the full length of the Confederate defenses. Now uncertain over the sudden Union bombardment, Hanson rode to the rear to round up numerous stragglers and to seek instructions.

The impatient Iowans of the 2nd were strung out from their double column by General Smith himself. Five companies stood shoulder to shoulder in the first line. Behind them 30 paces formed a rank equal in size. To the right Lauman was organizing the 52nd and 25th Indiana, both drawn to the rear of the forward position of the 2nd Iowa. The 7th and 14th Iowa acted as a reserve.

The entrenchments facing Lauman and Smith had been made formidable both by nature and Southern volunteer and slave labor. Although the slope was steep the distance to be transversed was comparatively safe. This was made possible by the absence of Confederate artillery, a fact which had been noticed and taken advantage of by Smith. In the rifle pits 130 Confederates were spread thin over 1,000 feet of front. With their own point of attack selected, 650 spirited Iowans with ample support prepared to grapple for the ridge.

The order came: "Fix bayonets! Forward and without firing," and passed from mouth to mouth down the two lines. As the pointed musket extensions whipped forth, the sun burst through the overcast, causing a sparkling glint on the blades. Many companies took the caps off their muskets. Uncontrollable now in their enthusiasm, the Iowans hailed this as an omen that they could not fail. Their disgrace would be redeemed at last.

To insure that this would remain a bayonet attack ramrod-stiff General Smith guided his war horse out in front of Tuttle's first five companies. Behind him in breathtaking cadence the 2nd Iowa relentlessly swept up the hill.

In the right flanking companies of the parallel lines there was a degree of minor confusion. A stone's throw away strode a solitary company, obviously not of their regiment. Actually it was Captain Rheinlander and his skirmish unit from the 25th Indiana. Just minutes before Lauman had jerked the 25th out of its position on the right and had marched it to closer support of the 2nd. Rheinlander, left without support or instructions, gamely kept abreast of the wall of steel on the left.[11]

The Tennesseans on the ridge were not asleep. The strange singing whine of bullets began to be heard over the slackening roar of Union artillery. Clipped twigs from limbs overhead pelted the Federal volunteers struggling to keep their ranks in order. A few of the balls had telling effect. Here and there Iowa hearts missed a few beats but the ever-present view of General Smith staring the enemy down and glimpses of that ferocious white mustache gave everyone courage. Still the Union masses had not unleashed a shot.

A few yards before the abatis the Confederates released their worst. Sensing the hesitation in the shock troops, Smith whirled around, at the same time doffing his forage cap and drawing his saber. "No flinching now, my lads," he said, placing the cap on the tip of the blade. "Here—this is the way! Come on!"

At the same moment as Major Chipman plunged forward into the earth with a wicked wound, Tuttle shouted instructions for the front rank to extend to the right and left so as to locate and take advantage of weak spots in the wooden barricade. The Rebels fired like machines. Captain Cloutman stumbled dead into the abatis. Captain Slaymaker hacked his path through the obstacles but fell with a body wound among the small advance party on the northern side. He died in minutes. Soldiers were shot in increasing numbers, sprinkling the incline with their bodies.

General Charles Smith, however, first emerged unscathed on the Southern side of the abatis. With the hat still on the point of his sword he waved the Iowans on through. They came too, axes and gun butts and bayonets finally blazing enough trails. Now while Lieutenant Colonel Baker and the second half of the 2nd paused on the downslope portion of the abatis, Tuttle made use of his hulking figure to secure a reformation of the advance line. The men had responded immediately, however, and no orders had to be issued. Now one deep, great cheer burst forth from the lungs of the 300 men as they charged uphill at a run.

In the rifle pits Captains Carson, Semple, and Martin and Major Turner took one look at the odds. Discounting the psychological edge the Yankees now held, they were outnumbered a good two-to-one by the shock force alone. With no reinforcements or assistance from Colonel Head it was decided to withdraw or be overrun.

Many Confederates were not quick enough. The confident Iowans burst into the works, keeping their perfect discipline, and bayoneted and clubbed those who did not drop their muskets immediately. In the center of the melee was James Tuttle, shouting, "Give them hell, boys."

General Smith had ridden back through the abatis once the 2nd had commenced its final charge. The second rank was now on its way to their support and the 52nd Indiana was marching raggedly up in reserve. Smith waved the 25th Indiana forward and sped to the east to bring up the 7th Iowa, the 14th Iowa, and the 12th Iowa from Cook's brigade.[12]

At the Union landing the *Pittsburgh* had just departed with Foote aboard. Commander Dove, now senior naval officer, read Grant's written plea. The flotilla was not in shape for offensive action and it would take time to prepare it. The clock read 2:30 P.M.

General Lew Wallace by this time had guided the brigade of Morgan Smith to a ridge north of Bufford Hollow, occupied by Fry's evacuated hospital. The two regiments drew into line of battle on the southern face of the ridge. Opposite them across a ravine rose the bluffs reportedly sheltering the advanced positions of the enemy, just south of the Wynn's Ferry Road. By then Wallace and McClernand had had second thoughts about their tactical dispositions and had decided their hand needed strengthening. In addition to support on the right flank from Cruft the two division commanders planned to advance artillery, supported by Ross's two regiments and three more just added to Thayer's brigade, to protect the left.[13]

In advance of the north arm of the "X" with his left just a little west of the intersection of that figure, Colonel Roger Hanson had placed the 2nd Kentucky in line. Behind on the crest of the arm mustered the 18th Tennessee, just arrived. The remnants of the right wing of the 30th Tennessee were shunted off to the south arm of the "X" to hold the trenches against Cook's developing threats.

Charles Smith's temper was getting the better of him. The

volunteer regiments were not as quick as he wished in marching to Tuttle's assistance. A volley of oaths passed his lips and was spread forth by the full weight of his lung power. The activity had brought with it a certain dryness in the mouth, and the general motioned for an aide to take out his canteen.

Not without some difficulty the 52nd Indiana had gained the works and the 25th Indiana had rejoined its detached company within the breastworks. One hour after the inception of the attack General Smith arrived to survey the former enemy defenses. They were good—logs on top with earthen breastworks beneath and slits in between. The general rode up to Tuttle, instructed him to take charge of the units within the captured works while he prodded the reserves into line, and rode back down the ridge.

Tuttle saw that Confederate reinforcements were obviously building up and knew what he must do. The north and east portions of the "X" had a certain dominance over the rifle pits now in his possession and should be seized for offensive and defensive purposes. He recalled his Iowans from their firing positions back to the crest of the ridge. He then pivoted his line so as to direct it toward the confluence of the "X," now in Southern hands. Here the Federals would dominate the road to the fort and be in a position to isolate it from the remainder of the garrison.

The Iowans plunged forward. Half of them strode along the hump and crest of the eastern arm; the left half of the attackers advanced through the upper reaches of the ravine which served the Confederacy as a natural moat. While their immediate opponents consisted of a crack regiment of the Rebel army, these Confederate troops did not possess the morale impetus which imbued the victorious Union striking force. The combatants of the 2nd Kentucky, while equal in number to the Iowans, were also jaded by the march from Wynn's Ferry Road.

The skirmish was short. Hanson was caught in advance of the best defensive positions. The rampaging 2nd Iowa this time let go a devastating burst of fire. The Kentuckians fled into the arms of Palmer's 18th Tennessee up the hill. After some fighting the Tennesseans too were pushed back until they stood on the river side of the crest of the northern arm. Tuttle, seeing the approach of numerous groups of Southern reinforcements, disposed his men to defend their newly won gains.

Smith meanwhile had been lending the benefit of his experience with the Confederate abatis to Colonel William Shaw of the 14th Iowa. Sections of timber had suddenly interposed themselves to their route and the general made a wide detour as the 14th struggled on up the hill. As Tuttle was securing his second ridge, Shaw and Smith met once more, this time within the rifle pits. The old veteran was quite pleased with the turn of events and swung his canteen by its strap over his head. Letting out a tremendous holler of joy, he offered the puzzled colonel a drink from his canteen.[14]

To the east activity had renewed itself. Captain Jasper Dresser had on orders returned to his battery position of that morning, accompanied by Ross's brigade. As he began a probing of the Confederate works, he found to his dismay that the Rebel artillery was opposite him in as great a strength as they had been at any time during the siege. Immediately all of them concentrated upon him and Dresser found himself compelled to expend ammunition at a rate more rapid than he had anticipated. A shell burst not far from the ear of a sergeant as he was pointing a gun, and the noncom slumped with a concussion. Two other gunners were shortly incapacitated with wounds. Ten minutes after he had initiated the engagement Dresser hitched up his guns and beat a retreat, feeling himself lucky to have escaped with so little damage.

Even though the high command was in a state of confusion which had negated the results of a morning of fighting, the

Confederates were not long in reacting to the incursion on their sensitive right flank. Colonel John Head spurred his horse cross country to bring up reinforcements from the garrison of the fort. General Buckner had arrived with the equivalent of a full battery of artillery and the 14th Mississippi and 3rd Tennessee. These, thrown into the fray, checked any further encroachment on the part of the Federal 2nd Division.

Union Colonel John Cook, having thrown forth his skirmishers, in force, trained his field glasses upon the section of the entrenchments within his view. Sweeping them along the crest, he was overjoyed to discern the national colors waving over the works near the sallyport which had bothered the Federals so. At the right of his line General Grant himself approached Colonel Crafts Wright of the 13th Missouri and suggested that in preparing for battle his troops divest themselves of blankets and knapsacks.[15]

Acting with dispatch and with his judgment at its keenest, Buckner placed Captain Porter, with the section of the battery he had brought with him, at his former position, which they reached in spite of a rapid infantry fire which killed many horses and forced them to haul their guns up by hand, and Captain Graves with a section on the Confederate part of the ridge that was being contested with the 2nd Iowa. Thus Graves from his frontal position was able to deal with the immediate threat, and Porter from his redan at the sallyport could strike out at support and reserves proceeding to the engagement.

Head called out Colonel Bailey and Colonel Sugg to bring their troops south from the fort at the double-quick. One reservation was that the 50th Tennessee was to leave half of its numbers within the fort to prevent any attempted coup on the fort itself. On his return to his regiment Head purposely kept his eye peeled for Buckner. Seeing the general busy, however, and recalling his disheartening treatment of the early morning hours, the Tennessee colonel decided not to consult his superior.

The effects of the Southern artillery bombardment were immediate. The organization of the supporting detachments in the rifle pits broke down as volunteers scattered for shelter. General Smith's attention consequently was diverted to silencing the enfilading cannon of Porter. Cook, realizing the seriousness of the barrage, sent a courier to Grant to seek permission to storm and sieze the battery.

As the Confederates lashed back with artillery and musketry Tuttle and his men began to suffer exceedingly. Four Confederate regiments, outnumbering the 2nd Iowa four-to-one massed on his front, firing into him all the while. On Tuttle's left the flank lay exposed, as the Iowans had not enough men to man the entire north leg of the "X." Even now it was reported that a body of troops was bearing on that sector from the north. To top it all off a lead ball passed through the colonel's sleeve and glove and struck the hilt of his sword with such force that Tuttle's arm was wrenched and paralyzed as the sword rebounded over his head.[16]

As the struggle drew toward a climax in the west, General Lew Wallace studied the position of the Confederate rear guard with care. General Grant had just come and gone, repeating his order to attack the Rebel hill. (Wallace could not resist harboring the suspicion that all this activity was just to keep the enemy occupied until nightfall would bring relief to a battered Union army.)

Through the center of the valley and up the northern side of the slope along Bufford Hollow ran a spur road off of Wynn's Ferry. The Rebel hill blocked access to this intersection. A sizable clearing bordered the road and the foot of the hill and as usual the territory to be transversed was defended by nature with thick underbrush and dense woods.

Owing to the nature of the country and lacking time for

complete reconnaissance of the flanks, Wallace decided to use Smith's brigade, in which he and many others had special pride and complete faith, as storm troops. The attack would be a direct approach.

The general trotted his horse down the line vigorously shouting, "You have been wanting a fight—you have got it. Hell's before you." The acting brigadier calmly drew on his cigar in an effort to light it, puffed on it, and turned to ask his brigade if they were ready. "Forward it is, then."

Supports were not immediately prepared. To the west stern-faced Colonel Leonard Ross had his hands full with the grape, cannister, and shrapnel raining down on him from Maney and his two associate batteries. Cruft had not the time to move all of his regiments to the right of Smith and had to follow the best he could the precipitous advance of the Missourian.

The 8th Missouri started off on the road from Bufford Hollow while the 11th Indiana moved to the left. The 44th Indiana of Cruft's command raced to catch up with the Missourians, while half of the 31st Indiana struggled to keep pace with the 11th. The bulk of Cruft's brigade marched as originally planned as flankers to the right, but behind schedule.

Through the open area Smith protected himself with only a token company of skirmishers, but as they reached the forest two flanking companies on either side of the front line were added as reinforcements. A quarter of the way up the ridge they took their first volley.[17]

Colonel Joseph Drake of the 4th Mississippi commanded in addition to his own regiment the 15th Arkansas, the 16th Alabama, and a Tennessee battalion, all of which totaled 1300 men that morning. After the attrition of the battle Drake found himself slightly inferior in numbers to the fresh and better-armed shock forces of Morgan Smith. Nonetheless, with the advantage of a strong natural defensive position, he resolved to hold the field and sent a messenger to General Johnson for reinforcements.

Bushrod Johnson had caught the crackle of musket fire and observers in the works had verified that there was substantial Federal activity in the vicinity of Drake's hill. Word, however, had also reached Johnson of the desperate engagement in Buckner's divisional sector. The commander of the left flank was reluctant to commit further troops to an area which might prove later in the day to be subsidiary. Instead he called for Forrest with the intention of dispatching him with a portion of the cavalry to reconnoiter and give assistance to Drake.

The 8th Missouri had been stopped cold. Young Captain Swarthout had been killed while doing his utmost to keep his company from being hit by the first volley. The Missourians were in a state of inertia, wanting to go neither forward nor backward.

To the left the 11th Indiana and the five companies of the 31st Indiana were stalled by distance and the terrain.

Morgan Smith himself had been momentarily distracted when an enemy bullet, fired high as usual when aimed downslope, had shot off his just-lighted cigar close to the lips. Calmly he took out a replacement and suddenly noted that he had no light. He called out for a match. A soldier ran up with one. Smith nodded, "Thank you. Take your place now." He nudged his horse up to the line where he ordered the men along its entire length to lie down; he dismounted himself.[18]

In front of Buckner the situation was growing graver for the Union. The 2nd Iowa was absorbing enormous losses. The color guard mustered not an unwounded man. Sergeant Doolittle, the color bearer, had been pierced by four musket balls. Corporal Pope had then snatched up the fallen staff, but in minutes tumbled down stone dead. Corporal Churchill took his place but was grievously wounded. Corporal Twombly took the flag from Churchill and shortly he was knocked down by a spent ball. Twombly, however, rose and waved the colors aloft once more.

On the left flank of the 2nd Iowa the reserves of about 500 garrison troops from the fort had arrived under Colonel Bailey. Fortunately for the North the 7th Iowa had reached this sector simultaneously. As Colonels Bailey and Parrott exchanged bursts of fire with the Iowans having the crest advantage, Captain Reuben Ross of the fort artillery directed two detachments to assist the infantry with cannon fire. As Ross himself brought up a howitzer with one gun crew, Captain Stankieuriz initiated a well-directed bombardment from a 9-pounder situated in the southwest walls.

Colonel James McPherson listened patiently while an excited aide from General Smith tried to picture graphically the havoc being wreaked by the Confederate guns. McPherson relayed the request for artillery support to Grant, while he personally instructed a section of two 10-pound Parrots to move forward and engage Porter. He then rode off to find Smith, who meanwhile had ordered Stone's Missouri battery to bring their guns into the works.

On the Federal firing line Colonel Tuttle had stepped atop a log and with his unparalyzed arm was beckoning to an Indiana regiment in the ravine behind him to hasten their ascent. At that moment a solid cannonball from one of Graves' pieces smashed into the log with all its impact. The timber jumped and spun, knocking the colonel off of his feet and sending him crashing ignominiously to earth on his back. His nearby subordinates rushed to his aid and Tuttle bravely tried to shrug off the effects of the accident, but by his stooped form everyone knew he was in pain.

At the same time a crisis occurred on the left. Stankieuriz and his 9-pounder had accurately maintained a steady barrage upon the 7th Iowa, which had lost the flower of its men at Belmont. Confederate Colonel Bailey had seen signs of weaken-

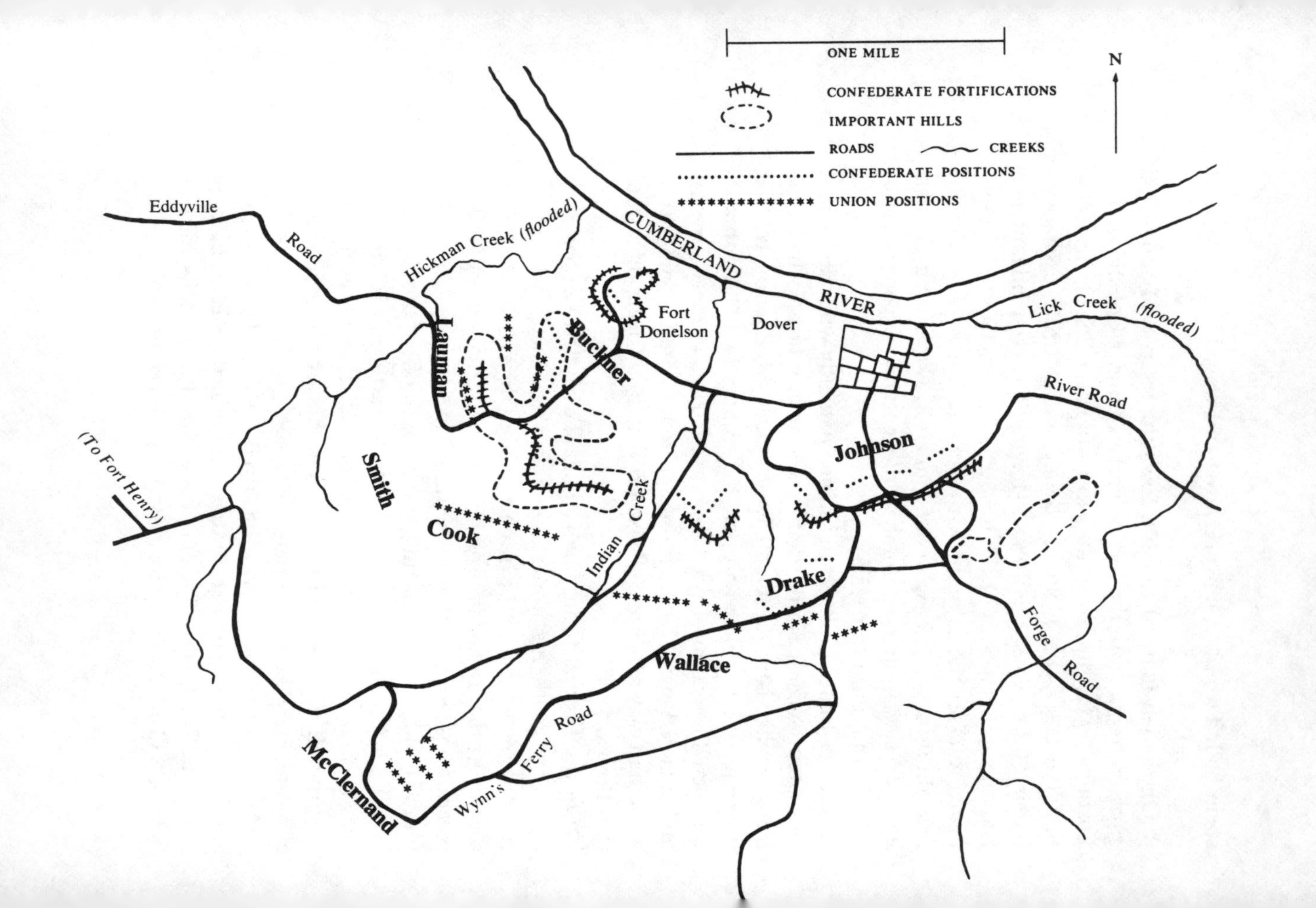
ONE MILE
N
CONFEDERATE FORTIFICATIONS
IMPORTANT HILLS
ROADS
CREEKS
CONFEDERATE POSITIONS
UNION POSITIONS
Eddyville Road
Hickman Creek (flooded)
CUMBERLAND RIVER
Lick Creek (flooded)
Fort Donelson
Dover
River Road
Lauman
Buckner
Johnson
Smith
Cook
Indian Creek
Drake
Forge Road
Wallace
(To Fort Henry)
McClernand
Wynn's Ferry Road

ing in the Union line and a slight advance brought their withdrawal. The Southerners had recaptured the end of the northern arm of the "X."[19]

In the ravine into which the 7th had retreated, chaos ensued. Because of Porter's enfilading barrage the 52nd Indiana had refused to advance beyond the first line of rifle pits. Now as the Iowans rushed downhill into their ranks, Confederates began to fire into their midst from the crest of the ridge. Naturally the volunteers of the Union replied in kind, but the smoke of battle made them careless and non-discriminating. The precedent of musket fire swept from left to right and before long some of the supports were firing into the backs of the 2nd Iowa.

Tuttle, still bent over from his back injury, became depressed. Ammunition was running extremely low and now his recruits were falling in large numbers to balls from their own army. Unable to render the activity which might remedy the situation, and with his left flank hard pressed, Tuttle ordered a retreat before his regiment could break of its own accord. It was a few minutes after 4:00 P.M.[20]

Colonel Nathan Bedford Forrest conferred with Colonel Drake. A brief scouting mission had informed the cavalryman of the masses of Ross's brigade edging in on Drake's right. On being asked, Drake reported that the frontal attack was making slow progress in the vicinity of the road, but that losses had been very slight. The old problem of ammunition had reappeared, however, and a prolonged engagement would require more of it or a retreat.

A perennial fighter, Forrest had seen enough of bloodshed that Saturday. He and his command had ridden back and forth across the battlefield more than once that day. At each turn Southern arms had been successful. Then the army had beat a quick retreat from the battlefield, leaving only a weak rear guard to watch over the field of spoils. He told Drake that

Johnson had sent him to scout and to act as the only assistance which could be lent from the works. He then informed the infantryman that he was taking all of his men back to General Johnson to report that he had advised Drake to retreat. Forrest then remounted and disappeared.

Drake pulled out gradually, hoping not to let the Federals recognize the diminished firepower. In his front the assault forces had crept forward practically on their bellies for nearly an hour but still had not achieved the upper hand.

On the right Cruft had enlisted the assistance of the 4th Illinois Cavalry, which dismounted eight troops of horsemen with their Sharp carbines in support of Cruft's flank sweep. Pressing forward at right angles to the Confederate positions, Cruft was crestfallen to see the last remnants of the Southern rear guard trotting off into the underbrush.

With thc timely reinforcement of the 44th Indiana, Morgan Smith reached the brow of his objective hill. On the left the 11th Indiana pulling in a pincers movement was able to snag two Rebels of the rear guard as prisoners. Confederate artillerymen, however, had their eye on this exposed encroachment. Their first shells were accurate and served to temporarily break up this aggressive assemblage. Their shells also had an undesired effect: the two prisoners were killed by shrapnel.[21]

Wounded Lieutenant Churchill of the 11th Illinois had passed a long uncomfortable afternoon. Once he had talked to a passing Southern cavalryman with a Colt carbine with a revolving chamber. More recently he heard a resumption of musket fire and suddenly a large body of retreating Confederates passed over and by him. Churchill held up his arm and no Rebel stepped on him.

As Smith's brigade followed Drake's men, Churchill saw the Confederates continue north through a ravine to a level spot along the Wynn's Ferry Road, where they regrouped. Their fire drove the Federals south of the position where

Churchill lay. An exchange of fire progressed over his recumbent form.[22]

A long train of men proceeded from left to right within the Confederate defenses. General John Floyd had been apprised of the danger in Smith's probe near the fort. The 42nd Tennessee from Heiman's brigade, stationed in Drake's trenches, and Simonton's brigade, double-timed through the slush and mud on their way to the hills on the right.

The 2nd Iowa had reached the rifle pits (of which they used the front for shelter) in a sorry condition but proud of their record. Thirty per cent of their number—33 dead and 164 wounded—had paid the penalty for winning their objective and almost winning the battle. Colonel Tuttle turned the command over to Lieutenant Colonel Baker.

Colonel Lauman, his languid eyes finally showing some fire, and General Smith attempted to rally the mixed regiments and regain the lost ground. The 52nd Indiana, badly demoralized, was ordered to the rear and replaced with their compatriots of the 25th. First it was necessary to overcome the two batteries which were raining death and fear among them. The Union batteries of Stone and Welker were now situated within the works and were given plenty of infantry support.[23]

With pleasure Smith observed Cook's brigade, given permission by Grant, advancing on the eastern part of Buckner's defenses along with the two Parrott guns supplied by McPherson. Within rifle range of the trenches but on the safe side of the abatis they forced a fire fight with Head of the 30th Tennessee, and Cook of the 32nd Tennessee, and Porter.

At this point the blue aggressor scored an advantage of sorts. From the east or from the south a Minie ball penetrated the artillery redan bordering the sallyport. It dug through the thigh of Captain Porter. As the battery commander was carried off to the hospital, a beardless youth of distinguished Kentucky name stepped forward to take charge of the guns. It would be Lieutenant Morton's battery for the time being.

In the valley south of the rifle pits a house, now surrounded by Union ambulances, had been turned into a hospital. In the line of fire of Graves' battery, it had come in for some shelling. One Yankee with more than a little courage climbed to the roof and waved a red flag—the Red Cross of the day.

Colonel J. J. Woods had just brought his 12th Iowa to Lauman's assistance. Porter's grape had hailed on his troops just as they were threading their way through the abatis and eight or ten of the regiment's number had been carried back to the hospital. There was little respite within the works. The abashed vanguard of the division was continuing to flinch before the crossfire set up by the Southern infantry across the ravine and Graves' battery now on the heights previously vacated by Tuttle. Only by constant encouragement and alertness was Woods able to maintain discipline in the 12th in the face of this demoralization on the battle line.[24]

General Ulysses S. Grant was not oblivious to the difficulties which were greeting General Smith. Through his field glasses he had observed the retrograde movement of the 2nd Iowa. His trained eye also had detected that everything was not running smoothly within the captured rifle pits. Apparently no assistance had been lent by a naval demonstration on the river and the army was showing signs of unravelling on both flanks. Impressed by the havoc being wreaked by the Confederate artillery, Grant called for his chief of staff, Colonel Webster, and directed him to ride to the right of the lines and order all Union forces there to retire beyond the range of enemy cannon and to throw up defensive breastworks. This, Grant hoped, would allow his roughly handled divisions to prevent a general retreat during the remaining minutes of daylight and to recuperate during the night. Then, with the aid of all the fresh reinforcements they could take whatever action would be necessary in the morning.[25]

Unaware of Grant's grave estimate of his defensive posture, Charles Smith struggled to restore order from the confusion among his followers. There was some respite when Stone's battery knocked out one of Graves' pieces. The 12th Iowa was finally pulled into the firing line and began to acquit itself well in returning the enemy's volleys. With the exception of the mauled 2nd Iowa Smith now had five regiments jammed into the small western arm of the "X." The two opposing division commanders now had equal contingents committed to the direct contest.

Colonel Cook, U.S.A., and his three regiments maintained their firing positions outside the abatis. The brigadier was gratified that his unit could stand up to the enemy in such fashion. Of course, the Rebel shot was passing in the main over their heads, shredding treetops and the flag of the 7th Illinois. Then, too, the two Parrott guns were beginning to have an effect in reducing the efficiency of Lieutenant Morton's guns.[26]

To the east the 11th Indiana was suffering the most from the fire fight between Drake and Morgan Smith. Cruft had moved his brigade up in support of Smith but was coming under heavy grape and shell fire from French's battery in the works. To the west Ross had been forced to the reverse side of the Wynn's Ferry Road ridge by a bombardment from Heiman's bastion.

To the east Brigadier General Lew Wallace lavished praise on Colonel Morgan Smith, who gradually reddened along the breadth of his large forehead. The two officers and their staffs were engaged in assessing the practicability of making some sort of assault upon the Southern works. Seeing a few scattered weapons lying strewn on the ground, they made the assumption that they had been dropped by their late antagonists and they began to evaluate upward the chances of securing a lodgement within the enemy's defenses. It was nearly five o'clock.

Minutes later after Colonel Smith had returned to the troops, black-bearded Colonel Webster rode up and halted at Wallace's side. Wallace turned and with astonishment listened to the command to withdraw. "The general does not know that we have the hill," he blurted.

"I give you the order as he gave it to me," replied Webster noncommittally.

Wallace turned away for a moment and glared reflectively at the Rebel lines. Then with a faint trace of a smile his face returned to the chief of staff. "Very well," he said. "Give him my compliments and say that I have received the order." In spite of himself Webster smiled at the obvious intention of the Indianan and obediently he rode off.[27]

A mud-splashed Colonel John Simonton could not restrain his disgust. His brigade had fought well that morning to redeem itself from its embarrassment at delaying the division's attack. Now they had been en route to reinforce Buckner in his life and death struggle. But suddenly, when almost at the foot of the final slope, a courier from Floyd had arrived and relayed the orders for the brigade to return to their positions on the left, as a threat was materializing there. Riding to the rear of the column, he complied.

Some time before General Pillow had been aroused from the deep sleep of the exhausted to be advised of the perilous situation of the army. Now at a few minutes after five in the company of General Floyd he approached the embattled regiments of Buckner's division. Once more the Kentuckian managed to control his temper, and he detailed a few of his impressions to his superiors, such as that he was outnumbered almost five to one. Then he seized upon the excuse that his men needed his direction and he returned to the battle. Neither Floyd nor Pillow gave any advice. Buckner, pre-occupied with keeping what he had, did not suggest any counterattack. With Simonton returning to the left and the Federals gradually regaining control of the infantry and getting artillery superiority, the opportunity to return to the previous status quo disappeared with the falling of darkness.

Some Confederate incursions had been made into the precipitous ravine separating the two contending arms of the "X." The 12th Iowa, however, aided by other regiments under the command of Lauman, succeeded in driving them to better cover. At the same time the nearby crossfire of muskets on their front and left and the battery of Graves on the right jangled the nerves of all those on the Union ridge. To the immediate right Morton's guns had finally been silenced, due primarily to the section supported by Colonel John Cook.[28]

The Confederate artillery around Dover had increased the accuracy and tempo of their salvos. Feeling the effect of the shell burst and charges of grape, Union regiments under the command of Cruft and Smith began to search for shelter.

Due to the orders of Grant and the determined and vigorous Southern resistance, Lew Wallace had made up his mind to retreat. Lieutenant Churchill observed both sides cease fire simultaneously and saw the Rebels retreat to their entrenchments. Cruft was ordered to camp under arms on the unexposed southern slope of the hill lately defended by Drake, while Smith would take the forward position in front of a crest of the hill. The latter in the afternoon engagement had lost some 80 men killed and wounded and had captured five prisoners.[29]

In response to the urgent message from Grant, received at 2:30, the *St. Louis,* followed at some distance by the *Louisville,* had chugged within range of the water batteries. Captain Ross of the fort's artillery had returned from the land side of the walls and offered a reply to the *St. Louis*'s shells. In a few minutes the gunboat withdrew, the *Louisville* never coming into action.

By tacit agreement the fire fight in the west terminated at dusk. For Buckner the 42nd Tennessee had come with its fresh 500 men to participate in the last 20 minutes of the fight. Buckner, however, had no thought for the offensive, and when General Smith consolidated his perimeter on the ridge by withdrawing a portion of his line a few paces, the musketry and artillery gradually drew to a close.[30]

At the headquarters of Albert Sidney Johnston a telegrapher tapped out a message. Since early in the afternoon the general had anxiously awaited further reports from Dover. None had materialized and he had decided that a report to the Secretary of War could no longer be delayed. The message read:

HEADQUARTERS WESTERN DEPARTMENT
Edgefield, February 15, 1862—5 :15 P.M.

HON. J. P. BENJAMIN

The attack at Fort Donelson was this morning renewed by the enemy at dawn and continued until 1 o'clock, when the conflict was still raging. We had taken some 200 prisoners, forced their positions, and captured four pieces of artillery. At that hour the enemy were still bringing up reinforcements for the attack. Our arms were successful, the field having been carried inch by inch, with severe loss on both sides. There is no intelligence since 1 o'clock.

A. S. Johnston

Night slipped its cloak over the armies of North and South. Both had suffered gains and losses since the dawn had brought its welcome relief from the wind and snow of Friday night. Nearly half of the Union line had been forced back, and the majority of this a great distance. Only five Union regiments were within hailing distance of the potential evacuation route of the Forge Road.

The Confederates in turn had forfeited a height which was of great tactical importance. The fort and its water batteries were now within range of the Federal cannon planted in the western arm of the "X." The approach of enemy infantry to an assault launching spot on the fort had eased. Also Union artillery could see in reverse a good segment of Buckner's eastern defenses, abandonment of which would threaten Heiman's central bastion.

As is common in battle both sides had made some glaring errors. The Confederates had taken advantage of more opportunities than had the Unionists. In spite of the inability of the sortie to get rolling in the morning, the absence of Grant (and the orders he had issued on his departure) and the lack of defensive initiative and leadership on the part of McClernand in not bringing reinforcements to his hard-pressed right started the tide running against the North.

The Confederates blundered right back by losing the impetus in their swinging left wing. After crossing the Forge Road it became entangled in the wilderness and never again realized itself as a dangerous and potent force.

Lew Wallace certainly must be commended for committing his brigades to McClernand's relief as soon as he did, but it turned out to be too late to spare that division. The South at the same time lost glorious opportunities for breaking the hinge of the Federal line in Buckner's half-hearted attacks and the intervals between them. Some excuse may be found here in the faulty planning of Friday evening.

At the climax, just after noon, numbers had the telling effect. In the morning Pillow's 7,000 infantry and cavalry with some assistance from Buckner's 3,800 had defeated about 16,000 Federal soldiers. At that crucial moment, however, Pillow's depleted division and Buckner's relatively fresh unit faced between six and seven thousand Union troops grouped in Cruft's and Thayer's brigades. While Cruft had been somewhat battered, 2,000 completely fresh Federal soldiers in three Illinois regiments were just joining Thayer and more were on the way. The Confederates knew this. Without the 2,000 men of Illinois it is conceivable that the Confederates could have pushed Cruft and Thayer aside and laid hold of all territory east of Indian Creek. Then with the assistance of Heiman and with psychology working on their behalf, it is not impossible that C. F. Smith with his under par division could have been driven from the field.[31]

Grant's behavior on this day was peculiar to say the least. His initial order early in the morning was predicated on assumptions he made about the Confederate leadership (which he was pushing into a corner) and allowed his field commanders no flexibility. His long delay in reaching Wallace and McClernand after leaving the gunboats is extraordinary under the circumstances. Then from that time until nightfall he alternated in displays of aggressive and defensive behavior, in optimism and in caution.

In view of the lack of prepared rations and the poor countryside, Floyd's army would not probably have been justified in beating an immediate retreat southeast from the battlefield. Yet to relinquish the field because of this misfortune was folly. In retrospect, from what we have seen of the conduct of the Union army, it seems improbable that it was in any condition, from its morale, fitness, or state of mind of its leadership, to push Pillow and Buckner back to the trenches. Even if Grant had decided to unleash Smith and attack the rifle pits, the Southern army, even with the loss of the fort and of Dover, would have been ready within hours to evacuate. By dark most of the contingents could have marched some distance and the rear guard could have disengaged and been some miles to the southeast by morning. Pillow in his apparent fatigue of mind caused the army a great disservice by withdrawing the two divisions from their advanced positions.

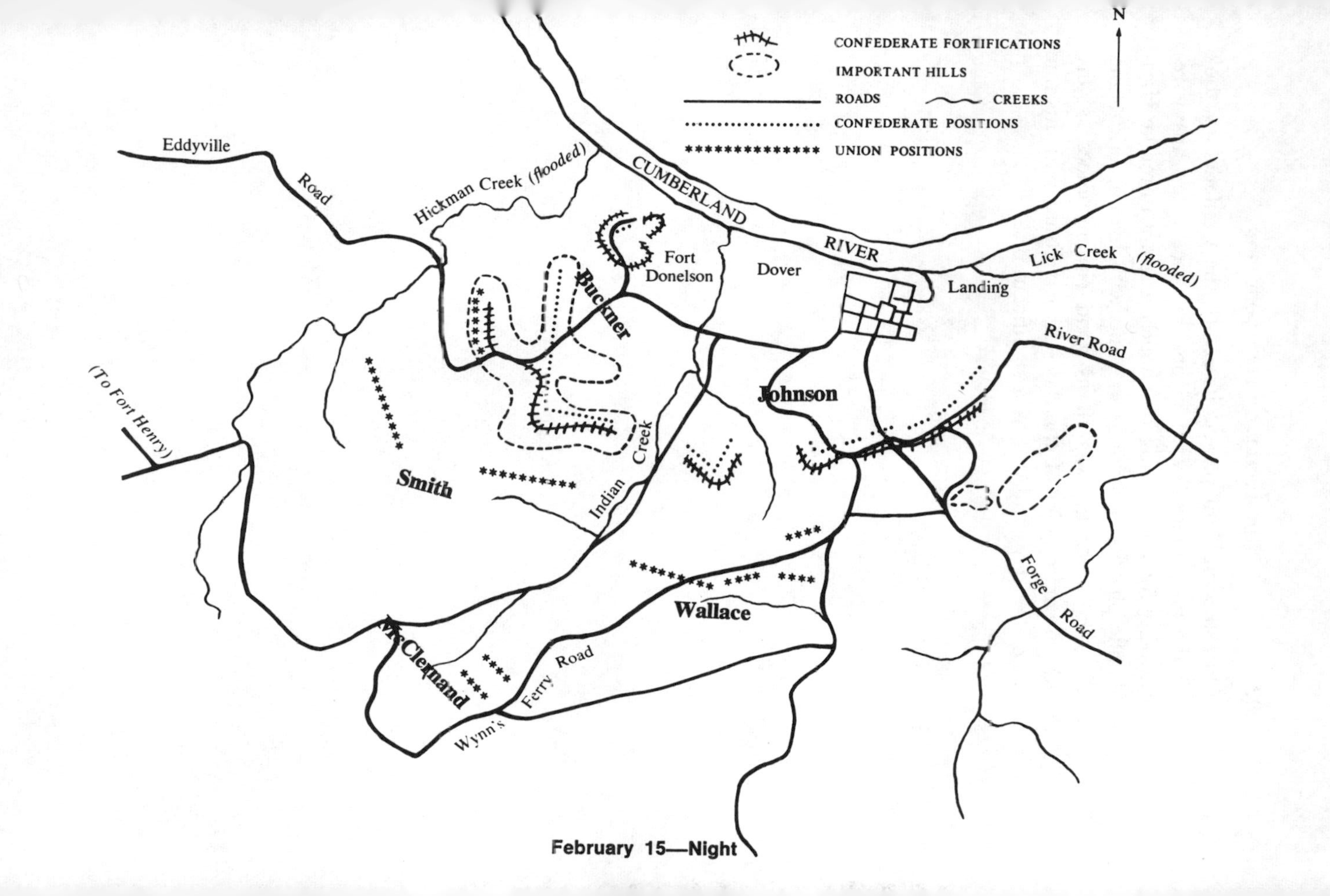

February 15—Night

Once the sun had passed its zenith the Confederacy took over the preponderancy of errors. Buckner bears heavy responsibility for not making one honest attempt to retake Hanson's rifle pits. By not doing so—and with his numerical and artillery positions he was in as good circumstances as any Southern commander of the day—he left Grant with his one profit of the day, and it was a significant one.

13

Nervous Relaxation

ACCOMPANIED BY A PARTY OF HORSEMEN, A TIGHT-FACED Ulysses Grant rode carefully through the dusk after a final inspection of the sites of Lew Wallace's two outlying brigades. Here and there around the landscape flitted the shadows of stretcher bearers answering the pitiful cries of the wounded. Rows of corpses lay outside of the hospitals. Suddenly the hand of the general signalled a pause and all the horses, skittish because of the many bodies, stomped to a halt.

A few feet away in the weeds lay the figures of a Federal lieutenant and a Confederate private. The officer was unsuccessfully trying to give his former antagonist a drink from his canteen.

Grant dismounted and asked if anyone in his escort had a flask of spirits. (The good doctor Brinton with his medical cache was not present.) There followed an embarrassed pause — everyone knowing Grant's weakness for and opinions about liquor. Finally a container of brandy came forth, and Grant himself gave first the Southerner and then the Northerner a swallow of the stimulant.

"Thank you, general," whispered the wounded Rebel. The lieutenant struggled to effect a weak salute.

Greatly moved, Grant called to Rawlins to send for stretcher bearers. In moments they arrived but cast their attentions upon the injured Union officer. "Take the Confederate, too," said Grant. "Take them both together; the war is over between them."[1]

At the same time various troop movements were taking place within the Union lines. Colonel Leonard Ross was retiring with his brigade, dragging with them the recaptured battery of Captain McAllister, but leaving Wallace's hill without any direct support. Also on orders of General McClernand, pursuant to Grant's directive to assume a tight defensive perimeter, the remnants of Richard Oglesby's brigade marched into a location for a camp behind William Wallace's unit, which was screening Indian Creek. Burial parties from all major engaged military contingents hastened toward the front. In John Cook's brigade bluecoats used the last flicker of sunlight to hunt for firewood. Charles Smith had been so heartened by the lodgement on the left flank that he had given Cook permission to build fires for the first night during the siege.[2]

Within the Confederate lines a pall of gloom pervaded the chilly air. The hopes of Friday evening had been dashed. The army appeared trapped, their right wing seriously threatened.

In the Southern high command nervousness was evident. All knew that a council of war was inevitable that night. To a man, in his own private way, each of the generals feared the outcome of the deliberations of that meeting. Each pondered his own personal path in the event of an unfortunate outcome in the discussions.

A heavy snow squall had materialized. At the Dover landing a heavy guard of Confederate soldiers ringed a motley huddle of shivering prisoners. Before their eyes streamed an interminable procession of Confederate wounded, either on stretchers or being assisted by the provost guard and medical assistants. One by one the steamers that had been anchored off the landing moved forward, loaded their hospital cargo, and wound their way upstream. As accommodations showed themselves available, the sick too were loaded on board. In all 1,134 Southern troops would leave the siege in this fashion. Near the end of the line were some 250 miserable prisoners of war. Floyd was taking no chances of feeding unuseable men or of forfeiting them in a retreat. By late evening every transport and steamer had disappeared from Dover.

As usual, gossip ran the length of the Rebel trenches. News, somewhat reliable, had come of the conflict sustained in Buckner's breastworks. As evening deepened Captain Jack Davis, relaxing in the ranks of the 7th Texas, heard an astounding report, bred in the wake of defeat, that the enemy army now numbered 80,000 effectives.

In spite of the poor visibility some of Forrest's command and a few other units on the left searched for wounded men of their own army. Some of them, their charity running low, occasionally took the opportunity to pot shot at parties of the Federal army on the mission of burying or recovering.[3]

Commanders and doctors were concerned with the problem of losses. During the siege the Confederate army had suffered more than 2,000 casualties, nearly all of them on Saturday. More than 500 Southern lives had been snuffed out, and about 1,500 recruits were convalescing from injuries received in battle.[4] Johnson's division, of course, had sustained the most. Nearly without exception each regiment in this unit had lost from 18 to 25 per cent. of their number during the morning strife. Leading the list were the 8th Kentucky, 26th Tennessee, and the 26th Mississippi.

Buckner's division lost in proportion to the fighting they

had done. Since the beginning of the investment the 32nd Tennessee had suffered 7 per cent. casualties, the 3rd Tennessee 12 per cent. and the 14th Mississippi 11 per cent., and the 2nd Kentucky 14 per cent. Porter's battery, on the other hand, had suffered a loss of nearly two-thirds.[5]

The Union army on the other hand had lost over 2,800 of its volunteers. Five hundred of these were dead and 2,100 were wounded. Eighty per cent. of these casualties had come on the 15th, showing that the Union army had been punished more heavily, even while on the defensive.

Leading all brigades in killed and wounded was Oglesby's with 863. William Wallace, excluding Morrison's two regiments, was down 547 men. McArthur had suffered 429 casualties. Lauman lost 357 up to then, and Cruft had lost 233. All other brigades had suffered relatively minor losses. Together the above brigades made up about four-fifths of the Union dead and wounded.

In Smith's Division the two brigades left to his command had lost about 360 soldiers, about three-fourths of their casualties during the entire campaign. On this Saturday the 2nd Iowa had suffered more than the rest of the division combined, and had more dead and wounded than any other regiment in the army, excepting the crushed 11th Illinois (which had lost more men than any Union regiment of the war up to that time). With none of the other units of the Second Division losing as much as 10 per cent, the Union counter-offensive was quite obviously a one-regiment affair.

Of Grant's army's entire casualty list, more than 2,400 men had been rendered ineffective while under McClernand's command. Lew Wallace, his division mounting in numbers almost by the minute, had lost 100 men in Smith's and Thayer's brigades.[6]

The Federal medical corps was having its troubles. Hospitals were in such short supply that Grant's and McClernand's headquarters had been requisitioned. Reserve medical supplies were almost non-existent. To top it all off, the steamer *Tuts* had been sent off with a cargo of wounded bluecoats and not a surgeon to attend them. Also there were about 400 wounded Confederates who were slowly being found and carried to the field stations.

On the far Union right Morgan Smith's search parties were collecting all the Northern wounded by the sound of screams or by the light of their lanterns or by the full moon which occasionally broke through the overcast. They found that these men principally belonged to the 8th, 11th, and 20th Illinois. Burial parties from Oglesby's brigade, attempting to dig trenches for their dead in the same area, were scared off by jittery or cocky Confederate pickets.[7]

In St. Louis, Henry Halleck, his usually wide child-like eyes narrow from paper work fatigue, prepared for bed. From his command headquarters that Saturday he had supervised the departure of three more brigades and three more batteries for Grant's army. He expected a total of 10,000 to reach Donelson by the 19th. All of these had been graciously sent by Buell. Halleck was still dickering with Buell to take himself and his whole army to Donelson. With the evacuation of Bowling Green, however, Buell had found enough in his own territory to keep himself busy.

As a reward for Grant and to ensure bureaucratic efficiency Halleck had that day notified the field general that he had been appointed to govern the brand new district of West Tennessee. Still concerned for the safety of the expedition (he estimated both armies at Donelson to have 30,000 troops), he had spent much of the day scouring the area for transports to dispatch reinforcements to Grant.

In Grant's military commands, records were a necessity to be dispensed with as much as possible. Therefore Halleck knew much better than he what the size of the army was before

Donelson. What Halleck did not know, however, were the losses sustained during Saturday's battle or indeed that a battle had transpired. With losses the Union army was somewhat over a thousand stronger than it had been Saturday morning.

Grant had arrived back at the Crisp house to find it crowded with wounded troops. A staff associate selected a nearby Negro slave cabin as second best and the general in charge of the army moved into these unpretentious quarters.[8]

The evening of the 15th promised to be the coldest yet, and nowhere, with the exception of Cook's brigade, was permission given for fires to be built. At least one brigadier, Jacob Lauman, was forced to endure the penetrating cold of the night without even a tent for shelter. Once again the invaders from the North steeled themselves for an interlude of darkness with little or no sleep. There was some solace : those who lived to campaign again would be called veterans.

As supper was being eaten within the Confederate entrenchments, Brigadier General Simon Bolivar Buckner had made a momentous decision. The Kentuckian had determined that his defenses, because of the positional losses sustained during the afternoon, were no longer tenable. He would advocate abandonment of them or surrender during the evening's council. Bailey's two regiments had already been sent back to the fort. With the exception of a select detail from Palmer's 18th Tennessee, very little or no work was being done to build new lines along the northern and eastern segments of the "X." Certainly the vaunted 2nd Kentucky, shaken and exhausted by their day's experience, did no construction, even though their colonel thought the new position stronger than the old one. Buckner did nothing to expedite any preparations to defend the territory on Sunday's dawn.[9]

14

The Incredible Conference

THE SPIRITS OF GENERAL ULYSSES GRANT HAD SUDDENLY taken a turn for the better. From the unit reports which had been flowing in, he announced his opinion that the Union army had suffered no more than 1,200 casualties since sunrise that day.

Lighting up his pipe Grant called for Captain Hillyer—the aide who wore his beard in similar style to the general's, only shorter. The captain was told to prepare to journey to the telegraph line at Fort Henry with a message to General Halleck. Grant then declared to the astonishment of everyone in the room that this message would definitively predict that Fort Donelson would surrender the next morning. They knew he planned to attack. At that moment the naval commander should have in his possession, they reasoned, the invitation to a river attack early Sunday morning.

Dr. Brinton, a close friend of Grant, closer perhaps than anyone in the room at the moment, rose from his rickety chair near the fire and walked over to the general's desk. "General Grant, what leads you to this conclusion?" he asked.

"First of all, the full haversacks of their army set me to thinking. They are pretty desperate and now we have beaten them. I know enough of Pillow and Buckner to assume they will now be ready to give up," Grant responded.[1]

Lieutenant Colonel Randal McGavock, assuring himself of an end to the fighting for the day, rode into Dover. The logical center for news was the headquarters tavern at the landing. On entering the command post he saw Floyd and Pillow sitting alone at a table. Floyd was writing. McGavock took a seat.

Floyd set down his pen and commenced to orally reveal the contents of his telegram report to Johnston. The conversation naturally turned to the battle and in the course of it McGavock suggested that from his vantage point with Heiman that brigade should have been allowed to attack and capture Thayer's battery. He further ventured the opinion that this would have routed the Yankees. Pillow grumbled that victory would have resulted if Buckner had made his move in time.

About this time Simon Bolivar Buckner entered the room. McGavock promptly departed from the company of generals, confident from the conversation that the battle would be vigorously renewed the next day.[2] Shortly thereafter Pillow excused himself, pleading fatigue and hunger.

At ten o'clock General Pillow had finished dinner with his staff. An invitation had been left with General Floyd, offering him the hospitality of Pillow's headquarters for any meeting which might be held that night. After all, Pillow's early arrival at Dover and his good fortune in having the leading citizen of the town, Major J. E. Rice, on his staff led him to accept Rice's offer of the best house in Dover as his headquarters. It was only fitting that the generals should meet there.

Shortly before Pillow had been in receipt of disturbing

news. Without his knowledge Floyd had sent all four steamers upstream. As the Tennessean brooded over the meaning of this, i.e., what was in Floyd's mind when he evacuated the wounded, why he had not taken Pillow into his confidence, and what this action would mean to the garrison, Bushrod Johnson came into the room, saying Floyd had just ordered his presence there.

Meanwhile General Floyd with the advice of Buckner was adding the finishing touches to the day's report. It was reticent in providing knowledge of future operations.

The enemy having invested our lines, it was determined to attack them, which we did this morning at 5:30 o'clock. General Pillow led the attack upon the enemy's right flank, and after a most obstinate and sanguinary conflict, succeeded in driving the enemy from his position and forcing him back towards his left flank. General Buckner led the attack on the right, in which many of his troops displayed commendable determination and courage. General Johnson led his command with spirit and firmness in the conflict. Nothing could exceed the steady and determined courage of many of our troops, with numbers much less than half. The enemy maintained a successful struggle, which continued for nine hours, and resulted in driving him from the field, with a loss on his part of 1,240-odd killed and wounded of whom 1,000 were killed. About 300 prisoners, six pieces of artillery, and 1,000 stand of arms were captured. Our own loss amounted to about 500 killed and wounded. They have a force of forty-two regiments.

As Floyd rose to prepare his journey to the Rice house, an aide deciphered the amended scrawl into a legible manuscript, dating it 11 p.m.[3]

In a matter of minutes Floyd and Buckner together made their appearance at the house. What Pillow did not fully realize was that the results of the battle of the 15th had led Floyd to form a close tie of reliance and kinship to Simon

Buckner. For one thing, reflection had convinced the senior general that Buckner had been correct earlier in the afternoon when he balked at retreating from the field they had just won. Now Floyd worried that the Federals would reoccupy the battlefield during the darkness. Second, what he had heard and seen of Buckner's personal and masterly direction of the defense of the right flank caused his unmilitary mind to feel deep admiration for Buckner.[4]

As the council of generals convened, the four leaders were alone in the comfortable sitting room of the Rice home. Pillow's aides were all either asleep or engaged in other errands. Colonel John Burch, however, sat in an adjoining room and heard much of the substance of the discussion.

The meeting began with a pleasant review of lessons to be drawn from the day's engagement. Pillow noted that without fail any future attempt at evacuation had better find the army fully stocked with rations, as the countryside to Charlotte could not support them. He also observed that he personally would not feel justified in leaving the field artillery and a holding garrison to be surrendered to the enemy.

Johnson, in halting fashion owing to his extreme fatigue, said that he did not believe that a retreat could have been successful that afternoon as the enemy was still in contact with their forces. He favored a night-time withdrawal.

Floyd opened his phase of the discussion with a passing reference to the knowledge of the arrival of heavy Federal reinforcements. This, he felt, made it imperative that the army consider no other alternative than evacuation. He assumed that the river road was still blocked by overflowed creeks and that the only feasible route again would be the Forge Road. He added that this was predicated on the assumption that the enemy had not returned to their lines of the morning.

Buckner reminded the council that he had from the beginning advocated evacuating the army with three days' cooked rations and he had not changed his opinion. With evacuation agreed upon the generals arose to assemble around the table to plan the details of the operation. Johnson, stating that the extreme tiredness from his constant duties during the day made the focussing of his attention impossible, asked to be excused from the meeting. He said that Pillow was as familiar with his division as he was and could handle those details. Floyd gave him permission to leave.[5]

As the generals drafted rough plans for ammunition and food supplies, the apportioning of blankets, and the fixing of the time, position, and order of march, a knock came on the exterior door of the house. Colonel Burch responded and found a messenger waiting for General Buckner.

The courier walked into the sitting room and handed a written note to the Kentucky officer. As Buckner read, his face grew solemn. He then interrupted the meeting with apologies. The reliable Captain Graves, it developed, had observed numerous enemy forces assembling before Buckner's right.

The planning session went on. It was decided to send out an order at one o'clock to prepare to assemble in an open field on the left flank at four o'clock. Just then another messenger for Buckner from Graves entered the room. Buckner read the note aloud. It stated that large troop movements could be detected flowing from Buckner's left position to his vulnerable right flank.

At that point Floyd remembered that no check had been made on the reoccupation of the Forge Road by the Union army. Thereupon Pillow sent an aide to locate some scouts and send them on this mission. Then, after working out the final details and turning them over to Pillow's staff for implementation, the council recessed until further evidence could be gathered on the route to take. It was 11:45.

The Rice house became a veritable beehive of activity. The sitting room became the domain of staff officers writing orders to various commanders and units. Pillow retired to his room to labor on his assignments.

North of Nashville Albert Sidney Johnston dashed off an optimistic telegram to Secretary of War Benjamin on the state of affairs at Dover:

> We have had to-day at Fort Donelson one of the most sanguinary conflicts of the war. Our forces attacked the enemy with energy and won a brilliant victory. I have the satisfaction to transmit the dispatch, after nightfall, of General Floyd, who was in command of our forces.

There followed the Virginian's message of 11 p.m.[6]

Some time thereafter, past 12:30, Floyd and Buckner came to Pillow's room and suggested that as a group they talk to Major Rice and others about the countryside they would have to trespass upon. Pillow agreed and invited the generals into his quarters. Rice was called in. Under questioning, primarily by Pillow, the aide-de-camp described the surrounding countryside, not, however, speaking in favourable terms of either road. At this moment Lieutenant Hunter Nicholson joined the group on the request of Pillow. Rice continued, saying that he knew of a doctor who knew more of the quality of the roads for some distance out than he did.

As the conversation with Major Rice was concluded, a staff officer announced the local doctor, J. W. Smith, previously referred to. As the doctor was giving the opinion that the roads were suitable for light baggage, someone called Lieutenant Nicholson out of the room. Meanwhile, Captain Gus Henry had been awakened from a deep sleep and ordered to report to Pillow's room. He entered shortly before the doctor departed to personally check on the fords over the river road.

Before Pillow could turn to Henry and Nicholson, a Major Jones, quartermaster, entered. Pillow got up from his chair and took Jones aside over by the wall. He explained the decision of the council to evacuate and followed it up with the intention of the army to destroy their excess stores.

"What time do you desire me to do this, sir?" inquired the quartermaster.

Pillow announced, "About daybreak; about 5:30 o'clock."

It was one o'clock. After their discussions with the local residents, the generals decided to call in Colonel Forrest and the medical director of the army for conference. Major Jeremy Gilmer came in. Pillow called for Burch and told him to wake Major W. H. Haynes.

It was but a matter of minutes before Lieutenant Charles Martin ushered in Colonel Bedford Forrest. The stuffy and smoky chamber was in a state of considerable confusion. Floyd and Buckner were sitting idly aside while Pillow attempted to take care of the people who were waiting for him.

At this moment Major Haynes opened the door. Pillow immediately walked up to him and passed on the information that the army was going to escape. As assistant commissary Haynes was expected to destroy the commissary stores at the last minute and then escape across the river.

"When shall I do this, general?" queried Haynes.

Taking out his watch, Pillow replied, "At 5:30 o'clock."

Haynes then left, followed immediately by Major Jones. Major Henry was then called forward by Pillow and told to gather up all the books and records of the army during the investment. He had been assistant adjutant general.

Several minutes after the departure of Henry, the leader of a party of two scouts sent out to explore the battle area of the morning on the left flank entered and reported. The troops in the lines had heard dogs barking out in the darkness, he said, and investigation had revealed many campfires glowing in the previously abandoned enemy lines. The Forge Road was blocked by Northern military units.

Pillow was on his feet, vehemently objecting to accepting

the evidence solely on the basis of bonfires. Instead he suggested that another team of scouts be sent out. In view of this outburst and the importance of verifying the information, Floyd agreed and ordered another pair of scouts sent out to determine the whereabouts of the Federals.

Walking over to consult with Forrest, Pillow learned that he had travelled a considerable distance up the Forge Road after dark while searching for wounded and saw no signs of the Unionists occupying their former positions. Pillow looked at the colonel searchingly and then instructed him to select two very reliable men of his command to check on the reports of the scouts. The general also asked Forrest to report on the condition of the river road running to Clarksville. Spotting Dr. Smith in the room, Pillow suggested that he accompany the mounted party as a guide.

Soon after Forrest left on his mission, the medical director of the army appeared. Floyd and Buckner plied him with a number of questions on how the army would fare in wading through water which they suspected would be several feet deep. The doctor replied that since frostbite cases were increasing since the temperature was near freezing and the high wind made the cold even more penetrating, and since the men were exhausted from fighting, he guessed that such a march would mean the death of more than half of the garrison. Profoundly shocked, the generals excused the doctor.

The two Confederate scouts dispatched by Floyd reached the breastworks of Johnson's division near the Forge and Wynn's Ferry Roads. Conversing with the men preparing their gear and rations for the evacuation, the scouts learned that hospital rescue parties had been withdrawn at midnight, but they had seen considerable Federal activity in the wilderness. Advancing further the pair discovered from pickets that there had been no absence of enemy targets that night. Progressing further, out into no man's land, the scouts heard and saw one of the last remaining mercy details from Morgan Smith's brigades searching the forest. Taking this to be a patrol, the scouts felt they had gathered all the needed evidence and returned to headquarters.

With a couple of picked men Forrest and Dr. Smith rode through the square, past the Dover landing byway, and down a short but steep embankment. During this interval Smith had spoken of his investigation of the road crossing of the Lick Creek slough. He suggested they turn off and journey up the bank a distance to the Hays ford. Forrest offered no objection. Coming to rough underbrush the group dismounted, not wanting to be heard by any outlying Union pickets. Reaching the ford, all waded across and discovered the creek to be only 18 inches deep. They remounted and returned to Forrest's regiment. Here the colonel ordered two other trusted cavalrymen to travel up the river road and then reconnoiter its environs to the south and west.

During all this time regiments of the Confederate army had been assembling southeast of the town in preparation for evacuation.

In the bitter cold, wounded Federal Lieutenant Churchill lay capless, his hair freezing to the snow.[7]

The report of the second pair of scouts fell upon the ears of a pensive council. All along each of the generals had feared that just this news of enemy reoccupation of their lost ground would be forthcoming. Thus resigned to what they had anticipated, no probing questions followed as to the methods by which the information had been gathered or the details of the observations.

Hardly had the scouts been dismissed when Colonel Forrest strode through the door with his couple of cavalrymen and Dr. Smith. They faced a rather dispirited audience, but nonetheless began their reports. Forrest estimated that the swamp of the slough extended for about a quarter of a mile but that the deep water was only 100 yards wide. The highest water came to the saddle skirts. Someone added that the mud was so soft that it came up to a man's knees. The water was also intensely cold, it was discovered.

The mounted scouts described the route taken on their reconnaissance. Large fires, they said, had been seen in the vicinity of some of the enemy's fires which had been observed on Friday night. A dull roar of personal conversation filled the room at this point; discussion centered on the fact that these men had explored only the Union far right and even at that their sightings confirmed earlier information.

Meanwhile Forrest suggested that perhaps these fires had been abandoned Saturday morning and had been fanned into their present state by the high winds then raging. Few in the room heard the cavalry leader's remark, and those who did deemed it futile speculation, unworthy of note. Most important, all three generals were convinced that a fierce struggle would be necessary in order to fight their way out the Forge Road.

The room quieted with apprehension, and then John Floyd spoke with deliberation. " Well, gentlemen, what is best now to be done? "

With Floyd looking directly at him Pillow felt constrained to make the first reply. " We can fight them another day in our trenches, and by tomorrow night we can have boats enough here to transport our troops across the river and let them make their escape to Clarksville."

At this point Major Haynes quietly slipped into the room and took a seat next to Lieutenant Nicholson. In measured tones Buckner was replying, " Gentlemen, you know the enemy occupy the rifle pits on my right and can easily turn my position and attack me in the rear or move down on the river battery. I am satisfied he will attack me at daylight, and I cannot hold my position half an hour."

Pillow quickly moved to dispute this dangerous opinion, " Why so, why so, general? "

Buckner tried dismissing this objection with a brief reply. " Because I can bring into action not over 4,000 men, and they demoralized by long and uninterrupted exposure and fighting, while they can bring any number of fresh troops to the attack."

" I differ with you. I think you can hold your lines; I think you can, sir! " Pillow returned heatedly.

Buckner responded in kind, " I know my position, and I know that the lines cannot be held with my troops in the present condition. You, gentlemen, know that yesterday morning I considered the 2nd Kentucky Regiment as good a regiment as there was in the service. Yet such was their condition yesterday afternoon that, when I learned the enemy was in their trenches—which were to our extreme right and detached from the others—before I could rally and form them I had to take at least 20 men by the shoulders and pull them into line as a nucleus for formation."

Floyd intervened decisively to prevent a verbal brawl. " I will have to agree with General Buckner on the nature of the situation in his own immediate front." Looking again at Pillow, he continued, " Our works cannot be defended. What shall we do? "

"We can still cut our way out and leave our dead and wounded on the field," the white-maned Tennessean replied.

" General Buckner, what is your opinion on cutting our way out? " Floyd questioned.

" In my opinion the cost would be too great. Was it not the purpose of General Johnston in defending Fort Donelson to accomplish the evacuation of Bowling Green? Has this not been already done? "

" General Johnston's army has reached Nashville," Floyd answered.

" I think then our army has done its duty," Buckner continued. " We have successfully defended our trenches, we have beaten off their gunboats, and we have fought them bravely in the open field. I think now that they have once again reinvested our works, our army has done all that it could. Our duty and our honor, gentlemen, can require no more.

" As to a sortie, to cut our way out would cost three-fourths of our men, and I do not think any commander has a right to sacrifice three-fourths of his command to save one-fourth."

" Certainly not," Floyd interjected.

After hearing Buckner complain all evening about the strength of the Union army and the demoralization and weakness of his own division and by strong inference of the Confederate army and seeing the vote against him, Pillow decided to beat a strategic retreat. " Gentlemen, as you refuse to make an attempt to cut our way out, and General Buckner says he will not be able to hold his position a half hour after being attacked, there is only one alternative left—that is capitulation. I am determined that I will never surrender the command nor will I ever surrender myself a prisoner. I will die first."

With the Pandorian word " Capitulation " finally uttered and released into the room, events moved swiftly. Floyd suddenly jumped on Pillow's wagon, " Nor will I; I cannot and will not surrender, but I confess personal reasons control me."

At this point Forrest, who had left the room briefly, slipped quietly through the door as Buckner was saying, " But such considerations should not control a general's actions."

" Certainly not," returned Floyd. " Nor would I permit it to cause me to sacrifice the command. Gentlemen, I cannot surrender. You know my position with the Federals. It wouldn't do; it wouldn't do."

Recognizing the handwriting on the wall, Buckner uttered the words Floyd and Pillow were waiting for: " Then I suppose, gentlemen, the surrender will devolve upon me. If the command of the army is turned over to me, I will surrender the army and I will share its fate," he concluded in noble, professional tones.

Floyd seized upon the opportunity of Buckner's willingness for a further advantage. " General Buckner, if I place you in command, will you allow me to get out as much of my little brigade as I can? "

" I will," replied Buckner, " provided you do so before the terms of capitulation are agreed on."

" Then, sir, I turn over the command," said Floyd to Pillow.

The words were barely out of his mouth when Pillow blurted, " I pass it."

With drama Buckner spoke smoothly, almost purring. " I assume it. Give me pen, ink and paper, and send for a bugler. I will send a flag asking for General Grant's quarters, that I may send a message to him. I will propose an armistice of six hours to arrange terms."

Gideon Pillow stood up stiffly from his chair preparing to leave this unhappy meeting. He felt a tug at his sleeve and looked into the angry eyes of Bedford Forrest. " General Pillow, I think there is more fight in these men than you all suppose, and, if you will let me, I will take out my command, no matter what the cost."

Pillow liked his spirit. " Yes, sir. Cut your way out."

Overhearing this, Floyd agreed and Buckner said quietly, " I have no objections."

Forrest then followed up his advantage. " Then I shall take out anyone who will follow me."

This brought an idea into the head of General Floyd. " Colonel, will you wait for me outside, please."

Forrest's dramatic display of boldness brought Pillow's mind to the protocol of his own position. " Gentlemen," he said weakly, " is there anything wrong in my leaving? "

" Every man must judge for himself of that," tersely replied Floyd.

After Pillow had gone through the door, Buckner, waiting for his materials, turned to Floyd, who was pondering what he would tell Albert Sidney Johnston. " General Floyd, surrender here is as bitter to me as it is to you or anyone else. I feel, however, that it is necessary here. At the same time I must for my own honor and sense of duty not separate myself from my own command. Their fortune is my fortune." This was the second time Buckner had mentioned honor and duty, professional West Point terms.

As Floyd was saying that he felt a similar loyalty to his unit, Colonel John Burch called to General Pillow in the hallway. " General, I cannot help but feel that your position in this meeting might possibly be misunderstood by the other generals." While he did not elaborate, Burch had uppermost in his consideration the fact that Pillow had decided not to surrender but rather flee.

Pillow answered him brusquely, " I don't think so."

" Just the same, General, I would recommend as a witness that you go back in there and talk to Generals Floyd and Buckner and leave no possibility that they could misunderstand your position."

Pillow paused for a moment, then nodded grudgingly in assent and re-entered the room. He found Floyd and Buckner waiting quietly for paper and writing implements. Lieutenant Hunter Nicholson and several of the generals' aides were in attendance. Major Haynes was just leaving, his orders countermanded by Buckner. The supplies were not to be destroyed but to be turned over to the Union army, as any professional gentleman officer would do.

Pillow seated himself between Floyd and Buckner and commenced clarifying his position. " Gentlemen, in order that we may understand each other, let me state what is my position. I differ with you as to the cost of cutting our way out, but if it were ascertained that it would cost three-fourths of the command, I agree that it would be wrong to sacrifice them for the remaining fourth."

Simon Bolivar Buckner eased himself back in the cushion of his chair and folded his hands simply in his lap. Then he opened his mouth; his tones were soothing but full of deeper meaning. " We understand you, general, and you understand us."

Floyd said only, " Yes." Pillow arose, motioned Nicholson to follow, and disappeared to pack what baggage he had.

Floyd was practically on his heels and located the impatient Forrest elsewhere in the building. " Colonel," he said, " I want you to lead my brigade out of this trap. Go back and organize your brigade and return to headquarters. I will have my men ready by then."

Forrest saluted and strode through the outside door. He paused by the lantern at the door, groped in his pocket for the watch purchased by his profits from the sale of slaves. It was three o'clock in the morning.[8]

15

Unconditional Surrender—The Beginning of a Legend

No one who ventured outside on that bitter winter night could mistake the fact that something was afoot in the Confederate encampment. Every half hour more gray regiments were assembling at the terminus of the earthworks on the left. Grumblings, however, were on the increase, since even the trenches were preferable to exposure to the biting wind out in the open.

In the Rice house General Pillow was locked in conversation with the owner over the best route out of the besieged town. The safest and quickest way, the major said, was across the Cumberland, but of course no one had any means of crossing it. He volunteered, however, to use his influence to see what could be done in that direction. In addition Pillow awoke Major Gilmer, informed him of the surrender, and invited him to join in the escape.[1]

In the cavalry encampment Lieutenant Colonel Nathan

Bedford Forrest sent for all the officers under his jurisdiction for a council. When they came together he explained to them the decision of the generals and of his own determination to escape and fight his way out if necessary. He wanted only those with him who were resolved to continue the fight for the Confederacy at any cost. Forrest was gratified to note that all of his own regimental officers stepped forward without hesitation. The Kentuckian Captain Williams also strode forward. Lieutenant Colonel Gantt and Captains Wilcox and Huey stood back. Sensing Colonel Gantt, an officer who had kept his command conspicuously out of the Saturday battle, to be the leader of the recalcitrants, Forrest urged him personally to continue to make his men useful to the South. Gantt stolidly refused.

At the Rice house General Buckner had completed penning his surrender note to General Grant. General Floyd, sitting quietly nearby, suddenly spoke up. Could Buckner delay the dispatch of the call for a parley for just a little time to allow him to escape? Buckner pondered the risks involved and agreed to return to Fort Donelson, re-copy his message in neater form and then send a courier with a white flag when daylight made him a little more distinguishable. Ill at ease, Floyd thanked him and left to visit his headquarters at the tavern to send a telegram to Johnston.[2]

Gideon Pillow's face had lighted up. Through some magical means which he did not question, Major Rice had brought over from the northern side of the Cumberland a small flatboat. Pillow gathered up his staff, had his colored servant carry his trunk with all of his baggage to the vicinity of headquarters near where the craft was tied up and rode there himself.

Meanwhile from the cavalry encampment and the Rice house news of the surrender spread like wildfire through the rows of tented enclosures and the huddled masses of newly marched regiments. Colonel W. A. Quarles of the 42nd Tennessee was dubious and not getting satisfactory information from his brigade commander, Colonel Heiman, and he determined to visit headquarters and personally ask for orders.

At the riverfront Pillow stood more than a little shaken. The flatboat measured only about 12 feet by 4 feet, and around him clustered ten men, two horses of the general's, and a trunk—all to be transported across the river. Looking at the manner in which the wind was whipping up the stream, Pillow knew the human cargo would have to come first. Therefore he rushed back to the tavern to enlist the aid of some of Floyd's staff to see that the rest of his contingent got favorable treatment in case the steamers returned.

Inside the doorway Pillow was hailed by Colonel Quarles, who had just heard the rumors of capitulation repeated. " General Pillow, sir, is it true that we are about to be surrendered? " he asked anxiously.

" I am afraid it is," Pillow replied distractedly.

" Can it not be prevented? Could we not fight our way out or something? "

Pillow looked the colonel square in the eye and said in tired, even terms, " No! I have fought against the surrender in the council, but my senior and junior in command overrule me. I can do nothing; I am powerless. The surrender has been positively determined on. Had I my way I would fight the troops. I believe I could get them out." [3]

The telegrapher at Dover drummed out a message to Nashville. He was completing a short report from General Floyd:

General A. Sidney Johnston:

Last evening there arrived in the river near Fort Donelson eleven transports, laden with troops. We are completely invested with an army many times our own numbers. I regret to say the unanimous opinion of the officers seems to be that we cannot maintain ourselves against these forces.[4]

Elsewhere in the town, however, Floyd had found a note of hope. On his desk was a routine telegram from Clarksville mentioning that two small steamers loaded with supplies should arrive at Dover some time before daybreak. Here was a more secure avenue for escape than a hazardous trip with the cavalry.

After making hasty farewells, General Gideon Pillow and his flock of aides cautiously boarded the raft. On shore stood the general's faithful Negro body servant watching the ten soldiers of the South, exclusive of the boatman, sit and bolster themselves for their ordeal. Soon after casting off the flimsy boat was lost in the morning murk of the Cumberland. The slave returned to the care of Pillow's horses and baggage.

North of the river at Nashville a staff officer of Albert Sidney Johnston quickly skimmed over the latest telegram from General John Floyd. Completely missing the significance of the guarded language, he decided it was not of enough importance to wake the general. He placed the time of 3:45 A.M. upon the paper and placed it where his superior would read it in the morning.

About four o'clock Colonel Forrest reported to Floyd at the headquarters tavern. There the former commanding general told him that there had been a change of plans and Floyd would take his brigade out by the Cumberland. Forrest inquired as to the whereabouts of Pillow and was told that he had already retreated. Floyd added that the cavalry was free to take any course Forrest now chose.[5]

Bushrod Johnson was now awake. A number of matters demanded his attention. The division and its reinforcements were becoming unruly, even for volunteers, with the persistent rumors that the garrison was about to be surrendered. Then too the regiments of Floyd's brigade were found to be marching toward town. On being questioned their officers reported this was on the order of General Floyd himself. Thoroughly alarmed, Johnson sent an aide to report to headquarters that his division was ready to march. Unknown to him this officer had run into extreme confusion in the town.

Forrest found his cantonment jammed with angry crowds of Confederate infantrymen. Hearing from adjoining cavalrymen that the horsemen were about to fight their way out from the promise of certain imprisonment, they demanded to be allowed to join the effort. The colonel was unwilling to jeopardize his risky undertaking with a straggling party of infantry, nor was he anxious to overload all of the steeds of his command. Someone from Porter's battery, however, had taken the chance of detaching the artillery horses from the guns, and this decided Forrest to permit some of the crowd to accompany him. One out of four cavalrymen was authorized to take a rider on behind him.

Forrest rode down the line of mounted riders to insure that everything was in readiness. Men on foot crowded in his way, pleading to be included in the retreat. Finally the colonel managed to spur his way through the throng back to the head of the column and issued the order to move forward. As the files began to pick up speed charitable cavalrymen indicated to hapless infantrymen that they would allow an extra load to mount up behind them.

Cautiously a party of scouts and skirmishers slid eastward through the darkness along the river road, eyes peeled for signs of enemy encroachment. At last one of the men who had accompanied the colonel earlier in the morning held up his hand in a signal for a halt. Then the officer in charge spread his detachment out along the western bank of the slough while a messenger reported to Forrest that the way was clear up to the bank of the overflow. Almost directly to the south the flicker of several fires could be seen.

When Forrest drew up with his reinforced regiment, he directed an augmented body of skirmishers to push through the slough and check on the far bank. Meanwhile the "grand guard," as one of the professional officers expressed it, paused in wait as a ready reserve. The mounting tension was finally relieved when a young courier rode recklessly through the deep icy water, waving his hat as a sign of success. Hearing that the crossing would be uncontested, Forrest led the main party through the ford and had it drawn up on the eastern side while he ascertained the progress of the rear elements.[6]

Meanwhile Simon Buckner was ordering back to their trenches the units which had gathered for the life and death sortie. In the melee of confusion of surrender reports, many regiments never received this order.

A soldier announced to the general that lookouts on the heights of the fort had sighted lights eastward on the river—lights that could only be the awaited steamboats. With the arrival of the steamboats the letter to Grant was completed; there only needed a few supplementary notes to be written. One officially told Bushrod Johnson what was going on:

> The command of the forces in this vicinity has devolved upon me by order of General Floyd. I have sent a flag to General Grant, and during the correspondence and until further orders refrain from hostile demonstrations with a view to preventing a like movement on the enemy's part. You will endeavor to send a flag to the posts in front of your position, notifying them of the fact that I have sent a communication to General Grant from the right of our position and desire to know his present headquarters.

For delivery of the vital proposals to the front, Buckner selected Major George Cosby, a regular army Kentuckian and one of his most trusted aides. As the major was not then at the divisional headquarters building, Buckner dispatched the missive to him with an accompanying explanation on separate paper. One told Cosby to take or have sent the letter to Grant by white flag. The bearer was also to inform the Union commanding general that Buckner's headquarters would thereafter be moved to Dover. As the courier turned to seek out Major Cosby, an afterthought occurred to Buckner and he recalled the man. On the front of another piece of paper he wrote a note ordering that a white flag be mounted on the fort proper but not on the batteries. This he hoped would prevent an attack at daylight in about an hour.[7]

At the wharf the *General Anderson* and her sister ship were being feverishly unloaded by Virginians of Floyd's brigade and what Negro help was available. One of the small vessels had been loaded with corn for the garrison and the other was stocked with ammunition, sugar, and flour. In order that the steamers could be utilized as transports it was necessary that these stores be put ashore for eventual disposal by Ulysses Grant and associates.

South of the hamlet Bushrod Johnson heard that a courier from General Buckner was looking for him. He began conducting a search for the messenger.

At that moment Buckner himself was engaged in a distasteful conference with one of his subordinates, Colonel John Head. Head notified the general that once the 30th had been ordered back to its camp, he had consulted the regimental surgeon about his own personal health. It seemed, Head related, that prolonged exposure had brought on a case of pneumonia and it was the doctor's opinion, he said, that prison life would be fatal for him. Head felt, he continued, obliged to seek the recommendations of his superior in this situation.

Buckner returned his old stock answer that this was a matter that Head must determine for himself. Buckner himself, he said, considered it his own duty to remain with his men and share their fate.

On his departure from the tavern Head walked rather slowly, then picked up speed. He had decided to try to leave on one of the steamers. After all, he told himself, he could be of no use to his Tennesseans in his "condition."[8]

After an inquiry from Lieutenant Colonel McGavock, Bushrod Johnson hurried to the Dover tavern headquarters to get some information. While McGavock paused outside observing the lights feverishly moving in all directions around the wharf where sat two anchored steamers, Johnson learned the fort had surrendered. He joined the colonel and the pair witnessed the progressive demoralization of troops in the town and saw groups going upriver.

On the river bank was a scene of utter disorganization. Most of Floyd's brigade was drawn up to march up the gangplanks. Major Brown of the 20th Mississippi (now reunited with McCausland's brigade after service with Baldwin and Johnson), had learned of the intention to embark on the steamers from one of Buckner's aides. Brown then went to Floyd to have these orders from an odd source verified, which they were.

At the landing various notions prevailed as to the order of march of the evacuation. Floyd intended to have the regiments embark according to the rank of their active commanding officer. Others had heard that the order of march from Bowling Green would be preserved. In any event Major Brown assumed that he was the junior major commanding a regiment, whereas in actuality a captain was in charge of the 56th Virginia.

Meanwhile, rank and file, absent without leave, poured into Dover, intent upon obtaining passage upon the boats. They turned into a rabble, pressing upon the not-too orderly lines of the Virginians. Floyd, nearly beside himself under the pressure of events, called upon Brown and the 20th to form a ring of bayonets around the wharf to keep those "unauthorized" from infiltrating aboard the steamers.

Sometime after five o'clock both steamers were under way with the first load to be ferried to the north side of the river. The 20th Mississippi, as the press of the refugees had relaxed, stacked their arms and waited with anticipation for the return of the ferries.[9]

Nathan Bedford Forrest asked an aide to strike a match. Viewing his watch, he knew it was not long until daylight. At that time it was likely Federals in great force would seek to seal off this dangerous exit from Dover. In spite of more than an hour of effort the horses were still in transit across the deep creek bed. The frigid water and the uncertain bottom had made a single file advisable and the temperature and depth of the water caused a high percentage of the animals to balk at the crossing. Forrest glanced back at the companies drawn up in the thickets behind him. The inactivity, the cold, and the biting wind were weakening their morale. In sudden decision he turned, rode up to Major Kelly and Adjutant Schuyler and told them to hold the nearby crossroads with a company. He then set out on the more northerly, less traveled route to the Cumberland Iron Works.

At 5 :30, the front-line veterans of the 7th Iowa were silently moving around at a stoop, performing early morning ablutions. Orders had been issued to prepare themselves for a renewed assault that morning and they were trying to get something in their stomachs before meeting the enemy in combat. Spirits were high, for since the early hours of Sunday morning deserters from the Confederate lines had scampered into Union lines, bringing word that Southern troops were being withdrawn. Whatever the portent of that move, it appeared that little resistance would be forthcoming to a grand attack upon the intervening defenses before the fort. Reinforcements were at hand. In the front lines were McArthur's decimated 12th Illinois and his 9th Illinois was in reserve.[10]

Suddenly just a matter of yards in front of them a bugle call shattered the morning stillness. To the volunteers this music from the enemy had no meaning, but then someone said he thought it signalled a parley or truce. Pickets tightened the pressure on their triggers until slowly a strip of white tent canvas gracefully protruded up from the enemy's ridge. As the pickets relaxed a Negro bearing a hickory pole and white flag and then an officer stepped across the intervening territory of no man's land.

Lieutenant Colonel James Parrott, commanding the 7th, had been alert from the first call of the bugle and now briskly walked to meet the messengers. Within close speaking distance Parrott and the two messengers drew to a halt. The Confederate officer was Major Nat Cheairs, commanding the 3rd Tennessee. He had been selected by Brown and instructed by Cosby. Major Cheairs saluted and informed the colonel that he bore a message from the Confederate commanding general relative to the capitulation of Fort Donelson and vicinity. Parrott replied that he would conduct the major to his superior. The Tennessee plantation owner bowed slightly to the Iowan and the two strode off leaving the flag bearer in the care of the pickets.

In spite of the reports of the Rebel deserters Colonel Jacob Lauman was not in the best of spirits that morning. The night had been spent huddled at the base of a large tree, without even a tent to shelter his body. Even sharing the "comforts" of the men could go too far. Then as one of his aides began preparing breakfast and the brigadier began hustling out his shaving equipment word flashed that a Confederate officer was approaching. Soon Cheairs and Parrott showed up. Lauman wasted no time on details but rushed Cheairs with his aide by horse to the quarters of General Charles Smith.[11]

Major Kelly and Adjutant Schuyler, pursuant to orders, led their company down the path taken by Colonel Forrest. In deference to the many still cursing their horses through the foreboding waters a guide was left at the crossroads to point the way of the command. Among those still on the Dover side of the obstacle were Captain Bidwell, Lieutenant Burt, and 36 men of the gallant artillery of the Dover army.

As the countryside became discernible in the growing light of day, General Lew Wallace formulated plans for carrying the war to the enemy. Thayer's fresh brigade and Wood's battery would reinforce Cruft's brigade in a grand assault on the Confederate positions. This would of course be after the men had eaten a hearty and warm breakfast.

Bushrod Johnson returned to his division still in a partial daze. In his pointed-roof tent he found an aide holding the letter from Buckner which had been left by the messenger. As a matter of curiosity he unfolded the paper and looked over the contents. Johnson decided to ignore the request to send a white flag to Union lines demanded of him there. After all the note to Grant had been sent some time previous to this and the bearer must have found his man. Furthermore no Union military forces were in view before the key part of his entrenchments.[12]

Spectators on the bank of the Cumberland were overjoyed to view one of their transports making her approach to tie in at the dock and in the distance her consort's outline was faintly discernible as her boilers churned in her race against time. Once again lines formed in anticipation of evacuation. This time certain companies of the 20th Mississippi stood in the forefront.[13]

The fire in the Crisp fireplace was low but it was keeping the house's occupants warm. By that hour the sickening smell of hospital had been dissipated by the odor of burning wood. In a straight-back chair near the flickering blaze Surgeon Brinton dozed fitfully. The whole night he had slept on the floor in close proximity to the chair, then he had awakened and walked around, and seeing it was near sunrise he did not return to his blankets but sat in the chair and soon fell asleep again.

The door opened, squeaking as it did so. Brinton jolted, then looked up in surprise. One of the last persons he expected to see at that hour of the morning was General Charles Smith, but there the trim, rangy figure stood, cursing softly and beating his arms against his torso. With him was Major Cheairs.

The doctor came to his full senses when Smith abruptly announced that the Rebels were proposing a truce for the purpose of surrender and one of the commanding general's aides hastened to rouse Grant out of his featherbed. As Smith advanced to warm himself by the flames, he asked the doctor if he had a drink to ward off the chill morning air. Knowing exactly what Smith had in mind and deeming the circumstances warranted breaking into the medical stores, Brinton groped in his bag and pulled out the flask. Smith took the container without hesitation and took a swig. The flames threw light on his boots and he told how he had scorched his socks by sleeping with his head in the saddle and his feet too close to the fire.

Meanwhile around the corner Ulysses Grant piled himself into his uniform. Unshaven, coat unbuttoned, he emerged into the cramped main room for his rendezvous with history. The whole staff was up and quietly watching his every move. Major Cheairs stepped forward, introduced himself to Grant and handed him the letter. Cheairs then retired out of earshot. Grant saw that the seal was broken and knew that the division commander had already read its contents. Seating himself, he held the envelope and tugged at the paper within and read:

HEADQUARTERS
Fort Donelson, February 16, 1862

Sir:

In consideration of all the circumstances governing the present situation of affairs at this station I propose to the commanding officers of the Federal forces the appointment of commissioners to agree upon terms of capitulation of the forces and post under my command, and in that view suggest an armistice until 12 o'clock today.

S. B. Buckner
Brigadier General C. S. Army

Brig. Gen. U. S. Grant
Commanding U. S. Forces near Fort Donelson

Grant looked up at Smith. "What answer shall I send to this, General Smith?" The old war horse muttered something about no terms to armed rebels and immediate and unconditional surrender. Grant laughed somewhat self-consciously and asked for some writing paper. An excited and flustered aide shoved some poor quality legal-size paper onto the table but at the moment no one really noticed or cared.

For about three minutes hardly a sound was heard in the small sitting room of the Crisp house as General Grant wrote and pondered. Finally he leaned back in his chair and announced, "This is what I am writing, General Smith." He then read:

Sir:
Yours of this date, proposing armistice and appointment of commissioners to settle terms of capitulation, is just received. No terms except unconditional and immediate surrender can be accepted. I propose to move immediately upon your works.
I am, sir, very respectfully, your obedient servant,

U. S. Grant
Brigadier General, Commanding

Smith commented, "It's the same thing in smoother words."[14]

Grant liked to come to decisions quickly and here he had done so. In spite of the sudden awakening, the situation within the Confederate entrenchments had become very obvious to his incisive mind. With the two senior generals not exercising command matters must be worse than Buckner let on. Grant had known Buckner as a military compatriot and friend. Buckner was a patrician of the type which was slow to see reality. The best way to get a reaction from him was to get him angry or to shock him. If his military condition was what Grant suspected it to be, Buckner would be forced into surrendering the garrison immediately. Grant wanted none of protracted negotiations which would allow Dover to be evacuated or reinforced. Grant held the cards at the moment and he showed them. The gracious closing was an afterthought to salve the feelings of a friend.

As Major Cheairs threaded his way under escort back to the Dover tavern with the verbal threat from Grant that the Federals would attack in one hour and 50 minutes, Brigadier Simon Bolivar Buckner chafed under the building tension. For a time which was beyond counting for his few waiting staff officers, the general peered out the north window onto the scene at the wharf. The first steamer, he saw, had been reloaded and was backing into mid-stream. The second vessel prepared to take on its complement.

Impatiently Buckner stalked back to the center of the dining room. Outside the tumult rose as the gangplank was lowered. This increased the nervousness of the new commander of Dover and Fort Donelson. It reminded him of the rumors filtering into his headquarters that talk was rife among the junior officers that someone should effect a coup de main and defend the entrenchments. Other news told of soldiers spiking artillery to prevent their being used by the North. This was contrary to Buckner's code of gentlemanly surrender.

What irked him most was that Floyd was pressing his deadline. The messenger should be returning at any minute. This would place Buckner in a compromising position *vis à vis* an honorable surrender. An escape or evacuation could not be tolerated from a surrendered fortress. A tour as instructor of ethics at the Point had made Buckner unusually aware of the protocol of the situation, and he was not about to stretch a point for an amateur like Floyd. He dispatched an officer to further warn and prod General Floyd.[15]

East of the bluffs of Dover a straggling line of hurrying men flowed toward the overflowing creek. Private James Woodward had tried to place himself aboard a transport but had found the last one just leaving. He had stayed for the return of the first boat but found it impossible to get aboard. He then set out for the road to Clarksville and found an unattended horse on the way. Mounted, he passed a good number of fellow Confederates walking their way to freedom.

Major Nat Cheairs reined up before the tavern and hitched his horse. Except by the anxious men inside the building he was unnoticed as everyone in the vicinity vied with one another to secure passage aboard what well might be the last ship from Dover. He strode through the doors to General Buckner, who as a matter of form did not advance.

Deliberately the general unfolded the rough paper and read. In spite of his upbringing he could not control his wrath and embarrassment at the bluntness and boldness of Grant's reply. For a second he was tempted to disregard his own counsels and resist. Reason immediately reminded him that the positions of his own division were unfortified and that many regiments there had not yet returned to their posts. Surrender at Fort Donelson was to be ignominious. No proud General Buckner would march out at the head of his troops between rows of reviewing victorious troops. Instead, probably, they would be trundled north, packed like sardines aboard Yankee boats. He had been abandoned and humiliated. When the time came, he vowed, he would demand a court of inquiry and see that his fleet-footed superiors were punished.

Nevertheless, unless the army was to be overrun and

slaughtered, the surrender must be effected immediately. Except for a recitation of Grant's note the surrounding staff knew nothing of what was going through the general's mind. The general called Colonel Brown and the two retired to an adjoining room to compare notes.

Nearly an hour later Buckner called Cheairs and handed him the stiff note to be taken to Grant:[16]

Headquarters, Dover, Tennessee
February 16, 1862

To Brig. Gen'l U. S. Grant, U. S. Army
Sir:

The distribution of the forces under my command, incident to an unexpected change of commanders, and the overwhelming force under your command, compel me, notwithstanding the brilliant success of the Confederate arms yesterday, to accept the ungenerous and unchivalrous terms which you propose.

I am sir,

Your very obedient servant,
S. B. Buckner, Brig. Gen. C.S.A.

Buckner reached for another sheet of paper. Now was the time to deal with Floyd. Wasting no formality Buckner hurriedly scribbled that unless the boat at the dock departed immediately he would shell it, since the surrender was about to take place.

Floyd was not difficult to locate and as his eyes drifted back and forth over the lines, his fleshy face turned white. An associate read the note aloud and from that moment there was spreading panic among the disorderly throng at the wharf. Hangers-on with the general secured a bodyguard of troops with fixed bayonets which escorted Floyd and his coterie aboard the last steamer.[17]

Included in the parade up the gangplank were Colonel John Head, newly ill, and Colonel Daniel Russell of the 20th

Mississippi, who had been indisposed throughout the siege. Fulfilling a promise of more than two hours before, some of Floyd's officers saw that Pillow's colored servant and his two horses were escorted aboard. In addition two privates were given protection as they carried Pillow's trunk containing his papers and baggage.

From his point of vantage Major Brown of the 20th Mississippi estimated that there were only about 200 Virginians of higher priority than his remaining Mississippians so he sent his adjutant down to the boat to remind Floyd that the 20th was ready to move.

The adjutant found the general nearly beside himself in consternation. One of McCausland's regiments still on the landing, in the strange absence of many of its officers, had apparently completely lost its discipline and was fighting its way up the gangplank. Aboard the boat guards held them off as the steamer's captain with some concern pointed out to Floyd the risk of swamping. With some connivance the adjutant wormed his way aboard. Relaying the message to Floyd, the adjutant added that since there seemed to be room for all, the 20th could clear the bank and restore order. Quite obviously distracted, Floyd impatiently waved him away saying that he would have to see.

No sooner had the adjutant repeated the unsatisfactory statement of Floyd than an aide from Buckner asked Brown to report to the general's presence. Brown found Buckner somewhat upset. The general notified the major that unless the boat put off immediately he would have his cannoneers put a shell into its side. He added that the same information had some time before been dispatched to General Floyd. Buckner then continued to expound on his reasons for taking such a drastic action. The place was surrendered, he observed, and with a white flag flying from the fort no resistance could be offered to the advance of the Union gunboats. In addition, his own honor was at stake, and, not to be mentioned, the honor of the Confederacy. When Buckner had finished, Brown stepped outside to the street to behold that the *General Anderson* had already cast off, taking only a few of his regiment. A scattering of outraged Confederates discharged their muskets at Floyd's boat in their frustration.[18]

A polyglot crew of gray uniformed landlubbers were in midstream as the last transport from Dover pushed off. Captain Jack Davis and his companions had been aroused to indignation by the news of imminent surrender. At first they had demanded of their senior officers that they fight their way out, but the officers felt that they themselves had not this right. Crouched now in the flatboat, Davis voiced the opinion that a delay of two hours could have permitted the two steamers to take the garrison and all of its supplies to the north bank of the Cumberland. Even at that moment, he asserted, a solid force posted in the trenches could have held off the Yankees while a host of Southerners could have escaped.

The sun was visible over the horizon as the son of Colonel Russell took off from the landing with his fellow Mississippians, Adjutant Cooper and Lieutenant Conway. They hoped to determine if some exit could not be found to the east. Other parties from their regiment preceded or followed them. Nearby the 56th Virginia with its commander, who was lowest in seniority in Floyd's brigade, found over 100 of its number had been abandoned. Because of the physical condition of the men—hard fighting and constant strain during the morning—their officers had discouraged the recruits from undertaking the strenuous escape march.[19]

Major W. E. Rogers searched through the personnel of his 3rd Mississippi for a large white piece of cloth. It was his sad assignment from General Johnson, on orders of Buckner, to bear the message of surrender to the Federal forces in their immediate front.

Downstream from the falling fortress, a crew of muscular seamen pulled their oars to the chant of the coxswain. In the stern of the rowboat sat Commander Benjamin Dove, being rowed to the gunboat *St. Louis*. Behind him lay the *Carondelet,* which he had just left with the orders to stay put on account of their large number of wounded in poor condition. General Grant had asked for a movement on the fort in the morning and to facilitate the operation Dove was ordering the injured sailors from the *St. Louis* and his own ironclad, *Louisville,* to be lowered to boats to be carried aboard an adjacent transport. As the boat reached the gangway of the *St. Louis,* he estimated that it might be some time before the remnants of the gunboat flotilla were under way.[20]

On the other side of Dover Colonel Nathan Bedford Forrest called on his command to come to a halt. It had been riding steadily for more than an hour after the ordeal of the crossing. The horses needed a rest and time must be provided for the rear guard and stragglers to catch up. The colonel estimated that they were far enough from Dover on the Cumberland Road to risk the rest. Nevertheless he dispatched scouts to keep watch on the trail behind for signs of Federal cavalry pursuit. Forrest was not much concerned, however, because of what he had seen or, more accurately, not seen of the Yankee horsemen of Grant's army during the four-day siege. The Federal cavalry had been distinguished at Fort Donelson mainly for its absence.

Major Rogers signaled to the young lad at his side to sound his bugle. Then he grasped the staff of the improvised flag and began his sad duty. Minutes later Union pickets rose from the concealing brush, covered him with their rifles and guided him southwestward toward the Wynn's Ferry Road where Lew Wallace was conducting Thayer's brigade to the staging spot for his planned morning storming of the enemy lines. The notes of the parley call had rung clear through the crisp, cold air. Wallace was determined to beat McClernand to any credit for any part of a surrender and quickly dispatched his adjutant to locate and return with the Confederate envoy.

By this time every soldier in the Southern army garrison was awake and discussing the meaning of the surrender of the army. Pros and cons of the advantages of prison life to the continued active service in the fighting corps were debated back and forth. By and large though, the extremists who urged every man to join in overthrowing the traitorous regime of disloyal officers found no following in the Southern regiments. High faith was placed in the officer corps by the rank and file largely because they had in most cases elected the same to their positions and for the reason that most of the privates had little semblance of education.

The decision for escape was often made on a different basis. If a friend took the lead in urging flight, most likely his clique would follow him if his influence was great enough. In this fashion before the chill of evening had vanished from the morning many of the nameless Southern army were hiking through the gullies to the east to at least have a look-see at the odds of a safe departure. Some, like Colonel McGavock, even considered swimming the frigid Cumberland to freedom.

Messrs. Russell, Cooper, and Conway, officers of the 20th Mississippi, stepped gingerly through the icy Lick Creek water up to their chests. On the far side the trio wrung out what moisture they could from their clothing and commenced to jog in the direction of Nashville, hoping thus to keep warm and dry out their uniforms.

Orderly Sergeant James Chandler of the 27th Alabama (Heiman's Brigade) saw on awakening that a white flag had just been posted on the hill. A crony urged him and a friend to investigate what they could do in effecting a departure. The three set out for the river and skirted its flow heading eastward. Finding no craft for escape and the landing deserted, they continued toward the sun.

Facing Brigadier General Wallace, Major Rogers, the words nearly choking in his throat, announced that everything under the control of the army of the Confederate States had been surrendered unconditionally. In addition General Johnson had ordered him, he continued, to request that this knowledge be passed on along the Union line to ensure that no accidental hostilities would occur. Looking to the left and right, Rogers flushed with a mixture of anger and embarrassment at the joy which could not be controlled by the Federal officers.

Wallace called Lieutenant Ross of his staff to his side and introduced him to Rogers. Wallace notified the major that Ross would accompany him to the headquarters of General Grant. While the pair then rode down the Wynn's Ferry Road at high speed, the general designated specific aides to carry verbal orders to the brigade leaders to march upon the ceded trenches and take charge of public property and prisoners. Then he and his remaining staff rode slowly for the sake of safety toward the enemy lines until they saw a white banner decorating the earthworks. At that reassuring sight they spurred their steeds up the road toward the town of Dover. It was a few minutes after 6:30.

Private S. S. Morgan of the 14th Mississippi was with his regiment in the proximity of Dover when he made up his mind that he wasn't going to stand idly by and wait for a Yankee prison camp to come to him. He had not walked far toward the rising sun when he joined company with messmates James Grady, L. C. English, and Bence Tubb, all of whom were bent on the same purpose.

Sergeant Chandler and his two buddies had meanwhile come upon the banks of Lick Creek and had followed it to a point where they encountered other groups of soldiers determined on departure. All continued upstream until they bumped into a still larger knot of immobile volunteers. Here a footlog, most of it under water, had been discovered leading to the far side of the creek. Slowly and sometimes unsuccessfully a procession of troops endeavored to cross by treading on it.[21]

At seven o'clock Wallace and his escort had finally located Buckner's new headquarters. On the way sullen Confederate soldiers had been uncommunicative to his inquiries for information and hosts of straggling gray-uniformed men cluttered the roads all along the way. Now, however, he was able to dismount and pay his respects.

The sentry at the door asked his name and passed him and his associates on inside. On the lower level in the rear of the tavern several disconsolate Confederate officers sat huddled at a large table waiting for their breakfasts. Simon Buckner looked up, noticed his visitors, drew himself up to full dignity and stepped forward, at the same time motioning his guests to continue their entrance. After greeting the Union division commander, a pre-war friend, Buckner politely added, "General Wallace, it is not necessary to introduce you to these gentlemen. You are acquainted with them all."

At that all of the Confederate officers rose and walked over to Wallace and shook his hand. In turn Wallace introduced his staff officers. Buckner then graciously offered them a place at his table for corn bread and coffee while they awaited the arrival of General Grant. Wallace accepted with gratitude. He was hungry.

The *Louisville* and *St. Louis* had rounded the point to come within sight of Fort Donelson. From one of the casements of the *Louisville,* in the lead, came the shout that a white flag had replaced the Confederate colors over the batteries. Unable to believe his ears, Dove rushed to an embrasure with his glass to verify the report of the sharp-eyed lookout. Boilers and machinery were set to working at full speed and the *Louisville* signaled a tugboat which had been tagging behind to hasten to the side of the flagship.[22]

Major Cheairs stood by in the encampment of Smith's division as Brigadier General Ulysses Grant digested the contents of Buckner's final note. To satisfy his curiosity Grant asked the Tennessean how large an army the South had fielded on Saturday. Cheairs guessed seven or eight thousand. Grant scoffed and Cheairs replied hotly, whereupon the general apologized. Grant then began issuing orders to his aides for the occupation of the entrenchments.

Abreast of the fort Dove transferred from the gunboat to the tug for the purpose of going ashore. At that time a second white flag flying from the upper battery came to his attention. In the interim as the *Louisville* had raced against the current, Dove had retired to his stateroom to accouter himself in his best naval uniform glittering with gold braid.

Near the lower battery Dove stepped ashore. Down the hill at a slow run came a Confederate major, grasping the hanger of his sword as he ran. The Southerner, unhappy that the gunboats had fired on the white flag of the fort, drew up before the commander, unhooked the weapon and offered it to the naval officer. Dove shook his head, saying he could not accept this symbol because he had not yet consulted with General Grant on what course of action he should follow. He did request that the Confederate accompany him to the town, and the two walked up the gangplank onto the tug, which set off for Dover.

Along with many others of the Southern army Sergeant Chandler and his companions had crossed the footlog to the far side of the slough. Ahead of them lay a long hike to the nearest Confederate military post, but the outlook was optimistic, as no Union soldiers had yet made an appearance.[23]

The Federal forces had received the surrender news with acclamation. The cheering had conveniently interrupted the replenishing of ammunition stocks by some of C. F. Smith's regiments. Now as Union military units pressed cautiously on toward the town, reports kept filtering in of a steady egress of small groups and individuals in gray uniform toward the east. An occasional detachment took station across the avenues of escape, but in short order they moved on to prospects of better opportunity, i.e. loot.

The difficulties of transportation had left the regiments on the line in general poorly supplied during the four-day engagement. Now hungry bluecoats marching in military order caught sight of undestroyed supply dumps of Confederate provisions. At first individual volunteers broke off from the columns to snatch the best of the loot. Others fearing nothing would remain for them hungrily broke ranks and joined the rush. Those with appetites satisfied cast their eyes around for "souvenirs" anywhere they could be found. Discipline in the Union army was reaching a low point.

Meanwhile Grant continued to prescribe the methods by which he desired the lines to be taken over. Officers were to keep their charges under strict control. Private Confederate soldiers were to be disarmed and the weapons stacked in centrally guarded depots. Destruction of military property by the enemy was to be forcibly prevented. All exits from the post were to be sealed off.[24]

Commander Dove and his Southern major strode along the Dover wharf, just shortly before abandoned by the last enemy transport, toward a figure in blue who stood at the land end. The Federal officer notified him that General Buckner had made the tavern his headquarters. Dove thanked him and proceeded.

On the porch the resplendent commander paused to meticulously brush off flecks of dirt which had accumulated on his blue coat. His knuckles tapped at the large door and a voice from within the place invited him to come in. In one grand sweep he swung the outer door open and went down the stairs, preparing to accept the surrender of Fort Donelson in the name of the navy.

As heads expectantly craned around to ascertain the identity of the visitor, Dove drew to a halt. Sure enough a Confederate general was present, but a senior general of the Union army was sitting at the same table. Unconsciously Dove's mouth gaped open as at the same time he removed his cap. Puzzled, Wallace pushed back his chair, rose to his feet, and walked over to find out what was the matter with this strange intruder.

"I understand this place has surrendered," blurted out the commander .

Wallace signified that it had.

"Under what terms?" inquired Dove.

"I understand from General Buckner that there were no terms," responded Wallace.

Dove rejoiced and commented inconsequentially on the significance and glory of the success. Wallace politely voiced his agreement.

At that the embarrassed naval officer began to effect his retreat by first bowing, his eyes looking first to Wallace and then beyond to General Buckner. "I beg to be excused, gentlemen," he said.

No sooner had the door to the room closed, than Wallace returned to his leisurely breakfast. He looked at Buckner with an amused smile and then the latter spoke up, "Do you know him?"

Wallace's teeth shone brightly in contrast to his mustache and beard as he answered, "Never saw the man before."

"He's one of your navy—so much is certain," Buckner suggested. He then turned to one of his staff. "You had better follow him, Captain, and see that no harm comes to him."

Simultaneously Wallace muttered an aside to Lieutenant Addison Ware, "The navy seems to be abroad very early.

Perhaps they're looking for swords." The satisfaction of evening the score for Fort Henry was evident on all the Union soldiers' faces.[25]

As it was going on eight o'clock General Grant prepared to make his triumphal entry. Orderlies had brought forth the saddled horses of all his deputies and his own well-curried war horse. A detachment of picked cavalrymen was drawn up as escort along the road. All initial matters for the occupation having been handled, Grant was ready to meet General Buckner.

General Charles Smith had not yet advanced his division to seize the works, and as Grant passed at a slow trot, the infantrymen cheered their victorious leader. No grandstander, Grant received the applause by bending his head forward and raising his hand to the level of the horse's head periodically. At the front lines the drum-beating regiments followed on his heels into Rebel territory. White flags were conspicuously flying everywhere. As Southern infantry in line behind their stacked rifles glared at the intruders, Smith and Grant exchanged courtesies with Colonel John Brown, who had come forward with his sword. Leaving the Confederate with his sidearm, the generals proceeded to discuss with him the procedure of the turnover of command from one army to another.

From Buckner's position the commanding general and his party descended the long slope into the valley of Indian Creek. Along the side of the road lines of Secessionist foot soldiers lounged menacingly on their rifles and muskets, so much so that troopers drew their revolvers. No incidents occurred, however, and soon the mounted men were urging their mounts up the obverse slope which did not really terminate until they had reached the edge of town. They trotted through the muddy streets of the provincial village, skirted the courthouse where the American flag was being raised from the cupola and proceeded east for two blocks. Here the crowd of loitering

Confederates had thickened, but several squads of blue infantry had the situation under control.

They made a left turn under their guide's direction and sighted their goal, almost undistinguishable from its surrounding buildings except for the small herd of horses tethered before it. A detachment of Union troops had taken station around the building and at the end of the dock, which was a continuation of the street, a tug flying the Stars and Stripes had tied up.

Grant's eye caught sight of an odd party of three standing in the roadway before the tavern. One man was in crumpled army blue, another in equally wrinkled Confederate gray, while the third wore a crisp naval uniform bristling with gold braid. At that moment the trio broke up as the naval personage made his way through the horses of the escort to the side of General Grant, who was by this time dismounting. He introduced himself as Commander Dove, temporarily in command of the Federal gunboats and asked if Grant had any orders. Giving his reins over to Captains Stewart and Schwartz of McClernand's staff Grant pondered, then suggested that all the gunboats be brought to the vicinity of the Dover landing to protect the eastern flank on the river. It was with some relief that the general observed that the commander carried no sword but his own. He would not collect swords from an enemy who had fought so honorably and well.[26]

There was the clomp of boots on the porch. A Federal lieutenant grasped the doorknob, put his weight to the door, and easily levered it open. He guided Grant to the stairs and shortly they entered the small basement room. Simon Buckner knew the moment had come. The fellow military schoolmate, the personal friend of the Mexican War and afterwards, the man who had brusquely offered the most degrading terms known to military protocol, the man who after receiving his message of acceptance of terms had kept him waiting for two hours would now meet him face to face in a matter of seconds.

Buckner was grateful for the long chat with Wallace; it had helped him to cool off. Buckner was now ready to receive his guest with his usual urbanity.

Grant came through the door, flashed his eyes over the many faces, finally aimed his look at Buckner, and waited uncertainly for a reaction. The Confederate commander was rising to his feet. Nudging his chair out of the way, he stepped around the table to within a couple of yards of Grant and bowed and smiled. "General, as they say in Mexico, this house and all it contains is yours."[27]

As Buckner was uttering these painfully obvious words, Brigadier General John B. Floyd walked heavily toward a shack housing the military telegraph in Cumberland City, Tennessee. The *General Anderson* and her consort had paused at this now front-line outpost to take on wood, but the refugee ex-commander would have ordered the lay-over anyhow. Pangs of discomfort and remorse had begun their ravages shortly after the precipitous departure from the dock at Dover. As Floyd had gradually taken hold of himself, he regretted the abandonment of sizable numbers of his own brigade infantry and of all three batteries of artillery and their complements which he brought from Russellville and from Virginia. Finally after a while it had occurred to him that perhaps Johnston deserved a more full report than he had dispatched. Possibly too he might have some explaining to do for some of his activities. He then sat down and wrote.

Floyd handed the operator on duty his message of defeat to the commanding general in the west and walked to prepare the maintenance garrison for evacuation. Over the wires the herald of doom to the Confederacy read:

This morning at 2 o'clock, not feeling myself willing to surrender, I turned over the command to General Buckner, who determined a surrender of the fort and the army, as any further resistance would only result in the unavailing spilling of blood. I succeeded in saving half of my own command by availing myself of two little boats at the wharf, all that could be commanded. The balance of the entire reserve of the army fell into the hands of the enemy. The enemy's force was largely augmented yesterday by the arrival of thirteen transports, and his force could not have been less than 50,000. I have attempted to do my duty in this trying and difficult position, and only regret that my exertions have not been more successful.[28]

The cavalry of Colonel Forrest were once more on the march. No signs of pursuit had as yet manifested themselves. The destination was Nashville via Clarksville, unless contrary orders diverted them elsewhere.

Almost directly opposite Forrest across the swollen Cumberland, General Gideon Pillow and his staff had secured horses from the cavalry detachment on the north side of the river and were riding rapidly toward Clarksville.

Ulysses Grant was quite willing to introduce this distasteful session with his old comrade in arms with pleasant conversation and Buckner was gracious enough to humor the victor in this inclination. Buckner's former instructor, C. F. Smith, was uncompromising in his attitude and conversation with the Rebel general. His refusal to even join the Confederates at breakfast made Buckner noticeably uncomfortable. Following Buckner's lead the talk had gone to recalling memories from the campaign in Mexico. General Wallace and his men had then departed on the excuse that the direction of the occupation by their division had to be attended to.

Grant questioned the Kentuckian on when he had arrived at Donelson. Buckner replied and the two compared notes on the initial days of the engagement. Smoking continuously, Grant remarked on the relatively easy march from Fort Henry to the vicinity of Fort Donelson. Buckner, momentarily forgetting that he had been in immediate command on the morning of the 12th as Pillow had been absent at Cumberland City, replied that the Union army would not have approached so easily had he, Buckner, been in charge of the Confederate army then. Smiling, Grant responded that he himself would have adopted more cautious tactics if he had knowingly been opposing his old schoolmate at West Point.

At this stage Grant brought himself to inquire what had happened to Pillow. The circumstances of the surrender since the conference had made this a sore point with Buckner and he answered between clenched teeth, "Gone."

"Why did he go?"

"Well," growled the Southerner, "he thought you'd rather get hold of him than any other man in the Southern Confederacy."

Grant's relaxed face broke into a smile. "Oh, if I'd got him, I'd let him go again. He would do us more good commanding you fellows."

Buckner managed a smile too. It did not travel from the heart, however, for he recognized that he had let his anger stretch the truth beyond an explicable point.

Shortly thereafter Grant eased into the details of the capitulation. For his information he asked about the numbers of men and equipment within the garrison. Buckner, as a Union aide made ready to note the figures, apologized for his ignorance but he had only been in command for a short time. He estimated that the troops numbered between 12,000 and 15,000. (He forgot to deduct Floyd's escapees, nor did he know of the individuals funneling to the east.) He had no precise information on the supplies and equipment. The Federals would have to take inventory on that themselves.

Buckner then turned to the subject of the late battle on Saturday. The Confederates were not in possession of the field and had not been able to bury their dead. They would be anxious to do so. The Illinoisan without hesitation authorized him to send out burial parties on their own.

On the matter of rations Buckner observed that his army had not been too well off here but that a quantity had just arrived that morning at the dock. Grant returned that Northern transports could easily move up sufficient quantities from the temporary Union base downstream to Dover. This would probably suffice until the Confederates were shipped north to detention camps.

Officers, continued Grant, would be permitted to retain their sidearms and body servants. Other Negroes, of whom there were a large number, however, would be impressed to do work on Federal service. Their owners would not have the return of them. The Confederate prisoners could also keep their clothing and blankets.[29]

A courier brought Albert Sidney Johnston Floyd's final telegram. The last of the Central Army was approaching the northern bridgehead of the Cumberland as the general sat magnificently on his charger perusing the contents of the news of disaster. The upshot of the message did not greatly disturb Johnston. His fickle mind had once again written off Fort Donelson and its contents when he had awakened that Sunday morning and found Floyd's first telegram awaiting him. Now he told himself that the final shock he had predicted more than a week ago had now arrived. More important, his main fighting force, the Central Army, less than 20,000 troops, was not closely pursued and was safe from entrapment.

A spark of interest flickered over some of the wording of the dispatch. Floyd did not explain why he had turned his command over to Buckner with any satisfaction. He indicates that the command was relinquished because surrender was imminent, yet Floyd places the burden of responsibility for surrender on Buckner while he himself indicates that he concurred in this decision.[30]

Strange indeed, yet Johnston dismissed this from his mind in his great concern to prepare Nashville for its abandonment to its fate. Just as no message of inquiry had been sent to Fort Donelson on what the current status had been there, so no message went to Richmond on the surrender of this bulwark and its garrison, which Johnston himself had estimated several days previous to stand at 17,000. Perhaps some encouraging news would come in later which would sooth the politician's ire.

Outside in the rain the governor of Tennessee galloped through the rainy streets of Nashville announcing the surrender.

Buckner and his staff rode among the increasingly wild Federal throngs which were swelling the streets of Dover. Grant was taking over the tavern as his own headquarters and Buckner had gone to his quarters upstairs in the tavern.[31]

In preparation for his own report Grant had his aides collating information on captured supplies and materials. Commissary officers were ordered to include the Confederate prisoners in their issue of rations. Southern burial parties were to be permitted on the Saturday battlefield. All arms not belonging to Rebel officers were to be collected, he reiterated.

It was nearly ten o'clock as a petulant patrol of the Union army slogged northward through the beginning rain along Lick Creek. In the west from a distance they could hear the noise concommitant with the seizure of the spoils of war. Instead of sharing in these, this patrol was sent by some conscientious officer to assure the sealing off of the Confederate encampment from the outside. The volunteers were unhappy and reluctantly obedient.

A rumble of suppressed voices came from ahead. The Federal officer in charge silently spread out his men and they swept in as a fan on the suspicious region. Before them lay a small cluster of Confederates on their side of the creek. Their focal point was a submerged log on which several were struggling through the high water. A number of shots were fired in the air and soon most of the drenched Southerners had returned to the Union side of the creek. Fort Donelson and Dover had effectively become a Union prison camp.[32]

Between the creeks Hickman and Lick 10,000 Confederate soldiers were hemmed in and shut in a loose but formal detention. With the advent of the occupation by Union brigades Southern officers issued orders restricting their followers to their own specific camps. This succeeded in keeping the incidents between the "betrayed" Rebels and their conquerors to a minimum, although most of the prisoners gave up their knives and pistols with reluctance.

Some Southern officers who received the word permitted details to venture out on the overgrowth with pick and shovel to hunt for and bury their own valiant dead. Especially prominent in these parties were the regiments who had suffered the most grievous losses on the 15th. Federal groups bent on a similar duty for their own deceased were criss-crossing the area. The scene raised mixed emotions but some Union volunteers were not beneath taunting their sudden "prisoners" and on occasion depriving them of the use of their tools. So by and large the Confederate dead were buried less deep than the two feet which was the rule of thumb for the Federal details. So hurried in some cases was the Southern digging that Rebel corpses protruded their feet through the mounds of the pits and burial trenches.

Lieutenant J. O. Churchill had at daybreak seen the first Federal search parties appear in his vicinity. Nevertheless it was ten o'clock before he was evacuated to a hospital.[33]

Captain Reuben Ross' dark features grew murky as a Union detail from the 2nd Iowa amid the fanfare of a bugle call raised the Stars and Stripes on the water battery flagpole of Fort Donelson. It seemed that a lot of work and sweat and bloodletting had gone for nothing. Then as he averted his grim eyes from the scene, a current of somber satisfaction eased over Ross' mind. The river batteries were the enemies of the Union Navy. It was the Union Army that was taking their possession. Fort Donelson had done its duty—actually more than had been expected of it. It had fended off the ironclad gunboats.

Word was abroad through the Confederate tents that Forrest and some others had apparently made good their escape. As postmortems once again raised their pitch, some observers in the Confederate ranks could not help observing that the large number of horses still within the Southern lines could have made possible the evacuation of the bulk of the army over the dreaded flooded slough. Some solace was taken in the fact that many regimental flags had been hidden or burned.

Individual freedom and lax discipline had become the rule in the Union army at Dover. Divisions, brigades, and regiments all intermixed in their desire not to miss the spoils or the sights. After all the war might not last long enough now to provide any like experience in the future. One reporter was seen striding along the earthworks, his head bent low, taking notes as if the parapets would soon melt.

Many took it upon themselves to interview the more communicative Confederates. The diehard Secessionists provided material for amusing letters home. A good number of the Southern volunteers drawled that they were now tired of the war and would like to return to their farms and see to the planting. Some skeptical Yankees smelled a hoax when some under-educated wearers of the gray professed with seeming sincerity to believe that they had been fighting for the Union all along.[34]

In Buckner's divisional front a group of curious youngsters from the 7th Iowa were examining the fine firing pieces of the vaunted 2nd Kentucky. An inscription on the stock of one of the rifles led one soldier to utter a shout of astonishment. In 1859 the old abolitionist John Brown had issued arms to certain of his followers who were going east with him from Iowa and the Kansas war. In a short time these weapons had found use in the abortive rebellion at Harpers Ferry. At the time of the secession of Virginia these arms were shipped to the Confederates stockpile and eventually went west to equip the 2nd Kentucky.

In the capital of the divided nation, the President of the United States, even knowing his son, Willie, lay only hours from death, was showing his interest in the campaign in a message to Henry Halleck:

> You have Fort Donelson safe, unless Grant shall be overwhelmed from outside. . . .Our success or failure at Fort Donelson is vastly important, and I beg you to put your soul into the effort.

Meanwhile Halleck himself was writing McClellan. "Fort Donelson is the turning point of the war, and we must take it at whatever sacrifice."

With the many problems on his mind, organization of his command was not one of the foremost for Ulysses S. Grant. His concern for the safety of nearly denuded Fort Henry had led him to send Lew Wallace with two brigades, accompanied by artillery and cavalry hotfooting it back to the Tennessee to defend that post against any expedition from Columbus.[35]

In addition, estimates on the spoils of victory had been assembled. Henry Halleck deserved the good news and an account of the activities which led up to the success. In his new headquarters in the Dover tavern Grant had been etching out the story of the siege in a long (for Grant) report which amounted to nearly two pages of handwriting. On orders the *Conestoga* gunboat was standing by to speed this and other necessary messages on to Cairo.

In space he had left at the beginning of the letter Grant scratched in the line which would turn the North upside down with rapture and joy:

We have taken Fort Donelson and from 12,000 to 15,000 prisoners, including Generals Buckner and Bushrod Johnston; also about 20,000 stand of arms, 48 pieces of artillery, 17 heavy guns, from 2,000 to 4,000 horses and quantities of commissary stores.[36]

After this U. S. Grant certainly would not be forgotten.

Epilogue

Sidney Johnston awaited further developments on Monday before he notified Secretary of War Benjamin of the debacle. To disguise the delay he announced in the telegram that Fort Donelson had surrendered at 4:10 P.M.[1]

Both Pillow and Floyd had arrived from Clarksville with the wounded and prisoners that morning. Johnston never questioned giving either further responsibilities, for Pillow marched off from Nashville with a new command and Floyd was handed the major task of evacuating the capital of Tennessee and of maintaining the rear guard, a job which he turned over to the trusted Forrest on his arrival. The Central Army marched south.

On Tuesday the Union army had oriented itself to the role of jailer to the extent that Bushrod Johnson no longer had direct charge over his division. He therefore in company with another officer took a walk near sundown over the brow of Heiman's hill and, finding no sentries, kept walking down the road to Charlotte.[2] Reinstated as a general in the Confederacy, he was severely wounded at Shiloh, but returned to service and surrendered at Appomattox.

Later in the day Buckner was permitted to write a report

to Johnston. In it he played the role of a martyr who had been left in the lurch by his superiors and asked for an inquiry.

Later as the Confederates were being shipped by stages north, Buckner entered the ship cabin of General Grant. In the course of the conversation the captor offered the Confederate the use of his private purse in his present difficult circumstances. Buckner was touched by this effort to repay their eight-year-old debt but said that he would get by.

Somehow newspapers in the North had received the erroneous impression that Grant was a devotee of the cigar. The general soon became flooded with boxes of cigars, and in a short time the cigar would become an actual personal symbol.

Henry Halleck was slow to congratulate Grant on the victory, although he did not deny praise to Foote, who had a lesser part. In addition he began to complain on the quality of reporting done by his front-line battle leader. Statements went to Washington that the army of Western Tennessee was disorganized if not outright demoralized, an observation which had more than a trace of truth. Finally he suspended the just-appointed major general for unauthorized cooperation with Buell. Tired of harassment, Grant wrote that if his superiors had not confidence in him he would tender his resignation.

By this time, however, Halleck had been given overall command in the west and he could not afford an internal wrangle within his department. Buell, after the rapid Confederate evacuation of central Tennessee, had taken the direct route to Nashville, occupying it on the 24th, and the two major Union armies still had not effected their junction.

Meanwhile, with the abandonment of Columbus, Henry Foote was directing the naval operations against the next Confederate bastion on the Mississippi, the area of New Madrid. Every time he stepped on his painful foot the Flag Officer recalled the effectiveness of the Rebel river batteries at

Fort Donelson. In this campaign he proceeded cautiously and deliberately, but in the long run very successfully.

In Richmond the stigma of defeat and surrender combined with the circumstances set forth in Buckner's report led to the focusing of official ire upon Floyd and Pillow. On March 11, the capital had both officers suspended from active duty, pending further investigation and more detailed reports on certain phases of the struggle from them both.

For a time Floyd tried to redeem his honor but his feeling of guilt over the operations at Fort Donelson was too overpowering. One of his last attempts at reinstatement came in August after Buckner's exchange when Floyd wrote his former subordinate congratulating him on his return to the Confederacy and emphasizing his own high opinion of Buckner. He did not hesitate to include mention of the misfortunes which had befallen him, but it was to no avail and he retired to private life in Virginia where he died the following year.

Pillow, of course, was not one to give in so easily. Voluminous reports and letters, complete with depositions from associates at Dover, deluged the War Office at Richmond. While his first battle report had been extremely matter of fact, indicating no guilty conscience, after his suspension praise of Buckner and rationalizations began to creep into his correspondence.

Historically speaking, neither Pillow nor Floyd in all of their explanations ever laid strategic blame for their predicament at the door of the departmental commander, Albert Sidney Johnston. Viewed from the perspective of the times this fact is not surprising. In March when the official charges were levelled Johnston was still their immediate superior who had shown confidence in them. Also it was possible that their initial explanations would suffice. After April 6, it was too late. At Shiloh General Albert Sidney Johnston had become the first national martyr of the Confederacy and was unassailable.

In August Pillow, still not exonerated, received orders to report to the army of General Braxton Bragg. Shifted to the Mississippi area, Pillow once again submitted his resignation when General Earl Van Dorn did not assign him to any military duty. At the same time he recited and reviewed all of his past "wrongs," including one that the government had given the Tennessee regiments organized by Pillow to his old antagonist, Leonidas Polk. To his surprise in October the resignation was accepted by Richmond. His bluff dramatically called, Pillow hurriedly responded that he had not really resigned.

Fortunately for the Tennessee lawyer this farce came to an end in December. The famous General Joseph E. Johnston had just come to command between the Mississippi and the mountains and called for the services of his old division commander in Mexico. This was in spite of Pillow's dismissal for insubordination in the Mexico City campaign by Scott. Dubious of Pillow's usefulness in the field, Johnston assigned him to a new job of collecting and organizing conscripts in the military district.

Immediately Pillow began to efficiently round up draft dodgers, recruit volunteers, and collect army stragglers. The Army of Tennessee especially prospered, but the goddess of controversy once again devoted special attention to this gentleman and in early 1863, the Secretary of War closed Pillow's office because of the methods he was using. In June, Johnston tried again, giving Pillow essentially the same job for three states. Once again the generals were satisfied, but civil rights in a states' rights conscious area had been tread upon and Pillow was making overtures to extend his "successful" methods to other regions with a corresponding augmentation in his power and the troops at his disposal. Once again a dispute with the Secretary of War arose and in disgust Pillow resigned his post in October, 1863. About the same time he wrote a last letter to President Davis and finally left the service for good. After the war Pillow, like many another ex-Confederate officer, tried to regain financial security. He died 16 years after the zenith and nadir of his career at Fort Donelson.

As the days passed with military uneventfulness, "Unconditional Surrender" Grant was becoming even more of a popular image. Reports emanating from the highest circles in western Tennessee had increased the estimate of the bag of Southern prisoners at Fort Donelson to 21,000. This conveniently conformed with Grant's fears early in the campaign that the siege forces were outnumbered by the garrison.

History has rather readily accepted this total, based largely on the number of rations given by the commissary general of prisoners at Cairo to a segment of the defeated army as it passed. This number was 14,623.[3] The lieutenant of the Mexican War, now brigadier general, had found the men under his control doubling in the past ten days. Without a natural flair for organization and without experience for so wide a charge, Grant never did get around to enumerating the Confederate prisoners. As for the commissary department, corruption was not an unknown vice in these regions, and what was a better area to practice on than enemy prisoners of war? The figure might easily have been inflated to compensate for past or future deficits. In addition, Johnston's estimate of 17,000 men at Dover is unacceptable since, as it has been seen, his figures were too high from the beginning.

Actually much of the management of the Confederate army in detention went over to Simon Buckner. As the transportation became available for carrying the prisoners north, Grant asked Buckner to have certain quotas ready at the landing for deportation. In his complete report to the War Department after the exchange in August, Buckner states that only 9,000 men were surrendered.[4]

Returning as the shining knight who had been abandoned

but who had chosen to share the foreboding fate of his men, Buckner was promoted to major general and immediately assigned command of the vital Mobile district, the Department of the Gulf. Later he joined Bragg in Kentucky and received the Department of East Tennessee. After that he fought in the battles of Murfreesboro, Chickamauga, and Knoxville. In July, 1864, at the request of the Department of Trans-Mississippi commander, he was transferred to that district and was promoted to lieutenant general. Here in the last days of the war he acceded reluctantly to a drive to install himself as military commander west of the Mississippi. When this coup fizzled, he surrendered the last corps of the Confederate States Army on May 26, 1865.

After the war Buckner entered politics and in time became governor of Kentucky and candidate for vice-president on the gold Democratic ticket. The last of the senior Confederate officers, Buckner died in 1914.

Lloyd Tilghman also returned to the Confederacy through the medium of exchange. In May of 1863, however, he was killed in Mississippi at Champion's Hill.

All of the surrendered garrison who survived the prison camps were exchanged. John Calvin Brown was shot at Perryville and again at Franklin but emerged as a major general. The bookseller, William Baldwin, became a brigadier but had the misfortune to be captured again at Vicksburg. After parole he died in a riding accident the next year. The lieutenant colonel of the 8th Kentucky, Hylan Benton Lyon, contrived to escape from besieged Vicksburg with his command. After joining forces with Forrest, Lyon returned to his favorite service as artillery commander at the Battle of Chattanooga.

Adolphus Heiman died of illness in Mississippi that November. Randal McGavock succeeded him in command of the 10th Tennessee but was killed by Grant's army at Raymond, Mississippi in 1863.

Roger Hanson enjoyed his release for a shorter span than most, because on the second day of the battle of Stones River he received a mortal wound while at the head of his brigade. After the exchange Hiram Granbury rose from major to colonel of his 7th Texas. After being made a brigadier he was killed storming the Federal works at Franklin. Joseph Palmer of the 18th Tennessee received wounds at Murfreesboro and Jonesboro. Promoted to brigadier general, he surrendered in North Carolina with Johnston. Major George Cosby became a brigadier in 1863.

Nathan Bedford Forrest, of course, became the most famous of all the Confederates at Donelson. While serving well at Shiloh, he did not become the legendary cavalry leader until given independent raiding assignments where he at once achieved spectacular successes against adverse odds. In a strange twist of history the low point in his military career came in April, 1864, when he stormed Fort Pillow, Tennessee (which the Federals as a tribute of their low esteem had not renamed) and massacred the predominantly Negro garrison.

A weak rival of Forrest in the East was John McCausland, who with his cavalry captured and burned Chambersburg, Pennsylvania, and cut his way out from Appomattox with his brigade before the surrender. His associate brigadier at Dover, Gabriel Wharton, later also received his star and served with Early in the valley of the Shenandoah.

Of the major Union participants Andrew Foote felt great discomfort from his ankle injury suffered at Fort Donelson and refused further promotion. Complications continued him on inactive duty and he died in 1863.

During Grant's temporary dismissal General C. F. Smith, a favorite of Halleck's, had succeeded to the command of the army. Under his direction the force moved up the Tennessee to Pittsburg Landing. Here in late March a painful leg injury and the results of exposure at Donelson made him relinquish his command. Within a month Smith had died in bed a few miles from the Shiloh battlefield.

On that battlefield on April 6, W. H. L. Wallace, who had received the nod for promotion to brigadier general, had been shot while unsuccessfully attempting to effect the retreat of his division. Within a few days of Smith he died in the same house.

John McClernand also fought at Shiloh, where his performance was not outstanding. Succeeding months found him still under Grant's Army of the Tennessee and his ambitions grew. Appointed a major general within weeks of Grant he exercised his connections with Washington to obtain an independent command on the Mississippi. He managed to undertake a successful expedition into Arkansas, but Grant reappeared on the scene to make him a subordinate corps commander within Grant's army. Then during the siege of Vicksburg McClernand overplayed his hand in the newspapers and was suspended by Grant and resigned the next year and went back to law.

On the first day at Shiloh, Lew Wallace was camped four miles downstream from Pittsburg Landing. In moving up he became lost or misdirected and arrived too late to be of any help. This misfortune left a mark on his military record which bothered him and evidently others. In spite of being appointed major general for his services at Fort Donelson, he was out of favor with Halleck and fought again only when Jubal Early threatened the District of Columbia in 1864. After the war Wallace served in the diplomatic service and as governor of New Mexico, where he dealt with Billy the Kid. He also continued writing novels, among them *Ben-Hur*. He died in 1905.

With Halleck's assistance James McPherson had a rapid rise up the military scale. Slightly over a year after the capture of Fort Donelson, he commanded one of the three corps of the Army of the Tennessee. Less than a year and he was directing that army itself. Then on July 22, 1864, Southern rifle balls killed him instantly on the outskirts of the Atlanta entrenchments. James B. McPherson was the only Federal army commander to be killed in action in the Civil War.

Under him in that fatal campaign served the bellicose politician of the 31st Illinois as a corps commander. Up to the very end of the war "Black Jack" John Logan was one of William T. Sherman's hardest fighting generals. On the death of McPherson he had temporarily been given the command of the Army of the Tennessee and in December Grant, remembering no doubt Logan's fighting spirit at Donelson on the 15th of February, appointed him to replace the ponderous George Thomas at Nashville. By the time he arrived, however, Thomas had scattered John Hood's army to the winds.

With the country at peace Logan switched his allegiance to the Republican Party. A year after the end of war he was prosecuting his former commander in chief, Andrew Johnson, for impeachment in the U. S. Senate. After serving in the Senate Logan tossed his hat into the ring for the Republican Presidential nomination but settled for the Vice-Presidential nod. When Cleveland and Hendricks won, Logan again became senator and died in office in 1886, at the age of sixty.

Amiable and competent Richard Oglesby later fought at Shiloh and Corinth and was promoted to the rank of major general. In 1864, the people of Illinois elected him governor on the Lincoln slate and he served in that office through 1873. He was then appointed to a term in the United States Senate. In 1885 he was again elected governor of Illinois. Oglesby died in 1899.

In October, 1862, John McArthur was one of the three division commanders defending Corinth against the assault of the Confederate army. Of the other Union brigadiers James Cruft, Jacob Lauman, Morgan Smith, Isham Haynie, and John Thayer all eventually became generals.

The enigmatic "lost" Colonel James Shackelford had great staying power and rose up the military ladder to general, where he was in on the conclusion of the chase of John Hunt Morgan's cavalry in Ohio. Other promoted colonels were the wounded Michael Lawler, Thomas Ransom, and James Tuttle. Additional promotions came to Leonard Ross, George McGinnis, J. D. Webster, and Elias S. Dennis of the 30th Illinois.

The wounded Lieutenant James O. Churchill was in the hospital from February until July. His promotion to first lieutenant had come on the day he was wounded and he was promoted to captain toward the end of his hospital stay. After his release from the hospital he remained on crutches until January of the following year. Upon leaving the service he held a position with the government as cashier for U. S. Customs and received a life-time pension as well because of disability remaining from his wound.[5]

Many units from both sides continued their service for their respective causes. The 9th Illinois, first engaged on Saturday the 15th, was destined to suffer more casualties in the Civil War than any other Union regiment. At Donelson it had more fatalities than any other regiment and 1½ months later would suffer the highest casualties of any regiment at Shiloh. The 8th Illinois, the 11th Illinois, the 18th Illinois, and the 2nd Iowa gave more of their complements at Fort Donelson than at any other battle, although all served at bloody Shiloh and other campaigns.[6]

U. S. ("Unconditional Surrender") Grant had the President and the people in his corner because of his victory at Fort Donelson. With this support he went through the war displaying such strategic and tactical skill that he received recognition as one of the great military captains produced on this continent. Three and a half years after the fall of Fort Donelson no one could touch him as a hero in the North.

Yet the road to fame begun at Fort Donelson and Fort Henry now descended from the clouds. First Grant got involved in the troubles of the Johnson Administration. Then, as Grant was elected President of the United States, John Rawlins, his close adviser, died. The next eight years found the greatest mis-management and corruption in American history. Having been played for a fool, Grant went on a world tour. On his return he allowed himself to be persuaded to try again for the Presidential nomination. Many had a vested interest in him and for a long time Grant deadlocked the convention of 1880. Finally Garfield came as a compromise and Ulysses Grant retired to private life.

Again an associate led him astray. Grant lent his name and money to an investment company which went bankrupt. The Grants were paupers. To regain solvency he turned to writing his memoirs. At the same time he contracted throat cancer.

In the late spring and early summer of 1885, the word had spread throughout the country that the famous general could not live much longer. A stream of distinguished visitors proceeded to the cottage in the small mountain town in the northern New York resort area.

Among the visitors in the last weeks was Simon B. Buckner. Grant's part of the conversation by that time was limited to scratching words and phrases on a pad. In the main they discussed the Academy days and the Mexican War and the post-war years. Fort Donelson was only fleetingly touched upon.

As he rode in the cab back toward the train station, Buckner could not refrain from musing on the ups and downs of this man's life. Thirty years before Grant had required a loan of him and now he could use one again. Before the War Between the States and after it his deeds were undistinguishable. Buckner removed his hat and wiped the sweat from the afternoon heat from his forehead. Wasn't it ironical that it was Fort Donelson that set Grant on the tracks of destiny! But then

Buckner had nothing to complain of. The surrender had not hurt his own career one little bit.

Grant was thinking how nice it was for the enemy he had most humiliated to pay him a visit. Yet his appreciation to the Kentucky gentleman was not as expansive as it should have been, for Ulysses S. Grant never knew how much he owed the completeness of the victory at Fort Donelson and thus his subsequent prominence in history to this visitor—Simon Bolivar Buckner.

Notes

CHAPTER 1

1. Kenneth P. Williams, *Lincoln Finds a General,* III, 75 (referred to hereafter as Williams). A conservative addition to these figures is from those incapacitated.
2. *War of the Rebellion: A Compilation of the Official Records of the Union and Confederate Armies* (O.R.), Series 1, Vol. III, 267–317.
3. Williams, 90.
4. O.R. VII, 814, 848.
5. *Ibid.,* 534, 561.
6. John Emerson, "Grant's Life in the West," *Midland Monthly* (May, 1898), 410, 411.
7. Williams, 189.
8. There is ample evidence that the idea of the strike against Fort Henry did not originate with Grant. For a discussion see Williams, Chapters V, VII and VIII.
9. O.R. VII, 574.
10. *Ibid.,* 577.
11. *Ibid.,* 608.
12. *Ibid.,* 581.

CHAPTER 2

1. O.R. VII, 689, 711.
2. Wilbur Foster, "The Building of Forts Henry and Donelson," *Battles and Sketches of the Army of Tennessee,* 1861–1865, quoted in Otto Eisenschiml and Ralph Newman, *The Civil War,* I, 148 (known hereafter as E & N).
3. Peter Franklin Walker, "Command Failure," *Tennessee Historical Quarterly,* (December, 1957), 338.
4. Williams, 200.
5. E & N, 150; O.R. VII, 137, 140.

6. *Ibid.*, 141, 132.
7. *Ibid.*, 122, 146.
8. *Ibid.*, 147, 152; Herschel Gower and Jack Allen, *The Life and Journal of Randal W. McGavock,* 585, 586.
9. Bruce Catton, *Grant Moves South,* 149 (known hereafter as Catton).
10. O.R. VII, 127.
11. *Ibid.*, 588.
12. U. S. Grant, *Personal Memoirs of U. S. Grant,* 173–175 (known hereafter as Grant).

CHAPTER 3

1. O.R. VII, 840, 859, 865.
2. *Ibid.*, 861, 863; Alfred Roman, *The Military Operations of General Beauregard,* I, 216–228.
3. Arndt M. Stickles, *Simon Bolivar Buckner, Borderland Knight,* 120.
4. *Ibid.*, 129.
5. O.R. VII, 366, 135.
6. *Ibid.*, 261, 367.
7. *Ibid.*, 389, 409.
8. *Ibid.*, 358.
9. *Ibid.*, 276.
10. Gower and Allen, *Pen and Sword,* 587.
11. Grant, 175; O.R. VII, 174.
12. Williams, 150; O.R. VII, 599.
13. *Ibid.*, 593–595.
14. Williams, 219.
15. O.R. VII, 130, 131.
16. *Ibid.*, 864, 865.
17. *Ibid.*, 859, 860, 865.
18. Ezra J. Warner, *Generals in Gray,* 90; O.R. VII, 840, 865.
19. *Ibid.*, 865.
20. O.R. LII(2), 266.
21. O.R. VII, 389.
22. *Ibid.*, 276, 352.
23. S. M. H. Byers, *Iowa in War Times,* 95 (known hereafter as Byers).
24. *Ibid.*, 96; O.R. VII, 598.
25. Williams, 220.
26. O.R. VII, 865, 278.
27. Stickles, *Borderland Knight,* 127; Warner, *Generals in Gray,* 75.
28. Stickles, 40, 41.
29. O.R. VII, 852.
30. *Ibid.*, 867.
31. Williams, 221.
32. O.R. VII, 410.
33. *Ibid.*, 279.
34. This landmark is also known as the Dover Hotel. I use "Dover Tavern" to avoid confusion with other multi-suite residences in

town and because it receives such appellation in many contemporary military documents.

While there is evidence that Pillow eventually established his quarters at the Rice House, the convenience of the Dover Tavern evidenced by its use by other generals leads me to believe he initially occupied the Tavern-Inn.

35. O.R. VII, 358, 279, 268–69.
36. Gower and Allen, *Pen and Sword,* LBF.
37. O.R. VII, 595.
38. *Ibid.,* 600.
39. *Ibid.,* 601.
40. Lew Wallace, *Autobiography,* 376, 377.
41. O.R. VII, 601.
42. *Ibid.,* 594, 604.
43. *Ibid.,* 342, 346.
44. The modern name is Erin Hollow; evidence is that this ravine was known as "Aaron Hollow" in the nineteenth century.
45. O.R. VII, 293.
46. *Ibid.,* 383.
47. *Ibid.,* 355.
48. Lew Wallace, "The Capture of Fort Donelson," *Battles and Leaders of the Civil War,* I, 404, 405 (referred to hereafter as Wallace).
49. O.R. VII, 612.
50. *Ibid.,* 604.
51. O.R. LII(2), 269. I can find no direct evidence that Buckner and Floyd journeyed to Cumberland City this day. There is evidence that Floyd had learned much about this post on the eleventh (O.R. VII, 272) and I have surmised that Buckner accompanied him to influence his judgment. The proximity of the place to Clarksville makes it most likely he would visit the site of his new concentration along with his second-in-command. It also provides a reason for Floyd not acknowledging Johnston's dispatch.
52. O.R. LII(2), 269.
53. O.R. VII, 328.
54. Stickles, *Borderland Knight,* 132.
55. O.R. VII, 383; John Allan Wyeth, *Life of General Nathan Bedford Forrest,* 44. (Mentioned hereafter as Wyeth.)
56. O.R. VII, 397, 398.
57. The details of this initial confrontation cannot be fully documented; this account is based on the mission of Buckner (O.R. VII, 328), the situation of Pillow, and the personalities and histories of the pair.

CHAPTER 4

1. O.R. VII, 329, 383; Wyeth, 44.
2. O.R. VII, 170; Grant, 176.
3. John H. Brinton, *Personal Memoirs of John H. Brinton,* quoted in E & N, 153, 154. (Hereafter this will be known as "Brinton" with the page numbers from E & N.)

4. O.R. VII, 272.
5. Brinton, 153.
6. O.R. VII, 183.
7. Wyeth, 44.
8. O.R. VII, 183, 184, 188, 383, 384; Wyeth, 44.
9. O.R. VII, 329, 384.
10. *Ibid.*, 162; Wallace, 406.
11. Henry Walke, "The Western Flotilla at Fort Donelson, Island Number Ten, Fort Pillow, and Memphis," *Battles and Leaders of The Civil War,* I, 430, 431.
12. O.R. LII(2), 271.
13. O.R. VII, 191, 276.
14. *Ibid.*, 193, 184, 212.
15. *Ibid.*, 329, 360. War Department marker at Fort Donelson National Military Park.
16. *Ibid.*, 351, 276.
17. *Ibid.*, 211.
18. *Ibid.*, 360, 190.
19. *Ibid.*, 184.
20. *Ibid.*, 193, 212, 220, 215.
21. *Ibid.*, 329.
22. O.R. LII(2), 271. Johnston's son (William Preston Johnston, *The Life of General Albert Sidney Johnston,* 438) writes that Johnston telegraphed Floyd on the afternoon of the 12th that he knew nothing of the wants of Pillow or Floyd or the position of Buckner. According to the quotation, he continued, " 'You do. You have the dispatch. Decide. Answer.' " Floyd's reply was that he and Buckner still intended a concentration at Cumberland City.
23. O.R. VII, 367, 377.
24. *Ibid.*, 352, 384.
25. *Ibid.*, 607.

CHAPTER 5

1. O.R. VII, 339.
2. *Ibid.*, 262, 267.
3. *Ibid.*, 330, 267. There appears to be no actual record of Floyd visiting the fort, but in as much as Floyd inspected Buckner that morning it is inconceivable that he could neglect the vital batteries.
4. *Ibid.*, 407.
5. *Ibid.*, 338, 359, 360, 343.
6. *Ibid.*, 184, 172.
7. *Ibid.*, 220, 223, 191, 184, 172.
8. Walke, 431; O.R. VII, 393, 398.
9. *Ibid.*, 184, 172, 193, 188, 209, 368.
10. *Ibid.*, 172, 191.
11. Walke, 431; O.R. VII, 396; O.R. LII(2), 272.
12. O.R. VII, 227, 231, 232, 352, 342, 343, 330.
13. *Ibid.*, 220, 267, 346.

14. *Ibid.,* 391, 389.
15. *Ibid.,* 172, 184.
16. *Ibid.,* 227, 232.
17. As a contrary reference, Wallace says they used Henry rifles (407).
18. Walke, 431; O.R. VII, 393, 394, 396, 398, 391, 389; O.R. LII(2), 272.
19. O.R. VII, 172, 203, 204, 212.
20. Walke, 431, 432; O.R. VII, 394, 398, 391.
21. *Ibid.,* 227, 228, 232, 220.
22. *Ibid.,* 204, 212.
23. *Ibid.,* 370.
24. *Ibid.,* 204, 205, 212, 368. Unit positions come from a map in Fort Donelson National Military Park files by Edwin C. Bearss.
25. Wallace, 412; O.R. VII, 212, 213, 214. Haynie's reports are too general and inaccurate to be of much use here.
26. *Ibid.,* 213, 368; Wallace, 412.
27. *Ibid.,* 173, 213, 368. Union accounts indicate only one retreat, but Heiman recalls two repulses. Although his account was written later, I have assumed he held a better overall picture of the battle than did any of the Federal commanders.
28. *Ibid.,* 370, 204, 360.
29. *Ibid.,* 204, 206, 202, 368.
30. Brinton, 159.
31. O.R. VII, 162, 165, 202, 206, 368, 360, 213, 168.
32. *Ibid.,* 173. There is here implied a criticism of Grant for not ordering such, presumably on McClernand's suggestion.
33. Brinton, 159, 160; O.R. VII, 609, 613; Wallace, *Autobiography,* 382, 383.
34. O.R. VII, 347.
35. *Ibid.,* 173, 174, 225, 226, 208, 190.
36. Wyeth, 45; Emmett J. Crozier, *Yankee Reporter,* 204, 205.
37. O.R. VII, 376, 379.
38. *Ibid.,* 194, 338, 199.
39. *Ibid.,* 360, 376, 368, 369, 330, 393, 398.
40. *Ibid.,* 228, 174, 201.
41. *Ibid.,* 379, 343.
42. *Ibid.,* 190, 188, 194, 215, 174.
43. *Ibid.,* 878, 879; O.R. LII(2), 272, 273; *A Compilation of the Official Records of the Union and Confederate Navies,* Series I, XXII, 611. (Hereafter this volume is cited as O.R.N.)
44. Walke, 432; O.R.N., 592.
45. O.R. LII(2), 273; Brinton, 154; O.R. VII, 613.

CHAPTER 6

1. Wallace, *Autobiography,* 379, 383, 384.
2. O.R. LII(2), 273.
3. O.R. VII, 221.
4. O.R. VII, 185, 174.

5. *Ibid.,* 343, 352.
6. Catton, 159; O.R. VII, 613.
7. Walke, 432.
8. Wallace, *Autobiography,* 384; O.R. VII, 209, 206, 201, 199.
9. *Ibid.,* 225, 369, 390.
10. *Ibid.,* 299; Wallace, *Autobiography,* 387.
11. *Ibid.,* 330, 282.
12. Wallace, *Autobiography,* 387–389.
13. O.R. VII, 330, 338, 381.

CHAPTER 7

1. Williams, 235; Grant, 179.
2. O.R. VII, 122.
3. O.R.N., 591.
4. O.R. VII, 408.
5. *Ibid.,* 399, 280.
6. O.R.N., 592.
7. Walke, 432.
8. Wyeth, 46; O.R. VII, 401.
9. *Ibid.,* 408; Walke, 432.
10. *Ibid.,* 433.
11. O.R. VII, 393, 395, 396.
12. Walke, 432.
13. Wyeth, 47; O.R. VII, 393.
14. *Ibid.,* 276, 377; O.R. LII(2), 274.
15. O.R.N., 591–593.
16. Walke, 432, 433.
17. O.R.N., 589, 584, 585; Jesse Bowman Young, *What a Boy Saw in The Army,* in E & N, 156; O.R. VII, 408.
18. *Ibid.,* 395; Wyeth, 47.
19. O.R.N., 612.
20. O.R. VII, 400, 395, 396, 255, 263. Distances in military reports usually vary widely and, as with times of day, judgments must be made. Ross, Pillow and Bidwell give us figures of 250–200 yards and Gilmer quotes 300 to 400 *feet.* I have considered the accuracy of the reporters and have reached a conclusion of 200 yards, which is a median when compared to the data of Foote, Culbertson, Walke and Bailey. The gunners and engineers had prior opportunity to sight and measure distances from landmarks.
    O.R.N., 393.
21. O.R. VII, 400, 393.
22. Walke, 434; Frank Moore, ed., *Rebellion Record,* IV, 172.
23. Walke, 434; O.R.N., 592.
24. O.R. VII, 384, 408.
25. O.R. LII(2), 274; Walke, 434, 435. The "4:10" is actually Gilmer's and seems to best correspond to the length of the battle. O.R. VII, 263.

26. *Ibid.,* 281, 393, 395, 396. The purported conversation has been assembled from the reports of Pillow, Culbertson, Bidwell and Ross.
27. O.R.N., 584, 591, 592, 593; Walke, 436.
28. O.R. VII, 255; O.R.N., 593.

CHAPTER 8

1. O.R. VII, 343.
2. *Ibid.,* 252; Wallace, *Autobiography,* 390–392, 394–395.
3. O.R. VII, 175, 185, 214.
4. *Ibid.,* 208, 195.
5. *Ibid.,* 185.
6. *Ibid.,* 223, 229.
7. *Ibid.,* 206, 207.
8. *Ibid.,* 206.
9. *Ibid.,* 215.
10. *Ibid.,* 225; Byers, 97.
11. O.R. VII, 268, 330, 263.
12. *Ibid.,* 285, 286, 365.
13. *Ibid.,* 282, 286. All conversation details of this conference cannot be fully documented but may be surmised from attitudes established from official reports. This is particularly true of Buckner.
14. *Ibid.,* 268, 286.
15. Ibid., 286, 369.
16. *Ibid.,* 369, 384. This conversation is invented, but could very easily have occurred between two distinguished Tennesseeans who had been in the garrison several days.
17. *Ibid.,* 331, 347, 350, 352.
18. *Ibid.,* 361, 371.
19. *Ibid.,* 276, 277, 387.
20. *Ibid.,* 265, 365.
21. *Ibid.,* 199.

CHAPTER 9

1. O.R. VII, 360.
2. *Ibid.,* 377.
3. *Ibid.,* 361, 286.
4. *Ibid.,* 369.
5. *Ibid.,* 347, 344, 352, 343.
6. Grant, 179.
7. Moore, *Rebellion Record,* IV, 184; O.R. VII, 339, 361, 286. Determination of the route used by Pillow in marching on McArthur was made from an 1865 U.S. Army topographical map of Dover and from a personal battlefield investigation.
8. *Ibid.,* 339, 384.
9. *Ibid.,* LII, 11.
10. O.R. VII, 286, 339.
11. *Ibid.,* 333, 344, 377.

12. *Ibid.,* 339, 361, 380.
13. *Ibid.,* 218.
14. *Ibid.,* 380, 277.
15. *Ibid.,* 339, 219, 380.
16. *Ibid.,* 219, 339, 277, 361.
17. *Ibid.,* 185, 219.

CHAPTER 10

1. O.R. VII, 340, 186, 373, 339.
2. *Ibid.,* 186, 339, 373, 375, 311, 276.
3. *Ibid.,* 218, 361, 176.
4. Charles Whittlesey, *War Memoranda,* 31; Grant, 179.
5. O.R. VII, 369, 373, 376.
6. *Ibid.,* 340. This is on Baldwin's authority, as Drake filed no report.
7. *Ibid.,* 190, 340, 217, 168; O.R. LII, 11.
8. O.R. VII, 191, 331.
9. *Ibid.,* 373, 371, 176.
10. *Ibid.,* 217, 218.

CHAPTER 11

1. O.R. VII, 237; Wallace, 420.
2. O.R. VII, 218, 216; LII, 11.
3. O.R. VII, 216, 217, 219, 176, 186.
4. *Ibid,* 190, 340, 237, 243.
5. *Ibid.,* 373, 374, 371, 190.
6. *Ibid.,* 385, 331.
7. *Ibid.,* 243, 250.
8. *Ibid.,* 374, 331, 344, 345; Moore, *Rebellion Record,* IV, 184.
9. O.R. VII, 251.
10. It is hard to account for all of the time Grant spent in his absence from the field on the 15th. This seems to be a logical guess for a portion of it.
11. *Ibid.,* 350, 331, 207, 248.
12. *Ibid.,* 373, 186, 372.
13. *Ibid.,* 189, 186, 246.
14. All we definitely know of the headquarters operations is that Hillyer was dispatched to Grant. Since Rawlins had to be briefed later by Lew Wallace on McClernand's requests, we can assume he was not there and that Webster gave the order.
15. O.R. VII, 186, 176.
16. *Ibid.,* 190, 186, 189.
17. *Ibid.,* 251, 189.
18. *Ibid.,* 376, 189, 186, 220.
19. *Ibid.,* 199, 345, 350, 352, 201.
20. *Ibid.,* 376, 177, 247, 249, 187.
21. *Ibid.,* 385, 278.

22. *Ibid.*, 242.
23. *Ibid.*, 186, 199.
24. *Ibid.*, 247, 244, 249.
25. *Ibid.*, 199, 332, 244, 248.
26. Wyeth, 52; O.R. VII, 176, 177.
27. *Ibid.*, 247, 199, 186, 385, 176; Wyeth, 52, 53.
28. O.R. VII, 187, 177.
29. Grant, 180; O.R. VII, 167.
30. *Ibid.*, 245, 248, 199, 247.
31. *Ibid.*, 314, 387, 340, 167.
32. *Ibid.*, 242, 244, 245.
33. Grant, 180.
34. O.R. VII, 247, 244, 201, 199, 195.
35. Whittlesey, *War Memoranda,* 34, 35; Hamlin Garland, *Ulysses S. Grant.*
36. O.R. VII, 248, 385, 200, 196.
37. *Ibid.*, 340, 196, 200; J. O. Churchill, letter in *Fort Henry and Fort Donelson Campaigns Source Book,* 840. (Hereafter to be cited as Churchill.)
38. O.R. VII, 200, 376; Churchill, 840, 841.
39. Wyeth, 52; Churchill, 841.
40. O.R. VII, 242, 208; Wallace, *Autobiography,* 401.
41. Churchill, 841; Wallace, *Autobiography,* 402; Wallace, 420; O.R. VII, 374, 200.
42. *Ibid.*, 263, 264, 356, 331, 348, 282.
43. *Ibid.*, 348, 356, 352, 385, 340, 332.
44. *Ibid.*, 343, 356, 370.
45. *Ibid.*, 208. The identification of the 11th Illinois and 44th Indiana as the emergency rear guard is an educated guess, as I have been unable to identify the Federal units opposing Forrest and Hanson.
46. Wyeth, 53; O.R. VII, 343, 369.
47. *Ibid.*, 356, 343, 340; Wyeth, 53.
48. O.R. VII, 208, 343, 263, 266; Wyeth, 53.
49. O.R. VII, 283, 290; Wallace, 420.
50. O.R. VII, 340, 348, 252; Wallace, 420.
51. O.R. VII, 332, 252; Wyeth, 53, 54.
52. O.R. VII, 353, 340.
53. *Ibid.*, 332, 292.
54. *Ibid.*, 350, 353, 356, 314, 385.
55. *Ibid.*, 381, 179, 244, 237, 348.
56. *Ibid.*, 353, 356, 344, 345, 348.
57. *Ibid.*, 253, 345, 356, 332, 353.
58. *Ibid.*, 332, 269, 273, 290, 316; James A. Connolly, "Major Connolly's Letters to His Wife, 1862–1865," *Transactions of the Illinois State Historical Society for the year 1928,* 220–224.
    The quotations between Floyd and Buckner are not actual but reconstructed.
59. The quick arrival of Morgan Smith, and C. F. Smith's artillery bombardment and quickly organized assault indicates prearrange-

ment to some degree. Colonel Webster must have joined Grant at the headquarters.

60. O.R. VII, 333, 250, 361; Catton, 158.

CHAPTER 12

1. Grant, 181.
2. O.R. VII, 253.
3. *Ibid.*, 354, 369.
4. *Ibid.*, 283, 291.
5. Grant, 181; Moore, *Rebellion Record,* IV, 174; O.R. VII, 618.
6. Wallace, 421, 422; Catton, 164–166.
7. *Ibid.*, 169; O.R. VII, 178, 179.
8. *Ibid.*, 221; O.R. LII, 8.
9. Pillow is not mentioned in any reports for the next few hours and, in view of the fact he had little or no sleep in the last two days, it seems likely he would take the opportunity to catch some sleep.
10. O.R. VII, 238; Wallace, 422, 423.
11. Byers, 98, 99; O.R. VII, 344, 288.
12. Wallace, 423; Byers, 99, 100; O.R. VII, 377.
13. Williams, 244; O.R. VII, 238.
14. Byers, 100; O.R. VII, 344, 354, 228, 229.
15. *Ibid.*, 192, 378, 221.
16. *Ibid.*, 333, 378, 223, 224, 221; Byers, 100, 107; Lieutenant Morton in *Fort Donelson Source Book,* 1357.
17. O.R. VII, 238, 239, 233, 211, 245; Wallace, 424.
18. O.R. VII, 361, 362, 233, 239; Wallace, 424.
19. Byers, 103; O.R. VII, 392, 226, 163, 231
20. *Ibid.*, 229; O.R. LII, 9.
21. O.R. VII, 362, 233, 239, 245, 249.
22. Churchill, 843.
23. O.R. VII, 370, 374, 230, 226; Byers, 102; O.R. LII, 9.
24. O.R. VII, 221, 349, 357, 223; Charles C. Nott, *Sketches of The War,* 33.
25. Grant, 181; Wallace, 425.
26. O.R. VII, 226, 223, 224, 221.
27. *Ibid.*, 234, 211, 233; Wallace, 425.
28. O.R. VII, 374, 333, 224.
29. *Ibid.*, 243, 245, 233, 169; Churchill, 844.
30. O.R. VII, 401, 371, 354; O.R.N., 588.
31. O.R. VII, 355. Unit strength is based on average regimental rosters, where other information is lacking.

CHAPTER 13

1. Catton, 167.
2. O.R. VII, 180, 187, 196, 222; Moore, *Rebellion Record,* IV, 174.
3. O.R. VII, 381, 302, 291, 159, 409, 385, 187.
4. *Ibid.*, 291. Pillow here estimates losses at around 2,000. Wyeth (70) guesses 400 killed and 1,500 wounded.

5. O.R. VII, 374, 342, 337, 345, 351, 355, 357; Morton in *Source Book,* 1358.
6. O.R. VII, 167–169; William F. Fox, *Regimental Losses in the American Civil War,* 426, 427.
7. O.R. VII, 242, 291, 233, 187.
8. *Ibid.,* 620, 617, 619, 621, 242; Adam Badeau, *Military History of U. S. Grant,* 51, 47.
9. Byers, 100; O.R. VII, 392, 354, 344, 333, 334.

CHAPTER 14

1. O.R. VII, 159; Brinton in E & N, 165, 166.
2. McGavock in Gower and Allen, *The Life and Journal of Randal W. McGavock,* 592.
3. O.R. VII, 287, 293, 255, 256. It has been assumed that Pillow's headquarters were now at the Rice House.
4. O.R. VII, 273, 269.
5. *Ibid.,* 288.
6. *Ibid.,* 255.
7. Churchill, 844.
8. This account of the surrender conferences can only be documented by examining together the accounts of the various participants and observers and comparing them. There are two source books: (1) Wyeth, 56–65; (2) O.R. VII.
   The testimony from the latter source is as follows: Floyd, 269, 270, 273, 274, 275; Pillow, 283, 284, 287, 288, 289, 302, 303, 304, 305, 307, 325; Buckner, 327, 333, 334, 335; Johnson (365) states he was not present at the conference, but it seems evident he was there at the first stage; Forrest, 386, 295; John Burch, 293, 294; Gus Henry, 296, 297; W. H. Haynes, 297, 298; Hunter Nicholson, 209, 300.
   In determining details and sequences I have assigned the following order of accuracy (from greatest to least): Haynes, Nicholson, Pillow, Henry, Burch, Forrest. The conversations are either as recorded verbatim by an observer or put into quotations from paraphrases.

CHAPTER 15

1. O.R. VII, 264.
2. *Ibid.,* 295, 386, 298, 300.
3. *Ibid.,* 302, 305, 306, 326, 327.
4. *Ibid.,* 256.
5. *Ibid.,* 274, 306, 386. There is no evidence of any immediate reaction from Johnston, so we must assume he did not see the telegram in time.
6. *Ibid.,* 362, 363, 295, 386.
7. *Ibid.,* 363, 160, 161.
8. *Ibid.,* 414, 363, 378, 379.
9. Gower and Allen, *Pen and Sword, Journal of Randal W. McGavock,* 593; O.R. VII, 381, 275.

10. *Ibid.,* 295, 386, 222.
11. "The 'Confederate Sins' of Major Cheairs," *Tennessee Historical Quarterly,* (June, 1964), 121. An eyewitness from the 2nd Iowa contradicts the major when he says he was accompanied by a party from his regiment. (Hereafter this is to be cited as "Cheairs."); O.R. LII, 10.
12. O.R. VII, 396, 390, 239, 263.
13. *Ibid.,* 381, 382.
14. Brinton in E & N, 166; Cheairs, 122; O.R. VII, 160, 161; Thomas J. Newsham quoted in Catton, 174, 175. I accept Cheairs' version.
15. Cheairs, 122; Stickles, *Borderland Knight,* 162; O.R. VII, 382.
16. Wyeth, 61, 62; Cheairs, 122.
17. O.R. VII, 161, 275, 382.
18. *Ibid.,* 379, 415, 302, 382; Moore, *Rebellion Record,* IV, 173.
19. O.R. VII, 409, 416, 275, 364.
20. *Ibid.,* 239; O.R.N., 588.
21. O.R. VII, 239, 416; Gower and Allen, *Pen and Sword,* 593; Wyeth, 60, 61.
22. Wallace, 428; O.R.N., 588.
23. Cheairs, 122; Virgil C. Jones, *The Civil War at Sea,* I, 383; Wyeth, 61.
24. Gower and Allen, *Pen and Sword,* 593; O.R. VII, 328, 336, 337.
25. Jones, *The Civil War at Sea,* I, 383.
26. O.R.N., 588; O.R. VII, 180: McClernand believed Schwartz and Stewart were the first in Dover.
27. Grant, 184; Garland, *Ulysses S. Grant,* 192.
28. O.R. VII, 275, 303.
29. Wallace, 428; Grant, 184, 185; Garland, *Ulysses S. Grant,* 192; O.R. VII, 625; Catton, 177.
30. Johnston (O.R. VII, 259, 922) claimed that 16,000 or 17,000 men were sent to Donelson, while he kept only 14,000, and only 10,000 of which were effectives (March 18, 1862). This seems apparently inaccurate for both armies. Reversing the figures might be more justifiable. He errs in the number of effectives detached from his effective command of 22,000 (922). Hardee's report for January gives an "aggregate present" of 24,500 to 30,500 (*Ibid.,* 852). Simultaneously, Tilghman reports 4,600 at Donelson and Henry (855).
31. O.R. VII, 258; A. L. Crabb, *Nashville, Personality of a City,* 59; Wallace, 428; Whittlesey, 42. When the *New Uncle Sam* steamed upstream, Grant shifted headquarters.
32. O.R. VII, 625, 626; Wyeth, 63.
33. *Ibid.,* 71, Whittlesey, 42; Connolly, "Letters," 220–224; Churchill, 845.
34. Byers, 106; Crozier, *Yankee Reporter,* 205; Connolly, "Letters," 220–224; Grant, 185.
35. Byers, 105; O.R. VII, 624, 625, 626.
36. *Ibid.,* 625; Williams, 257.

EPILOGUE

The most important single source for this biographical material is Ezra J. Warner, *Generals in Gray*. Standard biographical sources provide the remaining material with the following notable exceptions:

1. O.R. VII, 256.
2. *Ibid.*, 364.
3. Grant, 185, 186.
4. O.R. VII, 335.
5. Obtained from pension documents, Washington, D.C.
6. William F. Fox, *Regimental Losses in the American Civil War*.

Bibliography

Badeau, Adam. *Military History of Ulysses S. Grant,* Vol. I. New York : D. Appleton and Company, 1867.

Bounds, Rev. Ben H. *Memoirs.* Copy of unpublished manuscript in the library at Fort Donelson National Military Park.

Brinton, John H. *Personal Memoirs of John H. Brinton.* New York : The Neale Publishing Co., 1914.

Byers, S. M. H. *Iowa in War Times.* Des Moines : W. D. Condit & Co., 1888.

Catton, Bruce. *Grant Moves South.* Boston : Little, Brown & Co., 1960.

Cheairs, Nat F. "The 'Confederate Sins' of Major Cheairs," *Tennessee Historical Quarterly,* XXIII (June, 1964), 121–124.

Connolly, James A. "Major Connolly's Letters to His Wife, 1862–1865," *Transactions of the Illinois State Historical Society for the Year 1928.* Springfield : 1928. pp 220–224.

Crabb, A. L. *Nashville, Personality of a City.* Indianapolis : Bobbs Merrell, 1960.

Crozier, Emmet. *Yankee Reporters,* 1861–1865. New York : Oxford University Press, 1956.

Deaderick, Barron. *Strategy in the Civil War.* Harrisburg. The Military Service Publishing Co., 1946.

Eisenschiml, Otto and Newman, Ralph. *The Civil War,* Vol. I. New York : Grosset & Dunlap, Inc., 1956.

Emerson, John. "Grant's Life in the West," *Midland Monthly,* May, 1898.

Fort Henry and Fort Donelson Campaigns Source Book. Fort Leavenworth : The General Services School, 1923.

Foster, Wilbur F. "The Building of Forts Henry and Donelson" in Bromfield L. Ridley, *Battles and Sketches of the Army of Tennessee*—1861–1865. Mexico, Mo. : Missouri Printing and Publishing Company, 1906.

Fox, William F. *Regimental Losses in the American Civil War.* Albany : Albany Publishing Co., 1889.

Gower, Herschel and Allen, Jack (ed). *Pen and Sword, the Life and Journal of Randal W. McGavock.* Nashville : Tennessee Historical Commission, 1959.

Grant, Ulysses S. *Personal Memoirs of U. S. Grant.* New York : Charles L. Webster & Company, 1894.

Johnston, William Preston. *The Life of General Albert Sidney Johnston.* New York : Appleton, 1879.

Jones, Virgil Carrington. *The Civil War at Sea,* Vol. I. New York : Holt, Rinehart, Winston, 1960.

Moore, Frank (ed.). *Rebellion Record,* Vol. IV. New York : G. P. Putnam, 1862.

Newsham, Thomas J. "Operations Before Fort Donelson," *Magazine of American History.* XV (January, 1886) 40–42.

Nott, Charles C. *Sketches of the War.* New York : Anson D. F. Randolph, 1865.

Roman, Alfred. *The Military Operations of General Beauregard in the War Between The States,* 1861–1865, Vol. I. New York : Harper, 1884.

Stickles, Anrdt M. *Simon Bolivar Buckner, Borderland Knight.* Chapel Hill : University of N. Carolina Press, 1940.

Walke, Henry. "The Western Flotilla at Fort Donelson, Island Number Ten, Fort Pillow, and Memphis," *Battles and Leaders of the Civil War,* Vol. I. New York : Century Company, 1884.

Walker, Peter Franklin. "Building a Tennessee Army, Autumn,

1861," *Tennessee Historical Quarterly*. XVI (June, 1957), 101–114.

——— "Command Failure: The Fall of Forts Henry and Donelson," *Tennessee Historical Quarterly*. XVI (December, 1957), 338–340.

——— "Holding the Tennessee Line," *Tennessee Historical Quarterly*. XVI (December, 1957), 228–242.

Wallace, Lew. "The Capture of Fort Donelson," *Battles and Leaders of the Civil War*. Vol. I. New York: Century Company, 1884.

——— *An Autobiography,* Vol. I. New York: Harper, 1906.

Warner, Ezra J. *Generals in Gray*. Baton Rouge: Louisiana State University Press, 1959.

The War of the Rebellion: A Compilation of the Official Records of The Union and Confederate Armies. Series I, Vol. III, VII and LII. Washington: Government Printing Office, 1882.

The War of the Rebellion: A Compilation of the Official Records of The Union and Confederate Navies. Vol. XXII. Washington: Government Printing Office, 1908.

Whittlesey, Charles. *War Memoranda*. Cleveland: William W. Williams, 1884.

Williams, Kenneth P. *Lincoln Finds a General*. Vol. III. New York: Macmillan Company, 1952.

Wyeth, John Allan. *Life of General Nathan Bedford Forrest*. New York: Harper & Brothers, 1899.

Young, Jesse Bowman. *What a Boy Saw in the Army*. New York: Hunt and Eaton, 1894.

Index

Alabama, 16th, 267
Alabama, 27th, 101, 231, 254, 323
Alps, 72, 93
Anderson, Adna, 24
Arkansas, 15th, 267
Armstrong, Corporal, 223
Arn, Frederick, 207, 210, 216

Bailey, J. E., 84, 93, 97, 98, 265, 269, 288
Baker, Lieutenant Colonel, 261, 273
Baldwin, William, 51, 79, 83, 86, 93, 115, 129, 130, 164, 168, 169, 171, 173, 174, 176, 177, 179, 180, 181, 183, 185, 187, 191, 192, 194, 195, 217, 222, 229, 230, 231, 232, 237, 239, 311, 345.
Barn Hollow, 168–170, 173
Battery A (U.S.), 238, 239, 244, 253, 314
Beaumont, Captain, 37, 45, 95
Beauregard, P. G. T., 21, 30, 33
Bedford, Lieutenant, 135
Belmont, Mo., 17, 18, 22, 23, 35, 204, 206, 221, 240, 269
Benjamin, Judah, 149, 278, 294, 340
Benton, 214
Bidwell, R. G., 37, 45, 95, 136, 140, 146, 147, 148, 314
Bingham, Captain, 214, 221
Birge's Sharpshooters, 54, 94, 114, 128
Blair, George, 207
Bowling Green, Ky., 19, 21, 30, 32, 33, 34, 47, 55, 60, 61, 78, 129, 154, 287, 299, 311
Boyce, Lieutenant, 204
Brandon's Hotel, 38
Breckenridge, John, 49
Brinton, John, 67, 69, 107, 108, 110, 283, 289, 314, 315
Brockaw, John, 105
Brown, John (abolitionist), 337
Brown, John C., 45, 59, 75, 81, 125, 129, 150, 161, 166, 174, 175, 176, 227, 228, 230, 231, 233, 238, 239, 241, 242, 244, 245, 313, 319, 329, 345
Brown, William, 184, 311, 320, 321
Browne, J. B., 114
Brush, Captain, 185, 202

Buchanan, James, 43
Buckner, Simon B., 32, 42, 43, 45, 75, 76, 78, 81, 85, 90, 93, 112, 116, 125, 127–130, 144, 150, 157–161, 164–166, 254, 341, 342, 344, 345, 350, 351; at Clarksville, 48, 49, 52, 56, 57; Cumberland City plan, 56, 61–63, 67; arrives at Dover, 64, 65; first commands garrison, 66, 68, 71, 73, 74; occupies vacated trenches and launches attack, 171, 186, 194, 196, 198, 204, 206, 208, 210–212, 220–222, 224, 226–228, 235, 236, 238–246, 248, 249; defends right flank, 265, 268, 273, 276, 278–280, 282, 285, 288; final conference, 290–294, 296, 298–301; surrender, 302, 305, 309, 310, 316–321, 325, 327–330, 332–335, 337, 339
Buell, Don Carlos, 18, 21, 30, 39, 40, 46, 47, 60, 81, 82, 123, 154, 157, 195, 287, 341
Bufford Hollow, 217, 219, 224, 266, 267
Burch, John, 292, 293, 295, 302
Burns, Lieutenant, 102
Burt, Lieutenant, 314
Butter, W. R., 75

Cairo, Ill., 15, 20, 39, 42, 46, 53, 55, 61, 126, 213, 338, 344
Carondelet, 72, 73, 87, 89, 95, 97, 116, 120, 126, 134, 137–139, 143, 145, 146, 148, 322
Carson, Captain, 261
Carter, Lieutenant, 187, 190
Casseday, Alexander, 196, 205, 206, 227, 244
Central Army of Kentucky, (*see* Hardee, William)
Chandler, James, 323, 324, 326
Charlotte, Tenn., 129, 158, 162, 292, 340
Cheairs, Nat, 243, 313, 315, 317, 318, 319, 326
Chetlain, Augustus, 187, 188
Chipman, Major, 261
Churchill, Corporal, 268
Churchill, J. O., 223, 224, 272, 273, 277, 297, 336, 349
Cincinnati, 26, 28, 132
Clarksville, Tenn., 32, 34, 35, 42–44, 47, 48, 52, 53, 55, 56, 58, 61, 68, 78, 82, 159, 296, 307, 318, 332, 340
Clough, Lieutenant Colonel, 182
Cloutman, Captain, 261
Columbia, Tenn., 35
Columbus, Ky., 16–18, 21, 33, 111, 240, 338, 341
Conestoga, 26, 126, 133, 135, 143, 338
Conway, Lieutenant, 321, 323
Cook, Edward, 59, 65, 227, 228, 230, 231, 239, 243–246
Cook, John, 26, 78, 86, 90, 92, 93, 112, 124, 257, 262, 265, 266, 273, 275, 277, 278, 288
Cook, Sergeant, 135
Cooper, Adjutant, 321
Corinth, Miss., 19
Cosby, George, 309, 310, 313, 346
Crigler, Captain, 196
Crimean War, 40
Crisp house, 30, 74, 117, 120, 121, 123, 167, 248, 255, 288, 314, 316
Cruft, Charles, 30, 122, 123, 125, 128, 129, 151, 193, 195, 197–199, 201, 202, 207, 208–211, 214, 216–220; 238, 242, 250, 262, 267, 272, 275, 277, 279, 280, 286, 314, 348

Culbertson, Jacob, 64, 95, 98, 116, 135, 137, 142, 147
Cullum, Chief-of-Staff, 126
Cumberland City, Tenn., 25, 34, 52, 61, 62, 66–68, 71, 78, 84, 331, 333
Cumberland Iron Works, 312
Cumberland River, 16, 19, 24, 33, 34, 41, 42, 44, 45, 50, 56, 61, 67, 72, 81, 89, 90, 112, 118, 121–123, 133–135, 141, 154, 157, 236, 304, 305, 317, 321, 332, 334
Cumberland Road, 322, 323
Cunningham, Major, 182

Davis, Jack, 136, 140, 185, 321
Davis, Jefferson, 122, 134
Davidson, Colonel, 51, 86, 130, 161, 164, 165, 168, 169, 187
Dennis, Elias, 196, 203, 349
Dixon, Joseph, 64, 73, 84, 87, 90, 95, 96
Dockery, Corporal, 135
Donelson, Daniel, 47, 48
Doolittle, Sergeant, 268
Dove, Benjamin, 143, 262, 322, 325–328, 330
Dover Cemetery, 38
Dover Tavern, 35, 51, 118, 163, 311, 317, 325, 327, 330, 338
Dover, Tennessee, 22, 24, 35, 38, 42, 43, 45, 50, 53, 56, 57, 59, 63, 64, 67, 71, 73, 74, 76–78, 82, 85, 93, 100, 116, 126, 128, 133, 151, 154, 158–160, 164, 178, 241, 248, 255, 258, 277, 278, 280, 284, 285, 290, 294, 286, 306, 307, 310, 311, 313, 317–319, 322, 324, 326, 327, 329, 330, 334, 336, 337, 342, 344, 346
Doss, W. L., 171, 196, 205, 206, 228, 238
Drake, Joseph, 51, 78, 86, 168, 171, 177, 181, 193, 188, 191, 194, 208, 224, 242, 251, 267, 268, 271–273, 275, 277
Dresser, Jasper, 73, 82, 87, 89, 112, 114, 185, 242, 264
Dudley Ridge, 170

Eastland, O. R., 175
English, L. C., 324
Erin Hollow, 57, 81, 86, 88, 89, 94, 101, 107, 185, 228, 230, 237
Erwin, William, 205, 217, 220
Essex, 27, 39, 132, 133

Farquharson, Robert, 240
First Division (U.S.), (*see* Mc Clernand, John)
Florence, Ala., 19
Floyd, John B., 32, 33, 40, 42–44, 51, 52, 56, 57, 59, 61, 340, 342; Cumberland City plan, 61–63, 65–69, 73, 78; commands at Dover, 84, 85, 90, 93, 97, 98, 115, 118, 121, 123, 124, 126; first conference and evacuation plans, 128–130, 132, 134, 138, 141, 145, 149, 157, 159–162, 164, 182, 197, 216, 221, 241, 246, 248–251, 254, 256, 273, 276, 280, 285; final conference, 290–296, 298–301; evacuation, 302, 303, 305–307, 309–311, 317–321, 331, 333, 334
Foote, Andrew, 16, 20, 21, 23, 26–28, 39, 46, 47, 53, 55, 60, 111, 126, 167, 185, 198, 213, 214, 255, 262, 341, 346; naval assault on Fort Donelson, 132, 133, 136, 142, 144, 147
Forge Road, 129, 130, 153, 158,

168–170, 173, 177, 180, 186, 192, 202, 207, 278, 279, 292, 293, 295, 296, 298
Forrest, Jeffry, 211
Forrest, Nathan Bedford, 59, 63, 66, 67, 69, 70–72, 74, 81, 114, 129, 130, 137, 141, 144, 160, 164, 169, 177, 181, 194, 202, 208, 211, 212, 221, 222, 224, 228–235, 238, 239, 242, 268, 271, 272, 285, 295–298, 300, 301, 303, 305, 307–309, 312, 313, 322, 332, 340, 345, 346
Fort Donelson, Tenn., 19, 26–37, 40–47, 49–56, 60–62, 65, 66, 70–73, 78, 90, 111, 118, 120, 123, 126, 154, 159, 161, 162, 182, 256, 287, 289, 294, 299, 305, 306, 313, 315, 317, 318, 322, 325, 328, 332, 334, 335–340, 342, 344, 347, 349–351; river batteries, 37, 45, 50, 64, 93, 95–98, 133–149
Fort Henry, Tenn., 19–21, 25–33, 38–41, 52, 57, 59, 60, 63, 66, 69, 70, 72, 111, 123, 126, 132, 141, 146, 154, 238, 249, 278, 289, 329, 332, 338, 349
Fort Heiman, Ky., 25, 26, 39, 60, 111
Freeman, Lieutenant, 125
French, D. A., 86, 89, 112, 113, 275
Frequa, John, 140–142
Fry, Thomas, 209, 217, 224, 225, 262

Galena, Ill., 101
Gantt, Lieutenant Colonel, 45, 50, 153, 305
General Anderson, 310, 321, 331
Gilmer, Jeremy, 36, 37, 45, 51, 57, 74, 157, 226, 229, 230, 233, 235, 295, 304
Gordon, Thomas, 239, 241
Grady, James, 324
Granbury, Hiram, 186, 346
Grant, Ulysses S., 16–23, 341, 344, 347–351; at Fort Henry, 28–31, 38–40, 42, 44, 46, 53–55, 60; marches on Fort Donelson 67–69, 71, 72, 74, 82; invests garrison, 86–88, 90, 94, 98, 108, 110, 111, 117, 120, 121, 123, 125, 126, 129, 132, 134, 150, 151, 154, 157, 163; visits Foote, 167, 168, 181, 182, 185, 187, 192–194, 197–199, 201, 213, 214, 218–221, 240; directs closing stages of battle, 248, 249, 252–258, 262, 265, 266, 269, 273–275, 277, 279, 280, 282–284, 286–288, receives surrender, 289, 290, 301, 309, 310, 314–317, 319, 324, 325–327, 329, 330–334, 335, 338, 339
Graves, Rice, 92, 97, 101, 102, 106, 112, 166, 186, 222, 238, 244, 245, 265, 274, 275, 277, 293
Green, Captain, 76, 83, 112, 113, 116, 227
Green River, Ky., 30
Gumbart, Conrad, 73, 88, 89, 112, 115, 180, 193, 199, 201, 203, 204, 207, 209, 213
Guy, J. H., 86

Hale, Captain, 188
Hall, John, 145
Halleck, Henry, 20, 21, 29, 30, 39, 40, 46, 53, 55, 60, 81, 82, 111, 120, 126, 132, 157, 287, 288, 289, 338, 341
Hanson, Roger, 51, 64, 78, 91,

116, 125, 150, 159, 166, 173, 222, 229, 231–234, 259, 262, 264, 282, 346
Hardee, William, 19, 33, 34, 47, 49, 55, 61, 78, 142, 158, 182
Harpers Ferry, Va., 338
Hauger, Joseph, 113
Haynie, Isham, 97, 99–103, 105–109, 154
Haynes, Milton, 37, 38, 45, 73, 84, 93, 128
Haynes, W. H., 50, 56, 295, 298, 302, 348
Hays ford, 297
Head, John, 36, 51, 81, 138, 160, 164, 166, 173, 261, 265, 273, 310, 319
Heiman, Adolphus, 25, 27–31, 36, 38, 40, 50, 74, 77, 78, 81 89, 97, 100, 101, 103, 104, 106, 108, 109, 112, 127, 158, 160, 161, 164–166, 171, 182, 231, 239, 254, 273, 280, 306, 323, 345
Heiman's hill, 154, 185, 229, 235, 275, 279, 340
Henry, Gustavus A., 25
Henry, Gus A., Jr., 49, 294, 295
Henry, R. W., 180
Hickman Creek, 30, 50, 64, 74, 78, 129, 249, 336
Hill, William, 183
Hillyer, W. S., 201, 219, 289
Hitchcock, General, 40
Hopkinsville, Ky., 19, 34, 59
Huey, Captain, 305

Illinois,
2nd Cavalry, 70, 257
4th Cavalry, 127, 272
7th, 92, 93
8th, 70, 153, 180, 182, 199, 201–203, 287, 349
9th, 169–171, 178, 185, 191, 192, 312, 349
11th, 127, 162, 204, 209, 210, 213, 216, 219, 222, 223, 226, 230, 272, 286, 287, 349
12th, 171, 185, 188, 191, 312
17th, 54, 101–107, 109, 257
18th, 70, 76, 78, 88, 113, 117, 153, 180, 182, 185, 191–193, 202, 204
20th, 127, 204, 205, 209, 217, 219, 220, 287
29th, 70, 153, 186, 193, 199, 203, 204
30th, 70, 153, 192–196, 202, 203
31st, 70, 153, 186, 193, 206–213, 216, 217
41st, 171, 174–177, 181, 185, 188, 191
43rd, 54
45th, 101, 104, 107, 109, 154, 204, 230
46th, 238
48th, 97, 101–103, 105, 107, 109, 127, 154, 198
49th, 54, 101, 103–107, 109, 257
57th, 238
58th, 239
Indiana,
11th, 267, 268, 272, 275
23rd, 123
25th, 54, 90, 91, 94, 99, 259, 260, 262, 263, 273
31st, 207, 208, 210–212, 216, 219, 267, 268
44th, 198, 210, 211, 214, 217, 218, 221, 230, 267, 272
52nd, 54, 92, 257, 259, 262, 263, 271, 273
Indian Creek, 37, 38, 74–76, 78, 81, 92, 97, 110, 115, 128, 151,

166, 238, 242, 254, 280, 284, 329
Iowa,
2nd, 46, 55, 122, 125, 128, 150, 153, 156, 257–260, 262–265, 268, 269, 271, 273–275, 286, 336, 349
7th, 94, 259, 262, 269, 271, 312, 313, 337
12th, 153, 262, 274, 275, 277
17th, 54, 90, 91, 94, 99, 121, 259, 262, 264

"Jack," 69
Jackson, Andrew, 48
Jackson, Captain, 86, 117, 238
Johnson, Andrew, 49
Johnson, Bushrod, 24, 33–36, 38, 44, 45, 47, 74, 76–78, 83, 85, 116, 152, 158, 159, 163–165, 173, 174, 177, 181, 188, 191, 192, 194, 202, 210, 216, 221, 237, 239, 242, 249, 250, 268, 272, 291–293, 307, 309–311, 314, 321, 324, 339, 340, 345
Johnston, Albert Sidney, 32–34, 40–42, 45, 47, 48, 52, 55–57, 61, 68, 73, 78, 84, 90, 118, 120, 124, 134, 138, 141, 148, 158, 250, 278, 290, 294, 302, 305, 306, 334, 335, 340–343
Jones, Lieutenant (U.S.), 192–194, 199, 201
Jones, Major (C.S.), 294, 295

Kelly, D. C., 70, 71, 137, 141, 312, 313
Kentucky,
1st Cavalry (C.S.), 49
2nd (C.S.), 49, 51, 64, 117, 125, 150, 166, 186, 228, 229, 231–234, 243, 259, 262, 263, 286, 288, 299, 337, 338
8th (C.S.), 116, 180, 186, 204, 285, 345
17th (U.S.), 208, 210, 211, 218, 250
25th (U.S.), 197, 199, 201, 203, 204, 207

Lauman, Jacob, 78, 86, 90–92 94, 95, 98, 99, 116, 125, 128, 257, 258, 260, 273, 274, 277, 286, 288, 313, 348
Lawler, Michael, 76, 77, 184, 192, 204, 349
Lexington, 20
Lick Creek, 74, 152, 183, 297, 323, 324, 335, 336
Lillard, John, 176, 180
Lincoln, Abraham, 43, 122, 338, 348
Logan, John, 206, 208–211, 213, 214, 216, 217, 219, 226, 348
Louisiana, 1st Cavalry, 62
Louisville, 126, 135, 136, 140, 143, 144, 182, 277, 278, 322, 325, 326
Louisville, Ky., 81
Lyon, Hylan, 180, 186, 204, 345

Maney, Frank, 38, 51, 74, 76, 77, 86–89, 93, 101–103, 105, 109, 116, 127, 128, 267
Marks, Sam, 185, 202
Marsh, C. C., 205, 206, 219, 220
Martin, Captain, 261
Martin, George, 146
Massie, Lieutenant, 102
McAllister, Edward, 108, 112, 113, 152, 197, 198, 204, 230, 231, 233, 235, 284
McArthur, John, 78, 86, 110, 115, 117, 121, 152, 153, 156, 170, 171, 173, 177, 181, 185, 191–193, 209, 224, 286, 312, 348

McCausland, John, 83, 85, 116, 153, 168, 174, 177, 180, 187, 208, 217, 229, 311, 320, 346
McClellan, George, 21, 40, 44, 46, 81, 154, 338
McClernand, John A., 22, 26, 39, 54, 60, 63, 67, 69, 70, 72–74, 76, 78, 86–90, 93, 94, 97, 99, 100, 101, 108-110, 112, 115, 118, 120, 121, 124, 129, 151–153, 156, 158, 162, 168, 174, 180–182, 185, 187, 192–195, 197, 198, 201, 206, 208, 219–221, 237, 242, 253, 255–258, 262, 279, 280, 284, 286, 322, 330, 347
McCord, Lieutenant Colonel, 253
McGavock, Randal, 38, 53, 57, 90, 311, 323, 345
McPherson, James, 29, 108, 199, 269, 273, 347, 348
Memphis, Tenn., 19, 33, 59
Mill Spring, Ky., 16, 18
Mississippi,
  1st, 165, 180
  3rd, 180, 321
  4th, 267
  14th, 166, 173, 186, 196–198, 204, 228, 238, 243–245, 265, 286, 324
  20th, 114, 117, 129, 130, 163, 173–176, 179, 184, 202, 239, 242, 311, 314, 320, 323
Mississippi, Department of, 40
Missouri,
  1st Light Artillery, 152
  8th, 267, 268
  13th, 124, 265
Moore, W. P., 243
Morgan, S. S., 324
Morrison, William, 76, 78, 86, 93, 94, 97, 99–105, 108, 112, 117, 126, 154, 197, 286
Morton, John, 274, 275, 277
Mudd, John, 70, 257, 258

Nashville, Tenn., 19, 25, 33, 34, 38, 41, 42, 47, 49, 51, 53, 56, 88, 118, 120, 149, 157, 158, 163, 250, 256, 294, 299, 306, 323, 332, 335, 340, 341, 348
Nebraska, 1st, 122, 125, 238, 253
Nevins, Major, 216
New Uncle Sam, 60
Nicholson, Hunter, 294, 298, 302, 303
Nowlin, J.. W., 183

Oglesby, Richard, 22, 69, 70, 72, 74, 76, 78, 86–89, 93, 94, 110, 112–116, 124, 129, 152, 153, 177, 178, 180–182, 184, 186, 191–193, 199, 201–203, 206, 208–211, 219, 230, 244, 284, 286, 287, 348
Ohio,
  20th, 182
  58th, 125, 239
  68th, 125, 238
  76th, 125, 238
Ohio River, 23, 61, 214
Osborn, Lieutenant Colonel, 207

Paducah, Ky., 16, 20, 22, 170
Palmer, Joseph, 45, 75, 81, 91, 166, 205, 206, 228, 230, 231, 239, 241, 243–246, 253, 254, 264, 288, 346
Paris, Tenn., 21, 74, 111
Parker, Captain, 116
Parrott, James, 269, 313
Peytonia Iron Furnaces, 127
Pillow, Gideon, 17, 34–36, 42–45, 47–49, 56, 57, 59, 60, 63–65, 77, 81, 83–86, 100, 110, 116, 118, 121, 128, 129, 134, 135,

146–149, 157, 258, 276, 279, 280, 333, 340, 342–344; reaches Dover, 49–53; leaves for Cumberland City, 66–69; return to Dover, 73–76; sabotages sortie, 130; directs offensive, 158–165, 168, 171, 173–175, 177, 179, 180, 186, 187, 189, 194, 195, 208, 210, 211, 216, 221, 224, 226–231, 233, 239–243, 245, 246, 248, 254; final conference, 290, 291, 293–296, 298–301; evacuation, 302–307, 320, 332
Pinery Road, 37, 74
Pittsburgh, 121, 126, 133, 135, 136, 138, 140, 142–144, 147, 262
Polk, Leonidas, 17, 19, 34–37, 42, 241
Pope, Corporal, 268
Porter, Captain, 75, 91, 92, 94, 112, 238, 265, 266, 269, 271, 273, 274, 286, 308
Post, John, 203, 207
Pugh, Isaac, 174–178, 181, 188

Quarles, W. A., 230, 306

Ransom, T. G., 162, 164,210, 212, 213, 216, 219, 222, 223, 349
Rawlins, John, 27, 46, 54, 55, 60, 123, 199, 225, 226, 284, 350
Reed, Hugh, 198, 214, 217, 221
Rheinlander, Captain, 260
Rhoades, F. L., 70, 199, 203
Rice House, 258, 291, 293, 295, 304, 305
Rice, J. E., 165, 290, 294, 305
Richardson, Henry, 127, 156
Richmond, Va., 40, 45, 335, 342, 343
Ridge Road, 67, 69, 70
River Road, 164, 165, 168
Rogers, W. E., 321, 322, 324
Ross, Leonard, 257, 262, 264, 267, 271, 275, 284, 349
Ross, Reuben, 63, 64, 73, 87, 93, 96–98, 116, 134, 135, 142, 146, 269, 277, 336, 337
Russell, Daniel, 319, 321
Russellville, Ky., 32–34, 42, 48, 49, 60, 331

Sacramento, Ky., 59
St. Louis, 111, 126, 133, 135, 138, 140, 142, 144, 147, 185, 197, 218, 277, 322, 325
St. Louis, Mo., 20, 30, 39, 46, 55, 81, 126, 287
Schuyler, Adjutant, 312, 313
Schwartz, Captain, 88, 330
Second Division (U.S.), (*see* Smith, Charles)
Semple, Captain, 261
Shackleford, James, 197, 199, 201–203, 349
Shaw, William, 91, 99, 264
Sherman, William T., 40
Shuster, Lieutenant, 96
Simonton, John, 165, 169, 180, 182, 183, 186, 187, 193, 199, 207, 217, 223, 273, 276, 277
Slaughter, Robert, 199
Slaves, 57, 111, 288, 310, 333
Slaymaker, Captain, 261
Smith, Charles, 20, 22, 26, 32, 54, 71, 76, 86, 90, 110, 112, 115, 128, 129, 151–153, 156, 242, 248, 249, 256–262, 264, 267, 269, 273–275, 278, 280, 284, 286, 315, 316, 326, 329, 332, 346
Smith, Francis, 101, 104–106
Smith, John E., 101, 104, 107, 154, 230
Smith, J. W., 294, 296, 297

Smithland, Ky., 58, 118, 123
Smith, Morgan, 26, 256–258, 262, 267, 268, 272, 275–277, 286, 287, 296, 348
Smith, Thomas, 101, 198
Sparkman, Lieutenant, 135
Spence, D. H., 181
Stankieuriz, Captain, 269
Stevenson, Ala., 33
Stewart, Captain, 53, 97, 99, 100, 125, 256, 330
Stone, Captain, 269, 273, 275
Sugg, Colonel, 265
Swarthout, Lieutenant, 268

Taylor, Ezra, 88, 89, 108, 112, 115, 127, 197, 230, 242, 253,
Telegraph Road, 45, 63, 67, 70, 127
Tennessee,
- 3rd, 45, 166, 171, 198, 204, 205, 231, 237, 238, 241, 243, 244, 265, 286, 313
- 9th (battalion), 50
- 10th, 38, 57, 81, 101, 345
- 18th, 45, 81, 91, 125, 205, 206, 228, 237, 241, 243, 244, 262, 264, 288, 345
- 26th, 86, 115, 176, 180, 285
- 30th, 81, 107, 109, 160, 164, 167, 173, 262, 273
- 32nd, 59, 65, 81, 227, 228, 237, 241, 243–245, 253, 273, 286
- 41st, 93, 228, 238, 240, 245
- 42nd, 100, 106, 109, 116, 171, 230, 273, 278, 306
- 48th, 101, 231, 254
- 50th, 265
- 53rd, 101, 104, 106, 109

Tennessee River, 19, 21, 23–25, 28, 32, 33, 39, 40, 46, 47, 53, 58, 62, 67, 81, 118, 120, 123, 132, 157, 338
Texas, 7th, 114, 116, 180, 183, 186, 199, 207, 285, 346
Thayer, John, 125, 128, 129, 236, 238, 239, 242, 244, 253, 279, 280, 286, 332, 348
Third Division (U.S.), (*see* Wallace, Lew)
Thompson, Egbert, 135, 140, 224, 225
Tigress, 54
Tilghman, Lloyd, 24–28, 30, 36, 52, 345
Torpedoes, 26, 27
Tupper, Ansel, 191
Turner, Major, 261
Tuts, 287
Tuttle, James, 46, 128, 150, 154, 156, 259–261, 263, 264, 266, 269, 273, 274, 349
Twombly, Corporal, 268
Tyler, 126, 133, 135, 143

Veatch, James, 91, 92, 98
Virginia,
- 36th, 193, 195, 199
- 50th, 208
- 51st, 38
- 56th, 311, 321

Voorhies, Colonel, 101, 105

Walke, Henry, 72, 87, 90, 98, 121, 126, 133, 137, 143, 145, 146, 148
Wallace, Lew, 54, 60, 67, 76, 111, 123, 125, 127, 129, 151, 152, 154, 187, 190, 192, 193, 225, 226, 236–238, 249, 255–258, 262, 266, 267, 275–278, 280, 283, 284, 286, 314, 322, 324, 325, 328, 330, 332, 338, 347
Wallace, W. H. L., 22, 73, 74, 78, 88, 97, 100, 108, 110, 116, 117, 120, 121, 127, 152, 162, 196–

198, 209–211, 216, 220, 222, 230, 231, 233, 236, 237, 242, 284, 286, 347
Ware, Addison, 328
Washington, D.C., 23, 60, 341
Webster, J. D., 108, 199, 201, 249, 253, 254, 274, 276, 349
Welker, Captain, 112, 113, 273
West Point Academy, 22, 44, 221, 318, 333
West Tennessee, District of, 287, 341
Wharton, Gabriel, 38, 45, 76, 138, 168, 173, 176, 177, 181, 183, 184, 187, 191, 194, 241, 346
White, John, 212, 217
Wilcox, Captain, 305
Williams, Captain, 305
Woods, J. J., 153, 274
Woodward, James, 318
Wright, Crafts, 124, 265
Wynn's Ferry Road, 76, 77, 86–88, 100, 112, 116, 151, 153, 156, 158, 159, 164–167, 171, 185, 186, 195, 198, 207, 209, 210, 220, 222, 223, 225, 226, 229, 230, 236–239, 249, 259, 262, 263, 266, 272, 275, 296, 322, 324

"X" (ridge), 36, 37, 50, 64, 65, 74, 75, 81, 259, 262, 263, 266, 271, 275, 279, 288

Young, Jesse, 134, 139, 140